Global Fintech Revolution

Global Fintech Revolution

Practice, Policy, and Regulation

Lerong Lu

OXFORD
UNIVERSITY PRESS

Great Clarendon Street, Oxford, OX2 6DP,
United Kingdom

Oxford University Press is a department of the University of Oxford.
It furthers the University's objective of excellence in research, scholarship,
and education by publishing worldwide. Oxford is a registered trade mark of
Oxford University Press in the UK and in certain other countries

© Lerong Lu 2024

The moral rights of the author have been asserted

All rights reserved. No part of this publication may be reproduced, stored in
a retrieval system, or transmitted, in any form or by any means, without the
prior permission in writing of Oxford University Press, or as expressly permitted
by law, by licence or under terms agreed with the appropriate reprographics
rights organization. Enquiries concerning reproduction outside the scope of the
above should be sent to the Rights Department, Oxford University Press, at the
address above

You must not circulate this work in any other form
and you must impose this same condition on any acquirer

Published in the United States of America by Oxford University Press
198 Madison Avenue, New York, NY 10016, United States of America

British Library Cataloguing in Publication Data
Data available

Library of Congress Control Number: 2024932328

ISBN 9780198850144

DOI: 10.1093/9780191884597.001.0001

Printed and bound in the UK by
Clays Ltd, Elcograf S.p.A.

Links to third party websites are provided by Oxford in good faith and
for information only. Oxford disclaims any responsibility for the materials
contained in any third party website referenced in this work.

This book is dedicated to my wife and daughter.

Preface

The world is undergoing unprecedented technological breakthroughs in most business areas. Electric vehicles produced by Tesla and BYD are as common as petrol cars on the roads of big cities. AI-driven language processing tools like ChatGPT can write emails, essays, and computer codes as well as a well-educated person. Metaverse aided by VR and AR equipment such as Apple Vision Pro enables people to work, play, and socialise in the same way as we do in the real world. Pharmaceutical companies like Pfizer and Moderna use biotech to produce advanced vaccinations to help us end the Covid-19 pandemic. Clearly, technological innovations play a key role in driving economic growth and social advancement. The financial industry is no exception. This book is a timely work to examine the ongoing Fintech revolution across the world. Fintech denotes the close interaction between the financial services industry and the latest information technologies like big data, cloud computing, blockchain, and AI. The Fintech revolution has given rise to various novel financial services, products, institutions, and business models, such as app-based banking services, mobile payments, crowdfunding, P2P lending, cryptos, CBDCs, robo-advisors, and insurtech. Fintech has transformed the landscape of traditional financial activities relating to banking, investment, and insurance, while also reshaping the practice of financial regulation and compliance with the adoption of RegTech. Obviously, Fintech is able to cut the costs of delivering financial services, improve business efficiency, and provide high-quality and convenient service options for financial consumers. Nonetheless, Fintech presents multiple regulatory challenges for global policy-makers, legislators, and financial authorities in relation to data security, consumer protection, and financial stability.

This book uses a brand new analytical framework, known as Lu's Analysis Model, to help readers understand the complex phenomenon of Fintech, especially the dynamic and multidimensional Fintech ecosystem. It attempts to assess the global Fintech revolution from four distinctly different yet closely related perspectives to offer in-depth and critical discussion of the subject. First of all, the book conducts the analysis from the financial consumers' perspective to see how they benefit from Fintech innovations in terms of receiving more affordable, speedy, and convenient services with better customer experience. It studies the challenger banks and online P2P lending platforms, as well as digital money and payment systems as examples that bring real changes to people's lives. It also demonstrates the unchanged nature of finance while its delivering method is being modernised continuously. Second, the book examines the Fintech revolution from the financial corporations' perspective to understand how existing players and start-ups seize new opportunities to grow their businesses to the next stage. It considers Fintech businesses in different shapes that offer innovative products and services to consumers, including incumbent banks, financial holding companies, Fintech start-ups, BigTech firms, and Metaverse platforms. Moreover, it addresses the latest corporate finance and governance issues relevant to Fintech corporations, such as DCSS and SPACs. Third, the book discusses the Fintech revolution from the governmental perspective and analyses the risks and problems associated with novel Fintech activities and relevant legal, ethical, and regulatory challenges posed. It assesses the strategies and practices of global Fintech regulators, such as the regulatory sandbox and RegTech. The book makes some valuable suggestions for governments and regulatory bodies dealing with Fintech. Fourth, the book evaluates the Fintech revolution from the societal perspective to recognise its values for our welfare and society. It argues that Fintech, if properly regulated, contributes to a more equal, democratic, inclusive, and sustainable financial system that is working for everyone.

This book should appeal to a diverse readership across law, business, finance, economics, computer science, and sociology disciplines. It will be useful for academics, university students, researchers, practitioners, policymakers, and think tanks who are interested in the theoretical, practical, and regulatory implications of the global Fintech revolution. In detail, this interdisciplinary and comparative study is a must-read for economists and legal scholars who are investigating the rise of the Fintech ecosystem and governmental responses. The book can be used as a textbook for university courses relating to Fintech practice, policy, law, and regulation for undergraduate and postgraduate students from either business schools or law schools. Finally, the book should be of interest to legal, finance, and IT practitioners who work in international financial centres, such as London, New York, Hong Kong, and Singapore, as it offers them a holistic view of the latest financial industry developments and increases their professional knowledge in Fintech.

The book is the intellectual product of my research and teaching in the area of Fintech over several years (2016–2023). I would like to express my gratitude to the following people. First of all, I would like to thank my colleagues and students at the Dickson Poon School of Law, King's College London for their valuable feedback and comments on my research relating to Fintech. I have the privilege to serve as the founding director of the LLM Law and Technology programme (2020–present) at King's, and have been teaching the LLM course 'Law and Policy of Fintech' to over 120 postgraduate students each year. I am heavily indebted to my family, especially my wife and daughter. Without their love, encouragement, and support this book could not have been completed. I also thank the editors at Oxford University Press for their enormous support and patience during the publication process. Finally, I would like to thank the editors from Sweet & Maxwell for their permission to reproduce the following articles in this book: Lerong Lu, 'Financial Technology and Challenger Banks in the UK: Gap Fillers or Real Challengers?'. *Journal of International Banking Law and Regulation* (2017) 32: 273–282; Lerong Lu, 'How a Little Ant Challenges Giant Banks? The Rise of Ant Financial (Alipay)'s Fintech Empire and Relevant Regulatory Concerns'. International Company and Commercial Law Review (2018) 28: 12–30; and Lerong Lu, 'Solving the SME Financing Puzzle in the UK: Has Online P2P Lending Got the Midas Touch?'. *Journal of International Banking Law and Regulation* (2018) 33: 449–460.

Lerong Lu
London, June 2023

Contents

List of Figures   x
List of Tables   xi
List of Abbreviations   xii

1. Introduction   1
2. Understanding Fintech   11
3. Fintech Ecosystem—Part One: Global Fintech Hubs and Regulatory Solutions   45
4. Fintech Ecosystem—Part Two: Fintech Corporations, BigTech, and Metaverse   81
5. Fintech in Banking Institutions   132
6. Fintech in Online Lending Marketplaces   163
7. Fintech in Monetary and Payment Systems   195
8. Conclusion   236

Bibliography   242
Index   272

List of Figures

1.1 Lu's Analysis Model of the global Fintech revolution. 7
2.1 Cloud computing service models. 26

List of Tables

2.1	Comparison between weak AI and strong AI.	19
2.2	Main Fintech business segments and selected examples.	36
5.1	The world's top 20 banks by total assets.	134
6.1	The number of businesses, with employment and turnover figures, in the UK.	166
6.2	The five largest P2P lending platforms in the UK by loan volume.	171
7.1	The top five stablecoins by market capitalisation.	211

List of Abbreviations

AB	activity-based
ABCDE	artificial intelligence, blockchain, cloud computing, data (big data), and e-commerce
ABS	asset-backed security
AI	artificial intelligence
AIIB	Asian Infrastructure Investment Bank
AMER	Americas
AML	anti-money laundering
APAC	Asia Pacific
API	application programming interface
app	mobile application
APRA	Australian Prudential Regulation Authority
AR	augmented reality
ASIC	Australian Securities and Investments Commission
ATM	automated teller machine
AWS	Amazon Web Services
B2B	business-to-business
B2C	business-to-consumer
B2G	business-to-government
BaFin	Germany Federal Financial Supervisory Authority
BBA	British Bankers' Association
BBB	British Business Bank
BFP	Business Finance Partnership (UK)
BigTech	big technology company/companies
BIS	Bank for International Settlements
BoE	Bank of England
BTC	Bitcoin
C2B	consumer-to-business
C2C	consumer-to-consumer
CASS	Current Account Switching Service
CBDC	central bank digital currency
CBILS	Coronavirus Business Interruption Loan Scheme (UK)
CBIRC	China Banking and Insurance Regulatory Commission
CBRC	China Banking Regulatory Commission
CCPA	California Consumer Privacy Act
CEO	chief executive officer
CFPB	Consumer Financial Protection Bureau (US)
CFT	countering the financing of terrorism
CJEU	Court of Justice of the European Union

List of Abbreviations

CNY	Chinese yuan (renminbi)
CSRC	China Securities Regulatory Commission
DCSS	dual-class share structure
DeFi	decentralised finance
DFS	Digital Finance Strategy (EU)
DFSA	Dubai Financial Services Authority
DLT	distributed ledger technology
DMA	Digital Markets Act (EU)
DNA	data–network–activity
DSA	Digital Services Act (EU)
EB	entity-based
EBA	European Banking Authority
ECB	European Central Bank
e-commerce	electronic commerce
EMEA	Europe, Middle East, and Africa
EMV	Europay, Mastercard, and VISA
ERP	enterprise resource planning
ESG	Environmental, Social, and Governance
ESMA	European Securities and Markets Authority
EU	European Union
EV	electric vehicle
EY	Ernst & Young
FCA	Financial Conduct Authority (UK)
FDIC	Federal Deposit Insurance Corporation (US)
FHC	financial holding company
FinHub	Strategic Hub for Innovation and Financial Technology (US)
Fintech	financial technology
FLS	Funding for Lending Scheme (UK)
FOS	Financial Ombudsman Service (UK)
FSA	Financial Services Authority (UK)
FSB	Financial Stability Board
FSCS	Financial Services Compensation Scheme (UK)
FSDP	Financial Sector Development Programme (Saudi Arabia)
FTSE	Financial Times Stock Exchange
FX	foreign exchange
GDP	gross domestic product
GDPR	General Data Protection Regulation (EU)
GIC	Government of Singapore Investment Corporation
GPT4	Generative Pre-trained Transformer 4
HKMA	Hong Kong Monetary Authority
HNWI	high-net-worth individual
IaaS	Infrastructure as a Service
IADI	International Association of Deposit Insurers
ICBC	Industrial and Commercial Bank of China
ICO	initial coin offering
IMF	International Monetary Fund

insurtech	insurance technology
IoT	internet of things
IPO	initial public offering
KYC	know your customer
LSE	London Stock Exchange
M&A	mergers and acquisitions
MAS	Monetary Authority of Singapore
MCOB	Mortgage and Home Finance Conduct of Business Sourcebook
MiCA	Markets in Crypto-Assets Regulation (EU)
MIT	Massachusetts Institute of Technology
MMF	money-market fund
Nasdaq	National Association of Securities Dealers Automated Quotations (US)
NFC	near-field communication
NFRA	National Financial Regulatory Administration (China)
NFT	non-fungible token
NYSE	New York Stock Exchange
O2O	online-to-offline
OS	operating system
OTC	over-the-counter
P2B	peer-to-business
P2P	peer-to-peer
P2PFA	Peer-to-Peer Finance Association
PaaS	Platform as a Service
PBoC	People's Bank of China
PE	private equity
PICC	People's Insurance Company of China
PIPE	private investment in public equity
PIPL	Personal Information Protection Law (China)
PPI	payment protection insurance
PRA	Prudential Regulation Authority (UK)
PRC	People's Republic of China
PwC	PricewaterhouseCoopers
QR Code	Quick Response code
RBA	Reserve Bank of Australia
RBI	Reserve Bank of India
RBS	Royal Bank of Scotland
RegTech	regulatory technology
RFID	radio frequency identification
RLS	Recovery Loan Scheme (UK)
ROE	return on equity
SaaS	Software as a Service
SAFE	State Administration of Foreign Exchange (China)
SBA	Small Business Administration (US)
SDK	software development kit
SEC	Securities and Exchange Commission (US)
SGX	Singapore Exchange

SIB	systemically important bank
SLS	Start-Up Loans Scheme (UK)
SLSC	Shanghai–London Stock Connect
SME	small and medium-sized enterprise
SPAC	special purpose acquisition company
SSE	Shanghai Stock Exchange
SSRN	Social Science Research Network
Suptech	supervisory technology
TBTF	too big to fail
TFA	two-factor authentication
TOR	The Onion Router
UHNWI	ultra-high-net-worth individual
UK	United Kingdom
UN	United Nations
UPI	Unified Payments Interface
US	United States
USDC	USD Coin
USDT	Tether
VC	venture capital
VIE	variable interest entity
VR	virtual reality
WB	World Bank

1
Introduction

1.1 Background of the book: contextualising the Fintech revolution

Technological innovations play a key role in driving economic growth and social advancement. Thomas Edison invented the telegraph, light bulb, and motion pictures, among the 1,093 patents he obtained.[1] As a result, the United States (US) underwent a technological revolution and became a global superpower in the early 20th century. In 1908, Henry Ford created the Model T and the automatic assembly line, which sparked the mass production of cars and the modernisation of transportation.[2] In the 1970s, Bill Gates and Paul Allen founded Microsoft and began designing the operating system for microcomputers.[3] They produced the DOS and Windows operating systems, making personal computers accessible to billions of people. The popularisation of computers and the internet has significantly improved business efficiency and reshaped the way in which most people work, play, and connect. Since the turn of the 21st century, the world has witnessed a new wave of disruptive technological breakthroughs, including big data, blockchain, artificial intelligence (AI), the internet of things (IoT), 5G mobile network, quantum computing, neurotechnology, nanomaterials, virtual reality (VR), and augmented reality (AR).[4] Nowadays, technological innovations have happened faster than ever before, making it hard to predict what the world will look like even in 10 years.

There is no denying that technological advancements have greatly transformed business models and people's lifestyles. For instance, an increasing number of drivers have opted for electric vehicles (EVs) over petrol cars,

---

[1] 'Thomas Edison: Facts, House & Inventions—History', A&E Television Networks, 9 November 2009, http://www.history.com/topics/inventions/thomas-edison.

[2] 'Henry Ford—Biography, Founder of Ford Motor Company', Hearst Digital Media, 5 September 2019, http://www.biography.com/business-figure/henry-ford.

[3] Sophie Curtis, 'Bill Gates: A History at Microsoft', *Telegraph*, 4 February 2014, http://www.telegraph.co.uk/technology/bill-gates/10616991/Bill-Gates-a-history-at-Microsoft.html.

[4] OECD, 'OECD Science, Technology and Innovation Outlook 2023: Enabling Transitions in Times of Disruption', 16 March 2023, https://www.oecd.org/sti/oecd-science-technology-and-innovation-outlook-25186167.htm.

Global Fintech Revolution. Lerong Lu, Oxford University Press. © Lerong Lu (2024). DOI: 10.1093/9780191884597.003.0001

since EVs are more environmentally friendly and cheaper to maintain. The production and sale of EVs have been encouraged by governments in the United Kingdom (UK), US, European Union (EU), China, and Japan who are committed to achieving carbon neutrality in the 21st century.[5] In July 2020, Tesla surpassed Toyota as the most valuable carmaker when its market capitalisation reached $209.47 billion, despite Toyota having sold 30 times as many cars and generated more than 10 times as much income.[6] The Covid-19 pandemic had devastating impacts on the global economy, but we have also witnessed remarkable advancement in technologies across a wide range of industries, including biotech like Pfizer-BioNTech and Moderna vaccines, virtual worlds like Metaverse and digital assets, and online meeting facilities like Zoom and Microsoft Teams. In March 2023, the release of OpenAI's GPT-4 marked a milestone in the development of natural language processing, as AI and deep learning models now perform at levels comparable to humans on a range of academic and professional metrics.[7]

Like any other buzzwords in the technology industry, Fintech (financial technology) has been taking over headlines in recent years. Fintech describes the interplay between finance and technology. It refers to the application of internet technologies and innovations in financial services like payments, lending, wealth management, and insurance. The financial industry has seen significant change in terms of both the contents and methods employed in delivering financial services, as a result of the use of big data, cloud computing, AI, and blockchain. In 2022, Fintech attracted $92 billion in venture capital (VC) funding globally.[8] People have been debating whether Fintech is merely a passing trend or a genuine force for change. The answer is clear now. Evidently, the global Fintech revolution is transforming the traditional financial industry's landscape through cost savings, higher-quality financial services, more intelligent use of big data to assess credit risks, and the development of a more diverse and stable credit market.[9] Our daily lives have already been considerably impacted by Fintech—from the ease of using mobile payment apps like Apply Pay and Alipay to the simplicity of applying for a peer-to-peer loan through websites like Zopa and Funding Circle. Cities such as London, Frankfurt, New York, San Francisco, Beijing, Shenzhen, Singapore,

---

[5] Carbon neutrality means achieving net-zero carbon dioxide emissions, and over 110 countries have pledged carbon neutrality by 2050. See 'The Race to Zero Emissions, and Why the World Depends on it', United Nations, 2 December 2020, https://news.un.org/en/story/2020/12/1078612.
[6] 'Tesla Overtakes Toyota to Become World's Most Valuable Carmaker', BBC, 1 July 2020, https://www.bbc.com/news/business-53257933.
[7] 'GPT-4', OpenAI, accessed 1 June 2023, https://openai.com/research/gpt-4.
[8] Innovate Finance, 'Fintech Investment Landscape 2022', January 2023, https://www.innovatefinance.com/wp-content/uploads/2023/01/innovate-finance-Fintech-investment-landscape-2022.pdf.
[9] 'The Fintech Revolution', *The Economist*, 9 May 2015, pp. 13–14.

Dubai, and Mumbai have emerged as leading global Fintech hubs, where the majority of financial innovations and regulatory reforms are taking place.

Market players in the Fintech ecosystem, whether they are incumbent banking institutions or new tech start-ups, have been proactively embracing innovative technological solutions to update the offering of financial services. Digital transformation has been brought to every aspect of the financial industry, as disrupters challenge the old business models and fight for greater market shares. Fintech appeals greatly to financial consumers, particularly the young millennial generation who are tech-savvy and dissatisfied with old-fashion financial services. A survey found that more than a third of European consumers would switch banks or insurers if they did not provide cutting-edge technologies.[10] Fintech seems to create a win-win situation for both financial institutions and financial consumers. On the one hand, Fintech offers huge commercial opportunities for entrepreneurs who are capable of leveraging on novel technologies to build new financial products, services, and delivery models. We have seen the rise of many successful Fintech corporations, which have become unicorn businesses (i.e., unlisted companies with a valuation of over $1 billion) or high-profile public companies listed in New York, London, and Hong Kong—just to name a few: Ant Group, Lufax, Monzo, Revolut, Stripe, Wise, and LendingClub. They are likely to become tomorrow's leading financial institutions, similar to today's Goldman Sachs, HSBC, and Nomura. On the other hand, Fintech has brought enormous benefits to financial consumers, either individuals or businesses. They now enjoy more convenient, affordable, and accessible financial services and products, such as online peer-to-peer loans, digital banking services, mobile payment facilities, intelligent robo-advisors, and cryptocurrencies.

The rise of Fintech has displayed economic and social values. Despite the obvious improvement of efficiency in the operation of financial businesses, Fintech is said to contribute to a more equal, democratic, and inclusive financial world. The popularity of mobile money and payment systems, like the M-PESA in Kenya, helps the unbanked population access essential banking services with greater ease and lower costs. China's Alipay and WeChat Pay provide convenient, cheap, and secure mobile payment solutions for over 1 billion consumers, as the country has quickly become a cashless society. These are clear examples of how Fintech contributes to financial inclusion. Moreover, Fintech improves the equality of accessing financial resources for consumers and smaller businesses. Traditional financial institutions tend

---

[10] Emma Dunkley, 'Challengers Prise Open Grip of Larger Rivals', *The Financial Times*, 4 May 2016, p. 23.

to favour large corporate clients. After the 2007–2008 global financial crisis, banks have become increasingly reluctant to lend money to small and medium-sized enterprises (SMEs) due to the stricter lending criteria resulting from regulatory changes. Accordingly, there is a large financing gap which needs to be closed by alternative financing sources, such as online peer-to-peer (P2P) lending marketplaces. P2P lending and other crowdfunding methods have grown rapidly across the US, Europe, and Asia, becoming a feasible financing option for many SMEs and individual consumers and leading to greater financial equality. Finally, Fintech helps create a more democratic and decentralised financial system. In the old days, the power of making money has been monopolised by monetary authorities and central banks. Since 2008, the creation of Bitcoin (BTC) and other blockchain-based cryptocurrencies has indicated a new era in which private individuals and corporations are able to issue new money. Crypto transactions happen among users directly without the involvement of any financial intermediaries. Decentralised finance (DeFi) gives people more say on the operation and management of monetary and payment systems, providing insight into how money will function in the future.

Nonetheless, the proliferation of Fintech has posed a series of legal and regulatory challenges for policy-makers and financial regulators across the world, such as data protection, funds safety, prudential regulation, ethical business conduct, and anti-money laundering. Governments, academia, and international organisations (such as the World Bank (WB), International Monetary Fund (IMF), and Bank for International Settlements (BIS)) have been exploring how best to regulate Fintech to maximise their social values and enable their sustainable growth. Authorities need to strike a delicate balance between promoting innovation on the one hand and safeguarding consumer interests and financial stability on the other. There is constant discussion about whether the Fintech industry should be dominated by the free market or by government intervention. In practice, regulators have come up with some useful toolkits, such as the regulatory sandbox and regulatory technology (RegTech). The popular regulatory sandbox provides a controlled environment where Fintech companies can test new financial services, products, business plans, and delivery systems without confronting the usual regulatory constraints of carrying out regulated activities in a specific jurisdiction.[11] RegTech refers to the use of technological solutions to assist financial institutions in complying with regulatory and reporting obligations

---

[11] FCA, 'Regulatory Sandbox', November 2015, p. 1, https://www.fca.org.uk/publication/research/regulatory-sandbox.pdf.

in a fast, flexible, and cost-efficient manner.[12] RegTech helps financial regulators perform complex supervisory tasks more effectively, because they can use cutting-edge technologies to gather and analyse the information from the regulated entities and respond swiftly and precisely to the most recent market changes and real-time financial risks. Clearly, the making of policies and regulatory standards plays a vital and proactive role in shaping the direction of the global Fintech revolution, which is another focus of this book aside from the discussion of Fintech practices.

1.2 Objective and analytical framework of the book

The book intends to examine the causes and representations of the global Fintech revolution as well as its impacts on the financial industry and wider economy. It also explores the social values of Fintech, providing useful information for practitioners, researchers, and policy-makers. The book fills a major gap in the existing literature regarding the practice, policy, and regulation of Fintech businesses and relevant ecosystems. This interdisciplinary and comparative study should appeal to a large number of readers from diverse backgrounds in law, business, finance, computer science, and social study. It is recommended for academics, researchers, and think tanks who investigate the complicated phenomenon of the Fintech revolution and governmental responses. It can be used as a textbook for university courses relating to the study of Fintech's practice, policy, and regulation for undergraduate and postgraduate students from either business schools or law schools. The book also should greatly appeal to legal, finance, and IT practitioners working in global financial centres such as London, New York, Hong Kong, and Singapore, as it offers them a holistic view of the latest industry developments and increases their professional knowledge and skills. Finally, the book provides suggestions for public authorities like policy-makers, legislators, regulators, and international organisations when they make guidelines and new rules for the Fintech sector.

This book adopts an original analytical framework to help readers comprehend the complex nature of Fintech. The approach is extremely useful in studying the ever-evolving and multifaceted social phenomena, such as the Fintech ecosystem. The discussions in the book focus on four distinctive perspectives. First, the book conducts the analysis from the financial consumers'

---

[12] Deloitte, 'RegTech Is the New Fintech', 2016, https://www2.deloitte.com/content/dam/Deloitte/tw/Documents/financial-services/tw-fsi-regtech-new-Fintech.pdf.

perspective to see what benefits they could gain from Fintech innovations. Second, the book examines the Fintech revolution from the financial corporations' perspective to understand the new opportunities and challenges presented for the providers of financial services. Third, the book discusses the Fintech revolution from the governmental or regulatory perspective by analysing the risks and problems associated with innovative Fintech activities. Fourth, the book evaluates the Fintech revolution from the societal perspective to recognise Fintech's economic and social values. It should be noted that the discussions from four viewpoints are closely intertwined. The logic behind the analysis is that any Fintech services and products would be offered by a Fintech corporation, to a Fintech consumer, which is likely to be regulated by a Fintech regulator, either creating positive value for the society or causing negative effects. This analytical framework could be referred to as 'Lu's Analysis Model', as demonstrated in Figure 1.1, for use in future research of Fintech or the study of any other similar economic or social phenomenon.

1.3 Chapter outline of the book

This section introduces the chapter outline of the book, with a visualised explanation in Figure 1.1. After Chapter 1 'Introduction', the rest of the book proceeds as follows.

Chapter 2 'Understanding Fintech' conducts an inquiry into Fintech's conceptual meaning, nature, main forms, and special characteristics. It clarifies what types of financial institutions, activities, products, and services will (and won't) be covered by this novel concept. It would be necessary for readers to have a deep understanding of Fintech before studying relevant application scenarios, commercial implications, and regulatory challenges. As Fintech is a composite word of 'fin' (finance) and 'tech' (technology), Chapter 2 looks at these two components respectively. The 'fin' part represents the eternal nature of finance that finds the best way to match money supply and demand in our economy. The 'tech' part stands for various technological innovations in financial services, including AI, blockchain, cloud computing, data (big data), and electronic commerce (e-commerce). The chapter also summarises the common characteristics of Fintech, distinguishing them from traditional finance, such as disintermediation, automation, innovation, virtualisation, customer centricity, scalability, and accessibility. It argues that the growth of Fintech is adding true value to our society. Fintech makes the financial industry more efficient, equal, democratic, inclusive, and sustainable.

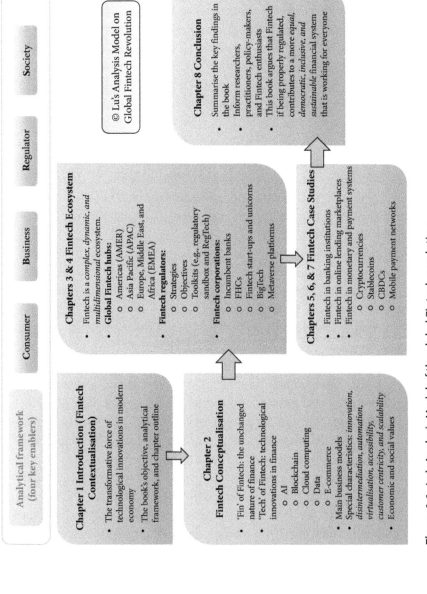

Figure 1.1 Lu's Analysis Model of the global Fintech revolution.
Source: The figure is compiled by the author

The book then investigates the so-called Fintech ecosystem in Chapters 3 and 4. Fintech has evolved from technology-driven financial products and services to more complex and multidimensional ecosystems with various players who interact with each other having a shared interest in the Fintech sector. The Fintech ecosystem not only refers to the venues where financial innovations take place, but also comprises the key players that collectively shape the industry's development path, such as Fintech corporations, financial consumers, financial regulators, governments, and investors.

Chapter 3 'Fintech Ecosystem—Part One: Global Fintech Hubs and Regulatory Solutions' discusses two elements of the Fintech ecosystem: the venues (global Fintech hubs) and financial regulators. It studies the competitive advantages, local features, and regulatory environments of global Fintech hubs in six continents, including San Francisco, New York, Sydney, Beijing, Shanghai, Shenzhen, Mumbai, Singapore, Paris, Frankfurt, London, Dubai, and Nairobi. It investigates Fintech regulators' strategies and toolkits, such as the regulatory sandbox and RegTech, and considers how financial authorities balance multiple policy objectives (e.g., promote financial innovation, ensure an adequate degree of consumer protection, and maintain financial stability) when supervising Fintech.

Chapter 4 'Fintech Ecosystem—Part Two: Fintech Corporations, BigTech, and Metaverse' continues to analyse the Fintech companies, as a key player in the ecosystem, that offer innovative products and services to consumers. Fintech businesses exist in various forms, ranging from smaller start-ups to successful unicorn corporations or financial holding companies (FHCs). In addition, big technology companies (BigTech), such as Apple, Amazon, Alibaba, Meta (Facebook), Alphabet (Google), and Tencent, rely on their technological advantages and customer base to offer financial services like banking, payments, investment, and digital currency. The rise of virtual worlds and digital assets like Metaverse, Web 3.0, and non-fungible tokens (NFTs) further contributes to the development of Fintech. The chapter critically discusses the opportunities, challenges, and risks for each category of Fintech corporation. It also evaluates the corporate governance issues relating to Fintech businesses, such as dual-class share structure (DCSS), and diverse financing options for Fintech corporations like VC, private equity (PE), initial public offering (IPO), and special purpose acquisition company (SPAC).

The book, by applying Lu's Analysis Model, carries out detailed and comprehensive case studies relating to Fintech innovations in three business segments in Chapters 5–7. The case studies pay attention to how financial innovations affect the traditional financial industry, what kinds of regulatory challenges are being presented, and how global policy-makers should react to such challenges.

Chapter 5 'Fintech in Banking Institutions' considers Fintech innovation in the banking industry, discussing a group of digital-based challenger banks that have quickly emerged after the global financial crisis of 2007–2008, such as Monzo, Starling, Revolut, N26, and WeBank. It examines the phenomenon of 'too big to fail', which indicates the market concentration and systemic importance of the largest banks across the globe. Digital banks or neo banks have no historical legacy and adopt a simplified and low-cost business model based on the internet and smartphone apps. Digital banks have strong competitive edges in distribution channels and the provision of bespoke services for clients such as retail customers and SMEs who are underserved by incumbent banks. This chapter discusses the economic, social, and cultural factors contributing to the rapid rise of digital banks and assesses their advantages over traditional bank. It also discusses how digital banks fit into the existing regulatory system, and identifies the pressing regulatory issues such as deposit insurance, capital requirements, financial security, and data safety.

Chapter 6 'Fintech in Online Lending Marketplaces' evaluates the alternative financing markets for smaller businesses and individual consumers, especially the rise of online P2P lending platforms globally. P2P lending improves the effectiveness of allocating financial resources and fosters financial equality among businesses of different sizes. The chapter considers the economic importance and financial dilemma of SMEs and illustrates the need for SMEs to have P2P lending as a vital fundraising option. It presents the online P2P lending markets in three countries with most active online lending transactions: the UK, the US, and China. The chapter claims that P2P lending has a number of advantages over bank lending because of the added value that financial disintermediation generates for both investors and borrowers, such as more diverse funding sources, higher investment returns, the expedited process, and increased transparency. Finally, it investigates the industry policies and regulatory frameworks governing online lending marketplaces.

Chapter 7 'Fintech in Monetary and Payment Systems' analyses the Fintech revolution taking place in international monetary and payment systems. Money is at the heart of any financial system. Since the turn of the 21st century, both the public and private sectors have proposed to create their own digital currency for the future economy, and the time has witnessed the explosive growth of digital money in a variety of forms. The chapter discusses the operating mechanisms, benefits, and limitations of three generations of digital money: blockchain-based cryptocurrencies, stablecoins, and central bank digital currencies (CBDCs). It assesses popular mobile payment networks around the world, including Fintech payment systems based on near-field communication (NFC) technology and quick response (QR) code. It also analyses the global initiative of building a cashless society proposed by governments and financial authorities. Clearly, the case studies on digital money showcase the breadth and depth of the global Fintech revolution. It implies that regulators and policy-makers could play a more proactive role in the development of the Fintech industry, rather than being reactive to market growth and financial innovations.

Chapter 8 'Conclusion' presents the key findings in the book to inform researchers, practitioners, policy-makers, and any Fintech enthusiasts. It provides readers with a comprehensive and critical understanding of the subject of the Fintech ecosystem and its economic and social implications. It focuses on the transformative force of Fintech, while also emphasising the importance of addressing legal, regulatory, and ethical considerations to ensure the sustainable growth of Fintech in the 21st century.

2
Understanding Fintech

2.1 Introduction

The term 'financial technology' (Fintech) has gained popularity across the globe. It has generated a lot of debate among academics, practitioners, policymakers, and the media. However, there is still disagreement regarding the precise definition of Fintech and the types of financial activities, institutions, and markets that the term actually covers. According to the Cambridge English Dictionary, Fintech refers to 'the business of using technology to offer financial services in new and better ways'.[1] Then the interpretation depends on how we perceive the 'new' and 'better' parts in financial services aided by technological breakthroughs. The Financial Stability Board (FSB) defines Fintech as 'technologically enabled innovation in financial services that could result in new business models, applications, processes or products with an associated material effect on financial markets and institutions and the provision of financial services'.[2] It emphasises not only the innovations and novel elements in financial services but also the significant effects that they have had on the financial industry and markets, which seems to be a more rigid definition. In general, Fintech denotes the latest technological innovations in the financial services industry, giving rise to various new-type financial services, financial products, and financial institutions that have been transforming the digital economy.[3] Fintech encompasses both front-end industrial applications and back-end technologies.

There is no questioning that Fintech is thriving. Each week, we can find a large number of news articles in *The Financial Times* and *The Wall Street Journal* about emerging Fintech firms and their products in relation to cryptocurrencies, quant investing, mobile payments, virtual banks, AI-based

---
[1] 'Financial Technology (Fintech)', Cambridge English Dictionary, accessed 1 June 2023, https://dictionary.cambridge.org/dictionary/english/financial-technology.
[2] FSB, 'Fintech', 5 May 2022, https://www.fsb.org/work-of-the-fsb/financial-innovation-and-structural-change/Fintech/.
[3] Lerong Lu, 'Promoting SME Finance in the Context of Fintech Revolution: A Case Study of the UK's Practice and Regulation'. *Banking and Finance Law Review* (2018) 33: 317, 319.

credit scoring, and so on.[4] So far, the economists and legal scholars have widely debated on the subject of Fintech, producing a substantial amount of academic work in this area. For instance, when we entered the keyword 'Fintech' into the search box of the Social Science Research Network (SSRN), it would come up with over 1,800 original research papers as of April 2023.[5] Governments in countries like the UK, Singapore, and China have become increasingly interested in fostering the growth of the Fintech sector as a key national strategy, as Fintech is thought to create job opportunities, improve business efficiency, and promote the competitiveness of their current financial industries.[6] At the international level, the United Nations (UN) has established a task force on digital financing with the goal of utilising digitalisation to build a financial system that is centred on the needs of citizens and to hasten the financing of the UN's Sustainable Development Goals.[7]

The purpose of this chapter is to examine the nature and meaning of Fintech and to provide clarification on the types of financial activities, products, services, and institutions that will fall within this concept. It would be necessary for readers to have a better understanding of Fintech before the book starts analysing Fintech's detailed application scenarios, relevant commercial opportunities, and regulatory challenges in the following chapters. As Fintech is a composite word of 'fin' (finance) and 'tech' (technology), the chapter will look at each component separately. Section 2.2 discusses the 'fin' part of Fintech, which represents the unchanged nature of finance that finds the optimal approach to match the supply and demand of money in our economy. Section 2.3 examines the 'tech' part, which indicates various technological advancements in financial services. It considers how AI, blockchain, cloud computing, data (big data), and e-commerce have been applied to or integrated with financial institutions and markets, as well as how they have helped create newer and more effective financial products, services, and infrastructure. Section 2.4 introduces the main business models of Fintech which have been launched by Fintech start-ups, existing financial institutions, BigTech, or a consortium of them. Section 2.5 outlines common characteristics of Fintech institutions and their services that set them apart from traditional finance, such as disintermediation, automation, innovation,

---

[4] For example, see 'Fintech', *The Financial Times*, accessed 1 June 2023, https://www.ft.com/fintech.
[5] The search is done via Social Science Research Network (SSRN), accessed 1 June 2023, https://www.ssrn.com/.
[6] HM Treasury, 'The Kalifa Review of UK Fintech', 26 February 2021, https://www.gov.uk/government/publications/the-kalifa-review-of-uk-fintech; PBoC, 'Fintech Development Plan (2019–2021)', August 2019; and 'Fintech and Innovation', Monetary Authority of Singapore, accessed 1 June 2023, https://www.mas.gov.sg/development/Fintech.
[7] 'Digital Financing Task Force', UN, accessed 1 June 2023, https://www.un.org/en/digital-financing-taskforce.

virtualisation, customer centricity, scalability, and accessibility. Section 2.6 discusses the key values of Fintech businesses, as the book argues that Fintech helps create a more democratic, equal, inclusive, and sustainable financial industry. Section 2.7 makes a conclusion for the chapter.

2.2 'Fin' of Fintech: the unchanged nature of finance

Despite the novelty of Fintech and its profound economic and societal impacts, we should never mystify the concept itself. In this chapter, we make an effort not to describe the terminologies in a strictly technical manner, as this book is primarily addressed to readers without technological background, such as legal practitioners, bankers, regulators, policy-makers, researchers, and law school or business school students. Therefore, relevant concepts and operating mechanisms relating to Fintech will be discussed in a straightforward and explicit manner that facilitates the understanding of most readers.

Fintech is nothing new in a sense that the growth of the financial industry has always been driven by significant technological innovations throughout history, including the telegraph, telephone, computer, and internet. According to some academics, the interaction between financial services and technology may have existed as early as the 19th century.[8] In fact, many of the financial services that we now take for granted were once major inventions in the 20th century. For instance, the Diners Club in the US created the world's first credit card in February 1950, allowing its users to make payments at a variety of venues such as restaurants and department stores.[9] In June 1967, the world's first automated teller machine (ATM) was unveiled at a Barclays bank branch in London, which allowed customers to withdraw cash after regular business hours when most banks were only open until 3:30 p.m. at the time.[10] As a departure from the conventional floor-based trading approach, the National Association of Securities Dealers Automated Quotations (Nasdaq) electronic marketplace was introduced in New York in 1971 to assist investors in trading stocks

---

[8] Douglas W. Arner, Janos Barberis, and Ross P. Buckley, 'The Evolution of Fintech: A New Post-Crisis Paradigm?' *Georgetown Journal of International Law* (2016) 47: 1271, 1273.
[9] 'Diners Club Credit Card History', Diners Club, accessed 1 June 2023, https://www.dinersclub.com/about-us/history.
[10] Barclays Bank, 'From the Archives: The ATM Is 50', 27 June 2017, https://home.barclays/news/2017/06/from-the-archives-the-atm-is-50/.

and bonds through the faster, less expensive, and more transparent computerised system.[11] This is not to mention the online banking and stocks trading platforms that only recently emerged in the majority of industrialised economies in the late 1990s or early 2000s, as middle-class households began to utilise personal computers and internet connections more frequently.

When we take a closer look at all these remarkable financial innovations, we will find that the essence and fundamental functions of financial services largely remain the same, regardless of how technologies evolve and innovate. In general, financial activities match money supply and demand in any economy, as they are supposed to facilitate risk management transcending diverse time and space.[12] Therefore, from a functional perspective, Fintech is playing an exact same role as traditional finance in our economy and society, despite their protean appearances and fancy notions invented by entrepreneurs and financiers. Fintech naturally applies to all established financial contexts, such as banking and lending, securities and investments, insurance, money, and payments, most of which will be covered in the later chapters of this book. For example, although bank lending is viewed as traditional finance and online P2P lending as Fintech, both achieve the same goal of directing savings from savers to small enterprises and individuals who are in need of credits. Additionally, although cash payments—that is, payments made with banknotes and coins—are considered traditional finance while mobile payments like Apple Pay, Google Pay, and Alipay are classified as Fintech, both of them serve a very similar function in commercial transactions by transferring money from customers to merchants. The same comparison can be drawn between high-street banks like HSBC and Barclays and digital-only banks like Monzo and Starling, as well as between physical banknotes like US dollars, Euros, and Chinese yuan and digital money like BTC, Tether, and CBDCs.

It is evident that in terms of functionality and scope of applications, traditional finance and Fintech are similar. Fintech, however, has the potential to help the financial services industry achieve its objectives and perform its tasks in regard to banking, securities trading, and insurance more successfully and efficiently. An appropriate metaphor might be that traditional finance can be compared to cold weapons such as bows and arrows, whereas Fintech can be compared to hot weapons like machine guns and missiles.

---

[11] Phil Mackintosh, 'Nasdaq: 50 Years of Market Innovation', Nasdaq, 11 February 2021, https://www.nasdaq.com/articles/nasdaq%3A-50-years-of-market-innovation-2021-02-11.

[12] Peter Christoffersen, *Elements of Financial Risk*, 2nd ed. (Cambridge, MA: Academic Press, 2012), p. 3.

Additionally, the distinctions between traditional finance and Fintech are similar to those between gasoline-powered cars and electric cars or between basic cell phones and smartphones. Though the two sets of concepts are grouped together in the same category, the latter offers greater features, more sophisticated functionality, or more economical solutions. When studying the phenomenon of Fintech, it is important for us to keep in mind that the nature of finance has never changed. Therefore, rather than considering Fintech to be a brand-new creation, it is more realistic to think of it as an upgraded version of traditional finance. Most of the time, Fintech is a relative concept, as people typically associate modern technology with inventions that occur after they were born.

Finally, when understanding the 'fin' part of Fintech, we should not ignore a less obvious feature of the Fintech industry compared with all of the fancy tech-driven innovations. It is that the growth of Fintech companies requires strong financial supports from banks, capital markets, VC, and PE funds. From the standpoint of corporate finance, the phenomenal growth of Fintech, particularly those unicorn companies, is impossible without ongoing and substantial investments from the industry funds around the world.[13] A total of 2,693 mergers and acquisitions (M&A), PE, and VC transactions contributed to the $135.7 billion global Fintech investments in 2019.[14] The amount invested in Fintech firms further climbed to $210.1 billion in 2021.[15] In this sense, the 'fin' component of Fintech could be understood as both the providers of new financial services and the recipients of financial investments on which businesses rely when launching new ventures.

2.3 'Tech' of Fintech: technological innovations in finance

As discussed, despite the fact that we are now living in the digital age, the nature of financial activities hasn't altered much over time. However, the concrete delivering mechanisms of financial services have changed substantially in the first two decades of the 21st century, owing to the fast development and proliferation of internet technologies. These technologies have significantly

---

[13] Unicorn companies refer to unlisted corporations that have a valuation of at least $1 billion. Most of them come from the tech industry. See Ningyao Ye and Lerong Lu, 'How to Harness A Unicorn? Demystifying China's Reform of Share Listing Rules and Chinese Depositary Receipts (CDRs)'. *International Company and Commercial Law Review* (2019) 30: 454.

[14] KPMG, 'Pulse of Fintech H2 2019', February 2020, https://assets.kpmg.com/content/dam/kpmg/xx/pdf/2020/02/pulse-of-fintech-h2-2019.pdf.

[15] 'Total Value of Investments into Fintech Companies Worldwide from 2010 to 2021', Statista, accessed 1 June 2023, https://www.statista.com/statistics/719385/investments-into-Fintech-companies-globally/.

increased the efficiency and effectiveness of providing financial services, and given consumers more options for the services they need as well as where and when to receive them. Obviously, Fintech not only results in larger profit margins for financial institutions, but also lowers the threshold and service costs for financial consumers, leading to greater affordability and financial inclusion. The remainder of this chapter will therefore concentrate on the examination of breakthrough technologies that are driving the current Fintech revolution.

The large-scale application of advanced technologies has been the driving force behind the rise of Fintech. They revamp or modernise the infrastructures used to run different financial activities. For instance, big data allows financial institutions to assess the creditworthiness of borrowers more accurately and timely by taking into account extensive sources of information including social media and online shopping records. Blockchain enables entrepreneurs to design and issue their own cryptocurrencies without the intervention of state agents. AI has made robo-advisors possible who can provide professional but low-cost financial advice for investors on stock selection and portfolio management. Clearly, the growth of Fintech has made banking, securities trading, insurance, and other financial industry sectors more affordable, quicker, and customer-friendly. Additionally, Fintech generates sizeable returns for shareholders and investors of both established institutions and new players who capitalise on the technologies to increase business productivity and profit margins.

The five key technological pillars that underpin Fintech developments will be covered in the following parts, including AI, blockchain, cloud computing, data (big data), and e-commerce. They are referred to as the 'ABCDE' of Fintech collectively. It should be noted, however, that none of these technologies precludes the others. In practice, multiple technologies typically work closely together. For instance, the application of most information technologies is likely to be data-intensive. Any use of AI and cloud computing would require the collection of massive amounts of data (big data).

2.3.1 Artificial intelligence

AI simulates human intellect in machines or robotics so that they can think and act like people.[16] AI is an area of interdisciplinary studies involving expert knowledge in computer science, mathematics, behavioural science,

---

[16] Stuart Russell and Peter Norvig, *Artificial Intelligence: A Modern Approach*, 4th ed. (London: Pearson, 2021), pp. 19–22.

psychology, linguistics, and so on. It suggests the breadth and depth of this emerging discipline as well as the joint efforts needed from scientists, economists, and lawyers to put AI theory into practice. AI can be applied in an extensive number of scenarios, including but not limited to natural language processing, intelligent database retrieval, automatic consulting systems, theorem proving, robotics, and automatic programming.[17] Nowadays, machines have become smarter, as they could be programmed to perform complex tasks and mimic various human behaviours, such as learning, reasoning, problem-solving, visual perception, speech recognition, decision-making, and language translation. As a result, it is expected that in the near future AI will revolutionise the majority of industries, including finance, healthcare, transportation, criminal justice, and smart cities.[18]

In fact, AI is not a brand-new idea developed in the 21st century. Rather, scientists have been working on it since the 1950s. Professor John McCarthy, a computer scientist at Stanford University, coined the phrase 'artificial intelligence' in 1956 when he hosted the first academic conference in this field.[19] However, the notion of AI has evolved continuously as technologies advance, in particular, with the mass production of computing hardware which enables stronger computing powers at lower costs.[20] In the old days, even some of the most fundamental features of personal computers, such as text recognition and maths calculator, would have been regarded as AI in the 1970s. However, the impression has greatly changed as AI is seen as machines, computers, or vehicles with more sophisticated and intelligent features, such as cars with autonomous driving, wearable devices with personal health assistance, and robo-advisers. These examples have demonstrated how the idea of AI, like that of Fintech, is always changing. As science and technology continues to advance, AI in 2050 is likely to be much smarter and more advanced than it is now.

The concept of AI can be further divided into strong AI and weak AI, depending on the functions and distinctive goals to achieve.[21] Weak AI refers to the machine intelligence that could only simulate basic human cognition

---

[17] Nils J. Nilsson, *Principles of Artificial Intelligence* (Burlington: Morgan Kaufmann, 2014), p. 2.
[18] Darrell M. West and John R. Allen, 'How Artificial Intelligence Is Transforming the World', 24 April 2018, Brookings Institution, https://www.brookings.edu/research/how-artificial-intelligence-is-transforming-the-world/.
[19] University of Washington, 'The History of Artificial Intelligence', December 2016, http://courses.cs.washington.edu/courses/csep590/06au/projects/history-ai.pdf.
[20] AI could not be achieved without sufficient computing power and big data. The development of AI has been facilitated by the growth of other technologies such as big data and cloud computing, providing voluminous information for machines to observe human activities and make predictions, as well as offering improved algorism and more computational capacity.
[21] 'Artificial Intelligence', Stanford Encyclopedia of Philosophy, 12 July 2018, http://plato.stanford.edu/entries/artificial-intelligence/.

and it has limited application in certain business areas. Although weak AI systems can be asked to accomplish different tasks, the scope of their operation is mostly set within a predefined range. Weak AI does not have its own mind. It seems to strictly follow the coding of its creators, despite the ability to quickly analyse a large quantity of data to find a practical solution. Apple's Siri, Amazon's Alexa, and Baidu's Xiaodu are some examples of a weak AI system. In contrast, strong AI is said to have its own mind. It stands for machine intelligence that matches the level of human intelligence and exhibits strong abilities of human cognition. Strong AI systems are able to learn, reason, solve problems, make independent judgement, formulate objectives, and communicate with other humans or AI. However, strong AI has been a hypothetical concept so far, as most of the projects are at the initial stage of experiment, such as self-driving cars and multimodal large language models (e.g., Generative Pre-trained Transformer 4 (GPT4)). Table 2.1 provides a summary of major differences between weak AI and strong AI models.

Recent years have seen the rapid growth and extensive application of AI across different business sectors including online search engines, medical diagnoses, and banking and finance. AI is likely to change most aspects of our work and life in the future, as it is projected to replace human jobs and improve the efficiency of production. It marks one of the major turning points in the history of AI that, in 2017, Google's AlphaGo defeated Mr Ke Jie who has been the world's top Go player.[22] This incident has shown that the intelligence of a robot could potentially match that of the smartest people on the earth. In the same year, Sophia, an AI-enabled robot created by Hanson Robotics in Hong Kong that can mimic 62 different human expressions, was granted full citizenship by the Saudi Arabian government.[23] During the Covid-19 pandemic, scientists and pharmaceutical companies have been using AI and machine learning to discover new drugs for curing the coronavirus. For example, Alibaba devised an AI algorithm that is able to diagnose coronavirus cases within 20 seconds with an accuracy rate of 96%.[24] The examples have demonstrated how intelligent and broadly applicable AI is to all business sectors.

---

[22] Go is considered as the most complex board game in the world as players take turns to place black or white stones on a 19×19 grid and compete to take control of most territories. See 'Google AI Defeats Human Go Champion', *BBC*, 25 May 2017, http://www.bbc.com/news/technology-40042581.
[23] 'Should Robots Be Citizens?', British Council, accessed 1 June 2023, http://www.britishcouncil.org/anyone-anywhere/explore/digital-identities/robots-citizens.
[24] 'AI Steps up in Battle Against Covid-19', *BBC*, 18 April 2020, http://www.bbc.com/news/technology-52120747.

Table 2.1 Comparison between weak AI and strong AI.

	Weak AI	Strong AI
Goals	To take over some vertical tasks from humans	To replace humans in most areas of work
Application and functionalities	Narrow. It has been programmed to provide a predefined range of functions. It can imitate humans' thinking and behaviours and complete some complex tasks	Wide. It has been developed to have the same (or even more) intellectual abilities as humans. It exhibits strong human cognitive abilities and can think, react, and accomplish any tasks like humans
Whether AI has its own mind	No	Yes
Whether AI needs further human instruction	Yes	No
Intelligence level	Low. It has been designed to look like intelligent humans	High. It has built-in advanced algorithms to enable it to think and behave just like intelligent humans
Capacities	Machine learning, voice and face recognition, suggestions for corrections in search engines, navigation systems, expert systems, to communicate in program language	Deep learning, logical thinking, to make decisions in the event of uncertainty, to make plans, to learn new knowledge and skills, to communicate in natural language
Examples	There are many examples including Apple's Siri, Amazon's Alexa, Google Assistant, and Baidu's Xiaodu	Limited examples as most projects are at the initial stage of experiment, such as self-driving cars and multimodal large language model (GPT4)

Source: The table is compiled by the author

Now, we will pay our attention to AI in the finance sector and Fintech. AI has been widely deployed in the financial industry. It has brought substantial changes to financial products, service delivery methods and channels, risk management, credit rating, and investment decision-making. At present, the application of AI in finance focuses on specific application scenarios, like smart payments, smart insurance claims, robo-advisors, intelligent customer service, intelligent marketing, smart investment research, and intelligent risk control. So far, intelligent customer services have been offered by an increasing number of financial institutions to provide better customer experience. In 2015, the Bank of Communications introduced intelligent AI robots called 'Jiao Jiao' as lobby managers in its bank branches in over 30 Chinese provinces and cities.[25] Jiao Jiao uses speech recognition, touch interaction, and body language to greet visitors, offer service advice, and check customers' accounts. Also, Ping An Bank, which employs 6,000 technology researchers, has replaced 80% of its customer support workforce with a 24/7 customer service system built using AI.[26]

According to a survey, 56% of hedge funds in the US have employed AI to inform their investment decisions, which has suggested the broad use of AI in the fund industry.[27] Moreover, JPMorgan has set up an AI research team headquartered in New York to explore cutting-edge technologies in relation to AI, machine learning, and cryptography to develop impactful solutions for the bank's clients and its own businesses.[28] Deloitte has found three traits that are shared by finance industry leaders in AI: integrating AI into their strategic plans, using AI to create potential for revenue and customer engagement, and having a portfolio strategy to acquiring AI.[29]

There is little doubt that the widespread use of AI is allowing us to improve society's overall wealth and productivity. However, AI has posed multiple legal, regulatory, and ethical challenges, making us rethink how machines and humans should interact and coexist in the future. For instance, millions of jobs are expected to be replaced by AI over the course of the next few decades, which could result in significant unemployment or even civil upheaval. According to an empirical study conducted in the US, throughout the 1990s and 2000s, adding one more robot for every 1,000 workers had resulted in a 0.2% decrease in total employment and a 0.4% decrease in salaries.[30] In an extreme scenario, AI might lead to a future without employment, but people tend to have a more conservative observation that AI is only likely to replace parts of the workforce, in particular those with low skill levels. According to a media survey, 37% of US workers between the ages of 18 and 24 were concerned that AI technology could lead to the loss of their jobs, compared to only 16% of workers over the age of 65.[31] It is probably

---

[25] Bank of Communications, 'Bank of Communications News', 29 September 2015, http://www.bocomgroup.com/BankCommSite/shtml/jyjr/cn/7158/7162/39814.shtml.
[26] 'From 1.0 to 4.0 Era, Ping An Bank Detailed the Transformation Path of AI Bank', Yicai, 27 June 2019, https://www.yicai.com/news/100240136.html.
[27] Peter Salvage, 'Artificial Intelligence Sweeps Hedge Funds', BNY Mellon, March 2019, http://www.bnymellon.com/us/en/what-we-do/business-insights/artificial-intelligence-sweeps-hedge-funds.jsp.
[28] 'Artificial Intelligence Research', JPMorgan, accessed 1 June 2023, http://www.jpmorgan.com/global/technology/artificial-intelligence.
[29] Deloitte, 'AI Leaders in Financial Services: Common Traits of Frontrunners in the Artificial Intelligence Race', 2019, https://www2.deloitte.com/content/dam/insights/us/articles/4687_traits-of-ai-frontrunners/DI_AI-leaders-in-financial-services.pdf.
[30] Daron Acemoglu and Pascual Restrepo, 'Robots and Jobs: Evidence from US Labor Markets', *Journal of Political Economy* (2020) 128: 2188, 2192.
[31] Jacob Douglas, 'These American Workers Are the Most Afraid of AI Taking Their Jobs', *CNBC*, 7 November 2019, http://www.cnbc.com/2019/11/07/these-american-workers-are-the-most-afraid-of-ai-taking-their-jobs.html.

because young workers are natives to the digital world, so they can better understand the potential impacts that AI is generating on their personal and professional lives. Employees in certain industries, such as advertising and marketing (45%), business support and logistics (42%), automotive (37%), and retail (34%), seem to be more concerned about AI and automation taking their jobs.[32] Nonetheless, if strong AI is becoming a reality, it will even put many knowledge-intensive and high-skilled jobs at risk, such as lawyers, doctors, investment bankers, and IT programmers. When AI is causing drastic social changes like this, we will need to rethink the meaning of work. It would be necessary for us to call for the government to safeguard the labour market and strengthen the social safety net in order to help the unskilled and jobless.

Furthermore, AI could lead to greater income and wealth inequality across the world as innovators are likely to earn the surplus while a large percentage of people face the job crisis.[33] Entrepreneurs and wealthy individuals are more likely to make use of AI to raise business productivity and cut down labour costs, leading to higher business profits and the further concentration of personal wealth. In contrast, ordinary people will probably be economically worse off when their jobs are going to be replaced by machines and robots. In addition, there are several ethical concerns raised by the widespread adoption of AI. It is possible that we will interact with more robots at work and in our daily lives, some of which may even resemble humans in appearance. However, it is still unclear whether we should treat these robots as machines or as human beings, and whether they should be given legal identities that allow them to own property and engage in contracts. Scholars and law-makers have widely debated the legal status of AI systems and whether we should admit their personhood.[34] It is clear that how we decide the legal standing of machines and robots will have a profound impact on the social norms and social originations in the future. Some people fear the arrival of the so-called technological singularity when AI overtakes human intelligence.[35] If that really happens, AI systems will be able to change their own programming and it is likely that they will pursue their own interests above their creators'. They might disregard human morality as it currently exists, and, as a result, AI systems might act in ways that are detrimental to human welfare and interests. In the worst case, they might try to eliminate all humanity, which would be extremely dangerous for human security. Last

---

[32] Ibid.
[33] Anton Korinek and Joseph E. Stiglitz, 'Artificial Intelligence and Its Implications for Income Distribution and Unemployment', National Bureau of Economic Research, December 2017, http://www.nber.org/papers/w24174.
[34] European Parliament, 'The Ethics of Artificial Intelligence: Issues and Initiatives', 11 March 2020, p. 20, https://www.europarl.europa.eu/thinktank/en/document/EPRS_STU(2020)634452.
[35] Murray Shanahan, *The Technological Singularity* (Cambridge, MA: MIT Press, 2015), p. 151.

but not least, using AI for military applications, such as creating intelligent weapons, may result in catastrophic consequences that risk human lives and undermine international peace.

2.3.2 Blockchain

Blockchain is a decentralised public ledger system that maintains a database of transactional records that are shared among network nodes, updated by miners, and tracked by all users.[36] In theory, the blockchain system, which is a decentralised method of storing and accessing data, is neither owned nor controlled by any one party. Let's look at 'block' and 'chain' separately to better understand the concept: 'block' stands for the digital information regarding commercial transactions, including but not limited to transactional parties, date, time, and price amount, while 'chain' means the way in which the information within each block has been stored as well as how each block is linked to another. Owing to blockchain's P2P feature, it is widely considered as an advanced way of data storing and sharing that is secure, transparent, easily accessible, and difficult to tamper. Blockchain has an enormous economic advantage over traditional means of keeping and processing data, for relevant transactions will not incur any transactional costs, though such a network does produce certain infrastructure costs which are to be shared by all users. Due to its unique characteristics, such as decentralisation, transparency, and immutability, blockchain has grown significantly in favour as the technology enabling public record-keeping in recent years.[37]

For a long time, we have been accustomed to centralised data services that possess the information of all users through one set of data servers. Accordingly, each user needs to interact with the sole centralised body to submit and retrieve information whenever they need it. For instance, banks and building societies represent the conventional centralised money system where customers deposit and withdraw cash through their official branches. Through factional reserve banking, banks merely keep a small percentage of deposits that they receive from customers and lend out the most of customers' funds, resulting in further money creation in the economy.[38] Meanwhile, when customers make any payments, it has to go through banks which collectively form a payment system. Centralised information or monetary systems,

---

[36] Melanie Swan, *Blockchain: Blueprint for a New Economy* (Sebastopol, CA: O'Reilly, 2015), p. 1.
[37] UN, 'Let's Learn Blockchain: Blockchain 101', 11 April 2018, https://unite.un.org/sites/unite.un.org/files/technovation/1_blockchain_101_ariana_fowler_consensys.pdf.
[38] Iris H.-Y. Chiu and Joanna Wilson, *Banking Law and Regulation* (Oxford: Oxford University Press, 2019), p. 2.

despite their dominant position in our society, have some drawbacks. For example, as the data are being kept in a single place, such a system is prone to the disruption caused by the breakdown of IT systems or any erroneous modifications, when all users are likely to lose access to their information. Moreover, the centralised system of storing data is susceptible to hacking and cyber-attacks. In contrast, within a decentralised information system like blockchain, data are held by multiple users who jointly own and manage the information. Blockchain is the underlying technology for BTC, Ethereum, Ripple, Litecoin, and other cryptocurrencies whose prices are highly volatile.[39] Instead of being issued by central banks, the virtual money has been created by users through the so-called mining process. If users of cryptocurrencies would like to send their money to each other, they do not need to go through any third parties and financial intermediaries, such as a bank.

Blockchain is also known for its transparency as all transaction data are made publicly available, making it possible for anyone to inspect the data at any time. However, the identities of users will be hidden by complicated cryptography, so people can only see other users' public addresses instead of their real account names, which protects the privacy of users but makes cryptocoins a hotbed for money laundering activities.[40] Moreover, the immutability of blockchain suggests that no one is able to tamper with the information once it is entered into the system, thanks to the hashing algorithm that takes an input of information at any length and then produces an output of information at a fixed length.[41] When initiating a transaction using blockchain, a party will create a new block which is to be verified by thousands of computers scattered around the whole network. The new block, after the verification process, will be added to the existing blockchain as a unique record and then it will be disseminated and stored across all computers within the same network. As a result, it is nearly impossible to falsify any records in the blockchain as this would need to change the data deposited in thousands of computers. Immutability is of great value to financial institutions, which are prone to embezzlement and where we have seen a number of scandals in the past as some senior bankers cooked the books and played around with the company accounts.

---

[39] BoE, 'What Are Cryptoassets (Cryptocurrencies)?', 19 May 2020, http://www.bankofengland.co.uk/knowledgebank/what-are-cryptocurrencies.

[40] For an examination of how BTC becomes a perfect tool for laundering criminal proceeds see Lerong Lu, 'Bitcoin: Speculative Bubble, Financial Risk and Regulatory Response'. *Butterworths Journal of International Banking and Financial Law* (2018) 33: 178.

[41] For the definition and examples of hash function (hashing algorithm) see University of Missouri–St. Louis, 'Hashing Functions and their Uses in Cryptography', accessed 1 June 2023, http://www.umsl.edu/~siegelj/information_theory/projects/HashingFunctionsInCryptography.html.

The blockchain technology has the potential to be applied across diverse industries and business scenarios, including banking, insurance, ticket selling, intellectual property protection, the sharing economy, supply chain management, property records, smart contracts, and IoT. For example, blockchain is ideally suited for facilitating international payments and money transfers since it helps with the tamper-proof documentation of sensitive data. In April 2018, Santander launched the world's first blockchain-based international money transfer service, which is known as the 'Santander One Pay FX', in a number of countries including Spain, the UK, Brazil, and Poland.[42] As a result of the reduction in the number of intermediaries in the payment process and elimination of the need for banks to manually settle payment transactions, international payments are now more efficient and affordable for retail customers. In November 2019, the US Securities and Exchange Commission (SEC) approved a pilot project led by Paxos, a financial infrastructure operator, which utilises blockchain to settle stock market transactions in a faster and cost-effective manner, when the current settlement standard normally takes two business days.[43] Moreover, the secure feature of blockchain renders it a useful tool for the accounting and auditing industry, where high regulatory standards exist in terms of validity and integrity. According to Deloitte, blockchain unveils the future for accounting, as companies, instead of keeping separate records based on transaction receipts, are able to record their transactions directly into a joint register and create an interlocking system of enduring accounting records.[44] It will significantly reduce the possibility of human errors and deliberately falsifying or damaging accounting data, as any entries will be distributed to all transactional parties with the protection of cryptography. Furthermore, blockchain can be used by regulators and financial institutions to combat money laundering and terrorist financing activities, as its immutable and decentralised nature greatly supports the daily work of 'know your customer (KYC)'.[45] The downside of applying blockchain at a larger scale, however, is that it might

---

[42] Santander, 'Santander Launches the First Blockchain-Based International Money Transfer Service Across Four Countries', 12 April 2018, https://www.santander.com/content/dam/santander-com/en/documentos/historico-notas-de-prensa/2018/04/NP-2018-04-12-Santander%20launches%20the%20first%20blockchain-based%20international%20money%20transfer%20service%20across%20-en.pdf.

[43] Alexander Osipovich, 'Blockchain Makes Inroads into the Stock Market's $1 Trillion Plumbing System', *The Wall Street Journal*, 7 November 2019, http://www.wsj.com/articles/blockchain-makes-inroads-into-the-stock-markets-1-trillion-plumbing-system-11573131600.

[44] Deloitte, 'Blockchain Technology: A Game-Changer in Accounting?', March 2016, p. 3, https://www2.deloitte.com/content/dam/Deloitte/de/Documents/Innovation/Blockchain_A%20game-changer%20in%20accounting.pdf.

[45] Loi Luu, 'With Blockchain, Knowing Your Customer Is More Important than Ever', *Forbes*, 17 May 2018, http://www.forbes.com/sites/luuloi/2018/05/17/with-blockchain-knowing-your-customer-is-more-important-than-ever/.

decrease the need for accountants, auditors, and bankers, resulting in certain job losses for professionals in the national and international financial centres.

2.3.3 Cloud computing

Cloud computing is the delivery of on-demand computing services over the internet ('the cloud') on a pay-for-use basis.[46] According to Microsoft, cloud computing refers to the supply of computing services, including servers, storage, databases, networking, software, analytics, and intelligence, through the internet to offer faster innovations, flexible resources, and economies of scale.[47] Cloud computing represents a major transformation of how modern businesses organise their IT resources. Traditionally, businesses need to set up their own on-site data centres, which requires heavy investments in hardware, software, and daily infrastructure management. In contrast, cloud computing allows any enterprises to use professional cloud services provided by large IT companies like Microsoft, Amazon, and Alibaba, instead of establishing and maintaining their own data centres. More corporations have chosen to outsource their computing and data storage departments to third-party IT companies in order to save costs and increase the capacity and speed of data storage and processing. It is suggested that the use of cloud computing could save up to nearly 70% of the lifecycle cost for a 1,000-server deployment.[48]

In practice, cloud computing is often provided as on-demand services. Businesses are allowed to request any amounts of computing power within a few seconds, which helps them meet the elastic needs of computing power during their daily business operation. Clearly, this flexible and productive arrangement has become a popular choice for corporations, large and small, around the world which have been moving their data analytic job over the cloud. For example, the aircraft-maker Boeing has been using Microsoft Azure to analyse aircraft fuel burn, plan flights, and predict maintenance costs,[49] not to mention most banks and financial institutions, like Goldman Sachs, Citigroup, and HSBC, that are now heavily reliant on cloud services. Cloud computing services could be beneficial for any businesses,

---

[46] 'What Is Cloud Computing?', IBM, accessed 1 June 2023, http://www.ibm.com/uk-en/cloud/learn/what-is-cloud-computing.
[47] 'What Is Cloud Computing? A Beginner's Guide', Microsoft, accessed 1 June 2023, http://azure.microsoft.com/en-gb/overview/what-is-cloud-computing/.
[48] Kevin L. Jackson, 'The Economic Benefit of Cloud Computing', Forbes, 17 September 2011, http://www.forbes.com/sites/kevinjackson/2011/09/17/the-economic-benefit-of-cloud-computing/.
[49] Barb Darrow, 'How These Fortune 500 Companies Are Moving to the Cloud', Fortune, 19 July 2016, http://fortune.com/2016/07/19/big-companies-many-clouds/.

as specialised IT companies have more resources in conserving and updating both hardware and software of data processing. It also makes the use of data safer and more reliable because extra backups and technology supports are offered by professional cloud providers, which would not be achievable by most companies that have limited budget and resources in this field.

Cloud computing services are broadly divided into three categories: Software as a Service (SaaS), Platform as a Service (PaaS), and Infrastructure as a Service (IaaS).[50] Each service has its own advantages and functionalities, which suit the needs of different corporate customers. Figure 2.1 illustrates the key differences between the three cloud computing service models. SaaS

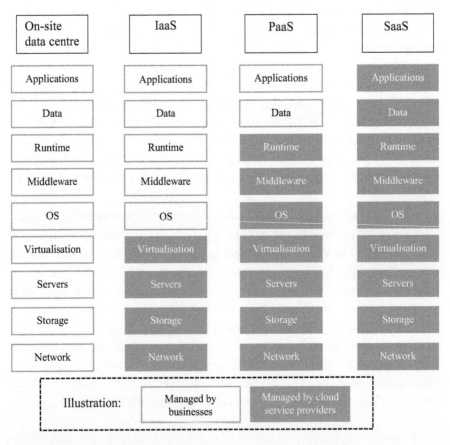

Figure 2.1 Cloud computing service models.

Source: The figure is compiled by the author

---

[50] 'IaaS, PaaS and SaaS Cloud Service Models', IBM, accessed 1 June 2023, https://www.ibm.com/cloud/learn/iaas-paas-saas.

is known as the cloud-based application service, as it allows businesses to rent the use of an existing app from the cloud service provider which manages underlying infrastructure, data, hardware, and software. SaaS is viewed as the most time-saving and cost-effective cloud solution for businesses customers, as it is a ready-to-use software service provided by third parties. Thus, users can access this service anytime on most devices connected to the internet. Some examples of SaaS include Microsoft Office 365, Google Apps, Dropbox, and Cisco WebEx. PaaS provides a platform for businesses and developers who can rely on it to create their own customised applications. Similar to SaaS, the servers, operating system (OS), data storage, and other data infrastructures will be maintained by the cloud computing service providers. Businesses only need to concentrate on the design and creation of applications built upon the existing PaaS framework. Examples of PaaS are AWS Elastic Beanstalk, Microsoft Azure, Heroku, and Force.com. IaaS provides businesses with computing resources similar to a traditional on-site data centre but removes their burden of managing such facilities. It offers greatest flexibility compared with SaaS and PaaS. Examples of IaaS are Amazon Web Services (AWS), DigitalOcean, Rackspace, Cisco Metapod, and Google Compute Engine.

Cloud computing services can also be categorised into public cloud, private cloud, and hybrid cloud, depending on the venue where business users store their data.[51] Public clouds are owned and operated by third-party cloud service providers that offer all hardware, software, and other technical infrastructures. The general public, individuals, or businesses do not have to purchase any hardware and they can access the cloud services remotely via internet on a pay-as-you-go basis. Some well-known public cloud providers include Microsoft Azure, AWS, Google Cloud Platform, AliCloud, Tencent Cloud, and Baidu Cloud. In contrast, private clouds are the cloud computing facilities used by a single business or organisation, which are more secure but expensive to operate. Private clouds, in most cases, are maintained as the private network by a company's on-site data centre, but they can also be hosted in a shared data centre or even in the public cloud providers' data centre. Hybrid clouds combine the features of both public and private clouds, which offer more flexible and adaptive computing solutions for corporate clients. Hybrid clouds allow their users to access extra public cloud computing resources if their private clouds reach the limit, which is an obvious advantage.

---

[51] 'What Is the Difference Among Public Cloud, Private Cloud and Hybrid Cloud?', Alibaba Cloud, accessed 1 June 2023, http://www.alibabacloud.com/knowledge/public-cloud-private-cloud-hybrid-cloud.

The application of cloud computing in financial services is likely to raise productivity for financial institutions and provide better products and services for consumers. Migrating to the cloud is favourable for most financial institutions as cloud computing resources bring a lot of benefits, such as agile innovation, risk mitigation, and cost reduction.[52] Due to fewer local data centres and greater operational efficiency, clouds that offer computing solutions to multinational corporations facilitate efficient and seamless data transfer during mergers and acquisitions, enable large financial institutions and start-ups to collaborate to create a Fintech ecosystem, and facilitate the development of a greener financial industry.[53] Moreover, the cloud transformation allows financial institutions to synchronise the whole enterprise and actively integrate different business units through data sharing, so they will have deeper and more sophisticated data analytics helping them make quicker and more uniform decisions to address customers' problems.[54]

So far, the financial services industry has already adopted a variety of cloud services and deployment models to suit its specific commercial and IT needs. We have seen an increasing number of bespoke cloud solutions for different financial segments. For example, there are banking-focused cloud services like core banking cloud service, lending and leasing cloud services, and revenue management and billing cloud services; insurance-focused cloud services like policy administration for life and annuity cloud services, health insurance cloud services, and rating and underwriting cloud services; and analytics cloud services like risk management cloud services, financial crime and compliance management cloud services, operational risk cloud services, and regulatory reporting cloud services.[55] Furthermore, the increasing data availability, coupled with more computational power, empowers Fintech platforms like P2P lenders and digital banks to better assess the credit profile of some borrowers who have been refused by large banks, improving their chance of obtaining an affordable loan.[56]

---

[52] Pinsent Masons, 'Banking on Cloud: A Discussion Paper by Pinsent Masons and the BBA (Now UK Finance)', December 2016, https://www.pinsentmasons.com/thinking/special-reports/banking-on-cloud.

[53] Institute of International Finance, 'Cloud Computing in the Financial Sector', August 2018, https://www.iif.com/portals/0/Files/private/32370132_cloud_computing_in_the_financial_sector_20180803_0.pdf.

[54] Deloitte, 'Cloud Computing: More than Just a CIO Conversation', 2019, p. 4, https://www2.deloitte.com/content/dam/Deloitte/ar/Documents/financial-services/Cloud-Banking-2030-Julio-2019.pdf.

[55] Oracle, 'Cloud Computing in Financial Services: A Banker's Guide', November 2015.

[56] Thomas Hale, 'How Big Data Really Fits into Lending', *The Financial Times*, 13 March 2019, https://ftalphaville.ft.com/2019/03/13/1552488421000/How-big-data-really-fits-into-lending/.

2.3.4 Data (big data)

Big data describes the large volume of data being collected, processed, and utilised by modern businesses in their daily operations. The concept encompasses structured, semistructured, and unstructured information, including but not limited to consumers' demographic and psychographic information, product reviews and commentaries, blogs, social media, and any other forms of data streamed continuously from mobile devices, sensors, wearables, and technical devices.[57] Obviously, the use of big data initially requires the production and accumulation of great amounts of data. Our personal computers, smartphones, tablets, and other electronic devices have been constantly generating all sorts of data, which can be processed by corporations, governments, and other organisations equipped with algorithms and analytical tools to extract valuable information for commercial purpose.

Internet companies, such as social media platforms and online shopping websites, are able to gather massive amounts of information from their users. Clearly, social media has become the primary source of information for many people, especially the millennial generation. As of the 1st quarter of 2023, Facebook (or Meta as it is known today) had 2.99 billion monthly active users.[58] On average, each user spent 50 minutes on Facebook every day, and 78% of US consumers claimed that they discovered the retail products they want to buy through Facebook.[59] Every second, internet businesses and tech giants produce petabytes of data, which is a goldmine for marketing and sales since data's commercial value should never be underrated. The e-commerce giant Alibaba and its affiliated Taobao and Tmall online shopping portals have been serving 700 million consumers globally.[60] Alibaba's data and cloud technologies have empowered millions of enterprises to sell their products directly to consumers located in any parts of the world, contributing to the digital transformation of manufacturing and retail industries in many countries including China. Evidently, big data is beneficial for most modern corporations as it reduces the time and monetary costs of business operations and helps companies make smarter decisions based on precise data analysis.

---

[57] PwC, 'Where Have You Been All My Life? How the Financial Services Industry Can Unlock the Value in Big Data', October 2013, http://www.pwc.com/us/en/financial-services/publications/viewpoints/assets/pwc-unlocking-big-data-value.pdf.

[58] Active users are those who have logged into Facebook (Meta) during the last 30 days. See 'Number of Monthly Active Facebook Users Worldwide as of 1st Quarter 2023', Statista, accessed 1 June 2023, https://www.statista.com/statistics/264810/number-of-monthly-active-facebook-users-worldwide/.

[59] James B. Stewart, 'Facebook Time: 50 Minutes a Day', *The New York Times*, 6 May 2016, B1.

[60] Alibaba, 'Alibaba Group Announces December Quarter 2018 Results', 30 January 2019, http://www.alibabagroup.com/en/news/press_pdf/p190130.pdf.

On the other hand, big data is also advantageous to consumers, since more tailored products and services can be created according to their real needs. A growing number of online retailers are advertising their products based on consumers' buying habits revealed by their previous activities on social media and shopping websites.

Big data presents both opportunities and challenges for financial institutions on various fronts, such as personalised customer service, fraud detection, risk measure, operational efficiency, and regulatory compliance. In a survey, 62% of business owners stated that big data has a significant potential to create competitive advantages.[61] With the aid of big data, banks and other financial institutions are able to provide improved and bespoke services for consumers. Market segmentation is of great importance to financial institutions, which divides existing and prospective customers into subgroups sharing common characteristics such as gender, age, marital status, occupation, income, and location. As a result, banks and Fintech companies can predict customers' demands depending on which categories of customer models they fall under. Big data is likely to give banks a better understanding of the types of loans and financial products their consumers are seeking. For example, Barclays has 17 million customers in the UK.[62] The information of banks regarding current accounts and credit card transactions can be used to identify market trends, growth opportunities, and customer behaviour based on actual spending. Financial institutions stand to benefit from increased customer satisfaction and higher profit levels when offering more individualised services to customers. According to Oracle, 84% of US executives claimed their businesses had noticed a rise in the demand for customers to have more individualised and customised experiences.[63] The survey further indicated that providing clients with a tailored experience could increase a business's annual revenue by 18%.[64]

Moreover, big data can enhance the fraud detection mechanism for financial companies. The growing use of online banking and mobile banking makes payment facilities, money transfer, and other banking services more convenient and affordable for consumers. However, the fast and easy services also expose customers to extra online fraud, which has become a global problem for financial regulators and law enforcers. Big data allows financial

---

[61] PwC, 'Where Have You Been All My Life? How the Financial Services Industry Can Unlock the Value in Big Data', October 2013, http://www.pwc.com/us/en/financial-services/publications/viewpoints/assets/pwc-unlocking-big-data-value.pdf.
[62] 'Insights by Barclays', Barclays, accessed 1 June 2023, http://insights.uk.barclays/.
[63] Oracle, 'The Era I Enterprise: Ready for Anything', April 2016, http://www.oracle.com/us/industries/oracle-era-ready-anything-2969053.pdf.
[64] Ibid.

institutions to record the spending habits and other financing patterns of customers, so they can easily detect unusual and suspicious online activities from users and request immediate account verification. This is likely to reduce the number of online frauds and prevent malicious actions. JPMorgan Chase employed the technologies to stop terrorist activities and identify fraud concerns among its own 250,000 employees.[65] The bank also relied on big data to identify fraudsters attempting to get into its customer accounts or cash machines. Apart from fraud detection, big data can be utilised to calculate and limit risk exposure relating to financial investments, providing suitable investment products for clients with different risk appetites. Finally, big data lies at the foundation of RegTech, which offers technologically advanced solutions to help financial institutions cope with onerous regulatory demands, improving the efficiency of financial compliance.[66] In summary, big data has been revolutionising many facets of the financial services sector by producing quicker, higher-quality solutions with less expense, based on the legitimate and effective collection and use of consumer data.

2.3.5 E-commerce

E-commerce refers to the commercial activities of buying and selling goods and services over an electronic network such as the internet, as well as relevant activities of transmitting funds and data relating to transaction parties.[67] E-commerce could be classified into four categories: business-to-consumer (B2C), business-to-business (B2B), consumer-to-business (C2B), and consumer-to-consumer (C2C).[68] In a strict sense, e-commerce is not a concrete technological term like AI or big data that we have previously discussed. However, the practice of e-commerce is highly technological, as the occurrence of relevant transactions depends on several technologies such as the internet, mobile network (e.g., 3G, 4G, and 5G), electronic funds transfer and payment system, supply chain and inventory management system, online marketing and sales, and electronic data collection and storage. Therefore, the development of e-commerce is intertwined with that of Fintech. In 2020, over 2 billion consumers bought goods and services online, as the total sales

---

[65] Richard Waters, 'Counter-Terrorism Tools Used to Spot Fraud', *The Financial Times*, 13 December 2012, https://www.ft.com/content/796b412a-4513-11e2-838f-00144feabdc0.
[66] The topic of RegTech will be discussed in detail in Chapter 3.
[67] Dave Chaffey, *Digital Business and E-Commerce Management*, 7th ed. (London: Pearson, 2019), p. 3.
[68] We also see e-commerce activities relating to business-to-government (B2G), but they are often considered as part of B2B in practice.

of e-commerce surpassed $4.2 trillion globally.[69] During the Covid-19 pandemic, more people chose online retail and payment due to the lockdown policies and safe shopping experience. In the US, e-commerce sales surged by $244.2 billion, or 43%, from $571.2 billion in 2019 to $815.4 billion in 2020.[70]

The rapid growth of e-commerce in the 2000s and 2010s is conducive to the rise of Fintech in three aspects. First of all, the completion of any e-commerce transaction needs the technical support of online or mobile payment facilities and digital wallets, which is a major business area of Fintech corporations. In the early days of PayPal, which is a leading online payment system, the company was primarily providing e-payment services for online retailers on eBay. PayPal had been the official payment provider for eBay for several years, when its payment system accumulated its first millions of users.[71] Prior to PayPal, consumers shopping online had to make payments to sellers by cheques or money orders via US mail. Similarly, Alipay used to be the exclusive online payment tool for Alibaba Group's shopping platforms including Taobao and Tmall dating back to 2003.[72] In the early 2000s, e-commerce and online shopping first gained popularity in China, but there existed a serious problem regarding the lack of trust between online retailers and shoppers who do not know each other. It has been perceived as the biggest hurdle of the online shopping industry, and that's why Alibaba launched Alipay to enable guaranteed transactions, increasing the safety of online purchases. In the present, Alipay and its parent company Ant Group (formerly known as Ant Financial) have developed into a fully fledged Fintech platform that offers mobile payment (Alipay), online banking (MyBank), wealth management (Ant Fortune), and credit rating (Sesame Credit), providing services to over 1 billion consumers, with a yearly transaction volume of US$17 trillion.[73] The success stories of PayPal and Alipay indicate that the rapid development of Fintech payment systems coincided with the exponential expansion of e-commerce in the early 21st century as it significantly

---

[69] 'E-commerce Worldwide', Statista, accessed 1 June 2023, https://www.statista.com/topics/871/online-shopping/.
[70] US Census Bureau, 'Annual Retail Trade Survey Shows Impact of Online Shopping on Retail Sales During COVID-19 Pandemic', 27 April 2022, https://www.census.gov/library/stories/2022/04/ecommerce-sales-surged-during-pandemic.html.
[71] 'Who We Are—History & Facts', PayPal, accessed 1 June 2023, https://about.pypl.com/who-we-are/history-and-facts/default.aspx.
[72] Lerong Lu, 'How a Little Ant Challenges Giant Banks? The Rise of Ant Financial (Alipay)'s Fintech Empire and Relevant Regulatory Concerns'. *International Company and Commercial Law Review* (2018) 28: 12, 14.
[73] Lerong Lu and Alice Lingsheng Zhang, 'Regulating Fintech Corporations Amidst Covid-19 Pandemic: An Analysis of Ant Group (Alipay)'s Suspension of IPO and Business Restructuring'. *The Company Lawyer* (2021) 42: 341.

sped up transaction times and improved the security of payments and money transfers between strangers.

Moreover, the development of e-commerce has encouraged more netizens to use digital banking and financial services like online banking and mobile banking, contributing to the proliferation of virtual banks such as Monzo, Starling, and N26. In order to satisfy customers' growing demand for e-commerce, banks have increased their online offerings to support online sales and purchases. Banks compete to provide services like the provision of online platforms that connect sellers and buyers, identity verification service, fraud detection features, electronic billing for cash management and remittance processing, and the provision of electronic procurement services to assist small businesses in negotiating volume discounts with suppliers.[74] Clearly, digital banking services are essential for conducting any e-commerce activities. Another area of Fintech businesses that benefits hugely from the development of e-commerce is the consumer credit or small business loan provider, as there is an increasing demand for finance from both online consumers and retailers. This has fuelled the growth of alternative lenders and P2P lending platforms such as Lending Club and Zopa. Finally, e-commerce facilitates the providers of consumer credits. The 'shop now pay later' feature, made available by Fintech platforms like Klarna, enables customers to split purchases into four equal payments, the first of which is due at checkout. With 150 million active users and more than 500,000 merchants across 45 countries, Klarna has rapidly established itself as the leading worldwide payments and shopping service provider.[75]

2.4 The main business models of Fintech

We have seen Fintech corporations organised under four different business models. Firstly, a sizable portion of Fintech services has been provided by tech start-ups or brand-new Fintech companies that have no prior financial industry experience. Examples are Monzo, Starling Bank, Tide, Stripe, and Klarna. It is observed that most Fintech firms that operate today had been set up from scratch by entrepreneurs in the past two decades (2000–2020). Compared with established financial institutions, Fintech start-ups benefit from low-cost and efficient operation since they do not possess legacy IT

---

[74] European Business Review, 'Ecommerce: Online Banking and Payments', 21 February 2022, https://www.europeanbusinessreview.com/ecommerce-online-banking-and-payments/.
[75] 'About Us', Klarna International, accessed 1 June 2023, https://www.klarna.com/international/about-us/.

systems and other heavy assets like a branch network and a large number of employees. Moreover, in many jurisdictions, novel Fintech businesses are subject to lighter regulatory scrutiny or receive favourable policy supports, such as the regulatory sandbox regime or Fintech seed funds. This could be another advantage for new Fintech businesses, but it also brings extra risks due to the potential regulatory arbitrage problem. However, there are also clear drawbacks for Fintech companies, as they don't seem to have the scale, reputation, or distribution systems to compete with conventional financial giants.[76]

Secondly, a large number of existing financial institutions have been actively testing and launching Fintech products and services in order to maintain their business competitiveness and market status. Large commercial banks (e.g., HSBC, Barclays, Wells Fargo, Citibank, and ICBC), investment banks (e.g., Goldman Sachs, Morgan Stanley, Credit Suisse, and Deutsche Bank), insurance companies (e.g., Allianz, AXA, Ping An, Aviva, and Prudential), accounting firms (e.g., PwC, Deloitte, Ernst & Young (EY), and KPMG), and hedge funds are quickly embracing all sorts of technological innovations. With more capital, clients, talent, and other resources at their disposal, large financial firms could scale up and solidify their market domination within a short period of time. Even some second-tier banks and smaller financial institutions have been trying to launch their own Fintech products or platforms to attract customers. For example, the UK's Clydesdale Bank and Yorkshire Bank released a smart mobile banking app 'B' which is able to learn the spending habits of its users automatically and offer tips to save money and make better budgets.[77]

Thirdly, tech giants (BigTech) around the world are relying on their technological advantages and huge customer bases to tap into the finance sector, creating a lot of innovative Fintech products, services, and platforms. BigTech are skilled at constructing their services, products, and ecosystems utilising information technologies. Most US BigTech like Alphabet, Amazon, Apple, and Meta, and Chinese BigTech like Alibaba and Tencent have long been involved in the financial services industry. Running their own financial services gives BigTech a significant advantage because they can quickly and thoroughly understand consumer demands thanks to their advanced analytics and network effects, as well as the valuable consumer data gathered

---

[76] Emma Dunkley, 'Fintech Start-Ups Put Banks under Pressure', *The Financial Times*, 12 September 2016, https://www.ft.com/content/ce8fa350-737f-11e6-bf48-b372cdb1043a.

[77] Rupert Jones, 'The Digital Upstarts Offering App-Only Banking for Smartphone Users', *The Guardian*, 14 May 2016, https://www.theguardian.com/money/2016/may/14/digital-app-only-banking-smartphone.

in their core businesses, such as social media, telecommunications, internet search, and e-commerce.[78] BigTech might swiftly join the financial sector by using such knowledge, capacities, and strategies. The successful operation of Apple Pay and Google Pay has already demonstrated that BigTech are significantly more competent at running payment systems than traditional banks and payment operators. Additionally, Meta's Diem project, which serves as a model for future digital currency, has drawn a lot of media interest.[79]

Fourthly, Fintech services and products are sometimes provided by a joint venture or consortium between large financial institutions and new Fintech companies. In most cases, the former would provide financial resources and a customer base, while the latter offers innovative technical solutions in financial services. Some incumbent banks have attempted to establish a cooperative relationship with Fintech start-ups, or even acquired certain stakes in them, in order to benefit from the rapid growth of the Fintech industry. In 2015, the Spanish lender BBVA spent £45 million purchasing 29.5% of the shares in Atom Bank, an online-only lender in the UK.[80] In China, commercial banks are accelerating their collaboration or forming strategic partnerships with Fintech companies, such as the alliance between ICBC, Alibaba and Ant Group.[81] This kind of partnership normally creates a win-win situation for both traditional banks and Fintech companies as they share the growing market and industry profits on a mutually beneficial basis.

Fintech has been reshaping every sphere of the financial system in terms of how consumers save, borrow, and invest money, as well as how institutions deliver their services. Therefore, how to classify various disruptive financial innovations has remained an important issue for practitioners, researchers, and policy-makers. Apparently, the Fintech industry has a lot of diversity, as it covers most areas of financial businesses like banking, online lending, payment, wealth and asset management, insurance, and virtual currency. As the book proceeds, readers will be impressed by the diversity and variety of Fintech. As discussed, the book does not aim to set a clear definition of Fintech, which seems to be an impossible task. The difficulty of defining Fintech mainly lies in the fact that innovation is a dynamic and multidimensional process. Today's extraordinary innovation is likely to become the industry

---

[78] Tobias Adrian, 'BigTech in Financial Services', IMF, 16 June 2021, https://www.imf.org/en/News/Articles/2021/06/16/sp061721-bigtech-in-financial-services.

[79] Hannah Murphy, 'Facebook's Libra Currency to Launch Next Year in Limited Format', *The Financial Times*, 27 November 2020, https://www.ft.com/content/cfe4ca11-139a-4d4e-8a65-b3be3a0166be.

[80] Martin Arnold and Emma Dunkley, 'BBVA Enters UK with Atom Deal', *The Financial Times*, 24 November 2015, p. 17.

[81] Alibaba, 'ICBC, Alibaba and Ant Financial Form Comprehensive Strategic Partnership Bringing Enhanced Fintech and Financial Services to Users', 16 December 2019, https://www.alibabagroup.com/en/news/press_pdf/p191216.pdf.

Table 2.2 Main Fintech business segments and selected examples.

Financial sector	Fintech applications	Examples
Banking	Digital-based bank, online-only bank, virtual bank, neo bank	Atom Bank, Monzo, Revolut, Starling Bank, Aldermore, Shawbrook, N26, MyBank
Lending	Online P2P lending, P2B lending, AI-based lending, crowdfunding	Zopa, Funding Circle, Lending Works, MarketInvoice, RateSetter, LendInvest, Iwoca, AvantCredit, Lufax
Payment	Online payment, mobile payment, money transfer	Apple Pay, Google Pay, Alipay, WeChat Pay, GoCardless, WorldRemit, TransferWise (Wise), PayPal, Stripe, Square
Insurance	Insurtech	Lemonade, Cuvva, Cyence, Safeshare, SPIXII, Slice Labs
Investment	Asset management, AI-empowered wealth management, robo-advisor, mobile trading, neo broker	Nutmeg, Wealthify, Trading 212, Betterment, Robinhood, Scalable Capital, Mint
Currency	Digital currency, virtual currency, cryptoassets, crypto exchange, stablecoin, CBDC	BTC, Ethereum, Ripple, Diem (Libra), USDT, Coinbase, Binance, Huobi, Bitstamp, E-CNY, Digital Euro

Source: The table is compiled by the author

norm in the near future, like the invention of the ATM in the 1960s. Therefore, it would be difficult to draw a clear line between innovative finance and traditional finance, as the former would gradually become the latter with the lapse of time. However, the book does try to capture the essence of Fintech, which refers to the technology-driven innovations in financial services. Table 2.2 summarises six main business segments of Fintech, and it is non-exhaustive.

2.5 The special characteristics of Fintech

Fintech not only delivers more convenient and affordable financial services for consumers, but also increases efficiency and profitability for financial institutions. Most Fintech companies are either working as a gap-filler in the financial industry (e.g., online P2P lending serves individual and SME borrowers rejected by mainstream banks) or preforming existing businesses in a better way (e.g., mobile payment platforms provide faster, cheaper services than traditional cash and card payments). We have already noted that technology has played a significant role in enabling modern finance. In a broad sense, almost anything in the financial services industry could be labelled as Fintech, as least when such financial products and services were firstly invented. However, the book endeavours to identify the common features of most Fintech businesses. They possess at least one of the following seven characteristics: innovation, disintermediation, automation, virtualisation, accessibility, customer centricity, and scalability.

2.5.1 Innovation

Innovation is the powerful delivery of creative ideas, which gives rise to new products, services, processes, and business models.[82] According to the perspectives of today's consumers, professionals, and investors, Fintech services and their providers must be innovative. As stated, innovation is a truly dynamic and constantly evolving process that never stops. Even the most ground-breaking financial innovations in the late 1990s, such as internet banking and online brokerage, are no longer viewed as revolutionary by today's consumers. Most people take such digital services for granted. Similarly, the greatest financial innovations from today, like cryptocurrencies and mobile payments, will soon become the norm for tomorrow's economy. Additionally, innovation must add value or increase the efficiency of providing financial services. It cannot be pursued solely for its own sake. Thanks to the thriving Fintech sector, both established institutions and start-ups put a lot of work into fusing the latest technologies like cloud computing, big data, blockchain, and AI with financial practices to generate real impacts.

2.5.2 Disintermediation

The majority of financial transactions need to go through specific financial institutions that function as intermediaries. The heavy reliance on financial intermediaries often leads to a situation where some traditional institutions like banks and brokers have obtained a dominant or even monopolistic market status. In contrast, financial disintermediation aims to remove banks, brokers, and any other third parties from the financial transaction process and interest relationships, enabling individuals and companies to conduct

---

[82] Marc de Jong, Nathan Marston, and Erik Roth, 'The Eight Essentials of Innovation', McKinsey Quarterly, 1 April 2015, https://www.mckinsey.com/business-functions/strategy-and-corporate-finance/our-insights/the-eight-essentials-of-innovation.

transactions or enter into investment agreements with each other directly.[83] For example, online P2P lending platforms, as a pure information exchange, directly match the investment need of savers with the capital demand of individual consumers and smaller businesses. Otherwise, savers would have to deposit their money into banks at first, and then banks would make loans from the pooled funds to any borrowers later. Also, cryptocurrencies tend to disintermediate traditional monetary and payment transactions by removing central banks and other authorities in the process of issuing and transferring money. Recently, financial activities based on DeFi have gained great popularity as they rely on distributed ledgers and smart contracts to offer financial services on a P2P basis, which are accessible to anyone as long as they have the internet connection.[84]

2.5.3 Automation

The level of automation in the financial sector has significantly increased due to the broad application of Fintech and AI. The financial services industry is currently experiencing a progressive replacement of human occupations, with increasing amounts of work being done by computers, machines, and robots. For example, algorithmic trading is rising rapidly among investment banks, hedge funds, and professional traders, as it refers to the process of using computers to execute securities transaction orders that involve automated or preprogrammed instructions to take into account variables like price, volume, and timing.[85] Moreover, most credit checks against potential borrowers are now performed by computers that have access to databases of credit information and use their computational capacity to analyse the big data to reach a decision in a matter of seconds. It is not only the quantity of automation but also its quality that is quickly improving. There is little doubt that the more intelligent machines enabled by data technologies and AI could assist financial institutions in making more accurate and efficient decisions when it comes to assessing the risks associated with lending and investing, as well as determining insurance premiums.

---

[83] Lerong Lu, 'Solving the SME Financing Puzzle in the UK: Has Online P2P Lending Got the Midas Touch?' *Journal of International Banking Law and Regulation* (2018) 33: 449, 454.
[84] 'What Is DeFi?', Coinbase, accessed 1 June 2023, https://www.coinbase.com/learn/crypto-basics/what-is-defi.
[85] 'Algorithmic Trading', IG, accessed 1 June 2023, https://www.ig.com/uk/trading-platforms/algorithmic-trading.

2.5.4 Virtualisation

Traditional finance relies on the branch network to reach clients and provide services. Major banks like HSBC and Barclays have thousands of physical branches on the high street of most towns, in addition to their headquarters and regional offices. However, a large number of Fintech service providers have limited or even no physical presence, as they could only be accessed by financial consumers via smartphone apps or online websites. Due to the lack of infrastructure legacies, many Fintech start-ups use the asset-light strategy. Online-based challenger banks like Monzo and Revolut are good examples representing the trend of virtualisation of financial services, as they do not possess any brick-and-mortar branches as traditional banks do.[86] The full digital presence has brought significant benefits in two aspects. On the one hand, it cuts the hefty costs of running the branch network, and on the other, virtual banks have no geographical boundaries for their business operation, so they can expand explosively within a short period of time.[87] In addition, all the virtual currencies (cryptocurrencies), as their name suggests, are fully digitalised and virtual, even the crypto exchanges themselves. The same is true for utilising traditional currencies like the US dollar, Chinese yuan, and British pound at a time when more and more people are turning to mobile payment systems like Apple Pay and Alipay, which are fostering the development of a cashless society. The trend of virtualisation of finance has been accelerated by the Covid-19 pandemic, as more people work, play, and shop online.

2.5.5 Accessibility

Most Fintech services are considered easily accessible and affordable for financial consumers, due to their online presence and low-cost business strategy. It echoes the widely held policy objective of financial inclusion, which calls for ensuring that all people and organisations have equal access to practical and reasonably priced financial products and services that satisfy their basic needs, including payments, transactions, savings, credit, and insurance.[88] It is obvious that the timely and economical provision of

---

[86] Lerong Lu, 'Financial Technology and Challenger Banks in the UK: Gap Fillers or Real Challengers?' *Journal of International Banking Law and Regulation* (2017) 32: 273, 277.
[87] Ibid.
[88] 'Financial Inclusion Overview', WB, accessed 1 June 2023, https://www.worldbank.org/en/topic/financialinclusion/overview.

financial services is contributing to a more sustainable global economy. At present, billions of population around the world are still excluded from the mainstream financial system, lacking access to essential banking and payment services. Kenya's M-PESA, as Africa's largest mobile money service and leading Fintech platform, offers an effective solution for the unbanked population to use basic financial services, including depositing, withdrawing, paying, and transferring money on a mobile device.[89] Clearly, with the aid of modern technologies, Fintech is able to provide more accessible and inexpensive financial services, benefitting consumers and businesses in both developed countries and emerging economies.

2.5.6 Customer centricity

In order to provide a positive customer experience, customer-focused businesses put customers at the centre of their organisational structure and corporate culture.[90] This increases customer loyalty and promotes company expansion. Compared with conventional financial institutions, Fintech companies tend to focus more on the real demands and experience of customers, based on which they design their products and ways of delivering services. It often leads to the simple and easy-to-use interface of Fintech apps like Monzo and Alipay, where users can easily identify and access various functions by fingertip. The simplicity and convenience of Fintech services was unimaginable in the past, when we needed to queue in a bank branch before talking to any staff member to convey our demands and then being served. Moreover, the majority of Fintech products and services are created so as to address specific consumer needs or pain points. For example, the undesirability of carrying heavy wallets to hold banknotes and plastic cards when consumers go out led to the creation of mobile payment tools. Moreover, Fintech companies are more customer centric because they value customers' engagement and feedback. Many of them have online community forums to collect costumers' suggestions and advice to improve product design and service quality.[91]

---

[89] 'M-PESA', Vodafone, accessed 1 June 2023, https://www.vodafone.com/about-vodafone/what-we-do/consumer-products-and-services/m-pesa.
[90] Denise Lee Yohn, '6 Ways to Build a Customer-Centric Culture', *Harvard Business Review*, 2 October 2018, https://hbr.org/2018/10/6-ways-to-build-a-customer-centric-culture.
[91] For example, see Monzo Community Forum, accessed 1 June 2023, https://community.monzo.com/; and Trading 212 Community, accessed 1 June 2023, https://community.trading212.com/.

2.5.7 Scalability

The term 'scalability' refers to an organisation's capacity to expand rapidly and respond to a growing workload by adding or efficiently utilising resources.[92] Fintech companies are agile in a sense that they, as challengers and latecomers, have to react to market demand quickly and precisely in order to survive and prosper. Most Fintech businesses are capable of scaling up their business operation within a short time, due to their simple, straightforward, and low-cost business models based on online distribution channels. The small capital requirement, coupled with the wide reach of the internet and mobile network, allows them to acquire millions of customers quickly. For instance, launched in 2012, the crypto exchange platform Coinbase today has 103 million verified customers who rely on the platform to transmit, utilise, and invest in cryptocurrencies.[93] In addition, it collaborates with 14,500 institutions and 245,000 ecosystem partners in more than 100 nations. In contrast, it took traditional stock exchanges (such as New York Stock Exchange (NYSE), London Stock Exchange (LSE), and Shanghai Stock Exchange (SSE)) several decades to establish their customer base and global reach. Apparently, Fintech companies are good at building ecosystems with business partners, clients, and even regulatory agencies. Some Fintech firms like PayPal and Stripe have adopted the application programming interface (API) system, which opens their digital platforms to appropriate third parties who can offer a variety of financial services to users. It is likely to speed up market penetration, increase competitiveness, and enrich customer experience by offering more consumer choices. Fintech ecosystems are powerful as they embrace openness and accessibility, which partly explains why they have grown so quickly in the 2010s.

2.6 The economic and social values of Fintech

This chapter will now highlight the economic and social values brought by Fintech after discussing the nature, forms, and distinctive features of the Fintech industry. Most Fintech companies have displayed a commitment to innovation and excellence, contributing to a more efficient and productive

---

[92] Deloitte, 'The Fintech Dilemma: When to Scale up Your Business?', accessed 1 June 2023, https://www2.deloitte.com/uk/en/pages/financial-services/articles/fintech-dilemma-when-to-scale-up-your-business.html.
[93] 'About—Coinbase', Coinbase, accessed 1 June 2023, https://www.coinbase.com/about.

financial system for the public good. Generally speaking, higher economic efficiency will lead to the creation of more wealth for individuals, businesses, and countries across the globe, which has indicated an advancement of society.[94] For consumers it also saves time and costs to access financial services, which could be spent on other economic activities to generate extra personal and social wealth. Moreover, the utilisation of big data, processed by AI and cloud computing, lends Fintech businesses a powerful strength in pricing risks, assessing creditworthiness of borrowers, and setting interest rates in a more accurate and intelligent manner. Data-driven financial services will be an essential component in tomorrow's digital economy. Moreover, Fintech is beneficial for solving a number of traditional dilemmas in economic theories. It is likely to address the information asymmetry problem between financial institutions and their clients, improving the transparency, competition, and efficiency of financial markets to help companies raise capital.[95]

What's more, Fintech is good for our society as it contributes to a more democratic, equal, and inclusive financial system. A lot of Fintech activities are known for P2P or disintermediated transactions, such as cryptocurrencies, online P2P loans, and other DeFi instruments. Relevant transactions have eliminated conventional institutions from the value chain, giving users more choice and freedom in creating and receiving financial services. Clearly, BTC and Ethereum are a more democratic way of making and using money, compared with fiat money monopolised by monetary authorities. Such decentralised cryptocurrencies have become increasingly popular as individuals and private corporations started to take over the power of creating money from the central banks. In 2008, Satoshi Nakamoto invented BTC by publishing an online paper advocating a new form of electronic cash that people can send to each other without going through disgraced banks.[96] Blockchain technology underpins the P2P nature of the BTC system. Crypto transactions take place directly between users, without the assistance of any financial intermediaries. It prompts economists and legal scholars to reconsider the meaning of money and whether the monetary system should be run by public or private entities.

---

[94] In a capitalist economy, prices suggest the equilibrium of supply and demand for any goods and services, which will continually change to allocate resources for the most efficient use. See James Dow and Gary Gorton, 'Stock Market Efficiency and Economic Efficiency: Is There a Connection?', *Journal of Finance* (1997) 52: 1087–1129.

[95] Information asymmetry has been a major concern for securities regulators cross the world, which also determines a company's cost of capital. See Richard A. Lambert, Christian Leuz, and Robert E. Verrecchia, 'Information Asymmetry, Information Precision, and the Cost of Capital'. *Review of Finance* (2012) 16: 1–29.

[96] 'Financial Technology: Friends or Foes?', *The Economist*, 6 May 2017, p. 12.

Fintech is conducive to fostering a more equal and fairer financial industry that works for everyone, especially ordinary consumers and smaller businesses. Traditional financial institutions and financial markets are said to serve large corporations primarily. After the 2007–2008 global financial crisis, banks have become increasingly reluctant to lend money to SMEs due to the stricter lending criteria as a result of regulatory changes. There is a big financing gap which needs to be closed by alternative financing sources outside the traditional banking sector, giving rise to an enormous online P2P lending marketplace in the US, Europe, and Asia. By allowing depositors and borrowers to interact with one other directly through online platforms, crowdfunding and P2P lending have displaced banks from the loan process. Due to benefits including the variety of funding sources, higher investment returns, the time-effective approach, and greater transparency, it has emerged as the most viable financing option for individuals and small businesses. The unequal bargaining power and discriminatory terms that are frequently seen in lending agreements between major banks and individual or corporate borrowers are expected to be addressed by online lending. It facilitates the building of an equal and unbiased financial system through the deeper and wider participation of consumers in the operation of financial activities.

Last but not least, through digital Fintech platforms like mobile payments and online banking apps, underserved financial customers can now access the financial services and products they require, leading to a more inclusive financial industry. The 2010s have observed the biggest change in payment methods and currencies thanks to the Fintech revolution. More people are using their mobile phones to make purchases, particularly those who live in large cities where 4G/5G networks are available, and more people are using smartphones and wearable devices. With over 2,700 banks as partners, Apple Pay has 127 million users worldwide, while Alipay has more than 450 million users.[97] The proliferation of Alipay and WeChat Pay enables the unbanked population in China to use modern financial services easily with nominal costs. As a result, the whole society is becoming highly connected, and the completion of financial transactions has been made easy. Consumers in Africa experienced the same thing when M-PESA allowed unbanked citizens in Kenya, Tanzania, Ghana, and South Africa to access fundamental banking services by any basic mobile devices. It not only boosts economic efficiency but also improves financial inclusion. Clearly, Fintech is beneficial for the sustainable growth of the financial industry and the wider economy.

---

[97] Helen H. Wang, 'Alipay Takes on Apple Pay and PayPal on Their Home Turf', *Forbes*, 30 October 2016, https://www.forbes.com/sites/helenwang/2016/10/30/will-alipay-dominate-global-mobile-payments/.

2.7 Conclusion

This chapter has examined the concept of Fintech and determined what it represents. Firstly, it has evaluated the 'fin' component of Fintech. From a functional standpoint, Fintech is performing similar functions to traditional finance in our economy, such as balancing the supply and demand for capital, pricing credit risks, and making investment decisions. However, Fintech tends to do the same jobs in a more intelligent, efficient, and cost-effective way as it embraces data analytics and AI. The chapter concludes that Fintech is a time-sensitive and relative concept, as today's Fintech innovation will soon become tomorrow's norm in the financial industry. Secondly, it assessed the 'tech' part of Fintech by examining the profound technological breakthroughs in the financial industry. AI, blockchain, cloud computing, data (big data), and e-commerce (ABCDE) have been the driving force behind most Fintech innovations and making Fintech distinctive from traditional finance. Technologies are the key to understanding Fintech, as they are genuinely new and disruptive, compared with the unchanged nature of finance. Thirdly, the chapter presented four different Fintech business models offered by various entities (i.e., Fintech start-ups, established financial institutions, BigTech, and joint ventures between any of the first three categories) and classified some typical Fintech businesses into six categories: banking, lending, payment, insurance, investment, and currency. Fourthly, it identified some common features of most Fintech companies and their business activities, including innovation, disintermediation, automation, virtualisation, accessibility, customer centricity, and scalability. Finally, it acknowledged key economic and social values that Fintech innovation has successfully brought, such as financial democracy, equality, and inclusion. It is safe to argue that Fintech helps create a more sustainable financial system and economy that benefits the majority of individuals, businesses, and nations.

3
Fintech Ecosystem—Part One

Global Fintech Hubs and Regulatory Solutions

3.1 Introduction

Fintech is more than innovative financial products and services. It represents a dynamic, multifaceted, and constantly evolving ecosystem that consists of multiple players interacting with each other and reshaping the financial industry collectively. The typical players in a Fintech ecosystem include financial regulators, Fintech corporations (e.g., established financial institutions, Fintech start-ups, and BigTech), consumers, and investors. According to EY, a well-functioning Fintech ecosystem is built upon four elements: talent, capital, policy, and demand.[1] This chapter primarily deals with two elements in any country's Fintech ecosystem. The first half of the chapter assesses global Fintech hubs, the important places where the current Fintech revolution is taking place. Fintech is a global phenomenon, as authorities in traditional financial centres like New York, London, Frankfurt, Hong Kong, and Singapore have been actively supporting the development of Fintech corporations and entrepreneurial environments.[2] Meanwhile, the time has witnessed the rise of some new Fintech hubs, which are not known for their financial industries. They manage to leverage on local strengths in technology and research capacity to become Fintech heartlands, such as San Francisco, Hangzhou, and Shenzhen. Accordingly, Sections 3.2–3.4 analyse the strengths, special features, and regulatory environments of global Fintech hubs in three geographical regions: the Americas (AMER), Asia Pacific (APAC), and Europe, Middle East, and Africa (EMEA).[3]

---

[1] 'Fintech and Ecosystems', EY, accessed 1 June 2023, https://www.ey.com/en_gl/banking-capital-markets/Fintech-ecosystems.

[2] For example, the Monetary Authority of Singapore (MAS) has been reforming its regulatory frameworks over blockchain and digital banking to increase the city state's attractiveness for Fintech start-ups and make it the world's most advanced financial centre. See Stefania Palma, 'Singapore Expands Fintech to Stay Ahead of Other Financial Centres', *The Financial Times*, 24 September 2019, https://www.ft.com/content/e7000952-b8fa-11e9-8a88-aa6628ac896c.

[3] The classification of global cities by three geographical regions (AMER, APAC, and EMEA) is commonly observed in the financial industry. See 'Office Locations', Goldman Sachs, accessed 1 June 2023, https://www.goldmansachs.com/our-firm/locations.html.

The chapter's second half focuses on the regulatory dimensions of Fintech, including regulatory strategies, toolkits, and policy considerations.[4] It identifies common regulatory themes for the Fintech sector, while detailed regulatory issues concerning specific Fintech business (e.g., virtual banking, online P2P lending, and digital money) will be addressed in the following chapters. Thus, Section 3.5 examines the practical application of regulatory technology (RegTech), as financial institutions and regulators rely on real-time data, complex algorithms, and AI to create advanced and cost-effective supervisory or compliance solutions. Section 3.6 assesses regulatory sandbox regimes throughout the world, allowing Fintech businesses to test novel products, services, and business ideas in a lighter regulatory setting to encourage innovation. Section 3.7 discusses the need to protect Fintech consumers and financial stability as two primary objectives for financial authorities and policy-makers to follow when they enact regulatory standards and policies to stimulate financial innovation. Section 3.8 draws a conclusion for the chapter.

3.2 Global Fintech hubs in the Americas

Despite the explosive development of Fintech activities, Fintech industries are not evenly distributed across the world. Innovative financial businesses and investment activities tend to concentrate in certain geographical regions like North America, West Europe, and Asia Pacific. Such regions have the highest number of Fintech companies, RegTech companies, and Metaverse companies, as well as more established financial institutions (e.g., banking, securities dealing, and insurance) and BigTech. They have strong Fintech industries and ecosystems, Fintech fund-raising opportunities, and best consumer experience. They see most active Fintech investments, due to the concentration of VC and PE funds. Besides these, Fintech corporations have also sprung up in other regional and global financial centres. For instance, there exist over 50 Fintech companies in the Middle East, including 20 in the United Arab Emirates.[5]

The 2010s has witnessed the rapid rise of so-called global Fintech hubs where the Fintech revolution is happening, due to their unmatched

---

[4] The reason why we discuss Fintech regulation and policy-making matters ahead of Fintech businesses (which is addressed in Chapter 4) is two-fold. On the one hand, policy and regulation plays an important and indispensable role in the development of Fintech sectors across the world, when governments tend to make supportive policies and regulatory rules to foster financial innovation. On the other hand, the discussion of regulatory topics is closely linked to the first part of the chapter—global Fintech hubs—where the regulatory environments are a key element to their success.

[5] Kadhim Shubber, 'UAE States Put Fintech Sector First', *The Financial Times*, 7 October 2016, p. 4.

advantages in terms of location, talent, capital, education, and technology. Accordingly, there have been a number of global Fintech hub rankings compiled by research institutions and consultancy firms throughout the world, such as Cambridge University,[6] Deloitte,[7] Findexable,[8] and Zhejiang University[9]. The chapter has consulted various private and official rankings to evaluate the unique strengths and regulatory environments of over a dozen global Fintech hubs located in all continents. In particular, this section considers the advantages and potential of global Fintech hubs in AMER.

The Fintech sector has experienced tremendous expansion in North America in the 2010s. With the largest banking sector in the world and stock exchanges like the NYSE and Nasdaq, the US financial services sector is large and diverse. After the global financial crisis in 2007–2008, American financial institutions are under increasing pressure to adhere to complicated new regulatory rules, such as the Dodd-Frank Act and consequent legal reforms.[10] In order to support Fintech businesses and other types of financial innovations, the US government and financial authorities have made a number of initiatives, including the direct provision of government subsidies and the policies that encourage private investments. For instance, the SEC has launched the Strategic Hub for Innovation and Financial Technology (FinHub).[11] FinHub coordinates the agency's oversight and response regarding emerging technologies in financial, regulatory, and supervisory systems, and it aims to interact with the private sector to foster innovation. Moreover, the US Small Business Administration (SBA) has launched a number of measures to support the growth of Fintech companies, including a proposal to permit Fintech start-ups to receive government-backed loans through SBA's

---

[6] Cambridge Centre for Alternative Finance, '2018 Global Fintech Hub Report—the Future of Finance Is Emerging: New Hubs, New Landscapes', 14 November 2018, https://www.jbs.cam.ac.uk/wp-content/uploads/2020/08/2018-ccaf-global-fintech-hub-report-eng.pdf.
[7] Deloitte, 'Connecting Global Fintech: Interim Hub Review 2017', April 2017, https://www2.deloitte.com/tr/en/pages/finance/articles/a-tale-of-44-cities-global-fintech-hub-federation-gfhf-connecting-global-fintech-hub-report.html.
[8] Findexable, 'Global Fintech Rankings Report: Bridging the Gap', June 2021, https://findexable.com/wp-content/uploads/2021/06/Global-Fintech-Rankings-2021-v1-23-June-21.pdf.
[9] Academy of Internet Finance, Zhejiang University, Zhejiang University International Business School (ZIBS), et al., 'Global Fintech Hub Report 2020', September 2020, https://www.cnfin.com/upload-xh08/2020/0911/1599789407455.pdf.
[10] The Dodd-Frank Wall Street Reform and Consumer Protection Act (Dodd-Frank Act) was passed in 2010, leading to the overhaul of US financial regulations, including the creation of new regulatory agencies like the Consumer Financial Protection Bureau (CFPB).
[11] The work of the SEC's FinHub includes the areas of distributed ledger technology (e.g., digital assets), automated investment advice, digital marketplace financing, and AI and machine learning. FinHub helps shape the SEC's regulatory response to technological developments in the financial industry through internal and external involvement. See 'Strategic Hub for Innovation and Financial Technology (FinHub)', SEC, accessed 1 June 2023, https://www.sec.gov/finhub.

renowned 7(a) programme.[12] Due to the strong innovation culture and government support, Fintech firms in the US have attracted major investments. They drew funding of $88 billion in 2021 as VC firms and other investors recognised Fintech's potential to completely transform the financial services industry.[13] It is obvious that the investments support the creation of new technologies and help the continued expansion of Fintech and RegTech businesses.

The US has two prominent Fintech centres: San Francisco and New York City. Silicon Valley in San Francisco's Bay Area is the world's most well-known technology, innovation, VC, and social media centre. San Francisco is situated in the northern part of California state. It has prestigious universities, including Stanford University, the University of California, Berkeley, and University of California, Los Angeles. Technology companies in San Francisco have a great chance to succeed since the city's culture values innovation, entrepreneurship, and the willingness to take risks.[14] The city has produced a long list of influential tech firms in the world, like Apple, Adobe, Alphabet (Google), Cisco, DropBox, eBay, Meta (Facebook), HP, Intel, Netflix, Oracle, PayPal, Tesla, and Twitter. Silicon Valley is also home to VC funds such as Sequoia Capital, Andressen Horowitz, Founders Fund, and Khlosa Ventures, which have poured billions of dollars into local tech star-ups. Apparently, the long-standing technological and capital strengths of Silicon Valley account for its leading position in technological innovation and the recent Fintech boom.

As a result, many American Fintech companies are headquartered in San Francisco or its nearby cities. Some local Fintech firms have become market leaders in their respective fields, such as PayPal, Square, and Lending Club. For example, PayPal is a world-leading online payment system enabling any business and individual with an email address to send and receive payments online securely, conveniently, and cost-effectively.[15] The network of PayPal builds on the existing financial infrastructure of bank accounts and credit cards to create a global, real-time payment solution. PayPal held customer money worth over $13 billion, exceeding that of many traditional banks in the US.[16] Square, valued at $26 billion, provides sellers with a diversity of

---

[12] SBA, 'SBA Authorized Fintech Lenders', 26 May 2020, https://www.sba.gov/document/report—sba-authorized-Fintech-lenders.
[13] 'Total Fintech Investment Tops US$210 Billion', KPMG, February 2022, https://kpmg.com/xx/en/home/media/press-releases/2022/02/total-fintech-investment-tops-us-210-billion.html.
[14] Cambridge Centre for Alternative Finance, '2018 Global Fintech Hub Report—the Future of Finance Is Emerging: New Hubs, New Landscapes', 14 November 2018, https://www.jbs.cam.ac.uk/wp-content/uploads/2020/08/2018-ccaf-global-fintech-hub-report-eng.pdf.
[15] 'About Us', PayPal, accessed 1 June 2023, http://www.paypal.com/uk/webapps/mpp/about.
[16] Telis Demos, 'As Industry Evolves, PayPal, Peers Rise Up', *The Wall Street Journal*, 2 June 2016, C1.

checkout hardware products, software products, and small business loans, and offers the Cash app for consumers, as the Fintech company has over 5 million users.[17] Lending Club has been the largest and most successful P2P lending platform in the US and globally, and originates around $2 billion loans per quarter.[18] In addition, many Silicon Valley tech giants are keenly embracing Fintech by making use of their current technological strength and vast customer base. For instance, Meta has been promoting Libra, its own digital currency, which it claims will help 1.7 billion people worldwide who lack bank accounts or find it expensive to send money.[19]

New York City is another top Fintech hub in the US. Over a century, New York has been one of the most prominent commercial and financial centres in the world, also famous for its manufacturing industry and international trade. New York is the largest city in the US, with a population of 8.6 million and a total gross domestic product (GDP) of $1.5 trillion, and this figure is expected to rise to $2.5 trillion by 2035.[20] The state of New York holds a number of top universities such as Columbia University, Cornell University, and New York University. It is near to other leading universities and research institutes located in the Northeast of the US, such as Harvard University, Yale University, Princeton University, the University of Pennsylvania, and Massachusetts Institute of Technology (MIT). The concentration of world-class higher education establishments provides New York with top-notch technology talents and professionals. Moreover, Wall Street in New York is a symbol of American capitalism where thousands of the largest banks, hedge funds, and securities brokerages are located, and they have been playing a key role in international financial markets. The NYSE ($23,089.20 billion) and Nasdaq ($11,719.82 billion) are the top two stock exchanges in the world in terms of the total market capitalisation of listed businesses.[21] In addition, New York holds some of the most valuable tech start-ups in the US, such as Infor which builds cloud-based enterprise resource planning (ERP) software products and WeWork which is a leading provider of shared work-space.[22] The

---

[17] Andrew Davis, 'How Square Became A $26 Billion Company', *CNBC*, 10 October 2019, http://www.cnbc.com/2019/10/10/how-square-became-26-billion-dollar-company.html.
[18] Aaron Back, 'LendingClub: Where's the Growth?', *The Wall Street Journal*, 5 May 2017, http://www.wsj.com/articles/lendingclub-wheres-the-growth-1494000744.
[19] Rory Cellan-Jones, 'Facebook's Libra Pitches to Be the Future of Money', *BBC*, 18 June 2019, http://www.bbc.co.uk/news/technology-48667525.
[20] Laura McCamy, '11 Mind-Blowing Facts about New York's Economy', *Business Insider*, 24 April 2019, http://markets.businessinsider.com/news/stocks/11-mind-blowing-facts-about-new-yorks-economy-2019-4-1028134328.
[21] Hong Kong Securities and Futures Commission, 'Market Capitalisation of the World's Top Stock Exchanges', September 2019, http://www.sfc.hk/web/EN/files/SOM/MarketStatistics/a01.pdf.
[22] Hurun Research Institute, 'Hurun Global Unicorn List 2019', 21 October 2019, https://www.hurun.net/en-US/Info/Detail?num=A38B8285034B.

financial system of the city is widely accessible to entrepreneurs in the area, making New York's Fintech sector one of the most vibrant in the world. There are over 690 Fintech businesses in New York.[23] For instance, Lemonade is a New-York-headquartered insurtech (insurance technology) company offering property and casualty insurance policies in the US and Germany.[24] It charges a flat fee for its services, and any leftover premiums are donated to charitable organisations. MoneyLion is another leading Fintech firm based in New York which is built to empower American citizens with fast, flexible lending and other bespoke financial services through proprietary data-driven platforms.[25]

There are other notable Fintech hubs in AMER aside from San Francisco and New York. In 2021, Fintech-related investments hit a record high in Canada ($7 billion) and Brazil ($5.2 billion).[26] Canada hosts over 1,200 Fintech companies, with Toronto being one of the top Fintech centres in North America.[27] The technology industry offers 80,000 jobs in Toronto, representing 10.2% of total employment in the city. Sizeable Canadian Fintech companies include FreshBooks (accounting management), Trulioo (identity verification and KYC), Borrowell (credit report and rating), Dapper Labs (blockchain and non-fungible tokens), Blockstream (BTC and cryptocurrencies), and KOHO (personal finance).[28] For the purpose of preparing for a prospective trial of national sovereign money, Canadian financial authorities, particularly the Bank of Canada, have been researching Fintech and CBDC.[29] Moreover, Fintech industries in Latin America and the Caribbean have seen fast growth: the number of Fintech firms in the region reached 2,482 in 2021, rising 112% from 2018.[30] The region now accounts for a quarter of the world's innovative Fintech platforms, led by Brazil and Mexico. A significant percentage of local Fintech offerings are related to insurtech and digital banking services that enable those who are excluded from the financial system to access basic financial services.

---

[23] 'Top Tech Companies in NYC', Built in NYC, accessed 1 June 2023, https://www.builtinnyc.com/companies/type/Fintech-companies-nyc.

[24] Oliver Ralph, 'Lemonade Aims Takes its Digital Fizz to German Insurance', *The Financial Times*, 11 June 2019, https://www.ft.com/content/6533b0ce-8c39-11e9-a1c1-51bf8f989972.

[25] 'What Is MoneyLion?', MoneyLion, accessed 1 June 2023, http://www.moneylion.com/about.

[26] 'Total Fintech Investment Tops US$210 Billion', KPMG, February 2022, https://kpmg.com/xx/en/home/media/press-releases/2022/02/total-fintech-investment-tops-us-210-billion.html.

[27] 'The Rise of Fintech in Canada: Home to a Vibrant Innovation Ecosystem', The Fintech Times, 30 March 2022, https://theFintechtimes.com/rise-of-Fintech-in-canada-innovation-ecosystem/.

[28] 'The 2019 Canadian Fintech Market Map', PwC, accessed 1 June 2023, https://www.pwc.com/ca/en/industries/technology/canadian-Fintech-market-map.html.

[29] 'Digital Currencies and Fintech: Research', Bank of Canada, accessed 1 June 2023, https://www.bankofcanada.ca/research/digital-currencies-and-Fintech/research/.

[30] Inter-American Development Bank, 'Study: Fintech Industry Doubles in Size in Three Years in Latin America and the Caribbean', 26 April 2022, https://www.iadb.org/en/news/study-Fintech-industry-doubles-size-three-years-latin-america-and-caribbean.

3.3 Global Fintech hubs in Asia Pacific

The Fintech sector is expanding rapidly in the APAC region. Countries like Australia, China, India, and Singapore are establishing themselves as leading Fintech players, with numerous ground-breaking financial service solutions being created for both consumers and corporate clients to address the specific needs of Asia's booming economies. The dynamic Fintech industry in Asia is led by Ant Group, which was launched by the e-commerce giant Alibaba in 2004 and has become the largest Fintech company, serving over 1 billion consumers.[31] Governments and financial regulators in the region have launched a lot of supportive policies and industry funds to spur innovation and investment in Fintech and RegTech businesses. Fintech firms in APAC attracted investments totalling $41.8 billion over 607 deals in the first half of 2022.[32]

Sydney, a premier Fintech hub in APAC and globally, will serve as the starting point for our introduction. Australia has over 800 Fintech corporations and its Fintech sector has grown significantly in recent years, thanks to the country's favourable regulatory environment, the highly qualified labour force, and the vibrant innovation culture.[33] Australia's Fintech market was worth $4 billion in 2020, up from $250 million in 2015.[34] The success of Australian Fintech firms is partly because of their geographical proximity to some of the fastest growing economies in the world, which has rendered the country a good choice for multinational companies to launch their head offices in the APAC region. Moreover, Sydney has a large talent base. The city is very student friendly and has top universities like the University of Sydney, University of New South Wales, and University of Technology Sydney. In 2022, Australia received $30.2 billion in Fintech investments, including the widely reported Afterpay-Block deal that was worth $27.9 billion.[35] The majority of Fintech companies in Australia either were founded or are currently being led by experienced financial services professionals who have a strong desire to find new and creative ways to offer customers better financial services in the areas of lending, blockchain, insurance, wealth management, and digital payments.

---

[31] Ant Group provides a variety of Fintech services like e-wallet, mobile payments, wealth management products, and personal credit rating. See Lerong Lu, 'How a Little Ant Challenges Giant Banks? The Rise of Ant Financial (Alipay)'s Fintech Empire and Relevant Regulatory Concerns'. *International Company and Commercial Law Review* (2018) 28: 12, 19.

[32] KPMG, 'Pulse of Fintech H1 2022—ASPAC', August 2022, https://kpmg.com/xx/en/home/insights/2022/08/pulse-of-Fintech-h1-22-aspac.html.

[33] 'What Is Fintech?', Fintech Australia, accessed 1 June 2023, https://www.fintechaustralia.org.au/what-is-fintech.

[34] Ibid.

[35] Elise Shaw, 'Fintech Investment Likely to Stay Subdued; M&A Could Pick up Investing', *Forbes Australia*, 23 February 2023, https://www.forbes.com.au/news/investing/Fintech-investment-likely-to-stay-subdued-ma-could-pick-up/.

In Australia, the policy-makers and financial regulators are supportive of the Fintech sector. The Australian Securities and Investments Commission (ASIC) has been running the innovation hub as an official initiative to provide practical support and informal assistance for eligible Fintech start-ups, helping them navigate Australia's regulatory framework.[36] The ASIC is dedicated to fostering innovation without compromising the core values guiding the country's financial services regulation and its existing licencing procedure. Moreover, it has an enhanced regulatory sandbox allowing entrepreneurs to test innovative financial services and credit activities.[37] Other regulatory bodies actively participate in the regulation of Australian Fintech, such as the Reserve Bank of Australia (RBA), which oversees Fintech companies running payment and settlement systems, and the Australian Prudential Regulation Authority (APRA), which is in charge of supervising banks, insurance companies, and superannuation funds. There is no doubt that Australia's strong regulatory framework, knowledgeable workforce, and supportive policies are all essential components that will support the ongoing growth of Sydney's Fintech industry.

China has been a front-runner in the Fintech arena. It has a number of principal Fintech hubs like Beijing, Shanghai, Hangzhou, Shenzhen, and Hong Kong. The development of technology and digital transformation remains a key national strategy for China, which is the second-largest economy (in terms of GDP) in the world. The People's Bank of China (PBoC), the country's central bank, has made a 'Fintech Development Plan' (2022–2025) to support the industry growth, focusing on sound governance and regulation, privacy and data protection, and low carbon and green Fintech, as well as the provision of fair and inclusive financial services.[38] In the long term, the Chinese government aims to pursue technology-driven economic developments to adopt smart technologies for improving the well-being of its citizens.

Beijing, as the capital city of China, is a leader of financial innovation in the APAC region. Beijing is not only a historical and culturally rich city but also a primary national centre for education, business, and politics. There are over 90 higher education establishments in the city, including prestigious institutes like Tsinghua University and Peking University. According to

---

[36] 'Innovation Hub', ASIC, accessed 1 June 2023, https://asic.gov.au/for-business/innovation-hub/.

[37] The Australian Securities and Investments Commission (ASIC)'s enhanced regulatory sandbox allows testing of a wider range of financial services and credit activities for a longer period of no more than 24 months. See 'Enhanced Regulatory Sandbox', Australian Securities and Investments Commission, accessed 01 June 2023, https://asic.gov.au/for-business/innovation-hub/enhanced-regulatory-sandbox/.

[38] PBoC, 'Fintech Development Plan (2022–2025)', 4 January 2022, http://www.pbc.gov.cn/en/3688110/3688172/4437084/4441980/index.html.

an official report in 2018, 226,271 university students graduated in Beijing, obtaining 118,287 bachelor's degrees, 64,207 master's degrees, and 14,252 doctoral degrees.[39] It provides numerous finance and IT talents for Beijing's Fintech industry which is heavily reliant on the city's abundant educational resources. Beijing has a prosperous economy as it hosts the headquarters of 56 companies in the *Fortune* Global 500 List.[40] Beijing Financial Street is viewed as the brain of China's financial industry as financial institutions on the street possess a combined amount of financial assets worth CNY99.5 trillion, accounting for 40% of the total financial holding in China.[41] The financial street is where central regulatory agencies, including the PBoC, China Securities Regulatory Commission (CSRC), and China Banking and Insurance Regulatory Commission (CBIRC), are located. The street also headquarters the Asian Infrastructure Investment Bank (AIIB), China's 'Big Four' commercial banks, People's Insurance Company of China (PICC), and China Life Insurance, as well as regional head offices of international financial institutions such as Goldman Sachs, Citibank, JPMorgan Chase, Morgan Stanley, VISA, Mastercard, Societe Generale, and Royal Bank of Scotland.[42] Beijing is also a favourable place for ultra-high-net-worth individuals (UHNWIs), as over 100 billionaires are currently residing in the city.[43]

Beijing, drawing on its strong talent, technology, and capital base, has become a city of technological innovations. It is home to the largest number of unicorn companies in the world, which means unlisted tech companies with a valuation of over $1 billion.[44] Beijing has 82 unicorn corporations, which is well ahead of rival cities like San Francisco (55), Shanghai (47), New York (25), and Hangzhou (19).[45] The examples of Beijing-based tech unicorns are ByteDance which operates AI-powered news platform Toutiao and video-sharing app TikTok. Moreover, Beijing has 58 leading Fintech companies that

---

[39] Beijing Government, '2018 Beijing Higher Education Graduates Employment Report', December 2018, http://jw.beijing.gov.cn/xxgk/zxxxgk/201812/t20181229_66964.html.

[40] The Global 500 List is the ranking of 500 largest corporations in the world by their revenues. The list is compiled and published by *Fortune* magazine on an annual basis. See 'Global 500', *Fortune*, accessed 1 June 2023, https://fortune.com/global500/2019/.

[41] 'Beijing Financial Street Financial Institutions Asset Scale Is Approaching RMB100 Trillion', *China News*, 29 April 2018, http://www.chinanews.com/fortune/2018/04-29/8503009.shtml.

[42] The 'Big Four' in China refers to the Industrial and Commercial Bank of China (ICBC), China Construction Bank, Agricultural Bank of China, and Bank of China. See Lerong Lu, 'Private Banks in China: Origin, Challenges and Regulatory Implications'. *Banking and Finance Law Review* (2016) 31: 585, 586.

[43] 'Beijing Overtakes New York as New "Billionaire Capital"', *BBC*, 25 February 2016, http://www.bbc.co.uk/news/world-asia-china-35657107.

[44] Ningyao Ye and Lerong Lu, 'How to Harness a Unicorn? Demystifying China's Reform of Share Listing Rules and Chinese Depositary Receipts'. *International Company and Commercial Law Review* (2019) 30: 454.

[45] Hurun Research Institute, 'Hurun Global Unicorn List 2019', 21 October 2019, https://www.hurun.net/en-US/Info/Detail?num=A38B8285034B.

have received total investments of $21.2 billion. It is home to JD Technology, the Fintech arm of the e-commerce group JD, and the company is devoted to the digitalisation of finance, city planning, business marketing, asset management, and agriculture.[46] Beijing houses leading Fintech platforms, such as Bitmain which produces application-specific integrated circuit chips for BTC mining and the firm accounts for 75% of global market share.[47] There are other large Fintech companies like Du Xiaoman Financial which is backed by the search engine giant Baidu and provides AI and big-data-powered personal consumer credit and investment services.

Shanghai, as the largest city in China, serves as an international financial centre and major Fintech hub.[48] It is the economic centre of the Yangtze River Delta region, one of the most economically developed areas in China. As a prime financial centre, the total transaction volume of the city's financial markets was around CNY1,645.8 trillion ($234.10 trillion) in 2023.[49] There are 1,605 financial institutions in Shanghai, 30% of which are foreign institutions.[50] SSE is the fourth-largest stock market in the world with a total market capitalisation of $4.59 trillion.[51] Based on its strong economic foundation and financial strength, Shanghai is said to become a key financial centre competing with New York, London, Hong Kong, and Singapore in the 2020s. Shanghai Municipal Government released an action plan to accelerate the building of its international financial centre when the city proposed to establish its strategic position as a Renminbi product-dominated financial market.[52] Shanghai has several leading universities in the country including Fudan University and Shanghai Jiao Tong University. At present, Shanghai's Fintech industry is the second-largest one in China, just next to Beijing. It holds the headquarters of top Fintech companies like PPDai, Lufax, and

---

[46] 'About Us', JD Digits, accessed 1 June 2023, https://www.jdt.com.cn/about/.
[47] 'About Bitmain', Bitmain, accessed 1 June 2023, http://www.bitmain.com/about.
[48] In the early 20th century, Shanghai was the largest financial centre in the Far East, but its status has fallen due to the socialist revolution in the 1950s. In the late 1970s, China started to re-embrace the market economy and underwent a series of economic reforms guided by the 'reform and open-up' policy, leading to the resurgence of Shanghai as an international financial centre. See Lu Lerong, *Private Lending in China: Practice, Law, and Regulation of Shadow Banking and Alternative Finance* (Abingdon: Routledge 2018), p. 21.
[49] Shanghai Government official website, accessed 1 June 2023, http://www.shanghai.gov.cn/.
[50] Ibid.
[51] Hong Kong Securities and Futures Commission, 'Market Capitalisation of the World's Top Stock Exchanges', September 2019, http://www.sfc.hk/web/EN/files/SOM/MarketStatistics/a01.pdf.
[52] Shanghai International Financial Centre is said to comprise six centres and one system: the global asset management centre, cross-border investment and financing services centre which mainly supports the 'belt and road initiative', financial technology centre, international insurance centre, global Renminbi asset pricing, payments, and settlement centre, financial risks management and stress-testing centre, and a world-class financial ecosystem. See PBoC, 'The Action Plan on Building Shanghai International Financial Centre (2018–2020)', 16 November 2018, https://jrj.sh.gov.cn/jcgk-ghjh/20220922/3ad0412a0a484a1797af008ec01bcd37.html.

ZhongAn Insurance. The city's Fintech firms have raised accumulated capital of $9.2 billion.[53] PPDai is the largest online consumer finance marketplace in China with 99 million registered users, offering small loans to consumers aged 20–40 with limited credit history.[54] Lufax, affiliated to Ping An Group, is a principal online lending platform with a valuation of $18.5 billion.[55] ZhongAn is an online-based insurance and insurtech company using AI and big data to simplify insurance underwriting, as the firm is able to price risk accurately and distributes its insurance services to the mass market purely through the internet.[56]

Hangzhou, as the capital city of East China's Zhejiang Province, is another key Fintech centre in Asia. Like Shanghai, Hangzhou is also located in the Yangtze River Delta region, which has the most developed private economy and financial markets in China, and it is just 100 miles from Shanghai. Hangzhou is well known for its prosperous private sector and high-tech industry and as the headquarters of China's largest e-commerce and tech company—Alibaba Group. In 2016, Hangzhou held the annual G20 summit, where the leaders of the world's largest economies gathered to discuss important issues relating to global economic cooperation.[57] Hangzhou has a number of higher education institutions, including Zhejiang University which is one of the most selective universities in China and is often referred to as the Cambridge of the East. Apart from Alibaba, Hangzhou has hundreds of tech firms, such as Hikvision, which is the world's largest supplier of video surveillance products, as well as Cainiao Logistics, Dahua Technology, Hithink Flush Information Network, and Mogu Inc. In total, Hangzhou holds internet companies with an overall valuation of RMB4.16 trillion ($603.58 billion).[58] Ant Group, the owner of Alipay mobile payment and Fintech platforms, is a leading Fintech company based in Hangzhou. Ant Group is one of the largest and most prominent Fintech companies globally, with more than 1 billion users. In 2019, Alibaba, as the parent company, completed

---

[53] Cambridge Centre for Alternative Finance, '2018 Global Fintech Hub Report—the Future of Finance Is Emerging: New Hubs, New Landscapes', 14 November 2018, https://www.jbs.cam.ac.uk/wp-content/uploads/2020/08/2018-ccaf-global-fintech-hub-report-eng.pdf.
[54] 'Company Profile', PPDai, accessed 1 June 2023, http://ir.ppdai.com/company-profile.
[55] Emma Dunkley and Nicolle Liu, 'Lufax Holds Off on Listing While Beijing Scrutinises Online Lenders', *The Financial Times*, 21 March 2018, http://www.ft.com/content/8a7bf706-2cbd-11e8-a34a-7e7563b0b0f4.
[56] Don Weinland and Oliver Ralph, 'Zhongan Launches Insurtech Concept to World', *The Financial Times*, 25 September 2017, https://www.ft.com/content/c9d10ada-9eb1-11e7-8cd4-932067fbf946.
[57] Tom Mitchell and George Parker, 'G20 Takes Up Global Inequality Challenge', *The Financial Times*, 4 September 2016, https://www.ft.com/content/cc70de98-72aa-11e6-b60a-de4532d5ea35.
[58] 'The Latest Valuation Ranking of Internet Enterprises in China', Hangzhou Net, 29 January 2019, http://appm.hangzhou.com.cn/article_pc.php?id=261153.

the restructuring of Ant Financial, paving the way for its IPO when the star Fintech firm was valued at $150 billion.[59]

Shenzhen, dubbed as the Silicon Valley of China, is a rising tech centre in Asia. The city has a 12 million population and is located in South China's Guangdong Province. Shenzhen forms part of the Pearl River Delta region as well as the Guangdong–Hong Kong–Macau Greater Bay Area which has an inter-city initiative to promote the growth of technology and innovation, infrastructure building, and financial cooperation in the region.[60] Shenzhen has a relatively short history as it only obtained city status in 1979, owing to China's reform and open-up policy to liberalise the economy and develop the private economy. After that, it grew rapidly from a small fishing village into a global city with large finance, technology, and modern manufacturing sectors. Shenzhen holds the second-largest stock exchange in China—the Shenzhen Stock Exchange—as well as the headquarters of several multinational companies such as Huawai, Tencent, ZTE, Vanke, Ping An Group, China Merchant Bank, DJI, and BYD. Due to its active capital market and financial industry, Shenzhen is ranked as the ninth-largest international financial centre in the world.[61] Shenzhen has a number of universities and colleges, including Shenzhen University, Southern University of Science and Technology, Shenzhen Technology University, and Chinese University of Hong Kong (Shenzhen). The city also benefits from high-quality talents who graduate from the nearby Bay Area cities like Guangzhou and Hong Kong. For instance, Frank Zhang, the chief executive officer (CEO) of DJI, the world's largest manufacturer of drones, started the business in his residence hall at the Hong Kong University of Science and Technology in 2006.[62] Shenzhen's status as a leading technology centre lends it a natural advantage in growing the Fintech industry, as local BigTech like Huawei and Tencent have expanded their business territories into finance. For instance, Tencent launched WeBank, an online-only bank and wealth management platform, as well as Tenpay, which is a third-party payment system similar to PayPal. In addition, Shenzhen has large Fintech companies such as JFZ Capital Management providing online wealth management services for high-net-worth

---

[59] Louise Lucas, 'Alibaba Restructuring Paves Way for Ant Financial IPO', *The Financial Times*, 24 September 2019, https://www.ft.com/content/267c395c-de94-11e9-9743-db5a370481bc.

[60] Shenzhen is considered as the window of the Chinese economy to the world as it connects mainland China and Hong Kong. It is a key city in the Greater Bay Area. See 'Greater Bay Area: China's Ambitious but Vague Economic Plan', *BBC*, 26 February 2019, http://www.bbc.co.uk/news/business-47287387.

[61] Z/Yen Group, 'The Global Financial Centres Index 32', 22 September 2022, https://www.longfinance.net/media/documents/GFCI_32_Report_2022.09.22_v1.0_.pdf.

[62] Jonathan Margolis, 'Chinese Drone Pioneer DJI Is Still Gaining Altitude', *The Financial Times*, 13 October 2015, https://www.ft.com/content/a0cfd67a-6dda-11e5-8171-ba1968cf791a.

individuals and Suishou Technology which devises smartphone apps relating to personal finance planning and credit card management.

Hong Kong has long been a key financial centre in the world as well as an important Fintech hub.[63] It is famous for its financial services industry, especially banking, capital markets, and insurance. At present, 73 of the world's 100-largest banks have a presence in Hong Kong.[64] As of September 2019, the total market capitalisation of all companies listed on the Hong Kong Stock Exchange amounted to $3.9 trillion.[65] The city is the top choice for many multinational companies to float their shares. It has made a total of $24.5 billion IPOs annually, just behind the largest stock markets in the US.[66] Furthermore, Hong Kong has the largest and freest foreign exchange (FX), future, and gold markets, as well as highly developed insurance and wealth management industries. Maintaining Hong Kong's competitive advantage in financial services, including Fintech, has been a key task for the city's government. According to Hong Kong's basic law, the city's mini constitution, the government shall provide an appropriate economic and legal environment for the maintenance of the status of Hong Kong as an international financial centre.[67]

Hong Kong's Fintech hub is distinguished by its diverse, resilient, and dynamic environment, which enables Fintech start-ups to quickly scale-up.[68] As of January 2023, over 3,700 start-ups and 800 Fintech companies were based in Hong Kong, including some unicorn Fintech firms like ZA International (which received a licence to operate as a virtual bank in Hong Kong), WeLab (an online financial business), and Airwallex (a provider of cross-border payment services).[69] Hong Kong has a sound legal regime and financial ecosystem that are supportive of the development of Fintech. It is one of the most open jurisdictions for Fintech companies to develop and extend cross-border operations because there are no FX controls or limitations on capital inflows and outflows. Moreover, a low and straightforward

---

[63] Hong Kong is a global city and special administrative region of the People's Republic China (PRC). It is located in the eastern Pearl River Delta in South China.
[64] Zia Khan, Harry Terris, Ben Meggeson, and Mohammad Taqi, 'The World's 100 Largest Banks 2023', S&P Global, 26 April 2023, https://www.spglobal.com/marketintelligence/en/news-insights/research/the-world-s-100-largest-banks-2023.
[65] Hong Kong Securities and Futures Commission, 'Market Capitalisation of the World's Top Stock Exchanges', September 2019, http://www.sfc.hk/web/EN/files/SOM/MarketStatistics/a01.pdf.
[66] Nicole Bullock and Jennifer Hughes, 'Hong Kong Wrestles with New York for Listings Laurels', *The Financial Times*, 29 December 2016, p. 13.
[67] The Basic Law of the Hong Kong Special Administrative Region of the People's Republic of China (Effective as of July 1, 1997), Article 109.
[68] 'Fact Sheet: Hong Kong Fintech Landscape', FintechHK, 13 January 2023, https://www.hongkong-fintech.hk/en/insights/news/news-2023/fact-sheet-hong-kong-fintech-landscape/.
[69] Ibid.

tax system, plus a number of generous government financing, support, and subsidy programmes are also advantageous to local Fintech start-ups.[70] In September 2016, the Hong Kong Monetary Authority (HKMA) launched the regulatory sandbox regime, in order to compete with regional rivals like Singapore in terms of Fintech innovations.[71] In June 2021, the HKMA released its 'Fintech 2025' plan with the intention of promoting the financial industry's adoption of technology and the provision of fair and efficient financial services that benefit Hong Kong citizens and the local economy.[72] The official plan has five areas of focus: all banks go Fintech (fully digital), future-proofing for CBDCs, creating next-generation data infrastructure, expanding the Fintech-savvy workforce, and nurturing the ecosystem with funding and policies. Obviously, the supportive industry policy will accelerate the growth of Fintech businesses in Hong Kong.

Mumbai, which is India's capital of commerce and finance, has rapidly emerged as a leading Asian Fintech centre as a result of the nation's expanding consumer market and economy. With the rapid development of digital infrastructure, rising smartphone adoption, and a sizable unbanked and underbanked population that calls for affordable and convenient financial services, the Fintech sector in India has seen substantial growth in recent years.[73] These factors have been taken advantage of by Indian Fintech firms to provide cutting-edge financial products and services, such as digital payments and remittance, lending, insurance, equity funding, and wealth management. In 2021, India had the third-largest Fintech ecosystem in the world, worth $31 billion.[74] The Indian Fintech sector has a diverse nature, with the participation of start-ups, established businesses, and conventional financial institutions. Both domestic and foreign investors have made considerable investments in the industry, including 1,040 Mumbai-based Fintech companies like Acko (insurance and banking infrastructure), SBI Payment

---

[70] Hong Kong has one of the lowest tax systems in the world. For example, the highest band for personal income tax was only 17% in the 2022/2023 tax year. See 'Hong Kong SAR. Individual—Taxes on Personal Income', PwC, accessed 1 June 2023, https://taxsummaries.pwc.com/hong-kong-sar/individual/taxes-on-personal-income.

[71] Hong Kong's sandbox regime focuses on the established banking industry as opposed to Fintech start-ups. It only applies to licenced banks that would like to use Fintech in their businesses, such as distributed ledger technology or robo-advisory. See Don Weinland, 'Hong Kong to Create Fintech "Sandbox" Allowing Bank Experiments', *The Financial Times*, 6 September 2016, https://www.ft.com/content/38a662ee-740f-11e6-bf48-b372cdb1043a.

[72] HKMA, 'Fintech 2025: Our Fintech Vision', accessed 1 June 2023, https://www.hkma.gov.hk/media/eng/doc/key-functions/ifc/fintech/HK_Fintech_2025_eng.pdf.

[73] India has an unbanked population of 191 million. See 'India Has Second-Largest Unbanked Population in the World', *India Times*, 15 June 2018, https://timesofindia.indiatimes.com/business/india-has-second-largest-unbanked-population-in-the-world/articleshow/64570254.cms.

[74] Ishwari Chavan, 'India's Fintech Market Size at $31 Billion in 2021, Third Largest in World', *India Times*, 10 January 2022, https://bfsi.economictimes.indiatimes.com/news/Fintech/indias-Fintech-market-size-at-31-billion-in-2021-third-largest-in-world-report/88794336.

Services (online payment), InCred (lending), and Fino Paytech (banking services). With official programmes like Digital India[75] and Unified Payments Interface (UPI)[76] assisting in the promotion of digital payments and financial inclusion, the Indian government has been encouraging the development of its Fintech sector. In addition, the Maharashtra government launched the Mumbai Fintech Hub as a formal investment platform to support the growth of the home-grown Fintech ecosystem.[77] The Reserve Bank of India (RBI) established the regulatory sandbox to allow Indian Fintech firms to test new financial products and services in a controlled setting.[78] The RBI also released a number of positive policies and regulatory rules for online lending and P2P payment systems. Despite a sound regulatory framework in place, the Fintech industry in India has to address urgent problems like regulatory ambiguity, privacy and data protection, and cyber-attacks.

Singapore has a thriving Fintech sector, and it holds the world's largest annual event and knowledge platform for the global Fintech community—Singapore Fintech Festival. During the 2010s, Singapore's financial services industry has grown explosively; it is now ranked as the third global financial centre in the world, next to New York and London.[79] The city-state of Singapore, located in Southeast Asia, aspires to serve as a gateway for foreign investors into the vibrant APAC region. The city is renowned for its Asian dollar market and its extensive and thriving capital markets, as well as first-class asset management offerings and private banking services for high-net-worth individuals. More than 150 international banks have their presence in Singapore, with a total asset size of $2 trillion.[80] The Singapore Exchange (SGX) has nearly 800 listed companies, 40% of which are foreign businesses incorporated in other Asian countries, Europe, or America.[81] It is the third-largest FX centre in the world, as its average daily trading

---

[75] The Government of India has started the 'Digital India' campaign to ensure that its services are made electronically accessible to its citizens through improved online infrastructure and increased internet connectivity, aiming at empowerment of the nation in the digital sphere. See Government of India, 'Digital India Programme', accessed 1 June 2023, https://digitalindia.gov.in/.

[76] The National Payments Corporation of India created the instant real-time payment system known as UPI. Transactions between individuals and merchants as well as between banks are made easier by the UPI interface. It allows for the immediate transmission of money between two bank accounts using mobile devices. See National Payments Corporation of India, 'Unified Payments Interface (UPI) Product Overview', accessed 1 June 2023, https://www.npci.org.in/what-we-do/upi/product-overview.

[77] Government of Maharashtra (India), 'Mumbai Fintech Hub', accessed 1 June 2023, https://Fintech.maharashtra.gov.in/.

[78] RBI, 'Enabling Framework for Regulatory Sandbox', 8 February 2018, https://rbidocs.rbi.org.in/rdocs/PublicationReport/Pdfs/ENABLING79D8EBD31FED47A0BE21158C337123BF.PDF.

[79] Z/Yen Group, 'The Global Financial Centres Index 32', 22 September 2022, https://www.longfinance.net/media/documents/GFCI_32_Report_2022.09.22_v1.0_.pdf.

[80] 'Banking', MAS, accessed 1 June 2023, https://www.mas.gov.sg/regulation/Banking.

[81] 'Why List on SGX', SGX, accessed 1 June 2023, https://www.sgx.com/securities/why-list-sgx.

volumes reached $929 billion in April 2022.[82] Singapore possesses two of the world's largest sovereign wealth funds: Government of Singapore Investment Corporation (GIC) and Temasek Holdings. According to one estimate, GIC managed $350 billion of assets, while Temasek had over $300 billion assets under its management.[83]

It should be noted that Singapore and Hong Kong have been competing as Asia's no.1 financial centre for a long time, as there exist lots of similarities between these two cities. Aside from their financial strengths, Singapore and Hong Kong both follow the English common law tradition and have an efficient and transparent legal system. Both cities have established themselves as international arbitration centres, as more global trade and investment shifts to Asia.[84] More recently, they have contended to gain the title of leading offshore Renminbi trading centre.[85] As the rivalry between these two cities has extended to the Fintech industry, the Singaporean government has made favourable policies to spur the further growth of its Fintech industry and capital markets. For example, the MAS has begun a number of initiatives to promote innovation and investment in the Fintech sector and has created a regulatory sandbox to assist in the development of Fintech and RegTech solutions.[86] In September 2021, the SGX officially started to accept the public listing of SPACs on its mainboard, in order to cement Singapore's status as a leading international financial centre and accommodate the financing demands from Asia's flourishing tech sectors.[87]

3.4 Global Fintech hubs in Europe, Middle East, and Africa

The chapter will now focus on prominent Fintech hubs in the EMEA region, beginning with major cities in the EU, such as Paris, Frankfurt, and Dublin.[88]

---

[82] 'Singapore Cements Position as Third Largest Global FX Centre', MAS, 28 October 2022, https://www.mas.gov.sg/news/media-releases/2022/singapore-cements-position-as-third-largest-global-fx-centre.

[83] Jeevan Vasagar, 'Singapore Fund Adds to UK Portfolio with Pound(S) 48.5m Deal', *The Financial Times*, 31 December 2016, p. 15.

[84] Jake Maxwell Watts, 'In Singapore, Making Law a Business', *The Wall Street Journal*, 3 January 2015, B4.

[85] Jennifer Hughes and Michael Hunter, 'Offshore Renminbi Rises from Record Low', *The Financial Times*, 5 January 2017, p. 20.

[86] MAS, 'Overview of Regulatory Sandbox', accessed 1 June 2023, https://www.mas.gov.sg/development/Fintech/regulatory-sandbox.

[87] Lerong Lu and Alice Lingsheng Zhang, 'Singapore's SPAC Listing Regime: A Game Changer or a Gap Filler?', *Securities Regulation Law Review* (2022) 50: 25, 31–34.

[88] The EU has 27 member states which together form a supranational political and economic alliance. In January 2020, the UK withdrew its membership from the EU, known as Brexit, and it is the only sovereign

Fintech businesses are a key driving force behind consumer satisfaction, modernisation, and growth in Europe's financial services industry.[89] In total, Fintech firms have generated about 134,000 jobs in Europe, and these are estimated to be worth nearly €430 billion as of June 2022, being a vital source of future economic growth in the region.[90] In the EU, Fintech-related legislation is a complicated and developing field. The EU has adopted a comprehensive strategy for Fintech regulation, with different regulatory bodies involved in supervising various facets of the sector. For example, the European Banking Authority (EBA) is in charge of guaranteeing efficient and uniform regulation and supervision of the banking industry throughout the EU. In accordance with the European Commission's Digital Finance Strategy (DFS), which was released in September 2020, the EBA's current Fintech working priorities include a variety of actions to support the scaling of innovative technology across borders while ensuring high standards of operational resilience and consumer protection in the financial sector.[91] Another EU agency tasked with preserving the integrity of the EU's financial markets is the European Securities and Markets Authority (ESMA) which establishes guidelines for applying EU regulations to Fintech firms active in the securities and derivatives markets.[92] The EU has proposed world-leading legislations and regulatory initiatives, which has pushed forward global regulatory convergence in Fintech.[93] Some well-known examples of EU laws in the digital sphere are General Data Protection Regulation (GDPR), Markets in Crypto-Assets (MiCA), Digital Markets Act (DMA), and Digital Services Act (DSA).

Paris excels in the Fintech sector and has a strong ecosystem for Fintech start-ups, making it a pioneer in financial innovation in Europe. Euronext, the biggest stock exchange in the EU in terms of market capitalisation and the volume of equity trading, is located in Paris, providing an ideal setting for Fintech companies to raise capital.[94] Paris, by hosting the Paris Fintech Forum which is an annual knowledge exchange and commercial

state having left the union. Therefore, we will discuss London, the UK's capital city, separately in the next part.
[89] 'Europe's Fintech Opportunity', McKinsey, 26 October 2022, https://www.mckinsey.com/industries/financial-services/our-insights/europes-Fintech-opportunity.
[90] Ibid.
[91] EBA, 'Financial Innovation and Fintech', accessed 1 June 2023, https://www.eba.europa.eu/financial-innovation-and-Fintech.
[92] ESMA, 'Report to the European Commission: Use of Fintech by CSDs', 2 August 2021, https://www.esma.europa.eu/sites/default/files/library/esma70-156-4576_report_to_ec_on_use_of_fintech_by_csds.pdf.
[93] 'EU Fintech Regulation: Key Themes and Trends', Freshfields, accessed 1 June 2023, https://www.freshfields.com/en-gb/our-thinking/campaigns/technology-quotient/Fintech/eu-Fintech-regulation-key-themes-and-trends/.
[94] 'Euronext Paris', Euronext, accessed 1 June 2023, https://www.euronext.com/en/markets/paris.

platform for digital finance and Fintech, has established extensive collaboration with global Fintech businesses and regulatory authorities.[95] Paris has world-leading education resources, as there are some top financial engineering programmes offered by prestigious universities, such as HEC Paris and ESSEC Business School, providing the city's Fintech sector with a large number of finance and tech talents. Leading Parisian Fintech companies include Le Swave (innovation Fintech platform), Alan (digital health insurance platform), Kayrros (data analytics), Payfit (payroll), and Ledger (cryptocurrencies platform).

Frankfurt is another key Fintech hub in Europe, with a burgeoning ecosystem of emerging firms and well-established players. The European Central Bank (ECB) and the German Federal Bank are both located in Frankfurt. As a reputable international financial centre, Frankfurt hosts many of the biggest international investment banks, asset management firms, insurance companies, and other financial institutions. The Frankfurt Stock Exchange, the world's 11th-largest stock exchange with a total market capitalisation of $1.9 trillion, is also situated in the city.[96] Many Fintech companies have launched their headquarters in Frankfurt because of the city's well-established financial sector, skilled workforce, and welcoming business climate, especially in fields like digital payments, blockchain technology, and online lending. Through Accelerator Frankfurt (which specialises in the fields of Fintech, RegTech, cybersecurity, insurtech, proptech, and blockchain) and other similar organisations, German start-ups have access to vast financing, mentoring, and networking opportunities.[97] Leading German Fintech companies are Trade Republic (investment broker), N26 (digital bank), Wefox (insurtech), Mambu (cloud banking infrastructure), and Scalable Capital (digital wealth management). Fintech innovation and development are also supported by Frankfurt's sound regulatory environment, which includes supervision from the German Federal Financial Supervisory Authority (BaFin) and its Fintech Innovation Hub programme.[98]

In addition to Paris and Frankfurt, Dublin has quickly emerged as a major financial centre and Fintech hub in Europe, and it has particular

---

[95] 'Paris Fintech Forum Communities', Paris Fintech Forum, accessed 1 June 2023, https://members.parisFintechforum.com/.
[96] Hong Kong Securities and Futures Commission, 'Market Capitalisation of the World's Top Stock Exchanges', September 2019, http://www.sfc.hk/web/EN/files/SOM/MarketStatistics/a01.pdf.
[97] Accelerator Frankfurt Program, accessed 1 June 2023, https://www.acceleratorfrankfurt.com/the-program/.
[98] 'Fintech Innovation Hub', Federal Financial Supervisory Authority, accessed 1 June 2023, https://www.bafin.de/EN/Aufsicht/Fintech/Fintech_node_en.html.

strength in fund administration, aircraft leasing, insurance, and wholesale banking activities.[99] The city is now home to a large number of financial services companies, as Ireland is the fourth-largest supplier of wholesale financial services in the EU. Dublin's Fintech sector benefits from Ireland's robust regulatory regime, skilled workforce, and a favourable tax regime (e.g., 12.5% corporate tax). Some top Irish Fintech start-ups are ION Group (treasury management solutions), Future Finance (student loans), Ecowatt (green investment platform), Brightflag (AI-based corporate legal operation), and Corlytics (RegTech). Fintech has received strong support from the Irish government, as its Finance Action Plan for 2021 has stressed four priority areas: sustainable finance, diversity, regionalisation, and digital finance.[100]

London is the capital city of the UK and a prime financial centre globally, as well as a leading Fintech hub known for financial innovations and sound regulatory practices. London and New York are perennial rivals for the title of no.1 international financial centre in the world, but due to Brexit uncertainties, London seems to have fallen behind New York in recent years.[101] London is a major centre of research and university education, as it holds 40 higher education institutions, including University College London, King's College London, Imperial College London, London School of Economics, and London Business School.[102] London has positioned itself as a leading financial innovation hub. In the 2010s, the UK has seen fast growth of its Fintech sector, which has been generating £20 billion annual revenue.[103] Many disruptive Fintech businesses, including Wise (Transferwise), Nutmeg, Monzo, Revolut, and Starling Bank, are based in London. Many of the most recent finance innovations were born and developed in London. For example, in 2005, the world's first online P2P lending platform, Zopa, was launched in London.[104] Clearly, the UK is one of the most attractive destinations for Fintech entrepreneurs and investors as the government, regulators, and industry

---

[99] 'Financial Services in Dublin', Dublin City Council, accessed 1 June 2023, https://dublin.ie/invest/key-sectors/financial-services/.

[100] Sean Fleming, 'Minister Fleming Publishes Ireland for Finance Action Plan 2021', Government of Ireland, 11 February 2021, https://www.gov.ie/en/press-release/101ac-minister-fleming-publishes-ireland-for-finance-action-plan-2021/.

[101] Cat Rutter Pooley, 'London Slips Further behind New York in Financial Centre Rankings', *The Financial Times*, 19 September 2019, https://www.ft.com/content/b8ab7f22-daac-11e9-8f9b-77216ebe1f17.

[102] London is not far from famous university towns like Oxford and Cambridge, and the top research universities located in London, Oxford, and Cambridge are collectively referred to as the Golden Triangle. See Sean Coughlan, 'Oxford Top of Global University Rankings', *BBC*, 11 September 2019, http://www.bbc.co.uk/news/education-49666979.

[103] EY, 'Landscaping UK Fintech: Commissioned by UK Trade & Investment', 6 August 2014, p. 6, http://www.ey.com/Publication/vwLUAssets/Landscaping_UK_Fintech/$FILE/EY-Landscaping-UK-Fintech.pdf.

[104] 'Our Story', Zopa, accessed 1 June 2023, http://www.zopa.com/about/our-story.

have worked together to stimulate and sustain the growth of the Fintech sector and ecosystem.[105]

Fintech has a strong presence in the UK in many areas, for example digital payments. Consumers in London frequently use contactless bank cards, Apple Pay, and Google Pay when they go shopping, dine in restaurants, and take underground trains. P2P lending is now popular in the UK, which has removed banks from the lending chain and provides a better deal for both investors and borrowers.[106] Investors at Funding Circle, for example, can earn an estimated annual return of 7.2%, which is much better than that of bank savings.[107] Also, the UK government-backed British Business Bank, via Funding Circle, has lent out £80 million to support small business borrowers who seek finance.[108] Moreover, UK Fintech firms have lowered the threshold for the traditional wealth management industry, making it an affordable option for ordinary people. For instance, Nutmeg provides inexpensive asset management services online, including diversified portfolios and stock ISAs, as well as pension schemes, with a £500 minimum investment.[109]

The success of UK Fintech could be largely attributed to its favourable government policies and flexible regulatory practices. According to a survey, the UK's financial regulatory regime is perceived as the most Fintech-friendly in the world, as the Financial Conduct Authority (FCA)'s sandbox regime is said to encourage innovation and competition whilst minimising financial risks.[110] The FCA has been implementing projects like Innovation Hub and RegTech Forum to encourage competition and growth in the financial services industry by assisting both large and small businesses that create new products and services that truly enhance the experience of consumers, and to support the development of new regulatory solutions.[111] Fintech has been on the UK's political agenda for a long time. As early as 2015, the UK government

---

[105] UK Department for International Trade, 'UK Fintech: State of the Nation', April 2019, https://assets.publishing.service.gov.uk/government/uploads/system/uploads/attachment_data/file/801277/UK-fintech-state-of-the-nation.pdf.
[106] Lerong Lu, 'Solving the SME Financing Puzzle: Has Online P2P Lending Got the Midas Touch?'. *Journal of International Banking Law and Regulation* (2018) 33: 449, 453.
[107] Funding Circle, accessed 1 June 2023, https://www.fundingcircle.com.
[108] Ibid.
[109] Using new types of low-cost investments like exchange traded funds, Nutmeg charges fees as low as 0.6% from its investors. See Emma Dunkley, 'A Tech Take on Wealth Management: Entrepreneurship: Nick Hungerford, Nutmeg', *The Financial Times*, 3 December 2014, p. 14.
[110] Caroline Binham, 'UK Regulators Are The Most Fintech Friendly', *The Financial Times*, 12 September 2016, https://www.ft.com/content/ff5b0be4-7381-11e6-bf48-b372cdb1043a.
[111] The staff at FCA, through RegTech Forum, regularly meet with start-ups, incumbent institutions, technology providers, and scholars to assess the impacts generated by RegTech and to understand where the regulator should focus its efforts. The FCA also develops other activities to promote the application of RegTech, such as Showcase Days and Digital Regulatory Reporting (working jointly with the Bank of English). See 'RegTech', FCA, accessed 1 June 2023, https://www.fca.org.uk/firms/innovation/RegTech.

announced its ambitious plan to build London into a global centre for Fintech.[112] In February 2021, the UK government published *The Kalifa Review of UK Fintech*, with the goals of promoting the development and broad use of Fintech and upholding the UK's standing in the global Fintech industry.[113] The favourable policies and regulatory frameworks have contributed to the long-term growth of Fintech and RegTech in the UK.

In addition to the EU and UK, other EMEA regions have witnessed certain Fintech hubs that are rapidly expanding. As the top financial centre in the Middle East and globally, Dubai has created a thriving Fintech industry, with a 30% annual growth rate in the area since 2017.[114] This could not be achieved without the city's reputation for having a top-notch regulatory environment for the Fintech sector. The Dubai Financial Services Authority (DFSA) aims to ensure that the regulatory system is sound, stable, secure, and growth-oriented for technological and innovative businesses.[115] Due to transformation of the payments, lending, insurance, and wealth management sectors brought by digital technologies and innovation, there has been a significant increase in the demand for Fintech services in the Middle East in recent years. The most heavily invested Fintech sectors in Dubai include payments and remittances, insurance, digital banking, crowdfunding, and cryptocurrency. There are currently 515 start-ups in the Fintech industry in Dubai, including some well-known businesses like TSLC (digital banking), Postpay (online lending), Bayzat (insurtech), and BitOasis (cryptocurrency).

Riyadh, as the capital city of Saudi Arabia, is another key Fintech hub in the Middle East. The Saudi Vision 2030 national economic development plan is the focal point of the Kingdom's extensive economic transformations, which includes the Financial Sector Development Programme (FSDP) aiming to build a robust, modern, and innovative financial services industry.[116] According to the FSDP, Fintech companies in Saudi Arabia would

---

[112] Peter Campbell, 'Osborne Wants London to Be Global Centre for Fintech', *The Financial Times*, 11 November 2015, https://www.ft.com/content/1f24a25e-886f-11e5-90de-f44762bf9896.

[113] *The Kalifa Review of UK Fintech* emphasises the potential to increase trade, develop highly skilled job opportunities throughout the country, and strengthen the UK's competitive position relative to other top Fintech centres. It lays out a number of suggestions for how the UK can capitalise on its current advantages, establish the ideal conditions for ongoing invention, and aid in the expansion of UK businesses. See 'The Kalifa Review of UK Fintech', HM Treasury, 26 February 2021, https://www.gov.uk/government/publications/the-kalifa-review-of-uk-fintech.

[114] Jackson Mueller and Michael S. Piwowar, 'The Rise of Fintech in the Middle East', Milken Institute, September 2019, https://milkeninstitute.org/sites/default/files/reports-pdf/Fintech%20in%20the%20Middle%20East-FINAL-121119.pdf.

[115] Encouraging innovation forms an important part of the Government of Dubai's strategic goals, and the city's good geographical position is a major factor in its success as a Fintech hotspot in EMEA. See 'Innovation', DFSA, accessed 1 June 2023, https://www.dfsa.ae/innovation.

[116] Saudi Vision 2030 is a strategic plan to diversify Saudi Arabia's economy, lessen its reliance on oil, and expand public service areas like health, education, infrastructure, leisure, and tourism. See Kingdom

reach a number of 230 by 2025, contributing 4.5 billion SAR ($1.2 billion) to the Kingdom's GDP and producing 6,000 new jobs.[117] In April 2018, the Saudi central bank and capital market authority launched Fintech Saudi to serve as a stimulus for the growth of the Fintech sector in the Kingdom.[118] In December 2022, Riyadh held the World Fintech Show, bringing together businesses, investors, lawmakers, government officials, and collaborators across the globe to redefine and re-energise financial services by employing the most cutting-edge technologies.[119]

Some cities in Africa also are involved in the booming Fintech industry. In 2021, there were 5,200 tech start-ups in Africa, half of which are Fintech companies.[120] Fintech was estimated to generate revenues of around $4–6 billion in 2020, with an average penetration level of 3–5%.[121] Nairobi, which is the capital and largest city of Kenya, is home to some of Africa's popular Fintech businesses like M-PESA. M-PESA is the favoured method of payment across the continent for both banked and unbanked individuals, providing approximately 51 million users with a cost-effective, safe, and convenient way to send and receive money, top-up airtime, pay bills, get the salary paid, obtain short-term loans, and complete other financial transactions.[122] Furthermore, Nigeria houses over 200 Fintech companies, with Fintech solutions provided by banks and mobile network providers.[123] Lagos, the biggest city in Africa and a major financial centre, has emerged as a thriving Fintech hub both locally and internationally. A young population, rising smartphone adoption, and a targeted legislative push to boost financial inclusion and cashless payments are making an ideal environment for a flourishing Fintech industry in Lagos and other Nigerian cities. Nigeria's thriving Fintech industry attracted more than $600 million in financing in 2019, accounting for 25% of all funds raised by African tech start-ups.[124] However, Nigerian authorities

---

of Saudi Arabia, 'Homepage: The Progress & Achievements of Saudi Arabia—Vision 2030', accessed 1 June 2023, https://www.vision2030.gov.sa/.
[117] Ibid.
[118] 'About Us', Fintech Saudi, accessed 1 June 2023, https://Fintechsaudi.com/about/.
[119] World Fintech Show, accessed 1 June 2023, https://worldFintechshow.com/.
[120] Max Flototto et al., 'Fintech in Africa: The End of the Beginning', McKinsey, 30 August 2022, https://www.mckinsey.com/industries/financial-services/our-insights/Fintech-in-africa-the-end-of-the-beginning.
[121] Ibid.
[122] M-PESA is the biggest Fintech platform in the continent of Africa and the most popular mobile money provider. Millions of people who own mobile phones but do not have bank accounts or only have restricted access to banking services are given financial services by M-PESA. See 'M-PESA', Vodafone, accessed 1 June 2023, https://www.vodafone.com/about-vodafone/what-we-do/consumer-products-and-services/m-pesa.
[123] Topsy Kola-Oyeneyin, Mayowa Kuyoro, and Tunde Olanrewaju, 'Harnessing Nigeria's Fintech Potential', McKinsey, 23 September 2020, https://www.mckinsey.com/featured-insights/middle-east-and-africa/harnessing-nigerias-Fintech-potential.
[124] Ibid.

have to address some weaknesses in the wider Fintech ecosystem, such as skill gaps in business management and marketing, to enable the continuous growth of Fintech in the country.[125] Apart from Nairobi and Lagos, other African cities like Casablanca, Cape Town, Johannesburg, and Kigali are seeing fast growth of Fintech industries that have received sizable investments and policy supports.

3.5 Regulatory technology (RegTech)

RegTech, which is an abbreviation for regulatory technology, describes the application of technological solutions to help financial institutions comply with regulatory and reporting requirements in a fast, flexible, and cost-effective manner.[126] RegTech also assists financial regulators in their efficient performance of onerous and complex supervisory tasks, as they could use AI, machine learning, blockchain, and other pioneering technologies to collect and analyse needed information of the regulated entities, providing a swift and accurate response to the latest market changes and real-time risks.[127] The official use of technology for regulatory, supervisory, and oversight purposes is referred to as supervisory technology (suptech).[128] It contributes to the stability and resilience of the entire financial industry. Clearly, RegTech is an advanced regulatory solution bridging government and financial authorities on the one hand, and established financial institutions and Fintech start-ups on the other.

Regulation and compliance in the Fintech sector need to be updated. It would be improper for authorities to simply restrict the growth of Fintech due to the increasing risks triggered by innovative technologies, products, and services. Instead, financial regulators, by upgrading their own regulatory toolkits, should focus on how to achieve safer and more sustainable development of Fintech and maximise the potential of technologies. Through

---

[125] 'State of Play: Fintech in Nigeria', *The Economist*, Intelligence Unit Report 2020, p. 3.

[126] Similar to Fintech which is the integration between finance and technology, RegTech refers to the synergy between regulation and technology. Overall, it assists firms in better understanding and managing compliance tasks and relevant risks by focusing on data and reporting where there has been an increased level of regulatory burdens for financial institutions. See Deloitte, 'RegTech Is the New Fintech', published in 2016, https://www2.deloitte.com/content/dam/Deloitte/tw/Documents/financial-services/tw-fsi-regtech-new-fintech.pdf.

[127] The objectives of RegTech could be interpreted differently, depending on whether it is serving financial regulators or financial institutions. For financial institutions, their primary purposes of using RegTech are to save costs, avoid regulatory incompliance and fines, and therefore improve profitability. For financial regulators, their goals in adopting RegTech are to improve the efficiency and effectiveness of risk identification and management at a macro level and ensure financial stability.

[128] 'BIS Innovation Hub Work on Suptech and RegTech', BIS, accessed 1 June 2023, https://www.bis.org/about/bisih/topics/suptech_RegTech.htm.

RegTech, the digitalisation and automation of regulatory processes is likely to reduce manual errors and improve the effectiveness of both supervision and compliance. Furthermore, we have to understand the relationship between Fintech and RegTech, as the former concept often includes, or overlaps with, the latter. In the eyes of financial institutions, RegTech is perceived as using Fintech to advance risk management, compliance, and reporting tasks. As for financial regulators, RegTech denotes the informalisation, intellectualisation, and modernisation of financial supervision, which suggests smart financial regulation in the Fintech era.

RegTech is distinctive from traditional financial regulation in several aspects.[129] First of all, financial regulators using RegTech can spot risks and regulatory discrepancies on a real-time basis.[130] The speed of supervisory response plays an important role in fulfilling policy objectives. RegTech is likely to transform financial regulation from a rigid regime that is mostly reliant on ex-ante authorisation and ex-post punishment to a more dynamic, instantaneous, and pre-emptive system that accommodates the fast-evolving financial sector. Secondly, RegTech could improve the predictability and accuracy of financial regulation. As regulators obtain large amounts of data in greater dimensions and complexity, they could use AI to build intelligent risk prevention tools and analytical models, leading to enhanced risk management of the whole financial industry. Thirdly, RegTech contributes to a more effective accountability mechanism in regulatory practices. For example, the regulatory decisions and actions on a blockchain-based system could be easily checked. Based on the standardisation of data and an automated process, the work of financial regulators could be closely monitored and audited to ensure regulatory accountability. Fourthly, RegTech improves the sustainability of financial supervision. The RegTech system can perform high-quality regulatory work on a 24/7 basis.[131] Thus, the quality of supervision won't be affected by the emotions, physical conditions, and personal cognitive level of regulatory staff. The data and modelling of any RegTech system can always be updated to adjust to the latest trends in financial markets and institutions. Finally, a well-designed RegTech system will show good compatibility and interoperability. By utilising software

---

[129] Financial regulation is a broad subject, and it consists of the regulation of banks and securities markets. See John Armour et al., *Principles of Financial Regulation* (Oxford: Oxford University Press, 2016), p. 3.

[130] Financial regulation is often found to be slow and falling behind market development, as the mismatch between finance and financial regulation leads to undesirable regulatory outcomes. See Dan Awrey and Kathryn Judge, 'Why Financial Regulation Keeps Falling Short', Columbia Law School's Blog on Corporations and the Capital Markets, 25 February 2020, https://clsbluesky.law.columbia.edu/2020/02/25/why-financial-regulation-keeps-falling-short/.

[131] 24/7 refers to any businesses that operate on a non-stop basis (i.e., 24 hours a day, seven days a week).

development kit (SDK) or API, RegTech systems, hosted by different financial authorities within a jurisdiction or internationally, could connect to each other and achieve data sharing and coordinated supervision.[132]

In practice, financial institutions can utilise various RegTech solutions to manage risks and comply with regulatory requirements. Popular applications of RegTech include compliance solutions relating to KYC, anti-money laundering (AML), and countering the financing of terrorism (CFT). For instance, ACA Group's Compliance Alpha provides financial firms with automated and continuous monitoring of a large number of sanctions and watchlists that include politically exposed persons and over 300 adverse media sources, with advanced name-matching algorithms.[133] The risk of non-compliance is decreased and time and money are saved when financial institutions use RegTech solutions to automate and streamline the AML and KYC process. Another area of RegTech application is conduct and prudential risk management. By offering real-time monitoring and reporting of risk factors and exposures, RegTech solutions are being utilised to assist financial institutions in better managing risks. Moreover, RegTech solutions are being used by firms to cope with excessive compliance tasks and facilitate regulatory reporting. They offer a central platform for tracking the latest regulatory changes, managing compliance requirements, and automating the process of monitoring compliance and reporting. For example, FundApps, founded in 2010, is a cloud-based RegTech company helping asset managers comply with ever-increasing regulatory requirements, and its clients include over 100 large financial institutions that hold $14 trillion in assets.[134] By using automated monitoring and compliance management software, clients of FundApps can stay aware of the latest disclosure requirements for major shareholding, short selling, and takeover panels, as well as be compliant with regulatory rules regarding sensitive industries investment, foreign ownership, and position limits.[135] Moreover, the RegTech solution provider Cappitech offers regulatory reporting and intelligence solutions for financial institutions, as it processes over 10% of the total EU trading volume and helps clients reduce 70% of total cost of ownership.[136] Automated reporting lowers the chance of errors and ensures that financial institutions can fulfil

---

[132] 'SDK vs. API: What's the Difference?', IBM, accessed 1 June 2023, https://www.ibm.com/cloud/blog/sdk-vs-api.
[133] 'AML Compliance Software: ComplianceAlpha RegTech Solution', ACA Group, accessed 1 June 2023, https://www.acaglobal.com/our-solutions/compliancealpha/aml-kyc-cip.
[134] 'About Us', FundApps, accessed 1 June 2023, https://www.fundapps.co/about-us.
[135] Ibid.
[136] 'Transaction Reporting with Cappitech', Cappitech, accessed 1 June 2023, https://www.cappitech.com/regulation/ppc-brand/.

their reporting duties on time and affordably. It also contributes to auditable record-keeping and promotes integrity in the industry. Finally, RegTech can effectively improve fraud detection and prevention for financial firms. By analysing vast amounts of data and utilising machine-learning algorithms, RegTech solutions are being used to detect and prevent fraud in real-time.

The above examples have shown how RegTech is being adopted by modern financial institutions to manage risks and comply with regulations. As the market needs change, new solutions are being created constantly in the RegTech sector. Clearly, RegTech solutions bring various benefits to financial institutions and regulators. Fintech companies and traditional banks could save significant costs by automating the compliance operation, since they are likely to use less manual labour and make fewer mistakes. In practice, compliance is becoming an increasingly expensive and resource-intensive work for any financial business. For both retail and corporate banks, the operating costs spent on compliance have increased by over 60% after the global financial crisis.[137] RegTech seems to be the answer to effective cost saving in relation to regulatory compliance. Also, RegTech solutions help financial institutions collect, process, and analyse financial big data quickly and precisely, which improves compliance outcomes and decision-making. Obviously, the application of RegTech is likely to increase accountability and transparency of financial transactions and reduce frauds and other financial crimes. It restores our confidence in the industry and rebuilds the trust between consumers and financial institutions.

Aside from the advantages, RegTech has certain limitations that need to be considered by both regulators and businesses. Before integrating RegTech into any existing compliance operation, financial institutions need to carefully assess the possible vulnerabilities and risks of technological solutions. RegTech is still in its infancy and most products are considered immature. Thus, most financial institutions have not fully embraced the technology despite its potential advantages. The limited adoption is partly due to the lack of industry standards for RegTech products, such as vendor due diligence, important performance indicators, and data privacy.[138] It means that certain RegTech products used by US companies could not be offered to EU businesses as they could not meet the EU's regulatory criteria or data protection law. The limited adoption and lack of industry standards are likely

---

[137] Deloitte, 'The Future of Regulatory Productivity, Powered by RegTech', 2017, https://www2.deloitte.com/content/dam/Deloitte/us/Documents/regulatory/us-regulatory-future-of-regulatory-productivity-powered-by-regtech.pdf.
[138] Bo Howell, 'Weighing the Pros and Cons of RegTech', Nasdaq, 26 April 2022, https://www.nasdaq.com/articles/weighing-the-pros-and-cons-of-RegTech.

to reduce the potential influence and advantages of RegTech. Moreover, the overdependence on RegTech could incur higher costs of staff training and infrastructure building. It also leads to increased operational risks and potential technical errors. Technologies like blockchain, AI, and machine learning, on which most RegTech solutions operate, can be complicated and challenging to apply. Given the fierce competition for talents in both public and private sectors, recruiting RegTech specialists could be difficult for financial regulators and institutions.[139] It takes a significant amount of time and capital to upgrade the compliance system and to equip existing staff with the necessary knowledge and skills to be able to operate such a system. This might result in unwillingness for large banks and financial institutions to adopt RegTech solutions, as they already face a heavy financial burden in fulfilling compliance duties. The estimated annual costs relating to financial crime compliance for global financial institutions reached $213.9 billion in 2021.[140]

It is not always as easy as we thought to integrate RegTech products with the financial institutions' current systems, for two reasons. First, most RegTech products only focus on providing compliance solutions in a small number of business areas. As a result, financial institutions need to purchase several RegTech products and deal with multiple RegTech providers. This is not convenient and will add to the cost of compliance. As the interoperability between new RegTech solutions is not satisfactory, it calls for a uniformed RegTech platform offering a wide spectrum of RegTech products which could satisfy the need of large financial institutions who prefer a one-stop shop for all regulatory solutions. Second, the integration between RegTech solutions and any firms' legacy systems is also challenging, as the latter has been built up over a long period of time by using several generations of tech solutions coping with a complicated dataset of compliance requirements.

Further, the increased reliance on technology is not fully safe. When there are any technology failures or technical issues, it might significantly impact the compliance posture of firms. In the worst scenario, the RegTech system itself could become a single point of failure in the entire compliance process.[141] In addition, effective RegTech solutions need to handle large amounts of sensitive financial data, which makes financial institutions susceptible to data breaches and cyber-attacks. Therefore, RegTech solutions must be securely built and compliant with data privacy laws in

---

[139] EBA, 'EBA Analysis of RegTech in the EU Financial Sector', June 2021, p. 33, https://www.eba.europa.eu/eba-assesses-benefits-challenges-and-risks-RegTech-use-eu-and-puts-forward-steps-be-taken-support.
[140] 'Global Spend on Financial Crime Compliance at Financial Institutions Reaches $213.9 Billion USD According to LexisNexis Risk Solutions Study', LexisNexis, 9 June 2021, https://risk.lexisnexis.com/global/en/about-us/press-room/press-release/20210609-tcoc-global-study.

any jurisdictions where the product users intend to operate. Last but not least, a big challenge for RegTech systems results from the uncertainty in the legal and regulatory environments. Like existing compliance systems, RegTech solutions must be able to quickly respond to changes in legislations, regulatory rules, and public policies, which have been evolving rapidly and frequently.[142] This is likely to cause difficulty for RegTech solutions to be regularly checked and updated to ensure their adaptability to the latest regulatory environment at national and international levels.

3.6 Regulatory sandbox

A regulatory sandbox refers to a safe space where Fintech companies can test innovative financial products, services, business models, and delivery mechanisms without directly incurring all the normal regulatory consequences of conducting regulated activities in a particular jurisdiction.[143] In practice, financial regulators typically demand that applicants include suitable safeguard mechanisms in their business models in exchange for more lenient regulatory criteria. These precautions include measures for protecting customers (such as demanding informed permission), financial restrictions (such as restricting the amount of money that a consumer can invest), and other risk control mechanisms.[144] A regulatory sandbox is an important tool for financial regulators to encourage disruptive innovation and foster competition, which could hardly happen in a tightly regulated financial industry dominated by large banks and financial institutions that could afford the high compliance costs. For those Fintech businesses that passed the test and satisfied regulatory objectives, they could apply to become licenced financial firms. However, if they did not achieve the goals of testing or caused negative impacts like consumer detriment or systemic risk, regulators could terminate the testing anytime. There should be immediate and effective communication between regulators and Fintech companies during the testing process. The regulatory sandbox illustrates how financial regulators could respond to the demands of Fintech firms developing novel solutions that might not

---

[142] For an overview of important regulatory changes for financial markets see 'Financial Services Regulatory Timeline Tool', Deloitte, accessed 1 June 2023, https://www2.deloitte.com/uk/en/pages/financial-services/articles/financial-services-regulatory-timeline-tool.html.
[143] FCA, 'Regulatory Sandbox', November 2015, p. 1, https://www.fca.org.uk/publication/research/regulatory-sandbox.pdf.
[144] 'Hong Kong Launches Regulatory Sandbox in Wake of Developments in Australia, Malaysia, Singapore, and the UK', Herbert Smith Freehills, 5 October 2016, https://hsfnotes.com/fsrandcorpcrime/2016/10/05/hong-kong-launches-regulatory-sandbox-in-wake-of-developments-in-australia-malaysia-singapore-and-the-uk/.

initially be compliant with existing legal and regulatory requirements, while ensuring that the activities are limited to acceptable parameters to preserve the integrity and stability of the financial system.[145]

As a popular regulatory toolkit, regulatory sandbox regimes have been adopted by financial regulators across the globe. In 2016, the UK was the first country to introduce a regulatory sandbox, which has consolidated London's position as a leading centre of Fintech and financial innovation.[146] As of December 2022, the FCA received over 550 applications to its regulatory sandbox in seven rounds of selection, and the regulator has moved to an always open model which allows Fintech firms to submit their applications throughout the year.[147] Further, the Australian Securities and Investments Commission (ASIC) launched an enhanced regulatory sandbox that enables natural persons and businesses to test innovative financial services and credit activities, without the need to obtain an Australian financial services licence or credit licence.[148] Other leading regulatory sandbox regimes across global financial centres are the HKMA's Fintech Supervisory Sandbox,[149] MAS's Regulatory Sandbox,[150] and DFSA's Innovation Testing Licence Programme.[151]

A regulatory sandbox regime could bring several benefits to the financial industry.[152] Firstly, it reduces the time and cost of transforming novel ideas to real products and services that could be rapidly replicated and delivered to consumers on a large scale. Regulatory uncertainty deters businesses from innovating. With the help of a regulatory sandbox, more and better Fintech products could reach the mass market quickly. Secondly, it helps innovative Fintech businesses have more access to financing resources (e.g., bank loans, VC, and PE funds), as their pilot projects are officially endorsed by the regulator, which enhances the credibility and reputation of such Fintech firms. Otherwise, investors would find it risky to put their money into the new

---

[145] Rosabel Ng et al., 'Inside and Outside Singapore's Proposed Fintech Regulatory Sandbox: Balancing Supervision and Innovation'. *Butterworths Journal of International Banking and Financial Law* (2016) 31: 596, 597.
[146] Caroline Binham, 'UK Regulators Are the Most Fintech Friendly', *The Financial Times*, 12 September 2016, https://www.ft.com/content/ff5b0be4-7381-11e6-bf48-b372cdb1043a.
[147] 'Regulatory Sandbox Accepted Firms', FCA, 16 December 2022, https://www.fca.org.uk/firms/innovation/regulatory-sandbox/accepted-firms.
[148] The ASIC's enhanced regulatory sandbox allows testing of a wider range of financial services and credit activities for a longer period of no more than 24 months. See 'Enhanced Regulatory Sandbox', ASIC, accessed 1 June 2023, https://asic.gov.au/for-business/innovation-hub/enhanced-regulatory-sandbox/.
[149] 'Fintech Supervisory Sandbox (FSS)', HKMA, accessed 1 June 2023, https://www.hkma.gov.hk/eng/key-functions/international-financial-centre/Fintech/Fintech-supervisory-sandbox-fss/.
[150] 'Overview of Regulatory Sandbox', MAS, accessed 01 June 2023, https://www.mas.gov.sg/development/Fintech/regulatory-sandbox.
[151] 'DFSA Innovation and Crypto', DFSA, accessed 1 June 2023, https://www.dfsa.ae/innovation.
[152] FCA, 'Regulatory Sandbox', November 2015, p. 5, https://www.fca.org.uk/publication/research/regulatory-sandbox.pdf.

business ventures, leading to harsher financing terms, higher costs of financing, or even a lower valuation for Fintech firms. Professional investors and VC funds have to factor the regulatory uncertainty and risks into the valuation formula. Thirdly, it enables financial regulators (such as the FCA, HKMA, and MAS) to work closely with Fintech businesses at an early stage of product development to ensure that proper consumer protection and prudential regulatory standards are built into the prototypes of Fintech products and services. Obviously, such an ex-ante regulatory approach is most economical and effective in supervising Fintech. Lowering the regulatory barriers and relevant costs for Fintech start-ups is the best way to encourage them to test new ideas. Meanwhile, an adequate level of protection for consumers and financial system stability will still be maintained, as the regulatory bodies are actively involved in the process of financial innovation. As we know, financial innovation defies conventional business models, services, and products, and thus it is difficult for challengers to innovate under the existing regulatory rules which were designed for the existing industry.[153] Accordingly, the sandbox regime could help Fintech firms test their products in a safer and more flexible environment without overhaul of the current regulatory system. Apparently, it is a win-win situation for the Fintech businesses, the regulators, and financial consumers.

A sandbox works as an ideal regulatory tool that could balance innovation with the protection of consumer interests and financial system safety. However, despite that some regulatory standards could be temporarily relieved for Fintech businesses when testing novel solutions, they still have to obey the basic laws (such as property law, contract law, data protection law, and banking law) in a given jurisdiction. In practice, the regulatory sandbox scheme has to be carefully designed in three areas to achieve the best regulatory effect. Firstly, financial authorities must prudently formulate the admission criteria to select the right Fintech activities to enter the scheme. The standard should not be too strict and narrow that it will prevent the majority of innovators from using the sandbox. Nor should it be too wide, which might lower the safeguard for consumers or flood the Fintech industry with incompetent players. Regulators need to assess if any financial innovation is making a substantial difference to existing products, services, and business models, and if it is bringing quantifiable benefits to consumers. Regulators also have to conduct due diligence with regard to applicants about their intention of using the sandbox and whether they have adequate resources invested in the

---

[153] Lerong Lu, 'Financial Technology and Challenger Banks in the UK: Gap Fillers or Real Challengers?'. *Journal of International Banking Law and Regulation* (2017) 32: 273, 281–282.

implementation of new ideas, the extent to which Fintech firms understand the current laws and regulations, and whether they have an effective internal risk-control mechanism. It is clear that no one should be overreliant on admission to a regulatory sandbox but should develop their own risk management and compliance methods. Moreover, the selection standards need to be consistent, straightforward, and transparent for any Fintech corporation, in terms of the criteria for accessing the sandbox and the fulfilment of regulatory goals.

Secondly, regulators need to provide a more tailored sandbox regime for different Fintech innovators, as their business models, products, and services could be highly heterogeneous. A one-size-fit-all approach for a regulatory sandbox is not workable in practice. A regulatory sandbox should be flexible enough to accommodate the diversity and special characteristics of each Fintech activity, and regulatory expectation should be agreed on a case-by-case basis. Fintech is an extremely broad term that could encompass everything from banking and insurance to robo-advisor. Fintech businesses are likely to encounter different challenges, depending on what kind of financial products and services they plan to offer and what kind of business models they operate. Fintech could be realised by established financial institutions offering updated services, or by start-ups and BigTech creating brand-new financial products. For new Fintech start-ups or tech companies that firstly tap into financial services, they would need to apply for a licence or regulatory authorisation before operating most financial services. This will inevitably cause significant costs for Fintech corporations, especially when the market demand and consumer interest is still unclear prior to the trial of new products. Therefore, there is a need for a special regime for such firms to test new ideas with a fast-track licencing process which is subject to more relaxed regulatory standards compared to a normal licence. However, once the pilot scheme finishes, applicants that embark on full financial services will have to convert their temporary licence to a full licence, allowing them to conduct businesses without restrictions. As for licenced financial institutions to test new ideas, their primary concern is that the regulators might take enforcement actions against the trial and even impose a hefty fine on anything they deem irregular. To assure existing financial institutions who embrace Fintech advance, it is necessary for the regulators to issue a 'no action letter' if they believe that the new activities will not violate existing requirements or run against regulatory objectives.[154] What is more, individual guidance could also

---

[154] FCA, 'Regulatory Sandbox', November 2015, p. 17, https://www.fca.org.uk/publication/research/regulatory-sandbox.pdf. A similar approach could be observed in other jurisdictions, such as the US: see

be given to Fintech businesses which help them interpret the applicable regulations regarding their testing products and services. Businesses that abide by the guidelines won't face penalties or enforcement actions from the authorities. There could even be exemptions or waivers made for entrepreneurs who would otherwise be breaking the law, encouraging the development of fresh concepts and allowing for more flexibility in testing new financial products. However, it should be highlighted that such a customised sandbox framework, which caters to each Fintech firm's needs, might consume a significant amount of resource for regulators.

Thirdly, there should be safeguarding mechanisms in place to protect consumer interests and financial system stability in any sandbox regimes. For example, Fintech customers, like those in the clinical trials for new medicine, should be informed of the testing, its risks, and potential compensations. It must require clear consent from consumers to be involved in the testing of new Fintech products and services. Fintech consumers in a sandbox should be entitled to no less than the same level of protection enjoyed by customers using similar services and products provided by a fully licenced and regulated institution. For example, Fintech consumers should be given access to a financial dispute resolution service (like the UK's Financial Ombudsman Service, FOS) and deposit protection scheme (the Financial Services Compensation Scheme, FSCS), like when they use normal banking and investment services. Before beginning the testing, Fintech companies should make sure they have enough capital and other resources to cover any losses to clients that may result from the operations. Finally, when deciding the regulatory perimeters for Fintech businesses testing novel solutions, regulators have to limit the scale of trial to ensure that it won't cause immediate risks to the stability of financial system.

3.7 Regulatory objective and strategy

When setting policies and regulatory rules to promote financial innovation and the growth of Fintech, policy-makers and financial authorities have to consider two primary goals: firstly, how to maintain an adequate level of consumer protection; and secondly, how to ensure that financial innovation won't lead to systemic risks and undermine the financial stability of one

---

US Consumer Financial Protection Bureau, 'Policy on No-Action Letters', 16 October 2014, https://www.federalregister.gov/articles/2014/10/16/2014-24645/policy-on-no-action-letters.

nation. Investor and consumer protection and financial stability have long been the two main objectives of modern financial regulation.[155]

This section will assess some regulatory mechanisms safeguarding the legitimate interests of Fintech consumers, especially in areas of fund safety, consumer education, dispute resolution, and personal data protection. In the Fintech sector, fund security is a critical issue which directly affects consumers' confidence in the businesses they are using.[156] Contrary to savings and payments by conventional banks and financial firms, the money transfers via Fintech platforms are not fully regulated. As a result, when such platforms fail, their customers' funds will not be adequately protected. There are even cases when consumers' money is taken advantage of through fraudulent schemes. For example, China's online P2P lending sector underwent a series of crises and platform failures in 2016, during which leading Fintech platform Ezubao defrauded $7.3 billion from over 900,000 investors.[157] In November 2022, the collapse of FTX, a Bahamas-based crypto exchange, resulted in the loss of billions of dollars of private and institutional investors around the world, including well-known financial firms like Sequoia Capital, SoftBank Group, and BlackRock.[158] Accordingly, some steps can be adopted by Fintech businesses to increase fund security, such as the use of custodian accounts for keeping clients' money which will be segregated from the operating cash of Fintech platforms.

Furthermore, raising consumer awareness and financial education is of vital importance to protect Fintech consumers. It is recommended that Fintech firms need to teach consumers how to use their services securely and safely, how to spot frauds, and how to make informed financial choices. Squirrel, Cleo, and Yolt are good examples of Fintech businesses in the UK who attempt to close the financial literacy gap by providing educational solutions to help British consumers handle their money more effectively.[159] In addition, Fintech companies should have a procedure in place for resolving

---

[155] John Armour et al., *Principles of Financial Regulation* (Oxford: Oxford University Press, 2016), p. 61.

[156] Banking and finance are essentially a business that is built upon confidence. See Stefan Ingves, 'Restoring Confidence in Banks', BIS Basel Committee on Banking Supervision, 4 March 2014, https://www.bis.org/speeches/sp140304.htm.

[157] Li Huang and Henry N. Pontell, 'Crime and Crisis in China's P2P Online Lending Market: A Comparative Analysis of Fraud'. *Crime, Law and Social Change* (2023) 79: 369–393, https://doi.org/10.1007/s10611-022-10053-y.

[158] Andrew Scurria and Soma Biswas, 'FTX Collapses into Bankruptcy System that Still Hasn't Figured out Crypto', *The Wall Street Journal*, 16 November 2022, https://www.wsj.com/articles/ftx-collapses-into-bankruptcy-system-that-still-hasnt-figured-out-crypto-11668550688.

[159] Manisha Patel, 'Banks Have a Responsibility to Fix the Financial Education Gap', The Fintech Times, 14 January 2020, https://theFintechtimes.com/banks-have-a-responsibility-to-fix-the-financial-education-gap/.

conflicts between businesses and consumers. In most cases, an internal customer service department with effective complaint handling or dispute resolution processes is desirable. Fintech firms also have to inform customers of the possibility of using external or official resources to handle complaints, such as filing the complaint to the UK's FOS.[160]

Ensuring data protection is another key task for financial authorities, which has significant legal and commercial implications for Fintech businesses. Fintech firms are collecting, storing, and processing an enormous amount of sensitive personal data and financial information, as big data plays an essential role in the function of most Fintech companies that specialise in retail banking, investments, and insurance. Complying with data protection laws has been a costly and resource-intensive job for Fintech companies, particularly when many jurisdictions have introduced strict data protection regimes to protect consumers, such as the California Consumer Privacy Act (CCPA), China's Personal Information Protection Law (PIPL), and the EU's GDPR. Meanwhile, we have seen a number of severe data leakage cases across the world in recent years. In April 2022, when a former employee of Cash App Investing left the business and downloaded corporate reports, sensitive information on over 8 million users was made public illegally.[161] In September 2022, Revolut, a leading European Fintech start-up, fell prey to a highly targeted cyber-attack that gave hackers access to the private information of tens of thousands of clients.[162] Some technical methods could be used to improve Fintech companies' data protection systems, reducing the likelihood of a data breach and paying expensive fines and litigation costs. Such methods include the encryption of sensitive data, implementation of access control,[163] regular testing of system malfunction, and publication of clear privacy policies. Last but not least, Fintech companies are advised to adopt the so-called data minimisation procedure, which means gathering

---

[160] UK financial consumers have access to a free and simple-to-use agency called the FOS which handles disputes between customers and companies that offer financial services. The FOS has the authority to make things right and settle conflicts fairly and impartially. See 'Our Homepage', FOS, accessed 1 June 2023, https://www.financial-ombudsman.org.uk/.

[161] Stacy Cowley, 'Block Says Cash App Breach Affected 8 Million Users', *The New York Times*, 6 April 2022, https://www.nytimes.com/2022/04/06/business/block-cash-app-data-breach.html.

[162] Carly Page, 'Revolut Confirms Cyberattack Exposed Personal Data of Tens of Thousands of Users', TechCrunch, 20 September 2022, https://techcrunch.com/2022/09/20/revolut-cyberattack-thousands-exposed/.

[163] Access control is a security method that limits who can access particular resources in a computing setting. It is a basic security principle that reduces risk to a company and other organisations and has two types: logical and physical. Different methods of access controls, such as two-factor authentication (TFA), are being implemented by Fintech firms to guarantee that only authorised personnel can access sensitive data. See 'What Is Access Control?', Citrix, accessed 1 June 2023, https://www.citrix.com/solutions/secure-access/what-is-access-control.html.

the minimal amount of information that is required to deliver the desired products and services and making sure that data are not kept for longer than is necessary.

Apart from the protection of financial consumers, authorities need to guarantee financial stability and resilience, as financial innovations are likely to cause systemic risks in some cases. Systemic risks are events like an economic shock or institutional failure that set off a chain of negative economic outcomes, such as the collapse of financial organisations or markets, or both.[164] This is a particular concern for regulators when dealing with large Fintech firms, conglomerates, or FHCs that engage in various banking and non-banking financial services and possess assets worth billions or even trillions of dollars.[165] Global regulators are especially wary of some form of systemic risks that could destabilise the financial system following the global financial crisis 2007–2008.[166] Consequently, prudential regulation at both micro and macro level has remained a top priority for financial regulators tackling novel Fintech businesses.

Technology is being adopted speedily in the Fintech sector, which is generating new risk factors that could eventually intertwine or combine to cause systemic risks. Such risks are frequently challenging to understand and predict, making them difficult to mitigate. According to research by the World Economic Forum, there are six categories of specific risk sources showing how technology could influence the development and amplification of systemic risks: digital interdependency, shared model vulnerability, entity-based regulatory insufficiency, conflict of national priorities, emerging source of influence, and new cause of financial exclusion.[167] In addition, the further development of BigTech providing financial services has given rise to urgent financial stability issues. It is because the financial businesses of tech giants do not always fall within the existing regulatory perimeter, and financial regulators seem to lack the data or analytical tool to ascertain the existence and magnitude of risks involved.[168] Therefore, possible systemic risks resulting from the operation of Fintech and BigTech should not be underestimated by financial regulators.

---

[164] Steven L. Schwarcz, 'Systemic Risk'. *Georgetown Law Journal* (2008) 97: 193, 198.
[165] For a discussion of Fintech conglomerates and FHCs like Ant Group see Chapter 4.
[166] Iris H.-Y. Chiu and Joanna Wilson, *Banking Law and Regulation* (Oxford: Oxford University Press, 2019), p. 13.
[167] World Economic Forum and Deloitte, 'Beneath the Surface: Technology-Driven Systemic Risks and the Continued Need for Innovation', 28 October 2021, https://www3.weforum.org/docs/WEF_Technology_Innovation_and_Systemic_Risk_2021.pdf.
[168] FSB, 'Fintech and Market Structure in the COVID-19 Pandemic: Implications for Financial Stability', 21 March 2022, p. 12, https://www.fsb.org/wp-content/uploads/P210322.pdf.

3.8 Conclusion

The chapter has investigated two pillars in any Fintech ecosystem: the place (global Fintech hubs) and the regulators. It has evaluated the comparative advantages, distinctive features, and regulatory environments of key Fintech hubs in different continents. Their successes can be credited to a number of factors, including but not limited to the favourable regulatory framework, supportive policies, skilled workforce, favourable tax structure, local technology industries, strong financial investments, and education. Then, the chapter has examined the regulatory dimensions of Fintech. It has assessed the use of RegTech for both financial institutions and regulators. RegTech not only helps financial businesses comply with regulatory and reporting requirements speedily and affordably, but also assists financial regulators in performing complex supervisory duties more efficiently and responding quickly to latest market changes. It has also looked at the design elements of international regulatory sandbox schemes and considered how they could be used as a powerful regulatory instrument to promote innovation while containing financial risks and minimising potential consumer harms. Finally, the chapter has highlighted two crucial objectives for policy-makers and financial regulators when they make any Fintech-related regulatory rules and policies to promote financial innovation: to ensure an adequate degree of consumer protection and to maintain financial stability.

4
Fintech Ecosystem—Part Two

Fintech Corporations, BigTech, and Metaverse

4.1 Introduction

This chapter continues to examine the key players in the burgeoning Fintech ecosystem, in particular the Fintech companies that offer innovative financial products and services to consumers, and how they cope with the regulatory oversight from financial authorities. Fintech corporations exist in different forms. They could be incumbent financial institutions that actively embrace Fintech to upgrade their existing offering of financial services, or newly launched start-ups that leverage on advanced technologies to fill the market gaps. Section 4.2 introduces multiple categories of Fintech corporations, from smaller Fintech ventures to sizable Fintech unicorn companies that are becoming new financial giants. Section 4.3 focuses on those Fintech corporations that have developed into large and complex conglomerates, or FHCs, by using Ant Group as an example to illustrate FHCs' business model and what challenges they pose for policy-makers and financial regulators. Section 4.4 discusses the corporate governance issues regarding Fintech corporations, focusing on innovations in business organisation such as DCSS and the Environmental, Social, and Governance (ESG) principle. Section 4.5 considers the corporate finance issues for Fintech corporations. It assesses traditional financing options like VC, PE, and IPO, as well as the rise of alternative listing arrangements like SPAC. The primary subject of debate is how existing capital markets' laws and regulations could be amended to meet the funding needs of Fintech companies. Section 4.6 studies BigTech that have started to offer financial services, and how best to regulate BigTech in finance to ensure market integrity, data protection, and financial stability. Section 4.7 evaluates the rise of Web 3.0 and virtual worlds like Metaverse and analyses its implications for the provision and regulation of financial services. Section 4.8 concludes the chapter.

4.2 Fintech corporations: established institutions, start-ups, and corporate unicorns

There exist various forms of business organisations that engage in the design and offering of innovative financial products, services, and business models. A large proportion of incumbent financial institutions, such as banks, insurance companies, payment operators, and securities brokers, have proactively adopted Fintech in their business operation and product development. They have competitive advantages in terms of the large customer base, brand name, capital reserve, and rich experience in finance. For instance, in January 2021, JPMorgan launched its digital-only consumer banking app in the UK by using the Chase brand, which employs incentives like 1% cashback, free overseas use of debit cards, and high interest rates on saving accounts to attract British consumers to try the new digital experience of banking.[1] Leading Chinese securities firm Huatai invested CNY2.3 billion ($331 million) in Fintech, and the upgrade of IT infrastructure in 2021 increased by 20.1% from CNY1.9 billion ($280 million), contributing to the full digitalisation of share brokerage services.[2] Moreover, insurance companies across the world have actively adopted Fintech to create new insurtech products. In September 2022, AXA introduced Moja, a novel digital insurance brand that seeks to disrupt the insurance industry by providing a digital-only option for customers who purchase insurance products or utilise relevant services via their smartphone or tablet.[3] The insurtech brand provides the greatest degree of simplicity and adaptability to accommodate customers' changing needs and budgets. When a lot of established financial firms use Fintech to the fullest extent in their businesses, Fintech quickly becomes an integral part of modern financial services. Today's disruptive Fintech will soon become the norm as the younger generation will see it as traditional finance when they grow up.

In contrast to traditional financial institutions that adopt technological transformation, most current Fintech corporations were the start-ups in the 2010s that have built their business models, products, and distributional channels from scratch. Many of them have taken advantage of resources

---

[1] 'JPMorgan Chase to Launch Digital Consumer Banking in the U.K.', JPMorgan Chase, 27 January 2021, https://www.jpmorganchase.com/news-stories/jpmorgan-chase-to-launch-digital-consumer-banking-in-the-uk.

[2] Feijun Hu, 'Securities Brokerage Financial Technology Competition', *Securities Times*, 20 June 2022, https://news.stcn.com/sd/202206/t20220620_4662547.html.

[3] 'AXA UK Retail Launches Moja—Its New Digital-Only Insurance Brand', AXA, 22 September 2022, https://www.axa.co.uk/newsroom/media-releases/2022/axa-uk-retail-launches-moja-its-new-digital-only-insurance-brand/.

like VC investment and proprietary technology to swiftly capture sizable market shares by using online distribution to reach millions of customers. Some Fintech start-ups have grown into a new generation of financial giants, such as Stripe, Monzo, Revolut, Coinbase, Robinhood Markets, Wise, and Klarna. They have either challenged the dominance of traditional banks and financial firms or filled a market niche in certain areas. Some successful Fintech companies have become a so-called unicorn corporation, which means unlisted tech companies with a valuation of over $1 billion.[4] Aileen Lee, a venture capitalist based in the US, created the term 'corporate unicorn' in 2013 to highlight the statistical rarity of such profitable business ventures. Only 0.07% of VC-backed technology start-ups have achieved the prestigious unicorn status.[5] There are variants of unicorn companies, which include decacorns with a valuation over $10 billion and hectocorns with a valuation over $100 billion. As of March 2023, there were 1,207 unicorn companies globally with a total cumulative valuation of $3,776 billion.[6] Fintech corporations account for 258 (or 21%) of all unicorn companies, representing the largest industry in the global economy that contributes significantly to innovation and wealth creation. Nonetheless, unicorns have geographically concentrated in a few countries, such as the US, China, India, the UK, Germany, France, Canada, Israel, and South Korea.

Authorities around the world have made guidelines to define corporate unicorns and provide relevant policy supports for their growth. For example, there is a growing consensus that the EU should take action to assist start-ups in realising their full potential by letting governments participate in the supply of VC. The European Commission has proposed to establish a €100 billion EU sovereign tech fund as well as a €10 billion EU sovereign green tech fund to help tech corporations scale up.[7] The Ministry of Science and Technology in China has published a ranking of unicorn companies and made official criteria to define them: (1) a unicorn company must be an enterprise incorporated in China with an independent legal entity; (2) it must be established within the last 10 years; (3) it must have received VC investments but have not gone public; (4) it must have a valuation of over $1 billion; and (5) those with a valuation over $10 billion are referred to as super unicorn or

---

[4] 'Technology Companies: The Rise and Fall of the Unicorns', *The Economist*, 28 November 2015, p. 57.
[5] Aileen Lee, 'Welcome to the Unicorn Club: Learning from Billion-Dollar Start-Ups', TechCrunch, 2 November 2013, http://techcrunch.com/2013/11/02/welcome-to-the-unicorn-club/.
[6] 'The Complete List of Unicorn Companies', CB Insights, accessed 1 June 2023, http://www.cbinsights.com/research-unicorn-companies.
[7] Giuseppina Testa, Ramon Compano, Ana Correia, and Eva Rückert, 'In Search of EU Unicorns—What Do We Know about Them?', European Commission, 25 February 2022, p. 5.

decacorn.[8] Moreover, global business leaders are prioritising financial investments and operational improvements to step up their game in the digital space and Fintech. The majority of Singapore CEOs believe that, due to Singapore's macroeconomic strength, attractive talent pool, and development potential, the country has the ideal conditions to inspire the next round of unicorn start-ups.[9] This demonstrates Singapore's continued commitment to becoming a smart nation and a recognised Fintech centre. Similarly, Saudi Arabia's Vision 2030 investment plan, which aims to support entrepreneurship and foster the development of Fintech, is likely to spur the growth of tech unicorns in the region, such as STC pay.[10]

The success of Fintech unicorn businesses has demonstrated economic implications in two aspects. On the one hand, tech unicorns are the best representative for the rapid progress and widespread use of advanced technologies like big data, cloud computing, blockchain, and AI. It clearly shows us how technology could ultimately become a commercial reality. On the other hand, the power of capital, which can quickly multiply the size of any company if entrepreneurs' bright ideas and business plans are supported by VC investors, is demonstrated by the presence of tech unicorns. The first generation of unicorn businesses established in the late 1990s or early 2000s, including Facebook, Google, Alibaba, and Tencent, have become global leaders in the tech industry, and publicly listed their shares on major stock exchanges in New York, London, or Hong Kong.[11] It is clear that an IPO of unicorns is the most coveted exit strategy for VC funds, generating huge investment profits for their financiers. More tech enterprises from all over the globe have recently joined the exclusive billion-dollar club. While the US unicorns like Databricks, Chime, and SpaceX have received a lot of media coverage, their Chinese peers have garnered less attention. China currently has a large number of VC funds and a thriving high-tech sector, both of which are the necessary conditions for fostering unicorn companies. In recent years, Chinese VC funds have been actively investing money in countries like the US and Israel—they provided $2.4 billion for Silicon Valley start-ups in early 2018, with a concentration on communications technology and biotech companies.[12]

[8] 'The Ministry of Science and Technology Officially Released the 2017 Unicorn List', People.cn, 24 March 2018, http://it.people.com.cn/n1/2018/0324/c1009-29886916.html.
[9] '2018 Annual APEC CEO Survey: Singapore Findings', PwC, 15 November 2018, https://www.pwc.com/sg/en/publications/apec-ceo-survey-sg-2018.html.
[10] Rayana Alqubali, 'Saudi Arabia Will See More Fintech Unicorns Soon, Head of Kingdom's Top Fintech Body Says', Arab News, 23 August 2021, https://www.arabnews.com/node/1915866/business-economy.
[11] Many tech unicorns have eventually grown into BigTech, which we will discuss later in this chapter.
[12] Don Weinland, 'Chinese VC Funds Pour $2.4bn into Silicon Valley Start-Ups', The Financial Times, 18 July 2018, http://www.ft.com/content/463b162a-8a3d-11e8-b18d-0181731a0340.

4.3 Fintech giants and financial holding companies: the case study of Ant Group

4.3.1 The rise of new FHCs

FHCs are large-scale financial groups or conglomerates that participate in banking-related activities but also provide non-banking financial services. In the US, FHCs are regulated by the Federal Reserve Board and may carry out a wide range of financial services, such as investment advisory services, merchant banking, securities underwriting and trading, and insurance product sales.[13] Some of the largest FHCs in the world include Citigroup, JPMorgan Chase, Bank of America, Mitsubishi UFJ, Mizuho Financial Group, HSBC, BNP Paribas, and ING Group, most of which control financial assets worth trillions of dollars. Global financial regulators have applied extra prudential regulatory criteria to FHCs, given their enormous sizes and the possibility of causing systemic risks. For example, the UK's Prudential Regulation Authority (PRA) in 2021 has suggested regulations for the application of current consolidated prudential requirements to FHCs in areas like record keeping, capital buffers, counterparty credit risk, and liquidity coverage.[14] The PBoC also issued trial measures on the enhanced regulation of China-based FHCs in 2020, asking companies to apply to be licenced as FHCs if their banking units hold over CNY500 billion in total assets or their non-banking units possess assets worth over CNY100 billion.[15]

In practice, most FHCs are well-established large financial groups headquartered in the US, Asia, and Europe. Many of them have a prolonged trading history of more than one century. For example, HSBC opened its first branch in Hong Kong in 1865, and Goldman Sachs was established in New York City in 1869. However, in the 2000s and 2010s, we have seen the spectacular rise of some Fintech corporations that have reached the status of unicorn companies or have further grown into multinational and trillion-dollar FHCs. Ant Group, headquartered in Hangzhou, China, is a typical example of the new generation of FHCs that have a relatively short history and mainly engage in Fintech-enabled banking and non-banking financial services. Ant Group, formerly known as Ant Financial Services Group (2014–2020),

---

[13] FHCs were created by the US Gramm-Leach-Bliley Act of 1999. Before becoming an FHC, a bank holding company must satisfy a number of regulatory standards and requirements. See 'Financial Holding Companies', Federal Reserve Board, accessed 1 June 2023, https://www.federalreserve.gov/supervisionreg/fhc.htm.

[14] PRA, 'Policy Statement 20/21—Financial Holding Companies: Further Implementation', September 2021.

[15] PBoC, 'Trial Measures on Regulation of Financial Holding Companies', Order No. 4, 11 September 2020, Article 6.

runs the world's largest mobile payment network, Alipay, which serves over 1 billion consumers and conducts $17-trillion-worth of transactions annually.[16] In 2003, Alipay was launched by Jack Ma (who also founded the e-commerce giant Alibaba Group). It has a humble beginning, as Alipay used to be an affiliated tool of Alibaba's online shopping platforms, Tmall and Taobao, to support the payments of online sales. The company name 'Ant' refers to the small insect, standing for the company's dedication to serving common consumers and small businesses. Since 2003, Ant Group has developed into a fully fledged Fintech empire operating in various financial sectors, including wealth management (Ant Fortune), mobile payments (Alipay), online banking (MyBank), and credit rating (Sesame Credit). Ant Group is a paradigm of successful Fintech corporations, exhibiting how start-ups could rely on technology and mass consumer markets to quickly scale up and become mainstream players to provide a better consumer experience and challenge the supremacy of established financial institutions. The case study of Ant Group sheds light on how best to regulate Fintech corporations and the new FHCs for global financial regulators and policy-makers.

4.3.2 The history of Ant Group: 2003–2009

The following sections examine Ant Group's growth path over the course of three time periods: 2003–2009, 2010–2019, and 2020–present. Let's start with the history of Ant Group from 2003 to 2009, to see how Fintech corporations solve the pain points of consumers. E-commerce and online purchasing first became popular in the early 2000s, but there was a problem with the lack of trust between online vendors and customers who did not know one another, which was thought to be the greatest barrier to the industry. As a result, Alibaba introduced Alipay in 2003 as a payment tool to help run its online shopping websites. Alipay offers guaranteed transfers, enhancing the security of online transactions.[17] Alipay, which acts as a payment intermediary between e-sellers and their customers, has resolved the long-standing trust problem in the thriving online shopping industry, aiding Alibaba's subsequent explosive development. In China, Alipay helped Taobao.com defeat eBay and even Amazon in the e-commerce market.[18] However, Alipay has remained an integrated payment tool of Taobao.com up to this point.

---

[16] Alipay, accessed 1 June 2023, https://global.alipay.com/platform/site/ihome.

[17] A customer must send funds to Alipay in order to make a purchase on Taobao.com. After getting the payment, Alipay will alert the online vendor to ship the goods. Alipay will release payment to the seller as soon as the customer receives the product and submits confirmation to Taobao.com.

[18] Mark Greeven et al., 'The Case Study: How Taobao Bested eBay in China: Dealing with a Powerful New Rival', *The Financial Times*, 13 March 2012, p. 10.

Alipay was spun off from Taobao.com in December 2004 and was independently run by Zhejiang Alipay Internet Technology Company.[19] Following that, Alipay began to offer payment services for other online retailers outside the Alibaba Group, as an independent Fintech payment system. As the annual transaction volume increased to CNY620 billion ($92.94 billion) in 2005, from CNY440 billion ($65.96 billion) in 2004, China's e-commerce industry witnessed rapid growth during this period.[20] Evidently, there needs to be a reliable and effective online payment system in place for e-commerce platforms to develop as rapidly as this. The same year, VISA and other major financial corporations joined forces with Alipay to form a cooperative network of payment service providers. Alipay started collaborating with a wide range of online companies, including gaming platforms, websites for reserving hotels and booking flights, and other B2C shopping sites.

Over 50 million individuals had registered their Alipay accounts as of early 2007, and over 300,000 businesses accepted Alipay as a form of payment.[21] Zhejiang Alipay Internet Technology Co. Ltd changed its company name to Alipay (China) Internet Technology Co. Ltd in 2008 when it started partnering with hundreds of international retailers from countries like Japan, South Korea, Australia, Singapore, Canada, and the US. Moreover, Alipay announced credit services for online vendors at Taobao.com who can borrow money up to CNY100,000 ($14,990.93), indicating that Alipay tapped into financial services outside of payment. These services were released in conjunction with China Construction Bank. The number of Alipay users reached 100 million in August 2008, with an average of 2 million transactions per day.[22] The same year, Alipay began to provide utility businesses with one-stop payment solutions so that their customers could pay their water, electricity, gas, and telephone bills via its portal. Additionally, it offered payment support for well-known B2C shopping platforms like JD.com and Amazon. Annual transactions through Alipay have surpassed CNY130 billion ($19.49 billion) as a result of the rapid growth.[23] By collaborating with prestigious travel companies like Ctrip, Elong, and Mango in 2009, Alipay grew its market share in

---

[19] The launch of Alipay's website (www.alipay.com) signalled the company's transformation from an online purchasing guarantee tool to a stand-alone payment system. See 'About Alipay', Alipay, accessed 1 June 2023, https://about.alipay.com/.
[20] Minjie Cao, '2005: A Key Year for China's E-commerce Industry', *Oriental Morning Post*, 7 May 2005, http://tech.sina.com.cn/i/2005-05-07/0948600190.shtml.
[21] At this time, the total annual transaction volume via Alipay was CNY47.6 billion ($7.14 billion), or 47.6% of the Chinese online payment industry. See 'Over 300,000 Businesses Accepted Alipay', *Beijing Times*, 1 February 2007, http://tech.sina.com.cn/i/2007-02-01/03591363850.shtml.
[22] 'About Alipay', Alipay, accessed 1 June 2023, https://about.alipay.com/.
[23] 'Taobao to See Transactions Top 100bn Yuan in 2008', *China Daily*, 16 June 2008, http://www.chinadaily.com.cn/bizchina/2008-06/16/content_6764882.htm.

the online travel booking sector. Additionally, it collaborated with YouBang Insurance to enter the internet insurance market. The number of Alipay users surpassed 200 million in 2009, as the figure doubled in just one year.[24] As of December 2009, 460,000 external companies (those not affiliated with the Alibaba Group) accepted Alipay. The highest-ever yearly transaction volume reached CNY287.1 billion ($43.04 billion), or 49.8% of the total market share.[25]

4.3.3 The history of Ant Group: 2010–2019

In the 2010s, as internet shopping continued to grow rapidly, Alipay was on an exponential growth trajectory. With 170 million registered users and revenues of more than CNY20 billion ($3 billion), which primarily came from online advertising and other fee-paying services, Taobao.com dominated 80% of China's e-commerce industry in 2010.[26] As a result, Alipay experienced consistent development as almost all purchases made on Taobao.com were executed via its platform. However, Alipay made the decision at this point to reinvent itself as a full-service provider of financial services. Alipay had over 550 million users as of December 2010, aiming to cover every aspect of daily living for Chinese citizens, including paying utility bills, credit card debts, administrative fines, tuition fees, and online charitable giving. At the same time, Alipay and UnionPay launched Instant Pay, a ground-breaking online payment service that enables credit card users to make payments without first creating an online banking account.[27] The first group of internet finance (Fintech) companies to receive third-party online payment licences was revealed by the PBoC in May 2010.[28] The central bank granted licences to Alipay and 26 other payment firms, which signifies the official support for the Fintech venture.

When Alipay introduced the Barcode Pay service in 2011, it extended its payment options from online to offline, enabling customers to use their smartphones and the Alipay app to make purchases in-person.[29] By scanning the barcode produced by their clients' Alipay apps, retailers can accept

---

[24] 'About Alipay', Alipay, accessed 1 June 2023, https://about.alipay.com/.
[25] Ibid.
[26] Mark Greeven et al., 'The Case Study: How Taobao Bested eBay in China: Dealing with a Powerful New Rival', *The Financial Times*, 13 March 2012, p. 10.
[27] 'Online Payment Entered into Instant Pay Age', *Xinhua*, 28 July 2011, http://news.xinhuanet.com/newmedia/2011-07/28/c_121733865.htm.
[28] Andrew McGinty and Mark Parsons, 'Third Party Payment Licences in China—Are They within the Grasp of Foreign Investors?', Hogan Lovells, 16 June 2014, https://www.hoganlovells.com/en/publications/third-party-payment-licences-in-china-are-they-within-the-grasp-of-foreign-investors.
[29] Steven Millward, 'Alipay Invades China's High Streets with Mobile Barcode Payments', Tech in Asia, 1 July 2011, https://www.techinasia.com/alipay-mobile-payments.

payments immediately. Shop owners had the option of using smartphones to scan the digital barcodes or, for a more professional look, a barcode-reading gun connected to the cash register. By providing a simple and affordable payment choice, Barcode Pay's launch benefits consumers and retailers alike. The barcodes automatically created by the Alipay app are unique and one-off since they are updated frequently to increase security. Each time users activate the service, they must set up a passcode. More recently, Alipay began to enable users to use fingerprint or facial recognition to confirm their identity. Customers can use the money in their Alipay accounts or link their credit or debit cards to the mobile app. Clearly, the introduction of Barcode Pay ushered in a new age of mobile payments.

Alipay broke the global record on 11 November 2011, processing 33.69 million transactions in just 24 hours, with the Tmall shopping platform's overall transaction volume totalling CNY3.36 billion ($500 million).[30] As a result, Alipay surpassed its US rival PayPal to claim the title of the world's biggest online payment system. Alipay acquired a special payment licence for working with investment fund firms in May 2012.[31] Thus, Alipay is accepted by 50 different fund companies, which accounts for 70% of the industry. Yu'E Bao (which means leftover treasure), a mobile wealth management tool offered by Alipay, was launched in June 2013 and quickly became popular. It received more than 30 million registrations within six months of its debut.[32] Many Chinese, especially the younger population, thought that Yu'E Bao was a great alternative to bank deposits. Its subscribers received a 5% annualised return in 2013, and they had the option of withdrawing their money whenever they wanted or using it to make online purchases. Investments made with Yu'E Bao are used to purchase money-market funds (MMFs) run by Tianhong Asset Management Company, a company in which Alibaba Group has equity.

Alipay received a licence from China's banking regulator in September 2014 to run MyBank, an online-only bank with no physical locations, which is a novel banking venture for the company.[33] On 16 October 2014, Ant Financial Services Group was established to replace Alipay (China) Co. Ltd.[34] The biggest global Fintech firm was created as a result, and Alipay is now part of Ant Group's business operations. In the same year, the daily number of

---

[30] In China, there is an internet shopping festival on 11 November, which is often referred to as the Single Day or Double Eleven event.
[31] 'About Alipay', Alipay, accessed 1 June 2023, https://about.alipay.com/.
[32] Simon Rabinovitch, 'Alibaba's Treasure Draws in Depositors', *The Financial Times*, 21 December 2013, p. 14.
[33] Lerong Lu, 'Private Banks in China: Origin, Challenges and Regulatory Implications'. *Banking and Finance Law Review* (2016) 31: 585, 592.
[34] 'About Alipay', Alipay, accessed 1 June 2023, https://about.alipay.com/.

transactions via Alipay exceeded 80 million and Alipay had 190 million active users. In early 2015, Ant Financial introduced Sesame Credit, a big data credit rating system that assigns credit scores to individuals and small companies based on their transactional data on Alibaba's shopping platforms and their payment history with Alipay.[35] Sesame Credit is particularly helpful for small businesses which have limited access to bank loans due to the lack of trading data, as now they can use their Sesame Credit score to apply for loans from various financial institutions.

Ant Group performs well in the capital market thanks to its promising business prospects. In July 2015, it finished its A-round of equity financing, attracting billions of dollars from China's National Social Security Fund, Guokai Finance, four Chinese insurance companies, Primavera Capital, and Shanghai GP Capital.[36] It put Ant Group at a valuation of $45 billion, similar to that of other successful tech companies like Uber and Xiaomi at that time. In April 2016, it closed its B-round of PE financing by raising $4.5 billion, and its valuation increased to $60 billion.[37] It then completed a $3.5-billion debt round to fund the company's international expansion, including the acquisition of MoneyGram, a cross-border payment service company based in Texas, for $1.2 billion.[38] After that, it was planning an IPO in the late 2010s, depending upon regulatory approvals.[39]

4.3.4 The history of Ant Group: 2020–present

In November 2020, the SSE and Chinese financial authorities abruptly halted Ant Group's IPO due to regulatory concerns that the company had not complied with capital adequacy requirements for its app-based lending business.[40] Initially, Ant Group proposed to launch a high-profile IPO, valuing the Fintech giant at over $300 billion, with a plan to raise $37 billion by simultaneously listing its shares on the SSE and Hong Kong Stock

---

[35] Gabriel Wildau, 'Alibaba Eyes Small Business Loans', *The Financial Times*, 29 January 2015, p.17.
[36] 'Ant Financial Completed A-round Finance with Valuation over $45bn', *Sina Finance*, 6 July 2015, http://finance.sina.com.cn/roll/20150706/030722596271.shtml.
[37] Gabriel Wildau, 'Ant Financial Raises $4.5bn in Record Fintech Private Placement', *The Financial Times*, 26 April 2016, https://www.ft.com/content/366490b4-0b7d-11e6-9cd4-2be898308be3.
[38] Arjun Kharpal, 'Exclusive: Ant Financial Close to Closing a Bigger-Than-Expected $3.5 Billion Debt Round for International Expansion', *CNBC*, 17 May 2017, http://www.cnbc.com/2017/05/17/ant-financial-debt-financing-round.html.
[39] Louise Lucas and Don Weinland, 'Alibaba's $60bn Payments Arm Stalls Planned IPO', *The Financial Times*, 16 May 2017, https://www.ft.com/content/25780a7c-3702-11e7-bce4-9023f8c0fd2e.
[40] Hudson Lockett and Primrose Riordan, 'Ant Group IPO Faces at Least 6-Month Delay after Beijing Intervention', *The Financial Times*, 5 November 2020, http://www.ft.com/content/35a95455-338a-4ede-bab3-fd0f098ac268.

Exchange. Increased regulatory requirements imposed by the CBIRC and PBoC, which mandate that internet platforms provide at least 30% self-funding for loans they plan to make, were the main cause of Ant Group's IPO suspension.[41] It only funded 2% of its total loans by itself, whilst the rest of the money (98%) came from bank loans or the sale of asset-backed securities (ABSs). Given the size of the Fintech giant's lending position and the involvement of the securitisation process, it is obvious that the highly leveraged operation of Ant Group's credit business contains huge financial risks, which are likely to destabilise China's financial system, leading to a potential financial crisis. Securitisation, which refers to the packaging and transfer of bank loans such as mortgages to standalone special investment vehicles that underwrite securities that will then be sold to global investors, has been identified as one of the main causes of the global financial crisis 2007–2008.[42]

Chinese regulators have imposed strict prudential regulatory rules on Fintech companies to preserve financial stability and to reduce financial risks so as to prevent a repeat of the financial catastrophe in 2008. According to the latest regulation, Ant Group is required to have at least CNY540 billion in capital on its balance sheet due to its projected CNY1.8 trillion ($271 billion) of outstanding consumer loans.[43] As a result, if it wants to maintain its core lending business and restart its long-delayed IPO, it must redesign its business model to account for the regulatory changes. In terms of prudential regulation and customer protection, the new regulation has forced Fintech firms like Ant Group to be supervised like banks. Thus, it is anticipated that Fintech firms' businesses will run more securely and present with fewer financial risks to the economy. On the other hand, stricter rules could impede further expansion of the Fintech industry. We all know that in order to innovate, sometimes it is necessary to break the rules, and that regulatory red tape is very likely to stifle technological advancement. Therefore, achieving an appropriate compromise between fostering financial innovation, preserving financial stability, and ensuring a reasonable degree of consumer protection is a main challenge for global policy-makers dealing with Fintech and financial innovation.

Most institutional and retail investors who had subscribed for Ant Group's new shares received a complete refund after the IPO was suspended.

---

[41] CBIRC, 'Interim Measures for the Administration of Online Micro-Lending Business (Draft for Solicitation of Comments)', 2 November 2020, Article 15(3).
[42] John Armour et al., *Principles of Financial Regulation* (Oxford: Oxford University Press, 2016), p. 7.
[43] Hudson Lockett and Primrose Riordan, 'Ant Group IPO Faces at Least 6-Month Delay after Beijing Intervention', *The Financial Times*, 5 November 2020, http://www.ft.com/content/35a95455-338a-4ede-bab3-fd0f098ac268.

Nevertheless, some experienced investors who had contributed to the pre-IPO round via Ant Group's offshore company, including BlackRock, GIC, Silver Lake, and Singapore's Temasek, were left with illiquid shares in the Fintech firm valued at $10.3 billion.[44] This demonstrates the underrated risks of making investments in the quickly growing Fintech sector. Financial investors are urged to use the ESG investing principle to evaluate the sustainability of Fintech companies before making any investment choices in order to address this issue.[45] The ESG investing approach focuses more on non-financial metrics as part of its analytical framework to identify material risks and growth opportunities.

In 2021, the Chinese government requested that Ant Group restructure its business model so that it could seek to become an FHC, which would be subject to stricter prudential regulations akin to those governing Chinese commercial banks. This has mirrored the global movement towards stricter financial regulation for internet and Fintech firms that pose risks to financial stability. On 12 April 2021, senior executives from Ant Group were summoned to a meeting with four Chinese regulators: the PBoC, CBIRC, CSRC, and State Administration of Foreign Exchange (SAFE).[46] Regulators have consequently collaborated to create a 'comprehensive and viable rectification plan' for Ant Group in order to address the regulatory incompliance and dangers in its business strategy.[47] In a press conference for Ant Group in April 2021, Pan Gongsheng, who was then the deputy governor of the PBoC, stressed that regulators need to uphold the principle of 'finance as foundation, empowered by technology' to oversee the Fintech sector.[48] Fintech platforms are required to serve the real economy and to prevent excessive financial risks. It is obvious that adopting revolutionary technology cannot be a justification for breaking statutes and regulations. In China, the Wild West of Fintech is expected to come to an end shortly as the industry is predicted to be more closely regulated, which is apparently good for its long-term growth.

---

[44] Mercedes Ruehll, Primrose Riordan, and Tabby Kinder, 'Global Investors in Limbo after Ant IPO Torpedoed by Beijing', *The Financial Times*, 15 January 2021, http://www.ft.com/content/f0950778-450e-4ef2-804d-7e16946ac4c0.

[45] Emiel van Duuren, Auke Plantinga, and Bert Scholtens, 'ESG Integration and the Investment Management Process: Fundamental Investing Reinvented'. *Journal of Business Ethics* (2016) 138: 525, 526.

[46] 'Ant Group Summoned to Meeting with Regulators; What Signal Did It Send?', *Xinhua*, 12 April 2021, http://www.xinhuanet.com/fortune/2021-04/12/c_1127321535.htm.

[47] Jing Yang, 'Jack Ma's Ant Group Bows to Beijing with Company Overhaul', *The Wall Street Journal*, 12 April 2021, https://www.wsj.com/articles/ant-group-to-become-a-financial-holding-company-overseen-by-central-bank-11618223482.

[48] CSRC, 'Press Conference for Deputy Governor of PBOC Mr. Pan Gongsheng Commenting on the Meeting between Financial Regulators and Ant Group', 12 April 2021, http://www.csrc.gov.cn/pub/newsite/zjhxwfb/xwdd/202104/t20210412_395827.html.

From 2003 to 2023, Ant Group has grown into a Fintech titan that has posed a threat to the operation of established banks and financial institutions as it seized the chance presented by the integration of finance and technology. The rapid expansion of Ant Group and other Fintech platforms, without sufficient and effective regulation, has given rise to various regulatory problems. Primary regulatory concerns include the anti-competition practice in the mobile payment sector and monopoly of information that infringes on the privacy and legitimate interests of consumers, as well as regulatory arbitrage when Ant Group seems to conduct traditional lending and investment businesses under the disguise of Fintech to evade existing regulatory standards. Evidently, regulators in China and beyond would like to send a clear message to all Fintech corporations about the intolerance of regulatory arbitrage that is likely to cause mounting financial risks and of any practices that harm consumer interests. Fintech firms need to carry out self-assessment and self-correction to bring their commercial activities in line with the existing regulatory framework to minimise systemic risks and protect financial consumers. Both traditional finance and innovative finance (Fintech) should fall under the same regulatory umbrella to create a level playing field in the financial industry.

4.3.5 Mapping the business model of Ant Group

As Alipay was converted into Ant Financial Services Group, it expanded its business scope from online payment to other financial services ranging from banking to credit rating. Equipped with the internet technology and innovative business model, Ant Group possesses obvious competitive advantages and has swiftly become a major player in the industry. In China alone, Alipay dominates the country's $5.5 trillion mobile payment sector, as it takes up 54% of the total market share.[49] It has been a strong contender to rival payment operators such as UnionPay, VISA, Mastercard, and PayPal. Moreover, the MMF behind Ant Group's Yu'E Bao holds assets worth $165.6 billion, exceeding JPMorgan's US government MMF ($150 billion) which used to be the largest investment fund in the world.[50] Obviously, Ant Group has built up a Fintech ecosystem not only replicating most functions of traditional banks but also providing novel financial services with high quality, lower cost, and

---

[49] Louise Lucas, 'Tencent Grabs Mobile Pay Share from Alibaba', *The Financial Times*, 2 May 2017, p. 14.
[50] Louise Lucas, 'Chinese Money Market Fund Becomes World's Biggest', *The Financial Times*, 26 April 2017, https://www.ft.com/content/28d4e100-2a6d-11e7-bc4b-5528796fe35c.

greater accessibility. This section focuses on four pillars of Ant Group's Fintech businesses: Alipay (mobile payment system), Ant Fortune (online wealth management), MyBank (online-based challenger bank) and Sesame Credit (credit rating service). The analysis pays attention to how Ant Group has disrupted conventional financial services and occupied significant market shares.

4.3.5.1 Pillar 1: Alipay—mobile payment system

Alipay is still at the core of Ant Group. Apart from serving as a major online payment processing tool for e-commerce, Alipay has become a common payment method for Chinese shoppers in store. The rapid shift to digital payment is mostly due to the popularisation of smartphones, as nowadays 95% of internet users in China go online via mobile equipment.[51] Most physical stores including supermarkets, restaurants, and clothes shops, as well as online-to-offline services like taxi-hailing and food-delivering apps, accept mobile payments offered by Alipay and WeChat Pay.[52] Both Alibaba and Tencent (the parent company of WeChat Pay) have signed up with millions of retailers in China and beyond to accelerate the transition towards the cashless society. For example, the US coffee chain Starbucks now accepts WeChat Pay at all of its 2,600 shops across China.[53] Outside China, Alipay's mobile wallet can be used in several countries including the US, UK, Japan, South Korea, and Australia. In the UK, a number of department stores including Harrods and Selfridges already accept Alipay.[54] Using mobile payment has become a trendy lifestyle for many people, in particular the millennials, whether they live in metropolises or small towns. It even becomes common for beggars on the streets to present a QR code to receive mobile payment donations instead of receiving banknotes and coins.[55] Clearly, mobile payment has been a vital element and the gateway to the entire Fintech ecosystem, as other Fintech services are offered within Alipay or WeChat Pay's e-wallet apps. According to one 2017 estimate, the market scale of China's mobile payment sector was around CNY38 trillion ($5.7 trillion), which was 50 times larger than that of

---

[51] 'The Age of the Appacus: Fintech in China', *The Economist*, 25 February 2017, p. 65.
[52] Leslie Hook and Gabriel Wildau, 'China Mobile Payments Soar as US Clings to Plastic', *The Financial Times*, 14 February 2017, p. 12.
[53] Louise Lucas, 'Tencent Grabs Mobile Pay Share from Alibaba', *The Financial Times*, 02 May 2017, p. 14.
[54] Justina Crabtree, 'How Alipay Is Helping London Stores Cash in on China's Golden Week', *CNBC*, 6 October 2016, http://www.cnbc.com/2016/10/06/how-alipay-is-helping-london-stores-cash-in-on-chinas-golden-week.html.
[55] Guo Kai, 'China's Mobile Payment Era: Costs and Benefits', *China Daily*, 11 May 2017, http://www.chinadaily.com.cn/china/2017-05/11/content_29295024.htm.

the US ($112 billion).[56] This is partly owing to the limited non-cash payment options at Chinese retailers, as credit cards are not as popular as they are in the US. China's mobile payment system has been extremely streamlined and convenient, allowing millions of businesses and consumers to complete transactions in a few seconds. Moreover, during the Chinese new year, people have the tradition of giving red envelops with some lucky money inside to each other. In recent years, red envelopes have been digitalised as people tend to send virtual red envelopes, a built-in function of Alipay or WeChat Pay apps, rather than traditional paper-made red pockets.[57] Around the world, mobile payment takes place in a variety of forms including NFC (or contactless), QR codes, and cloud-based pay, depending on different technologies adopted. In Europe, mobile payment services usually embrace NFC technology, which means shoppers swiping their smartphones over a chip reader.[58] In contrast, most mobile payment transactions in China have been conducted through QR codes generated by mobile payment apps. Consumers use their Alipay app to generate a one-off QR code, and then retailers will hold a special reading gun to scan the QR code and complete the transaction. Alternatively, some retailers print out their Alipay's accounts (presented as QR codes) near the counter for shoppers to use their smartphones' cameras to scan and make payment.

4.3.5.2 Pillar 2: Ant Fortune—mobile wealth management platform

Ant Fortune, a wealth management platform accessed via smartphone apps, is another pillar of Ant Group. In August 2015, Ant Fortune was released when the company set out its strategic plan to become a leading online financial services provider.[59] Financial consumers can use the Ant Fortune mobile portal to invest their money in MMFs, investment funds, fixed-term savings, crowdfunding projects, P2P loans, and stock markets (in Mainland China, Hong Kong, and the US). Without charging commission fees, Ant Fortune offers around 900 investment products from over 80 financial institutions.[60]

---

[56] Leslie Hook and Gabriel Wildau, 'China Mobile Payments Soar as US Clings to Plastic', *The Financial Times*, 14 February 2017, p. 12.
[57] Yuan Yang, 'Alibaba and Tencent Open New Front in Red Envelope War', *The Financial Times*, 30 January 2017, p. 16.
[58] Leslie Hook and Gabriel Wildau, 'China Mobile Payments Soar as US Clings to Plastic', *The Financial Times*, 14 February 2017, p. 12.
[59] Yue Wang, 'Alibaba Finance Affiliate Launches Fund Investment Smartphone App', *Forbes*, 18 August 2015, https://www.forbes.com/sites/ywang/2015/08/18/alibaba-finance-affiliate-launches-fund-investment-smartphone-app/#115f657f6301.
[60] Ibid.

It is operated as a financial supermarket providing one-stop investment experience for financial consumers. As Ant Fortune works as a financial broker to match investors' money with products offered by external institutions, it is not involved in investments or undertaking market risks. In this respect, the relationship between Ant Fortune and other financial firms such as banks, securities firms, fund companies, and P2P lending platforms is perceived as cooperative rather than competitive. Evidently, Ant Fortune has lowered the threshold of wealth management services by offering a variety of investment options to ordinary investors who have limited investment experience in the financial markets and possess only a small sum of capital. With the help of Ant Fortune, ordinary savers are able to establish their own investment portfolios by relying on its AI and professional advice.[61] Thus, Ant Fortune has solicited 25 million users since its debut, 81% of whom are under age 36.[62] Among hundreds of investment products available on Ant Fortune, attention shall be given to Yu'E Bao, a wealth management product based on MMFs and operated by Ant Group itself. Depositors who move their savings from bank accounts to their Yu'E Bao wallet can earn returns up to 15 times the banks' interest rates.[63] Yu'E Bao was launched in 2013 and in less than one year the investment scheme had attracted CNY400 billion ($59.96 billion) from Chinese savers, making it a principal rival to dominant state-owned banks.[64] Yu'E Bao is working like an add-on of the Alipay app, as users can deposit or withdraw funds effortlessly by a simple touch. MMFs have high liquidity similar to that of cash, whilst subscribers can earn handsome returns paid on a daily base.[65] As a result, Yu'E Bao became an instant success after its launch. Tens of millions of customers have chosen to use Alipay e-wallet and Yu'E Bao as their de facto banking accounts. The fast expansion of Yu'E Bao and other mobile wealth management platforms has contributed to the record-breaking value of MMFs in China—CNY4.4 trillion ($659 billion).[66] Obviously, MMFs have posed an enormous challenge to big banks and the traditional wealth management industry, which lost a large number of clients to these rising Fintech firms.

---

[61] Meng Jing, 'Ant Financial Gears Up for More Wealth Management', *China Daily*, 9 September 2016, http://europe.chinadaily.com.cn/business/2016-09/09/content_26748999.htm.
[62] Ibid.
[63] 'Foe or Frenemy? Internet Finance in China', *The Economist*, 1 March 2014, p. 75.
[64] Ibid.
[65] The return of Yu'E Bao is based on the interbank lending rate, which fluctuates freely over time.
[66] Chris Flood, 'China Tightens Money Market Regulation', *The Financial Times*, 1 February 2016, p. 10.

4.3.5.3 Pillar 3: MyBank—online-based challenger bank

China's banking sector has long been dominated by state-owned lenders which are reluctant to lend money to SMEs.[67] In order to break up the state monopoly and increase competition in the banking sector, the Chinese regulator has been encouraging qualified private investors to set up new banks. As a result, Alibaba partnering with other investors established a privately funded bank under the regulator's pilot reform plan. The banking arm of Ant Group is called MyBank which is an innovative online-only bank. In June 2015, MyBank obtained its licence from the CBRC, with a registered capital of CNY4 billion ($645 million).[68] Ant Group holds a 30% stake in MyBank, while Fosun International Ltd and Wanxiang Group own 25% and 18% of the new bank, respectively.[69] MyBank's primary customer base is SMEs which have been underserved by mainstream lenders. It is among the first group of new lenders that do not have brick-and-mortar physical branches, allowing them to lower the operation cost and provide more convenient services through online portals and mobile apps. By visiting MyBank's website or using its app, consumers can manage their current accounts (including investing money into MMFs), apply for credit loans, and transfer money between different banks without charge. Evidently, Fintech lends MyBank significant competitive advantages over traditional lenders. Due to the problem of information asymmetry, large banks often refuse to lend to SMEs because borrowers cannot provide valid information to demonstrate their credibility and thus fail to pass relevant credit checks. However, through tracking the trading history of small businesses that use Alibaba's e-commerce network, MyBank is able to evaluate the credit situations of small firms based on the accumulated big data. Big data, coupled with cloud computing, enables MyBank to make loan decisions in minutes. The business model of MyBank is described as '3-1-0', namely, making a loan application in three minutes, approving the application in one second, and zero human intervention.[70] The intelligent loan application process will consider 100,000 indicators by analysing big data, as well as go through over 100 predicting models and 3,000 loan strategies designed

---

[67] Lerong Lu, 'Private Banks in China: Origin, Challenges and Regulatory Implications'. *Banking and Finance Law Review* (2016) 31: 585, 586.
[68] 'Alibaba-Affiliated Online Bank Get Green Light from China Regulator', *Reuters*, 27 May 2015, http://www.reuters.com/article/us-alibaba-bank-idUSKBN0OC0- SI20150527.
[69] Ibid.
[70] 'MyBank Jin XiaoLong: SME Finance Is no Longer Difficult', *China Finance*, 9 July 2017, http://finance.china.com.cn/news/special/wtfh/20170709/4281638.shtml.

by Ant Group's financial engineers.[71] It is said to be far more accurate and efficient than the traditional credit checking process. Given its technological and data advantages, MyBank has been growing rapidly since its establishment. In 2016, it served over 800,000 SMEs with a combined loan volume of CNY45 billion ($6.75 billion), generating a net profit of CNY315.5 million ($47.30 million).[72]

4.3.5.4 Pillar 4: Sesame Credit—big data credit rating service

The last pillar of Ant Group is Sesame Credit. Sesame Credit offers credit rating services to millions of personal consumers, by utilising Alibaba's big data derived from Taobao and Tmall shopping platforms. China has not built up an official credit system for its citizens, so Ant Group decided to fill this gap by taking advantage of its enormous data reserve. Sesame Credit plays an important role in Ant Group's Fintech ecosystem, as it supplements the operation of other financial services. It can be accessed via Alipay's app or other cooperative merchants' websites. With the authorisation of users, Sesame Credit produces a credit score based on personal shopping data, payment history on Alipay, and other behavioural data from Alibaba's e-commerce platforms. Similar to FICO which aligns a credit core (300–850) to consumers by mathematical algorithms, Sesame Credit allocates a score ranging from 350 to 950 to Alipay users. The credit score can be employed by users to borrow loans from financial institutions and online P2P lending platforms up to CNY300,000 ($44,972.79).[73] Apart from that, consumers who have higher scores on Sesame Credit enjoy certain privileges like expedited airport security checks and free loaner umbrellas.[74] If one person's credit score is over 650 points, they do not need to pay a deposit when renting a car. There are also other benefits for high-score users, such as fast hotel booking without submitting credit card information to secure a room. Moreover, Chinese tourists can use Sesame Credit scores as proof of their financial capability, other than employment certificates and bank statements, when applying for foreign visas from countries like Singapore and Luxembourg.[75] Currently, Sesame Credit has been widely accepted by thousands of websites to verify

---

[71] Ibid.
[72] 'MyBank Earned 315bn Net Profit Last Year, Lower than Tencent's WeBank', *NetEase*, 8 July 2017, http://tech.163.com/17/0708/13/COR0623V00097U7R.html.
[73] 'Borrow a Loan up to CNY300,000 Using Sesame Credit', *Sohu*, 1 September 2016, http://www.sohu.com/a/113129483_444830.
[74] Cheang Ming, 'FICO with Chinese Characteristics: Nice Rewards, But Punishing Penalties', *CNBC*, 16 March 2017, http://www.cnbc.com/2017/03/16/china-social-credit-system-ant-financials-sesame-credit-and-others-give-scores-that-go-beyond-fico.html.
[75] 'Alibaba Unit to Start Credit-Based Visa Application Services for Luxembourg', *China Daily*, 16 July 2015, http://usa.chinadaily.com.cn/epaper/2015-07/16/content_21301110.htm.

users' identities and financial conditions, for example Airbnb. Conversely, some wrongdoings (e.g., late bill payment or traffic violation) will lead to the downgrade of credit scores, causing negative effects for its bearers.[76]

4.3.6 Fintech vs traditional bank: friend, enemy, or frenemy?

The financial industry has seen fierce rivalry between traditional banks and Fintech companies. Apparently, in some business areas, such as payment and saving, there exists direct competition between Ant Group and incumbent institutions. The widely popular Alipay has surpassed state-backed Union-Pay in terms of the number of processing offline payments.[77] It means that Alipay's virtual payment system is de facto the largest payment network in China. Previously, UnionPay had been leading the market of debit and credit card payments for two decades, as it was extremely difficult for competitors to break into China's payment sector. Even global payment providers like VISA and Mastercard failed to gain substantial market shares. Alipay, however, takes advantage of the popularity of smartphones to override credit cards, winning the favour of millions of consumers. In 2016, it earned CNY139 billion ($20.84 billion) from its payment service department.[78] Clearly, the company has made billions of payment fees that would otherwise be earned by UnionPay. Although the rise of Alipay could be catastrophic for the traditional payment industry run by dominant banks, it is beneficial for numerous businesses and consumers, who enjoy faster, safer, and more affordable payment services.

Moreover, Ant Group's wealth management products based on MMFs form a big threat to banks' deposit-taking businesses. As Yu'E Bao offers an eye-catching interest return for its subscribers, millions of savers have selected Alipay over other banks as the place to hold their current accounts. It has resulted in direct deposit losses in billions, if not trillions, for major state-owned banks, including the Big Four. As of June 2017, the total market scale of MMFs in China reached CNY5.11 trillion ($770 billion), rising 18.09% from CNY4.32 trillion ($647.61 billion) in the previous year.[79] Obviously, a

---

[76] Cheang Ming, 'FICO with Chinese Characteristics: Nice Rewards, But Punishing Penalties', *CNBC*, 16 March 2017, http://www.cnbc.com/2017/03/16/china-social-credit-system-ant-financialssesame-credit-and-others-give-scores-that-go-beyond-fico.html.
[77] Gabriel Wildau, 'Alipay Bypasses China UnionPay on Fees', *The Financial Times*, 1 August 2016, p. 14.
[78] Ibid.
[79] 'Outstanding Balance of Yu'E Bao Surpassed Merchant Bank's Personal Deposits', *Xinhua*, 5 July 2017, http://news.xinhuanet.com/finance/2017-07/05/c_1121264650.htm.

large proportion of the growth came from banks' deposits. Under strict state control, state-owned banks are only allowed to pay 0.30% annual interest for demand deposits and 1.35–2.75% for term deposits. In sharp contrast, the annualised interest rate of Yu'E Bao has varied between 2.3 and 6.7% over its history.[80] Yu'E Bao holds 260 million accounts, making it the no.1 e-wallet in the world. As a substitute for banks' current accounts, Yu'E Bao allows users to deposit, withdraw, and transfer money at any time without charge. The expansion of Yu'E Bao has eroded the profits of Chinese banks which have long been exploiting the interest rate margin between the official deposit rate and lending rate, set by the central bank to protect the interest of state lenders. In other words, Yu'E Bao has diverted lots of deposits from mainstream banks to its platform, which has been the main source of profits. In 2017, the market scale of Yu'E Bao was around CNY1.43 trillion ($214.37 billion), exceeding the total deposit amount of China Merchant Bank (CNY1.3 trillion, $194.88 billion), the fifth-largest lender in the country.[81]

Apparently, Ant Group has become a huge threat to existing banks in terms of payment and deposit businesses. The heated competition from Fintech firms has resulted in the decreasing profitability of Chinese banks in recent years.[82] Therefore, the relationship between Ant Group and existing banks, to a large extent, can be perceived as competitive. However, despite the rivalry status, Ant Group has also contributed to the development of the banking industry in some respects. For example, the online-based MyBank targets loan services for small and micro businesses, an area of business that has been ignored by state lenders for decades. Thus, MyBank seems to play a supplementary role in the banking arena by serving marginalised clients, and MyBank's business competes directly with the prosperous online lending sector which also considers SMEs as their main clients. In 2017, the P2P lending sector in China had an outstanding loan amount worth CNY816 billion ($122.33 billion).[83] It is clear that MyBank helps the banking industry expand its business boundary to contend with other Fintech firms. What is more, the development of Sesame Credit has led to the gradual establishment of China's personal credit system, which plays an important role in strengthening the country's financial infrastructure. At present, rating services provided by Sesame Credit are essential for banks lacking effective

---

[80] 'Yu'E Bao', TianHong Fund Management Company, accessed 1 June 2023, http://www.thfund.com.cn/fundinfo/000198.

[81] 'Yu'E Bao Reached 1.43 Trillion Yuan, Near to the Deposit Amount of Big Four', *Sina*, 1 July 2017, http://finance.sina.com.cn/roll/2017-07-01/doc-ifyhrttz1913643.shtml.

[82] 'Fitch: Chinese Banks' Profitability Is Likely to Decline Further', *Reuters*, 7 April 2017, http://www.reuters.com/article/fitch-chinese-banks-profitability-is-lik-idUSFit995515.

[83] Gabriel Wildau, 'China Curbs "Wild West" Loan Sector', *The Financial Times*, 5 April 2017, p. 6.

methods to gauge the credit conditions of numerous individuals and small businesses. Ant Group's big data, therefore, empower Chinese banks to make loans in a more efficient manner. In this regard, the businesses of Ant Group and existing banks seem to complement each other.

4.3.7 Regulatory concerns over FHCs

Financial regulation in the Fintech age should strike a good balance between encouraging industry innovation, protecting financial consumers, and preventing systemic risks. As an increasing amount of deposit has been transferred from existing banks to various Fintech platforms, including Ant Group, regulatory authorities have to reform and upgrade the monitoring framework to accommodate the latest developments of the financial industry. While pioneering Fintech services have brought greater convenience and better returns for consumers, their associated risks should not be underestimated. Hence, this section analyses three key legal and regulatory issues relating to Ant Group's Fintech businesses.

The first implication is that regulators must strike an equilibrium between encouraging innovation in Fintech and managing financial risks. Fintech innovation has challenged conventional business models, services, and products in the financial industry. It is difficult for industry disrupters to prosper and innovate under the existing regulatory rules which were designed for incumbent players.[84] The financial industry in countries like China has been strictly monitored by sector-based regulators. Nonetheless, the latest Fintech revolution has blurred the traditional boundary between different financial services. As shown in the case study of Ant Group, the Fintech giant participates in various financial activities covering deposit-taking, investment, payments, and credit rating. The new integrated business model, therefore, has challenged the efficiency and effectiveness of China's current regulatory architecture that splits clearly as regards to banking, securities, and insurance. Thus, the institutional structure of financial regulation has to be reformed to adapt to the Fintech era. The twin-peak model adopted by the UK and Australia, which concentrates on conduct regulation and prudential regulation simultaneously, might be an example for China's upcoming financial reform. At present, existing laws and regulatory rules, to some extent, lag behind the pace of technology advance and industry growth. The financial industry in China was considered as relatively conservative, with

---

[84] Lerong Lu, 'Financial Technology and Challenger Banks in the UK: Gap Fillers or Real Challengers?'. *Journal of International Banking Law and Regulation* (2017) 32: 273, 282.

limited financial activities and players, most of which have state backgrounds. Nonetheless, the upsurge in Fintech firms ranging from P2P lending and crowdfunding to mobile payment has been transforming the financial industry greatly. Chinese regulators, which regard financial stability as their top working priority, are wary of the Fintech explosion. Especially, some scandals in the Fintech sector in the 2010s have worried the regulators. In 2016, Ezubao, one of the largest online investment platforms, turned out to be a Ponzi scheme as it defrauded CNY50 billion ($7.5 billion) from 1 million investors across China.[85] Moreover, it is predicted that 90% of 4,856 online P2P lending portals in China have been struggling to survive due to the liquidity problem.[86] Therefore, how to encourage Fintech innovation and entrepreneurship while containing extra financial risks remains a complicated task for financial authorities. Regulators around the world have devised regulatory instruments to fit Fintech innovation into the existing regulatory framework. The most notable approach so far has been the so-called regulatory sandbox, which allows businesses to test novel products, services, business models, and delivery mechanisms under a temporary lighter regulatory environment.[87] A regulatory sandbox was firstly adopted by the UK's FCA and, as a result, it has been viewed as the most Fintech-friendly jurisdiction in the world.[88] The FCA has three operation objectives: protect consumers, enhance market integrity, and promote competition.[89] It is clear that the FCA puts the competitive objective at the centre of its regulatory framework, which stimulates industry disrupters to promote innovation and competition. Accordingly, a sandbox can help Fintech firms trial their products in a safer and more flexible environment without the overhaul of current regulatory systems. In today's economic climate, it seems a win-win situation for all parties, including Fintech businesses, financial regulators, and consumers. Apart from the UK, a number of jurisdictions are adopting a regulatory sandbox regime as a temporary method to regulate their Fintech industry, including Hong Kong, Singapore, and Australia. Moreover, RegTech (the application of new technologies in financial regulation) can be used by both regulatory authorities and regulated firms to manage risks and

---

[85] Fangjing Ma et al., 'Chinese Investors Seek Protection of Rights Over Ponzi Claims', *The Financial Times*, 3 February 2016, p. 6.
[86] Daniel Ren, 'China Regulators Warn that 90 Pc of Peer-to-Peer Lenders Could Fail in 2017', *South China Morning Post*, 19 February 2017, http://www.scmp.com/business/china-business/article/2072177/china-regulators-warns-90-pc-peer-peer-lenders-could-fail.
[87] 'Regulatory Sandbox', FCA, 27 March 2022, https://www.fca.org.uk/firms/innovation/regulatory-sandbox.
[88] Caroline Binham, 'UK Regulators Are the Most Fintech Friendly', *The Financial Times*, 12 September 2016, https://www.ft.com/content/ff5b0be4-7381-11e6-bf48-b372cdb1043a.
[89] Financial Services and Markets Act 2000 (UK), section 1B.

reduce costs relating to regulation and compliance.[90] Financial innovation should be promoted given that additional financial risks can be identified and addressed.

The second implication is that regulators need to enhance the protection of Fintech consumers, especially in the areas of data and fund safety. Fintech consumers are exposed to higher risks as a result of financial invention. The credit rating service offered by Sesame Credit has been kept under close scrutiny as it is said to threaten individuals' data safety and its services contain obvious conflicts of interest.[91] The Chinese central bank gave eight tech firms, including Alibaba and Tencent, temporary permission to develop their credit scoring systems, but has delayed granting full licences afterwards, because of potential conflicts of interest in the business model of Fintech companies. Most third-party credit scoring firms in the world like FICO are independent bodies which do not take part in core financial activities such as banking, investment, and payment. However, Ant Group not only operates Sesame Credit but also engages in a full range of financial businesses, which, therefore, questions its independence and objectivity in allocating credit scores. More importantly, the use of big data derived from users' shopping history on Alibaba's e-commerce platforms has raised controversies. Chinese regulation stipulates that, to collect personal information, it is required to seek the consent of the people relating to such information; otherwise, the information should not be collected, except where such information may have to be disclosed under laws and administrative regulations.[92] In practice, online shoppers accumulate a large amount of information when they view webpages, select goods, and make payments. Under most circumstances, shoppers are not aware of their footages being recorded by the platforms. Obviously, they accept some general terms and conditions before using the online shopping websites, but it lacks detailed rules in terms of what information users would like to be kept by Alibaba and other shopping sites. Also, consumers do not have control over how the information is being processed and disseminated. It requires that anyone using personal information has to reach an agreement with the people relating to such information about the purpose of use; the information shall not be used for other purposes outside the agreement; and the information shall not be disclosed to third parties

---

[90] Deloitte, 'RegTech Is the New Fintech', 2016, accessed 1 June 2023, https://www2.deloitte.com/content/dam/Deloitte/tw/Documents/financial-services/tw-fsi-regtech-new-fintech.pdf.
[91] 'No More Loan Rangers? Beijing's Waning Support for Private Credit Scores', *Reuters*, 4 July 2017, https://uk.reuters.com/article/ant-financial-credit-idUKL3N1JO05W.
[92] State Council of China, 'Administrative Regulation of Credit Investigation Industry', 2013, Order No. 631, Article 13(1).

without the permission of the people.[93] Despite the strict privacy law, the implementation process could have certain flaws, as on the internet the flow of information is extremely hard to trace and control. There are also hackers who steal personal information and sell it to potential buyers to make profits. In response to the urgent privacy issue, Sesame Credit has appointed a Chief Privacy Officer whose main duty is to build an inclusive privacy control mechanism throughout the process of credit rating.[94]

In addition to the privacy issue, how Fintech firms use and keep client money remains an important matter. As we know, depositors of traditional banks are protected under the official deposit insurance scheme. In China's case, its deposit insurance covers up to CNY500,000 (US$80,550) per saver per bank.[95] It means that if a saver's bank goes into financial difficulty, their money up to a certain limit will be automatically compensated by the state without any conditions. However, as savers move their funds from bank accounts to Fintech platforms like Ant Group's Yu'E Bao, their money will no longer be under the official protection. As a result, ordinary savers are exposed to higher market risks which they might not realise. In the eyes of most savers, Yu'E Bao is regarded as a safe alternative to bank saving and they never think about the possibility of platform failure and money loss. Therefore, financial regulators and Fintech companies are recommended to conduct investor education to help raise people's risk awareness. Moreover, Fintech platforms, with assistance from the central bank and financial regulators, can establish reserve funds in order to reimburse clients' losses in emergency situations.

The third implication is that Fintech regulators have to keep a close eye on the prevention of systemic risk and the maintenance of financial stability. The rapid growth of Fintech makes some Fintech giants and FHCs like Ant Group systemically important. As introduced, the amount of money managed by Ant Fortune is at the same level as that held by China's Big Four lenders. It suggests that the safety and soundness of Ant Group will have a significant impact on the overall financial stability. Although Ant Group has a strong technology background (the 'tech' side of Fintech) as it was initiated and supported by Alibaba which is a BigTech, it lacks sufficient experience and expertise in terms of operating financial businesses (the 'fin' side of Fintech). Whether it can manage to run such a large amount of money in a safe

---

[93] Ibid., Article 20.
[94] 'Sesame Credit Hired Chief Privacy Officer', *Sina*, 18 July 2017, http://tech.sina.com.cn/i/2017-07-18/doc-ifyiakwa4502600.shtml.
[95] Lerong Lu, 'Private Banks in China: Origin, Challenges and Regulatory Implications'. *Banking and Finance Law Review* (2016) 31: 585, 598.

manner and control relevant risks remains uncertain. Ant Group has realised the seriousness of this problem and therefore imported many financial and legal professionals from established institutions including Goldman Sachs and other large commercial banks and insurance companies.[96] Furthermore, the increasing deposit base of Yu'E Bao might result in potential bank runs. When savers move money from banks to Ant Fortune in a short time, banks could face sudden deposit loss and liquidity drain. As the insolvency of banks can trigger panic effects and destabilise the entire banking sector, financial regulators should prevent its occurrence by strengthening macro-prudential regulation and establish a comprehensive and effective financial safety net. It is apparent that the enormous scale of funds managed by Yu'E Bao has attracted heavy regulatory attention relating to its liquidity risk. Accordingly, the CBRC has been closely watching the operation of Yu'E Bao and tightened the regulatory rules regarding how much money per saver can hold under their Yu'E Bao accounts. The maximum personal quota was reduced from CNY1 million ($149,909.30) to CNY250,000 ($37,477.32).[97] Moreover, there is a rule restricting how many times users can transfer money between Yu'E Bao and their bank accounts within 24 hours (currently three times a day).

4.4 Fintech corporate governance: DCSS and ESG

DCSS refers to a corporate organisational structure designed with at least two publicly traded share classes which bear disproportionate economic interests and voting rights.[98] It is common for tech entrepreneurs across the globe to adopt DCSS. For instance, Meta, the US social networking company, has issued two classes of shares. Each of Meta's class A shares allows their holders to have one vote and, in contrast, the holders of Meta's class B shares are able to cast ten votes per share. As the ratio of voting power between class A and class B shares is 1:10, Mark Zuckerberg who is Meta's co-founder and CEO possesses less than 13% of the company's outstanding shares but

---

[96] For example, Douglas L. Feagin, manager of Ant Group's international business, was a senior partner at Goldman Sachs; Yu Shengfa, president of MyBank, was previously the president of Hangzhou Bank; Ying Ming, president of Ant Group's insurance sector, was the vice president of China Life Insurance; Chen Leiming, chief legal officer, was a partner at the US law firm Simpson Thacher & Bartlett LLP. See 'Senior Managers of China's Fintech Giants', *Sohu*, 12 April 2017, http://www.sohu.com/a/133541889_465942.
[97] 'Yu'E Bao Reached 1.43 Trillion Yuan, Near to the Deposit Amount of Big Four', *Sina*, 1 July 2017, http://finance.sina.com.cn/roll/2017-07-01/doc-ifyhrttz1913643.shtml.
[98] Lerong Lu and Shunqi Yang, 'Do Investors Vote with their Feet? Commenting on Deliveroo's IPO on London Stock Exchange and the Dual-Class Share Structure'. *Company Lawyer* (2021) 42: 332–333.

controls 58% of total votes.⁹⁹ Apart from US tech giants, an increasing number of Chinese tech companies like JD.com have opted for DCSS. Despite having only 16% of JD's shares, Richard Liu who serves as the CEO of the e-commerce and Fintech platform JD.com could exercise 83.5% of the company's combined voting power.¹⁰⁰ DCSS is undoubtedly a preferred corporate legal structure for tech entrepreneurs all over the globe, which helps them retain the control of businesses after introducing external investors.

The public share offering of Fintech companies with DCSS is now fully or partially accepted by global financial regulators and leading stock exchanges, such as the NYSE, LSE, and SSE. In general, investors in the US and Asia have actively embraced tech companies with dual-class shares, seemingly more interested in the potential financial gains than the actual voting rights which are often unused by retail investors. In April 2019, the video-conferencing software company Zoom floated its shares with DCSS on Nasdaq, with the share price increasing 72% in the first trading day.¹⁰¹ However, the debut of Deliveroo, which is an online food delivery company and a leading UK-based tech firm, on the LSE has shown another story. On 31 March 2021, when Deliveroo began trading shares on the LSE, its share price closed at 287p which was 26% down from the offering price.¹⁰² It has been one of the worst-performing major IPOs in London, particularly given that the current tech boom has significantly increased the valuation of tech companies and piqued investor interest. It seems that European investors are more sceptical of this novel voting rights arrangement. Thus, companies with DCSS have received mixed reaction from global investors.

In the 1890s, DCSS originated from the US when International Silver Company first offered a class of shares with no voting rights. In the 1920s, DCSS gained popularity but also faced some opposition from investors. In reaction to investor outcry in the US, DCSS was outlawed by the NYSE from 1926 to 1985. Later in the 1980s, DCSS was eventually deregulated as a result of its anti-takeover stance as well as the growing rivalry among the three US stock exchanges. Due to the increasing number of technology company IPOs in recent years, such as those by Fintech, biotech, and electric car

---

[99] Benjamin Robertson and Andrea Tan, 'Why Dual-Class Shares Catch on, Over Investor Worries', *Bloomberg*, 5 March 2021, https://www.bloomberg.com/news/articles/2021-03-04/why-dual-class-shares-catch-on-over-investor-worries-quicktake-klwbtryg.

[100] JD.com, Inc., 'Prospectus', US Securities and Exchange Commission, 2 December 2014, https://www.sec.gov/Archives/edgar/data/1549802/000104746914009683/a2222411z424b4.htm.

[101] Jordan Novet, 'Zoom Rocketed 72% on First Day of Trading', *CNBC*, 18 April 2019, https://www.cnbc.com/2019/04/18/zoom-ipo-stock-begins-trading-on-nasdaq.html.

[102] Tim Bradshaw and Attracta Mooney, 'Disaster Strikes as Deliveroo Becomes "Worst IPO in London's History"', *The Financial Times*, 1 April 2021, https://www.ft.com/content/bdf6ac6b-46b5-4f7a-90db-291d7fd2898d.

manufacturers, DCSS is currently gaining popularity on a worldwide scale. So far, DCSS has been endorsed by major stock markets in Asia, including Hong Kong, Singapore, and SSE's Star Market.[103] In order to solicit profitable IPO businesses, major financial centres have loosened the listing requirements in an effort to draw more tech companies with DCSS to float their shares. Furthermore, DCSS has been reviewed by some European authorities. In November 2020, the UK launched an official listing review, discussing the feasibility of permitting DCSS in the premium listing segment of the LSE.[104] In February 2021, the Kalifa Review of UK Fintech endorsed DCSS as a mechanism to improve the UK listing environment by fostering more competitive Fintech businesses.[105]

Policy-makers and scholars have engaged in extensive discussion about the legal structure's advantages, limitations, and regulatory challenges.[106] Due to some obvious advantages, technological companies have used DCSS widely. Firstly, it is acknowledged that DCSS is valuable for tech company founders whose equity interests and voting rights have been significantly diminished during their companies' growing stage, due to the necessity of obtaining significant funding from VC and PE funds. DCSS assists company founders in maintaining the control of the business when they seek external equity financing, especially for innovative Fintech companies. As a result, entrepreneurs can distribute equity shares while keeping their voting rights, creating a win-win situation for both company founders and investors. In most cases, VC investors care more about achieving high financial returns than having a say in the business. Secondly, DCSS could be an efficient defensive mechanism in hostile takeovers, as the corporate legal structure contributes to a stable management team for the company's long-term growth.[107] Therefore, senior managers and corporate executives can focus on long-term strategic planning for the company without being influenced by the market when most voting powers are concentrated in their hands. Finally, as for international stock exchanges and securities regulators,

---

[103] Lerong Lu, 'The Rising Star in the East: Unveiling China's Star Market, the Registration-Based IPO Regime and Capital Markets Law Reform'. *International Company and Commercial Law Review* (2020) 31: 394–412.

[104] 'UK Listings Review', HM Treasury, 19 November 2020, https://www.gov.uk/government/publications/uk-listings-review.

[105] 'The Kalifa Review of UK Fintech', HM Treasury, 26 February 2021, https://www.gov.uk/government/publications/the-kalifa-review-of-uk-fintech.

[106] Bobby V. Reddy, 'Finding the British Google: Relaxing the Prohibition of Dual-Class Stock from the Premium-Tier of the London Stock Exchange'. *Cambridge Law Journal* (2020) 79: 315, 319.

[107] In M&A, a hostile takeover is the acquisition of a target business by another company, which is often referred to as the acquirer, by approaching the target company's stockholders directly, through either a tender offer or a proxy vote. See Anil Shivdasani, 'Board Composition, Ownership Structure, and Hostile Takeovers'. *Journal of Accounting and Economics* (1993) 16: 167–198.

their acceptance of DCSS is likely to help the bourses attract more IPOs from novel companies, such as Fintech and BigTech, using that structure. This will give stock exchanges a clear competitive edge in international financial markets, boosting their business revenues and bringing in more liquidity and dynamism as global inventors are attracted by the listing of high-profile tech companies.

However, like every coin has two sides, DCSS structure also receives fierce criticism on several fronts. For instance, it has been attacked for breaching the fairness and equality principle as it goes against the classic doctrine of 'one share, one vote' in company law and corporate governance standard.[108] Fintech firms' corporate governance might suffer as a result. Concerns about corporate accountability are raised by DCSS, which heavily depends on shareholders' capacity to have a direct impact on the board. As a general rule, shareholders are given proportional voting rights based on their cash flow investment in the corporation. However, when DCSS is used to separates control from ownership, managers and executives may put their own interests ahead of the needs of the company. Some shareholders will be in a disadvantageous position since they have little or no say in corporate affairs. In addition, DCSS has a detrimental impact on shareholder participation because retail shareholders may feel that their participation is pointless in the absence of voting rights. Finally, DCSS is likely to incur extra agency costs in managing Fintech companies, as a result of the separation between control and ownership.[109]

Further, companies with DCSS might encounter resistance at a time when the investment concept of ESG has been integrated into the decision-making process of large financial institutions and investment houses.[110] In recent years, institutional investors have been using non-financial criteria to analyse business risks and growth opportunities, with a tendency to place more emphasis on the social values of businesses. ESG standards, also known as the sustainable or socially responsible investing approach, are being adopted by an increasing number of mutual funds, hedge funds, and robo-advisors to create new investment products. Therefore, DCSS corporate legal structure

---

[108] One share, one vote optimises the weight given to shareholders' interests in comparison to those of the controlling party, which promotes the selection of a capable management team. However, in a company control contest, the benefit to security holders is not always maximised by one share, one vote. See Sanford J. Grossman and Oliver D. Hart, 'One Share–One Vote and the Market for Corporate Control'. *Journal of Financial Economics* (1988) 20: 175–202.

[109] Kirby Smith, 'How Dual-Class Share Structures Create Agency Costs', Columbia Law School's Blog on Corporations and the Capital Markets, 5 January 2018, https://clsbluesky.law.columbia.edu/2018/01/05/how-dual-class-share-structures-create-agency-costs/.

[110] 'ESG Investing and Analysis', CFA Institute, accessed 1 June 2023, https://www.cfainstitute.org/en/research/esg-investing.

might not be entirely ESG-compatible. For example, the governance standard in ESG evaluates corporate management, executive compensation, internal controls, auditing, and shareholder rights. It is clear that the use of DCSS is detrimental to ESG investment in that many shareholders have been denied the opportunity to participate in crucial corporate decision-making as a result of their restricted voting rights. Thus it is anticipated that tech companies using DCSS will face protests and criticism over how they handle small investors and how they plan to use DCSS in the coming years. Governments and financial regulators must carefully balance the objectives of fostering tech innovation and entrepreneurship on the one hand, and attaining a socially responsible corporate culture on the other, in order to create a more competitive and attractive capital market for international investors.

4.5 Fintech corporate finance: IPO, SPAC, and capital markets regulation

Corporate financing channels can be generally divided into equity financing and debt financing.[111] Equity financing is the process by which businesses acquire funding by issuing shares to either current shareholders or any new investor in exchange for capital. The popular equity financing methods for Fintech corporations include raising money from VC and PE funds, issuing new shares to public investors on stock exchanges through IPO, or merging with listed entities like SPAC. In contrast, debt financing refers to the process of issuing debt instruments or borrowing money from banks or other financial institutions. Bank loans, online P2P lending, bond issuance, company credit cards, and invoice factoring are a few examples of how Fintech companies could finance their business needs by debt financing approaches. This section mainly considers equity investments in Fintech corporations, which amounted to over $1 trillion across 35,000 deals from 2010 to 2020.[112] Fintech investment, by making up 5% of the value of global equity deals, clearly outgrew non-Fintech deals.[113]

A number of countries have been reforming their listing rules and IPO criteria to help tech corporations raise funds. Companies choose to go public to raise new capital and increase their prestige, which also provides a way

---

[111] Eilis Ferran and Look Chan Ho, *Principles of Corporate Finance Law*, 2nd ed. (Oxford: Oxford University Press, 2014), p. 57.
[112] Giulio Cornelli et al., 'Funding for Fintechs: Patterns and Drivers', BIS Quarterly Review, September 2021, https://www.bis.org/publ/qtrpdf/r_qt2109c.pdf.
[113] Ibid.

of exiting businesses for some corporate controllers.[114] IPO is of particular importance for companies at a growing stage which need extra funding from international capital markets. For a long time, stock exchanges and financial authorities around the world have enacted stringent listing requirements regarding corporations' profitability and share ownership, preventing many internet and technological companies from the public offering of shares. However, circumstances have undergone a significant change recently, as securities laws and regulations are being reformed globally. For instance, China established the 'science and technology innovation board (star market)' within the SSE in 2019 to assist the fundraising of tech enterprises and enhance the global competitiveness of Chinese capital markets.[115] By having differentiated listing rules and strengthened information disclosure rules, the star market is specially designed for tech corporations based on their actual financing needs and special features, such as lack of profitability in the short term[116] and the use of complex legal structures like variable interest entity (VIE) and DCSS. In 2020, the UK authorities conducted a thorough review of their listing rules, aiming to improve the environment for companies, especially those in the tech sector and life sciences, to go for a public listing in London.[117] They plan to increase the efficiency of the entire listing process, redesign the prospectus regime, and liberalise other aspects of securities regulation regarding DCSS and SPAC. In addition, the UK and China jointly launched the Shanghai–London Stock Connect (SLSC), allowing eligible Shanghai- or London-listed companies to issue depositary receipts to access each other's stock markets, giving tech companies greater access to a wider pool of international investors.[118] Other jurisdictions like the US, Singapore, and Hong Kong have also been actively reforming listing standards to accommodate the financing demands of tech enterprises.

Apart from traditional IPOs, recent years have seen the rise of SPACs as an alternative route for Fintech corporations and other tech firms to raise capital. SPACs have gained popularity among international investors as a new asset class, and it is becoming a preferred listing choice for business owners worldwide, replacing conventional IPOs. In practice, obtaining a listing

---

[114] Eilís Ferran and Look Chan Ho, *Principles of Corporate Finance Law*, 2nd ed. (Oxford: Oxford University Press, 2014), p. 351.
[115] Lerong Lu, 'The Rising Star in the East: Unveiling China's Star Market, the Registration-Based IPO Regime, and Capital Markets Law Reform'. *International Company and Commercial Law Review* (2020) 31: 394, 399.
[116] This is due to heavy investments in research and development and the uncertain market prospect.
[117] 'UK Listings Review', HM Treasury, 19 November 2020, p. 19, https://www.gov.uk/government/publications/uk-listings-review.
[118] Lerong Lu and Ningyao Ye, 'Shanghai–London Stock Connect: Operating Mechanism, Opportunities and Challenges'. *Journal of International Banking and Financial Law* (2019) 34: 684, 685.

by merging with SPACs is akin to a reverse merger, when the target private company will be acquired by an existing public company, which bypasses the lengthy and complicated regulatory requirements associated with traditional IPOs. SPACs refer to a special corporate vehicle created by sponsors as cash shells which will be utilised to raise money via a public listing and have an acquisition strategy to purchase unspecified targets in the future.[119] In the US, SPACs are known as blank-check companies which lack underlying operating businesses and other substantial assets aside from cash and limited investments derived from the proceeds of their IPOs.[120] SPACs are a new type of financing arrangement combining the features and advantages of several corporate financing strategies, such as IPO, PE investment, M&A, and backdoor listings. Previously, technology companies, particularly those unicorns, would only consider a listing through SPAC when their primary IPO applications had failed the stringent regulatory checks.[121] However, more and more tech companies are now choosing SPAC over standard IPO as their preferred method of going public. In most cases, SPAC listings are less expensive than traditional IPOs. Underwriters usually charge 3.5–7% of the funds raised in a public offering for the majority of IPO projects, but for SPACs the listing fee is approximately 5.5%, including 2% to be paid at the time of listing and 3.5% to be deposited into a trust account with the funds raised.[122]

Due to the record-breaking $157 billion in global transaction volume in 2020, SPAC listing has received a lot of media coverage since that year.[123] In 2021, SPAC mania continued when US-based SPACs raised $156.7 billion through 612 IPO transactions.[124] Although the Covid-19 pandemic had catastrophic effects on the global economy, it also stoked investors' interest in emerging asset classes like SPACs. There are a number of reasons for the recent boom in the SPAC market, including shifting market dynamics, stricter rules governing conventional IPOs, and high demand for alternative ways to access the capital markets. Moreover, the celebrity effect has

---

[119] Ci Ren and Lerong Lu, 'Special Purpose Acquisition Companies (SPACs): The Global Investment Mania, Corporate Practices, and Regulatory Responses'. *Journal of Business Law* (2023), 1: 22, 23.

[120] 'What You Need to Know About SPACs—Investor Bulletin', SEC, 25 May 2021, https://www.sec.gov/oiea/investor-alerts-and-bulletins/what-you-need-know-about-spacs-investor-bulletin.

[121] Ningyao Ye and Lerong Lu, 'How to Harness a Unicorn? Demystifying China's Reform of Share Listing Rules and Chinese Depositary Receipts'. *International Company and Commercial Law Review* (2019) 30: 454.

[122] 'Considering an IPO? First, Understand the Costs', PwC, accessed 1 June 2023, https://www https://www.pwc.com/us/en/services/deals/library/cost-of-an-ipo.html.pwc.com/us/en/services/deals/library/cost-of-an-ipo.html.

[123] Patturaja Murugaboopathy, 'Global SPAC Deal Volumes this Year Surpass Total for 2020', *Reuters*, 9 March 2021, https://www.reuters.com/article/uk-usa-markets-spac-idUKKBN2B11WG.

[124] 'US De-SPAC & SPAC Data & Statistics Roundup 2022', White & Case, February 2023, https://www.whitecase.com/sites/default/files/2023-02/us-spac-de-spac-data-statistics-round-up-v2.pdf.

intensified the rising trend of SPAC by encouraging more retail investors to get involved. Sports and entertainment celebrities have been taking part in the SPAC boom by either starting their own SPACs or endorsing already-existing SPACs, which frequently results in extremely high market valuation. In February 2021, Slam Corp., a SPAC owned by baseball legend Alex Rodriguez, raised $500 million during its IPO on Nasdaq.[125] Some famous fund managers and investment banks, such as Goldman Sachs, Morgan Stanley, Blackstone, and Softbank, have become SPAC promoters and introduced their star projects, which further elevated the market sentiment.[126] Ordinary investors clearly underestimate the risks of SPAC investment because such shell entities have no operating businesses and only pledge to buy uncertain private companies in the future. Accordingly, the SEC's Office of Investor Education and Advocacy issued an investor alert warning stating that 'it is never a good idea to invest in a SPAC just because someone famous sponsors or invests in it or says it is a good investment'.[127]

The NYSE and Nasdaq have dominated global SPAC transactions. The SEC has made a lot of efforts in improving the regulation of SPACs in the areas of disclosure requirements, liability risks, and investor risk awareness.[128] The LSE, the second-largest SPAC market outside of the US that permits the use of special corporate entities for listing, has approved at least 50 SPAC listing applications over the past five years.[129] In an effort to draw in more tech unicorns and keep its position as a leading global financial centre after Brexit, the UK has been considering relaxing the SPAC-related listing regulations while enhancing investor protection.[130] Despite the relatively small sizes of alternative financing, the stock exchanges in Canada and a few European nations, including Italy and the Netherlands, also have their own SPAC models. A number of Asian stock exchanges have warmly welcomed the launch of SPACs. In South Korea and Malaysia, SPACs have been permitted to sell their shares publicly as an optional listing route for several

---

[125] Matt Egan, 'Celebs Including A-Rod and Ciara Are Getting into SPACs: What Could Go Wrong?', *CNN*, 23 February 2021, https://edition.cnn.com/2021/02/23/investing/spac-arod-kaepernick-celebrities/index.html.

[126] Amrith Ramkumar, '2020 SPAC Boom Lifted Wall Street Biggest Banks', *The Wall Street Journal*, 5 January 2021, https://www.wsj.com/articles/2020-spac-boom-lifted-wall-streets-biggest-banks-11609842601.

[127] 'Celebrity Involvement with SPACs—Investor Alert', SEC, 10 March 2022, https://www.sec.gov/oiea/investor-alerts-and-bulletins/celebrity-involvement-spacs-investor-alert.

[128] Ci Ren and Lerong Lu, 'Special Purpose Acquisition Companies (SPACs): The Global Investment Mania, Corporate Practices, and Regulatory Responses'. *Journal of Business Law* (2023) 1: 22, 31–34.

[129] 'SPACs: The London Alternative', Norton Rose Fulbright, May 2021, https://www.nortonrosefulbright.com/en-gb/knowledge/publications/94734f5e/spacs-the-london-alternative.

[130] FCA, 'Investor Protection Measures for Special Purpose Acquisition Companies: Changes to the Listing Rules (PS21/10)', July 2021, https://www.fca.org.uk/publication/policy/ps21-10.pdf.

years.[131] The HKEX has been debating whether to officially introduce a SPAC model, while stepping up law enforcement against illegal trading by shell companies.[132] Furthermore, the SGX declared new regulations in September 2021 to allow SPAC listing on its mainboard.[133] With the SGX becoming the first major Asian stock exchange to approve the listing of SPAC, it is fair to say that Singapore's SPAC model is a true game changer in international financial markets.[134] It not only gives Asia's tech companies and unicorns a long-awaited chance to enjoy better and more convenient financing options at home, but also accommodates the growing investment needs of Asia's retail, professional, and institutional investors, as well as family offices who want to access new asset classes to diversify their portfolios.

In practice, a typical SPAC listing involves two steps: (1) creating a SPAC as a shell entity and raising money through the shell entity's public listing; and (2) locating a target company and merging it with the listed shell, a procedure that is frequently referred to as de-SPAC. In the first step, SPACs will be set up by a management team known as sponsors. Professional managers with expertise in corporate finance, PE, or a relevant industry often act as sponsors to create SPACs. Investment banks, hedge funds, PE funds, successful entrepreneurs, and famous people like athletes, actors, and politicians are just a few examples of sponsors who think they can use their knowledge and reputation to raise money and find worthwhile companies to acquire. After the establishment of SPACs, there will be a formal IPO process for them, during which the sponsors and their investment bankers are required to set the offering price, underwrite shares, and hold roadshows, as well as finish the registration process by satisfying regulatory requirements and issuing a prospectus. Investors who purchase public units from SPACs typically pay $10 for each unit, which includes one common stock and one public warrant (or a portion of a warrant).[135] Warrants and common shares each have their own stock codes and are traded independently on stock exchanges. Some SPACs will create a crescent term to allow the constant change of the exercise price of warrants. When extra shares are issued in relation to a business

---

[131] Freny Patel, 'SPAC invaders', *Asia Business Law Journal*, 2 June 2021, https://law.asia/spac-invaders-asia/.

[132] Hong Kong Exchanges and Clearing Limited, 'Consultation Paper: Special Purpose Acquisition Companies', 17 September 2021, https://www.hkex.com.hk/News/Regulatory-Announcements/2021/210917news?sc_lang=en.

[133] SGX, 'SGX Introduces SPAC Listing Framework', 2 September 2021, https://www.sgx.com/media-centre/20210902-sgx-introduces-spac-listing-framework.

[134] Lerong Lu and Alice Lingsheng Zhang, 'Singapore's SPAC Listing Regime: A Game Changer or a Gap Filler?'. *Securities Regulation Law Journal* (2022) 50: 25, 31–35.

[135] Angela Veal, 'SPAC Warrants: 8 Frequently Asked Questions', Eisner Amper, 17 May 2021, https://www.eisneramper.com/spac-warrants-faqs-0421/.

combination at a price below the predetermined threshold, the provision seeks to adjust the warrant strike price. In such circumstances, the strike price will be altered to 1.15 times the greater of the following two prices: (1) the stock's market value or (2) the price of the newly issued shares.[136] At the beginning of SPAC registration, sponsors 'promote' will be issued, which usually represents 20% of the total publicly issued shares for a minimal purchase price of $25,000.[137] Sponsors promote aims to reward members of the management team, who are prohibited from receiving any commissions or bonuses prior to the completion of the de-SPAC transaction. It should be noted that, at this point, there are no substantial differences between the regulation of SPACs and other IPOs, including the laws governing issuance frauds. SPACs are featured for having their raised funds ring-fenced and administered by a trust account after their public offerings. The majority of the funds collected during the IPO will be deposited in a trust account which typically holds 90–100% of the total fund. Such funds can only be utilised to complete future M&As. The remainder of IPO proceeds directly held by the sponsors, or funds provided on an additional basis by the sponsors, will be used to cover the cost of SPACs' daily operations prior to the conclusion of de-SPAC transactions. The trust account's assets will normally be used for purchasing low-risk, short-term investments like short-term US Treasury bonds.

The second stage, in any SPAC transaction, involves completing the acquisition of target businesses within a set time frame, which is typically within 2 years with a maximum of 36 months after SPACs publicly float their shares.[138] If not, SPACs would have to go through the liquidation procedure and return the money to investors proportionately. An alternative option is that SPAC sponsors could ask shareholders for permission to prolong SPACs' lifecycle by another 12 months. The sponsors' subscribed warrants will expire automatically if the target business cannot be located before that date. SPACs will continue to operate as a regular listed company (the successor company) if a merger is completed within the allotted time. Prior to the IPO of SPACs, the acquisition objective won't be decided. This is because securities regulators, such as the SEC, will require SPACs to disclose relevant information about the target business and its financial situation if they have a particular

---

[136] Ramey Layne, Brenda Lenahan, and Sarah Morgan, 'Update on Special Purpose Acquisition Companies', Harvard Law School Forum on Corporate Governance, 17 August 2020, https://corpgov.law.harvard.edu/2020/08/17/update-on-special-purpose-acquisition-companies/.

[137] Ortenca Aliaj, Sujeet Indap, and Miles Kruppa, 'The SPAC Sponsor Bonanza', *The Financial Times*, 13 November 2020, https://www.ft.com/content/9b481c63-f9b4-4226-a639-238f9fae4dfc.

[138] This refers to the common US practices. SPAC regimes in different jurisdictions may set different maximum time limits.

acquisition target at the time of listing. It is likely to slow down the entire IPO process. Therefore, in the prospectus, directors and executives of SPACs typically state that objective assets won't be determined during the pre-IPO phase. After the IPO, the management team with the readiness of funding will start looking for a specific target and engage in a series of due diligence checks and extended talks. In order to prevent the dilution of founders' share equities, target companies will typically have a market valuation that is two to three times greater than that of the listed shell. But occasionally, instead of looking for an ideal target in the best interests of the investors, sponsors are likely to find a target company that will be simpler to combine within the time frame in order to cash in their rewards.

Once the acquisition target has been identified, SPACs will proceed to the crucial final stage of operation, the de-SPAC deal. The de-SPAC procedure is comparable to an acquisition of a publicly traded company. As an acquirer, SPACs must receive shareholder approval in accordance with SEC proxy rules once a potential opportunity of initial business combination is found.[139] The majority of SPACs' Articles also contain clauses stating that the acquisition plan must be approved by a majority vote of the initial shareholders. The details of the decision-making process, the financing sources, and the transaction contracts of the M&A deal must be disclosed before shareholders decide on the acquisition. After the acquisition announcement date, shareholders must be informed of the target company's financial position and business operations. The document known as Schedule 14A will include all the information being released. The US Supreme Court has long granted shareholders the right to challenge issuers for compensation in cases of false statements.[140] In other words, class actions from shareholders could happen at this point. There are extra information disclosure criteria during the de-SPAC procedure in addition to the comprehensive information provided in Schedule 14A. Under US law, listed companies must file Form 8-K and make current reports before conducting significant acquisitions.[141] The SEC, however, mandates that SPACs submit a special Form 8-K that should contain all the information equal to that needed in a Form 10 registration statement, unlike the ordinary Form 8-K issued by most listed companies. The SEC's

---

[139] However, there is no requirement that the target business abide by the SEC's voting rules. See 'De-SPAC Process—Shareholder Approval, Founder Vote Requirements, and Redemption Offer', GigCapital, 27 December 2019, https://www.gigcapitalglobal.com/de-spac-process-shareholder-approval-founder-vote-requirements-and-redemption-offer/.

[140] JI Case Co v Borak, 377 US 426 (1964).

[141] International Organization of Securities Commissions, 'Principles for Ongoing Disclosure and Material Development Reporting by Listed Entities', October 2002, https://www.sec.gov/about/offices/oia/oia_corpfin/princdisclos.pdf.

review of the disclosure papers has to be accepted, and SPAC sponsors must perform thorough due diligence. This Form 8-K is referred to as 'Super 8-K' due to the more stringent information-sharing requirements.[142] It ensures that the degree of information transparency in any SPAC listing is at least on par with that of a regular IPO. The proxy vote, in which shareholders decide whether to support or oppose the acquisition plan, marks the culmination of the de-SPAC procedure. The majority of the money raised by SPACs will be deposited in a third-party trust account, and the initial shareholders of SPACs have the right to either approve the acquisition transaction or redeem their shareholdings before the acquisition.[143] The sponsors shall try their best to prevent liability provisions under securities laws, such as making any false statements about the facts or leaving out important facts from registration statements. Finally, if shareholders decide to approve the acquisition plan, SPACs will combine with the target firms, as the entire merger process takes three to five months. With a new ticker symbol, the combined entity will continue to trade under the name of the target firm. At this point, the de-SPAC transaction is fully completed.

The success of SPACs can be attributed to a number of factors because they have benefits for most parties involved, including sponsors, investors, and the target business. Retail investors have long called for easier access to alternative investments like PE, private debt, hedge funds, commodities, structured products, VC, and derivatives.[144] We have observed a significant quantity of hot money chasing novel financial asset classes, such as crypto-assets and SPACs, during the Covid-19 pandemic. In April 2021, the price of BTC reached a record high of $64,000 as the IPO of Coinbase, a major cryptocurrency trading exchange, significantly lifted investor confidence.[145] Quantitative easing and other positive monetary policies have increased the amount of money supply into the financial markets, driving up the price of assets like SPACs. SPAC investors gain some advantages over other alternative investments, such as PE funds. For instance, any SPACs will have a deadline to finish an acquisition, which is between 18 and 24 months after

---

[142] Ramey Layne and Brenda Lenahan, 'Special Purpose Acquisition Companies: An Introduction', Harvard Law School Forum on Corporate Governance, 6 July 2018, https://corpgov.law.harvard.edu/2018/07/06/special-purpose-acquisition-companies-an-introduction/.

[143] All of these extra safety precautions are said to effectively prevent frauds in SPAC listings. See Daniel S. Riemer, 'Special Purpose Acquisition Companies: SPAC and SPAN, or Blank Check Redux'. *Washington University Law Review* (2007) 85: 931.

[144] Lauren Landry, 'What Are Alternative Investments?', Harvard Business School, 8 July 2021, https://online.hbs.edu/blog/post/what-are-alternative-investments.

[145] Barbara Kollmeyer, 'Bitcoin Surges to New High Above $64,000 as Investors Wait for Coinbase IPO', MarketWatch, 14 April 2021, https://www.marketwatch.com/story/bitcoin-surges-to-new-high-above-64-000-as-investors-wait-for-coinbase-ipo-11618381133.

the IPO. Investors will receive a refund of their original investment if the deal is not completed by the deadline. Also, the selection of qualified sponsors who will use their resources and experience to screen high-growth company targets is advantageous to investors. Additionally, the money of investors will be kept in escrow, which improves the security of investments. After the successful conclusion of de-SPAC transactions, the underwriting fees in the trust account will be given to underwriters. Undoubtedly, investors are attracted to SPACs' low-risk exit strategies like the redemption rights. The majority of funds can be taken out of the trust account to redeem public shares even if the transaction does not go through. As a result of their ability to sell their assets when the acquisition occurs, SPAC shareholders benefit from the high liquidity of their investments.[146]

Aside from the advantages for investors, the use of quick, cost-effective, and practical blank-check funding vehicles is beneficial for SPACs, their sponsors, and target businesses alike. Comparatively speaking, SPACs have a lower listing barrier than businesses choosing a traditional IPO. Private companies are increasingly looking for alternatives to traditional methods of accessing the capital markets, such as a direct listing of shares on a national securities exchange or a merger with a SPAC. In the US, it may only take eight weeks from a SPAC's creation to its IPO.[147] Investment bankers, attorneys, and accountants need to spend less time preparing the necessary documents for the IPOs of SPACs, allowing them to close more transactions and generate more incomes within the same period of time. When going public, SPACs only need to reveal a minimal amount of information and risk factors in their financial statements. SPAC sponsors have to provide some basic materials in advance of listing registration, like executive resumes that follow the registration templates.[148] Sponsors, on the other hand, are eager to create and operate SPACs primarily because of the prospective financial benefits. Incentives for sponsors include the chance to buy 20% of SPAC shares at the face value within a year of the de-SPAC deal. SPACs benefit from the larger financing scale and broader investor appeal, compared to PE financing, since they are listed on national stock exchanges. The sponsors and other parties, such as PE funds, hedge funds, and other private investors, will be able to buy minority shares through private placements, which is known as

---

[146] Johannes Kolb and Tereza Tykvova, 'Going Public Via Special Purpose Acquisition Companies: Frogs Do Not Turn into Princes'. *Journal of Corporate Finance* (2016) 40: 80.
[147] 'How Special Purpose Acquisition Companies (SPACs) Work', PwC, accessed 1 June 2023, https://www.pwc.com/us/en/services/audit-assurance/accounting-advisory/spac-merger.html.
[148] The securities regulator will not inquire about the operating years, asset value, or past performance of SPACs. Additionally, the SEC's feedback papers are frequently brief, so responding by SPAC sponsors is quicker as a result.

private investment in public equity (PIPE). PIPE replenishes the SPACs' cash reserves in order to quickly fund the business combination, once a tender offer is made to the target companies.[149] In contrast to a purchase by PE funds, where all cash is required, this portion of the additional shares can be used as the consideration for the acquisition.

Therefore, a growing number of private businesses, particularly BigTech and Fintech firms, have chosen to merge with SPACs in order to go public. Private businesses that opt for traditional IPOs will face a number of uncertainties, including the outcome of the listing application, the precise amount of time it takes to get listed, and the accurate issuer valuation. However, if all necessary disclosure and approval requirements are met, listing via de-SPAC only needs the agreement of two parties. The shells already have money available when SPACs make a tender offer to target businesses, and the acquirees do not need to obtain consent from a significant number of external investors. As a result, the SPAC listing method is less reliant on external market factors. Obviously, a quick listing option would be desirable for Fintech companies and BigTech, because of the high level of rivalry in the high-tech sector and the ongoing fast evolution of their businesses.[150] By choosing the SPAC model, tech companies can list their shares shortly after their establishment without having to accumulate years of accounting and performance reports to meet the onerous financial reporting requirements under an ordinary IPO process. By utilising capital markets to raise money and build corporate image, the fast listing option enables target companies to gain the first-mover advantage in a competitive industry. As a result, Fintech corporations are more likely to become market leaders in their respective financial service sectors. Furthermore, the target businesses' shareholders will have more options regarding the listing proceeds. The actual controllers can request cash plus share swap as the payment consideration when their companies merge with SPACs. Because shareholders do not have to wait until the end of the lock-up period to liquidate their shares, a portion of the profits can be cashed out straight away. In addition, SPAC parties may include a valuation adjustment method in the merger agreement, giving them more flexibility to change the consideration. Last but not least, the possibility of maintaining control of the target businesses' current shareholders is another advantage of SPACs. PE investors, on the other hand, frequently request preference shares and assert

---

[149] 'The Role of Private Investment in Public Equity (PIPE) in Financing SPACs Business Combinations', Allen & Overy, 1 June 2021, https://www.allenovery.com/en-gb/global/news-and-insights/publications/the-role-of-private-investment-in-public-equity-pipe-in-financing-spacs-business-combinations.

[150] Douglas W. Arner et al., 'The Evolution of Fintech: A New Post-Crisis Paradigm?'. *Georgetown Journal of International Law* (2016) 47: 1271.

multiple priority rights, which considerably reduces the founders' control over the business. In contrast, the founders' influence over the target company will largely stay intact, since under the SPAC model external investors will invest in the shell company rather than the real target company. As a result, the majority of investors only hold ordinary shares and have limited influence over corporate board decisions.

4.6 BigTech offering financial services

4.6.1 BigTech in finance: operating mechanism and benefits

After discussing various types of Fintech businesses and relevant corporate governance and finance issues, the chapter now looks at other new-type financial services providers, especially BigTech. Leading technology companies, known as BigTech, have an established standing in the market for digital services across the world.[151] BigTech in the US like Alphabet, Amazon, Apple, Meta, and Microsoft and their Chinese equivalents like Alibaba, Baidu, ByteDance, Tencent, and Xiaomi are examples of influential technology companies with established technology platforms and wide-ranging customer networks. BigTech are perceived as the most powerful business organisations in the world, and they have the highest market capitalisations compared with the largest banks and any other businesses. For instance, as of March 2023, Apple was worth $2.37 trillion, much higher than the market value of Goldman Sachs ($113 billion), Barclays ($31 billion), and ICBC ($230 billion).[152]

BigTech have benefitted from the so-called data–network–activities (DNA) loop.[153] They are able to collect and process large amounts of consumer data for analytics so as to create more and better services with specialised features. The variety of services is likely to increase network externalities, which will attract more consumers and lead to more user activities. More users will then generate more data, completing the self-reinforcing loop. BigTech's main business, however, is still in technology. Financial services make up a relatively small portion of their revenues, in contrast to Fintech companies that concentrate on the provision of financial services as their

---

[151] Jon Frost et al., 'BigTech and the Changing Structure of Financial Intermediation'. *Economic Policy* (2019) 34: 761–799.
[152] The share prices were derived from Yahoo finance, accessed 1 June 2023, https://uk.finance.yahoo.com/.
[153] Hyun Song Shin, 'Big Tech in Finance: Opportunities and Risks', BIS, 30 June 2019, https://www.bis.org/speeches/sp190630b.pdf.

primary undertaking. Only 11.3% of BigTech's earnings, according to the Bank for International Settlements (BIS), came from financial services, whilst 46.2% went to information technology.[154] However, BigTech's market share in finance is increasing quickly, as, by virtue of their size, resources, and organisational structure, BigTech have a significant capacity to speed up the transition towards financial service provision.

So far, BigTech have proactively entered the financial services industry. They are now providing a variety of services including payments, asset management, virtual currency, consumer lending, credit scoring, and insurance. Take payment services for example. Alibaba group launched Alipay to facilitate fast and secure transactions on its online shopping portals. Apple has made Apple Pay, a payment tool that enables users to make online or in-store purchases using apps on mobile iOS devices or the Safari web browser. Five out of ten Americans who responded to a poll said they had used Apple Pay in a store or restaurant in the previous 12 months, demonstrating the payment tool's popularity.[155] Alphabet and Amazon have introduced comparable smartphone payment technologies (i.e., Google Pay and Amazon Pay). Providing e-payment services can strengthen the business operations of BigTech by making secure transactions easier. The transaction data gathered from these payment services can create network externalities that improve user engagement, enabling BigTech to meet consumer needs more effectively in their primary business activities. This, in turn, can lead to more data being generated. Additionally, Meta made an effort to introduce its own stablecoins called Diem (previously known as Libra), which are based on blockchain technology, with the aim of creating a new digital payment and currency system. However, this initiative faced opposition from regulators in both the US and EU, as well as from the general public due to concerns related to financial stability, monetary sovereignty, privacy, and potential anti-competitive behaviour, leading to the termination of the project.[156]

BigTech are believed to bring a number of advantages to both customers and the financial sector, as they lead to increased efficiency and financial inclusion. BigTech lower the cost of financial services by using big data, AI, and other advancements in technology so that customers, particularly those who are unbanked, can access financial services with greater ease. For instance, BigTech are able to offer lending services to prospective client

---

[154] BIS, 'BIS Annual Economic Report', June 2019, p. 56, https://www.bis.org/publ/arpdf/ar2019e.pdf.
[155] 'Apple Pay—Statistics & Facts', Statista, December 2021, https://www.statista.com/topics/4322/apple-pay/.
[156] James Fontanella-Khan, Hannah Murphy, and Miles Kruppa, 'Facebook Gives up on Crypto Ambitions with Diem Asset Sale', *The Financial Times*, 27 January 2022, https://www.ft.com/content/e237df96-7cc1-44e5-a92f-96170d34a9bb.

groups that had previously been kept out of the financial system because of a lack of paperwork and information or logistical challenges. WeBank, backed by Tencent, offers Welidai microloan services to ordinary consumers, who can apply to borrow CNY500–300,000 and get a decision within five seconds.[157] It also provides Weiyedai loan products for SMEs, delivered fully online and based purely on company credits without collaterals, and small business borrowers could receive funds in 15 minutes.[158] Clearly, BigTech platforms have made lending easier by lowering the cost of information, enabling big data-based credit risk evaluation, and expanding the scope of lending activities. Traditional banks, in comparison, must go through a number of steps in order to grant loans and determine the cost of borrowing, such as evaluating the credit risk of borrowers by gathering paperwork and requesting collateral, which may be costly and time-consuming. Moreover, with the help of Coinstar, Amazon released Amazon Cash, which enables customers without bank accounts to store cash digitally and use it to make purchases from the Amazon online platform and its partners.[159] It performs similarly to a bank account and could support societal financial inclusion.

4.6.2 BigTech's risks and regulatory challenges

The financial activities of BigTech pose regulatory difficulties on a number of fronts, including financial stability, data privacy and consumer security, anti-competitiveness, accountability, and tax. Firstly, the foremost regulatory challenge of BigTech lies in their enormous sizes, which are likely to threaten financial stability. BigTech are large and powerful institutions, which are even more influential than well-established FHCs. They are engaged in a variety of commercial activities related to social networking, online search engines, and computer hardware. When combined, these activities may increase commercial risks and endanger the stability of financial system. BigTech are likely to grow to be systemically important, or too big to fail, in the near future.[160] While providing financial services, BigTech often partner with banks and other incumbent institutions. For example, Apple and Goldman Sachs have been working together to provide Apple Pay customers with a credit card that

---

[157] 'WeBank: Leading Digital Bank', WeBank, accessed 1 June 2023, https://res.webank.com/s/hj/www/assets/eng-5b9c186679.pdf.
[158] Ibid.
[159] 'Coinstar Teams with Amazon to Provide Amazon Cash Reload Sites', Coinstar, 15 May 2018, https://www.coinstar.com/press-releases/coinstar-teams-with-amazon-to-provide-amazon-cash-reload-sites.
[160] Agustin Carstens, 'Big Techs in Finance: Forging a New Regulatory Path', BIS, 8 February 2023, https://www.bis.org/speeches/sp230208.pdf.

is integrated into the Apple Wallet application.[161] The collaboration between BigTech and banks not only makes the financial system more complex but also creates new channels for the creation and distribution of risks.

Moreover, traditional financial services are becoming more and more dependent on BigTech solutions and their provision of cloud computing services, such as Amazon Web Services, Microsoft Azure, and Google Cloud Platform. Therefore, a systemic failure in the delivery of financial services could result from the breakdown of BigTech platforms and other technical problems. The world has seen the devastating consequences of major financial institutions collapsing during the global financial crisis 2007–2008. This event led to a market and institutional breakdown that had adverse effects on the overall economy, including a severe recession, rise in unemployment, and loss of consumer trust in the financial industry.[162] Therefore, it is necessary to strengthen the prudential regulation for BigTech who either provide financial services independently or collaborate with existing financial institutions. As an illustration, the Basel III framework, which is the global standard for bank capital and liquidity requirements, should equally apply to BigTech offering banking services in order to strengthen the regulation, supervision, and risk management of deposit-taking institutions.[163]

The protection of consumers using BigTech's financial services, particularly the appropriate handling of user data and privacy, is a second area of regulatory concern. The dominance of large tech companies over e-commerce, search, and social media networks gives them the ability to gather, process, and share vast amounts of data, which could lead to the creation of digital monopolies. The excessive use of data is likely to cause a series of problems, including price discrimination. This means that the extensive analysis of data by advanced algorithm empowers BigTech to determine the highest price a particular customer can afford, resulting in customised pricing for individual consumers at maximum rates.[164] BigTech may affect customer preferences because they seek to collect as much data as possible. While users enjoy the flexible and convenient financial services provided by BigTech, their confidential information may be made available to a variety of parties, which could cause issues with information security, data breach and leakage, and

---

[161] 'Apple Card', Apple, accessed 1 June 2023, https://www.apple.com/uk/apple-card/.
[162] Wenjie Chen, Mico Mrkaic, and Malhar Nabar, 'Lasting Effects: The Global Economic Recovery 10 Years After the Crisis', IMF, 3 October 2018, https://www.imf.org/en/Blogs/Articles/2018/10/03/blog-lasting-effects-the-global-economic-recovery-10-years-after-the-crisis.
[163] BIS, 'Basel III: International Regulatory Framework for Banks', June 2011, https://www.bis.org/bcbs/basel3.htm.
[164] Flynn Murphy and Qian Tong, 'China Tech Giants Accused of "Bullying" Consumers with Algorithms', *Nikkei*, 16 January 2021, https://asia.nikkei.com/Spotlight/Caixin/China-tech-giants-accused-of-bullying-consumers-with-algorithms.

cyber-crimes. Stricter regulatory frameworks for data sharing, like the EU's GDPR and China's PIPL, have been implemented to support technological innovation and promote transparency of BigTech's financial services as digital data flows across borders. Apart from data protection, regulators and policy-makers have to ensure fund safety for consumers. If BigTech retain significant amounts of consumer money, there should be a reliable system in place to make sure that the customers' financial assets are kept separate from the company's non-financial activities.

Furthermore, market monopoly and anti-competitive behaviour could be another significant area of risk when BigTech enter the financial services sector. BigTech are able to acquire a larger share of the market quickly due to their substantial user bases and cutting-edge technology. This lends BigTech a competitive edge, which is likely to alter the market structure and dynamism of the financial industry in the future. For example, major Chinese banks had to raise the interest rate on deposits to contend with the financial products based on MMFs offered by BigTech's digital wallets, which has elevated the banks' cost of funding.[165] Also, BigTech platforms could drive out potential rivals by taking advantage of network externalities and market monopolies, since their services have become essential for consumers using a variety of services like e-commerce, search engine, and network platforms. Finally, BigTech face accountability concerns as they could potentially shift their high-risk operations to other corporate entities subject to less regulation, such as foreign subsidiaries, affiliates, or shell companies. By doing so, they would not be required to comply with the laws of a specific jurisdiction and could avoid responsibility for conducting certain improper actions.

4.6.3 Exploring the optimal regulatory approach for BigTech

The regulatory approaches for BigTech providing financial services could be classified as activity-based (AB), entity-based (EB), or hybrid. According to the AB approach, all financial services of the same kind should be governed by the same set of rules and guidelines, regardless of who provides them. It can be summarised as 'same activity, same risk, same regulation'.[166] To avoid regulatory arbitrage, BigTech engaging in functions

---

[165] FSB, 'BigTech in Finance: Market Developments and Potential Financial Stability Implications', 9 December 2019, pp. 23–24, https://www.fsb.org/wp-content/uploads/P091219-1.pdf.

[166] Fernando Restoy, 'Regulating Fintech: Is an Activity-Based Approach the Solution?', BIS, 16 June 2021, https://www.bis.org/speeches/sp210616.htm.

resembling those of banks and financial institutions should be subject to the same laws and regulations that already apply to banking and other financial activities. Nonetheless, despite the ideal regulatory objective, the AB approach is likely to be less effective when applied to the supervision of BigTech providing financial services, for certain reasons. BigTech's potential risks stem from their business model, which uses the DNA loop to synthesise different commercial activities to achieve maximised profitability, especially the integration of their financial and non-financial businesses. This unique model is likely to make BigTech systemically important, posing a threat to financial stability. However, the distinctive features of their business model and related risks are not adequately addressed by the current policies and regulatory approaches. The AB regulation, instead of addressing the spillover effects of BigTech's overall business structure, focuses on very specific financial services that BigTech offer. In addition, while different institutions may offer the same financial service, they may do so in different ways, so the same activities may not result in the same risks as predicted. It all depends on the special characteristics of the service providers. Therefore, a bank and a BigTech providing a similar consumer loan or asset management services could present very different regulatory challenges for authorities.

The EB regulation is applicable to corporate groups with a licence conducting regulated financial activities.[167] Requirements are enforced at the entity level and may include conduct, prudential, and governance standards. Several supervisory actions aid in the implementation of EB regulation. Due to the limitation of the AB approach, scholars and regulators are starting to argue in support of EB regulation. We have seen some latest regulatory updates in this area, such as the EU's DSA and DMA which came into force in 2022.[168] While the DMA's main objective is to level the playing field for digital companies, the DSA seeks to provide a more secure online environment. The DSA has established new responsibilities for intermediary service providers. Therefore, regardless of where they are based, all online intermediaries offering their services in the market must adhere to these duties. In addition, the DMA has created a new category of substantial online platforms known as gatekeepers and set guidelines forbidding unfair and anti-competitive conduct on those platforms.

---

[167] Tobias Adrian, 'BigTech in Financial Services', IMF, 16 June 2021, https://www.imf.org/en/News/Articles/2021/06/16/sp061721-BigTech-in-financial-services.
[168] European Parliament, 'EU Digital Markets Act and Digital Services Act Explained, 14 December 2021, https://www.europarl.europa.eu/news/en/headlines/society/20211209STO19124/eu-digital-markets-act-and-digital-services-act-explained.

Apart from the EU's regulatory reform on BigTech, Chinese and US regulators have made a similar move. In 2021, Chinese authorities, including the State Administration for Market Regulation, took major regulatory action against BigTech platforms for anti-monopoly practices and data breach through the publication of guidelines, conducting investigations, and levying fines.[169] Likewise, the US congress released a list of suggestions for how BigTech should be regulated to prevent anti-trust activities.[170] What's more, the approaches of both segregation and inclusion have been suggested as feasible options for the regulation of BigTech. The concept of segregation would involve a monitoring framework for BigTech, where the financial services entities within the company would be separated from those that do not provide financial services. It would also require specific obligations to be imposed on these entities interacting and sharing data relating to financial activities. On the other hand, inclusion would not create a distinct boundary around financial entities within BigTech. Instead, regulatory requirements would be consolidated, and the emphasis would be to place consistent requirements on the entire BigTech to address the risks associated with interdependencies in its business model.

The third path is a hybrid of the AB and EB approaches. A research paper by the IMF suggested that while home supervisors should create an EB strategy to cover the global activities of BigTech, host supervisors could theoretically tackle local risks and concerns primarily through AB regulations.[171] A hybrid strategy could give regulators the proportionate power and flexibility they need to create a strong regulatory structure for BigTech. However, as prudential and conduct regulators have different mandates, goals, and regulatory focuses, there are worries that the cooperation between these two agencies would be challenging to accomplish. When assessing financial services providers, prudential regulators prioritise big firms and large transactions and tend to focus on system-wide risks. Instead, conduct regulators evaluate all types of behaviour violations, even those that occur at the most minute scale. Between these two, a proper level of coordination and cooperation is expected to be difficult. Additionally, BigTech operating in the finance service sector needs a more all-encompassing regulatory tactic that considers not only financial regulation objectives but also competition and data privacy

---

[169] 'China's Tech Giants Fall under Regulator's Pressure', *BBC*, 16 March 2021, https://www.bbc.co.uk/news/business-56410769.

[170] Jay B. Sykes, 'The Big Tech Antitrust Bills', US Congressional Research Service, 13 August 2021, https://crsreports.congress.gov/product/pdf/R/R46875.

[171] Parma Bains, Nobuyasu Sugimoto, and Christopher Wilson, 'BigTech in Financial Services: Regulatory Approaches and Architecture', IMF, January 2022, https://www.imf.org/-/media/Files/Publications/FTN063/2022/English/FTNEA2022002.ashx.

goals. Thus, to effectively address the multidimensional risks presented by BigTech, it is advised that the primary regulator of financial services work closely with the authorities of data protection and anti-competition in a given jurisdiction.

4.7 Metaverse, Web 3.0, and financial services

Metaverse has gained great popularity in the commercial world in recent years. In October 2021, Facebook changed its name to Meta because the social media behemoth thought that the Metaverse will be the upcoming revolution in social interaction and the replacement for mobile internet.[172] In 1992, science-fiction author Neal Stevenson first used the phrase Metaverse to describe the 3D virtual world in his book *Snow Crash*.[173] Metaverse, like the Internet, enables us to communicate with one another when we are not present in person and will bring us even closer to that experience.[174] The word Metaverse could be interpreted from two of its components. 'Meta' refers to something or someone who is more than normal or goes above and beyond. 'Verse' (universe) alludes to the entirety of space, time, and all of its objects, including galaxies, planets, stars, and all other types of matter and energy.

Therefore, the concept of 'Metaverse' refers to an imaginary version of the Internet that functions as a singular, all-encompassing, and interactive virtual universe, enabled by the use of VR and AR devices. VR is the term for the application of computer technology to the creation of a simulated world that can be viewed in 360 degrees.[175] VR provides a more immersive experience than conventional interfaces by immersing the user in the virtual world, and VR exists in three forms: semi-immersive, fully immersive, and non-immersive. AR refers to the real-time integration of digital information (i.e., contents created by computer) with the physical surroundings of the user.[176] Unlike VR, which creates a wholly artificial environment, AR users experience a real-world environment with generated perceptual information on top of it to improve the experience, visual effects, and other feelings. Based on VR and AR, Metaverse is the new method for interacting with

---

[172] 'Facebook Changes its Name to Meta in Major Rebrand', *BBC*, 28 October 2021, https://www.bbc.co.uk/news/technology-59083601.
[173] Neal Stevenson, *Snow Crash* (London: Penguin, 2011).
[174] 'What Is the Metaverse?', Meta, accessed 1 June 2023, https://about.meta.com/what-is-the-Metaverse/.
[175] 'What Is Virtual Reality?', Virtual Reality Society, accessed 1 June 2023, https://www.vrs.org.uk/virtual-reality/what-is-virtual-reality.html.
[176] 'What Is Augmented Reality or AR?', Microsoft, accessed 1 June 2023, https://dynamics.microsoft.com/en-us/mixed-reality/guides/what-is-augmented-reality-ar/.

others and exchanging knowledge in almost every area of our professional and personal lives. Metaverse is more like a 3D version of the internet that offers an immersive experience. It can be applied to different industries and scenarios, including entertainment, education, retail, and social networking. Goldman Sachs estimated that the Metaverse as a whole represents an $8 trillion potential market.[177] Massive financial investments in digital materials, the availability of digital assets, the hardware to create virtual spaces, and the digital infrastructure to link each virtual component will be necessary for the Metaverse to succeed.

The Metaverse movement is centred on the rapid progress of Web 3.0 technologies, which are at the forefront of a paradigm change in online commerce.[178] We have experienced three generations of internet technology over the past few decades. Web 1.0 is the term used to describe the original read-only internet format, in which a few content creators produce materials for a large audience, and everyone else could only use search engines to find, acquire, and consume those materials. Google Search, Yahoo, Baidu, and websites of mainstream media like the BBC, CNN, and NHK are notable examples of Web 1.0. Web 2.0 is an enhanced version of the internet, with more active user participation. The prevalence of smartphones and mobile internet led to the creation and further development of Web 2.0, which is known for its user-generated contents, mobile usability, and platform interoperability. Examples of Web 2.0 are social media and networking platforms such as Facebook, Twitter, Instagram, QQ, WeChat, Weibo, and LinkedIn.

Web 3.0 is the latest development of the internet, and there has not been a consensus on its meaning. It is known for decentralised data storage and sharing based on blockchain technology. We no longer need a centralised internet service provider thanks to the enhanced computing power and connectivity. More data and smart algorithm allow the making and execution of smart contracts based on the specific needs of each internet user.[179] Web 3.0 also encompasses the integration of virtual and real worlds, such as Metaverse, with the next level of connectivity empowered by data analytics and internet technologies. Further, the growth of AI and machine learning, especially in the field of natural language processing, has contributed to the rise of Web 3.0. A good example of an AI-enabled chatbot is ChatGPT, which was

---

[177] Candice Tse, 'GSAM Connect: Into the Metaverse', Goldman Sachs, 25 August 2022, https://www.gsam.com/content/gsam/us/en/institutions/market-insights/gsam-connect/2022/into-the-Metaverse.html.
[178] Jon M. Garon, 'Legal Implications of a Ubiquitous Metaverse and a Web3 Future'. *Marquette Law Review* (2022) 106: 163, 171.
[179] Max Raskin, 'The Law and Legality of Smart Contracts'. *Georgetown Law Technology Review* (2017) 1: 304, 309.

created by OpenAI, attracting 100 million users in the first two months after its debut.[180] ChatGPT and other advanced AI systems are likely to be a new start of Web 3.0.

As Metaverse is a full-function virtual world, there will be the provision of a variety of financial services similar to that offered in the real world. The recent time has witnessed financial institutions and Fintech platforms making strategies to embrace VR and Metaverse to improve operational efficiency and consumer experience. For example, VR training has been introduced by the Bank of America for the first time in almost 4,300 financial centres across the US.[181] A virtual banking environment is being used by 50,000 employees to practise a number of simple to complicated duties and simulate client interactions. South Korea's KB Kookmin Bank, to update the financial infrastructure in its Metaverse, created simulated financial towns, telecommuting centres, and virtual interaction areas.[182] The Fintech trading platform eToro introduced MetaverseLife as a smart portfolio with exposure to various Metaverse companies and platforms.[183] It is expected that consumers will be able to access most financial services in Metaverse in the near future.

NFTs are another area of Fintech application in Metaverse. These are used to verify authenticity and ownership of digital assets in virtual worlds, and are special digital identifiers that cannot be duplicated, replaced, or divided.[184] In practice, NFTs are stored in a public ledger or blockchain using the same technology as cryptocurrencies. They can represent any virtual assets like artwork, GIF images, videos, music, collectibles, avatars, video game skins, and tweets. NFTs are well liked in the digital art world because of their unique characteristics that enable online assets to have provable scarcity and unalterable ownership. NFTs are likely to have a large secondary market, as they can continue to be traded among collectors after being created by artists and internet users.[185] Every NFT has a provenance, allowing collectors to check for authenticity before making a purchase or placing a bid.

---

[180] Dan Milmo, 'ChatGPT Reaches 100 Million Users Two Months After Launch', *The Guardian*, 2 February 2023, https://www.theguardian.com/technology/2023/feb/02/chatgpt-100-million-users-open-ai-fastest-growing-app.

[181] 'Bank of America Is First in Industry to Launch Virtual Reality Training Program in Nearly 4,300 Financial Centers', Bank of America, 7 October 2021, https://newsroom.bankofamerica.com/content/newsroom/press-releases/2021/10/bank-of-america-is-first-in-industry-to-launch-virtual-reality-t.html.

[182] McKinsey, 'Value Creation in the Metaverse: The Real Business of the Virtual World', June 2022, p. 45, https://www.mckinsey.com/~/media/mckinsey/business%20functions/marketing%20and%20sales/our%20insights/value%20creation%20in%20the%20metaverse/Value-creation-in-the-metaverse.pdf.

[183] 'Invest in Virtual Worlds at MetaverseLife CopyPortfolio', eToro, accessed 1 June 2023, https://www.etoro.com/smartportfolios/Metaverselife.

[184] Usman W. Chohan, 'Non-Fungible Tokens: Blockchains, Scarcity, and Value', Critical Blockchain Research Initiative Working Papers, 24 March 2021, http://dx.doi.org/10.2139/ssrn.3822743.

[185] 'NFTs: Redefining Digital Ownership and Scarcity', Sotheby, 6 April 2021, https://www.sothebys.com/en/articles/nfts-redefining-digital-ownership-and-scarcity.

The rise of Metaverse has seen an increase in Fintech-related regulatory problems, especially when more businesses start selling digital goods and services. Questions will be raised about property ownership verification and possible theft or copyright infringement of verified transactions. Consumers are likely to face difficulties using cryptocurrency as payment for digital goods and services in Metaverse. It remains unclear if crypto assets are viewed as an ordinary property or a financial instrument. The latter option appears increasingly possible in some jurisdictions, leading to extra regulatory scrutiny. Moreover, the biggest regulatory hurdle for owners of Metaverse platforms would be complying with laws and regulations relating to data protection and privacy. As technologies are becoming more pervasively incorporated into everyday life for users, data generated by Metaverse will become significantly more valuable than it already is. Last but not least, how to safeguard intellectual property in Metaverse remains a key regulatory issue. When a piece of virtual work in Metaverse comes from a decentralised collaborative process carried out by various users concealed behind avatars, it could be practically difficult to identify the real creators. Such ambiguity is likely to alter how judges view fair use in future legal cases.

There are a large number of supporters for the wider application of Metaverse in our work and life. Metaverse has been a hot topic on Wall Street in the early 2020s because it has the potential to revolutionise trading and investments. It is likely to determine how the internet or even the business world develops in the future, creating a lot of new investment opportunities for investment bankers and fund managers. People regard Metaverse as the most important trend in the technology sector since the launch of Apple's iPhone, while some commentators think it could be the next dotcom bubble.[186] In any case, large corporations and investors do not want to miss out on any opportunities. BigTech and social media platforms are generally in favour of Metaverse because it is thought to increase interpersonal connections and workplace productivity. For example, Tencent plans to create and populate a Metaverse before its major competitors, such as NetEase and ByteDance (the parent company of TikTok), through a combination of corporate acquisitions and upgrading of its gaming and networking platforms.[187] Moreover, Metaverse appeals to the younger generations, such as Generation Z, many of whom prefer online gaming and social activities and want to make up for

---

[186] Bernhard Warner, 'Why Wall Street Thinks the Metaverse Will Be Worth Trillions', *Fortune*, 27 January 2022, https://fortune.com/longform/wall-street-Metaverse-web3-investors-roblox-meta-platforms-microsoft/.

[187] Priyanka Boghani, 'Tencent Poised to Lead China's Charge into the Metaverse', S&P Global, 17 March 2022, https://www.spglobal.com/marketintelligence/en/news-insights/latest-news-headlines/tencent-poised-to-lead-china-s-charge-into-the-Metaverse-69311462.

the loss of actual life during the Covid-19 pandemic by participating more in the virtual world.[188]

Metaverse also receives strong criticisms in several aspects. For example, the participation in Metaverse needs high-quality VR or AR hardware equipment, which could be expensive, contributing to greater inequality in the population and exacerbating the so-called digital divide.[189] Moreover, we have observed the issue of interoperability among numerous Metaverse initiatives. Given that each Metaverse project depends on proprietary technology and intellectual property, there hasn't been a widespread adoption of standardised technical standards for Metaverse. The lack of interoperability could impede the further growth of Metaverse and increase the time and monetary costs when users have to register for multiple Metaverse platforms devised by different tech companies. The technological readiness is also a concern, as some experts believe AI and blockchain are not yet ready to be deployed at the level anticipated. As a result, the potential use of Metaverse for commercial purposes might be overstated. At present, people are labelling any old project that involves gaming, VR, or NFTs with the tag Metaverse, according to critics who have cautioned that the concept is becoming overhyped.[190]

Furthermore, the rise of Metaverse could reinforce the problem of technology monopoly, as it is likely to strengthen the prestigious status and dominant market positions of BigTech who operate Metaverse. Finally, people tend to underestimate the negative consequence of excessive or addictive use of social media and online platforms. This might result in a number of regulatory and ethical issues in the virtual world, such as threats to user safety, online abuse, hate speech, and privacy concerns. For instance, in May 2022, in the Horizon Worlds, which is Meta's VR environment, a woman was reported being sexually assaulted by an unknown person.[191] Any unlawful or illicit activity that takes place in the real world is undoubtedly going to occur in

---

[188] Generation Z refers to people born between 1997 and 2012. See Michael Dimock, 'Defining Generations: Where Millennials End and Generation Z Begins', Pew Research Center, 17 January 2019, https://www.pewresearch.org/fact-tank/2019/01/17/where-millennials-end-and-generation-z-begins/.

[189] Digital divide means the unequal access to digital devices and technologies, like laptops, smartphones, tablets, and the internet.

[190] Harry Robertson, 'Wall Street Is Pumped About the Metaverse. But Critics Say It's Massively Overhyped and Will Be a Regulatory Minefield', Business Insider, 25 December 2021, https://markets.businessinsider.com/news/stocks/Metaverse-outlook-overhyped-regulations-facebook-meta-virtual-worlds-genz-2021-12.

[191] Adam Smith, 'Woman Says She Was Virtually "Raped" in the Metaverse While Others "Passed Around a Bottle of Vodka"', The Independent, 30 May 2022, https://www.independent.co.uk/tech/rape-Metaverse-woman-oculus-facebook-b2090491.html.

Metaverse in the future if the virtual worlds attract more users. Therefore, regulators and policy-makers must continue to consider how to police and govern Metaverse to make it a secure and civilised environment.

4.8 Conclusion

This chapter has completed the analysis of various vital players in the global Fintech industry. It has discussed the existing banks and financial institutions that proactively adopt Fintech to upgrade their services and infrastructure, the Fintech start-ups that rely on advanced technologies to build innovative business models and financial products, the new financial giants and FHCs that specialise in Fintech, BigTech that depend on their tech reserve and mass user base to tap into financial services, and the novel Metaverse platforms that enthusiastically engage in the provision of financial services and products. Despite the different forms of Fintech business organisation, they all echo the spirit of financial innovation and entrepreneurship. Fintech brings better consumer experience and increased business efficiency in the financial industry. With the collective efforts of all Fintech corporations, the global Fintech revolution has been made possible.

5
Fintech in Banking Institutions

5.1 Introduction

This chapter focuses on the Fintech revolution taking place in the banking sector. Following the global financial crisis, an increasing number of new digital banks have been founded with the help of cutting-edge information technologies, aiming to compete with established high-street lenders for a larger share of the market. The UK has a relatively concentrated banking sector, as the five largest lenders possess 85% of personal current accounts in the country.[1] Traditionally, people hold a belief that the bigger a bank, the safer it is. However, during the 2007–2008 financial crisis, this idea was challenged by the failure of some well-established banking institutions, like Lehman Brothers in the US and RBS in the UK. In early 2023, we saw the liquidity crisis happening to major banks, like Credit Suisse in Europe and Silicon Valley Bank in the US, after the Covid-19 pandemic.[2] This seems to suggest that large banks, having a complicated corporate structure and multifaceted business activities, often contain risks that are difficult to identify by their customers and even financial regulators. Besides, major banks have suffered significant reputational damage as a result of the financial crisis and other notorious scandals such as the Libor manipulation and mis-selling of payment protection insurance.[3]

At this time juncture, by taking advantage of people's distrust in incumbent institutions, some entrepreneurs have set up new digital banks that have neither historical legacies nor physical networks, such as Aldermore, Shawbrook, Atom, Monzo, Starling, Revolut, and N26. These challenger lenders try to cut the complexity of conventional branch networks, which requires heavy investments in property, equipment, and trained staff, in order to build

---

[1] The five largest banks in the UK are HSBC, Barclays, Lloyds Banking Group, Royal Bank of Scotland (RBS), and Santander. See Elaine Moore, 'Challengers Line up to Take on the Big Banks', *The Financial Times*, 14 July 2012, p. 3.

[2] Stephen Morris, James Fontanella-Khan, and Arash Massoudi, 'How the Swiss "Trinity" Forced UBS to Save Credit Suisse', *The Financial Times*, 20 March 2023, https://www.ft.com/content/3080d368-d5aa-4125-a210-714e37087017.

[3] Adam Jones and Jennifer Thompson, 'RBS Prepares for Libor Settlement Talks', *The Financial Times*, 3 November 2012, p. 10.

a simple, straightforward, and low-cost business model for modern banks. Some market disrupters have become an immediate success by providing products and services for customers who have been underserved by existing banks, such as retail customers and SMEs. The obvious competitive advantages enable challenger banks to grow fast and occupy market share. In recent years, the total lending volume of challenger banks in the UK increased by 31.5%, compared with a decline of 4.9% for the big five lenders.[4] Challenger institutions outfitted with Fintech are becoming more prevalent outside of the UK as well. German Fintech giant N26 operates smartphone-based banking services in 24 European countries, and also plans to tap the American and Asian markets. In 2019, N26 raised $300 million from PE investors led by the US's Insight Venture and Singapore's GIC, putting its valuation at $2.7 billion as the largest Fintech company in Europe.[5] What's more, China holds a number of innovative challenger banks operated without bricks and mortar, including Alibaba's Zhejiang E-Commerce Bank and Tencent's WeBank. The Chinese banking sector has been dominated by state-backed banks, but recently its financial regulators started to allow private investors to set up new banks in order to increase industry competition and provide more loans for capital-strapped entrepreneurs.[6]

Accordingly, this chapter provides an in-depth analysis of the rising digital-based challenger banks and relevant policy and regulatory implications. It consists of the following sections. Section 5.2 examines the phenomenon of 'too big to fail' (TBTF), which indicates the market concentration and systemic importance of the largest banks across the globe. It is said to negatively impact the industry competition and limit the service options for retail and corporate customers. Section 5.3 explains the concept of the digital-based challenger bank. Section 5.4 analyses the economic, social, and cultural factors contributing to the rapid rise of digital banks and assesses their competitive edge over traditional banks. Section 5.5 conducts case studies of successful digital banks in the UK, while Section 5.6 studies booming Fintech banks in China. Section 5.7 discusses how digital banks fit into the post-crisis regulatory system, emphasising prudential regulation and consumer protection. Section 5.8 identifies some pressing regulatory issues presented by digital banks, such as deposit insurance, capital requirements, financial security, and data safety. Section 5.9 draws a conclusion.

---

[4] Emma Dunkley, 'Challengers Prise Open Grip of Larger Rivals', *The Financial Times*, 4 May 2016, p. 23.
[5] Nicholas Megaw, 'Germany's N26 Becomes Europe's Top Fintech with $2.7bn Valuation', *The Financial Times*, 10 January 2019, http://www.ft.com/content/d945cfa8-1419-11e9-a581-4ff78404524e.
[6] Lerong Lu, *Private Lending in China: Practice, Law, and Regulation of Shadow Banking and Alternative Finance* (Abingdon: Routledge, 2018), p. 147.

5.2 Too big to fail: market concentration of global banks

There is no denying that a small number of the largest financial institutions in the world control the majority of banking assets and other financial resources. From Table 5.1 we can observe that the top 10 banks in the world hold a combined amount of assets of $28 trillion, among which the ICBC is ranked the largest bank with total assets worth over $4 trillion. It also reveals the geographical concentration of gigantic banks, with China possessing 20 of the world's top 100 largest banks, the US 10, Japan 9, the UK 6, France 6, Germany 6, Canada 5, South Korea 5, Brazil 5, and Australia 4.[7] In contrast, a lot of developing countries did not make the list. India only has one major bank (State Bank of India) in the list, although it has over 1.4 billion population. This suggests the inequality and uneven distribution of financial resources between countries in the traditional banking sector, which is a main trigger

Table 5.1 The world's top 20 banks by total assets.

Rank	Bank	Country	Total assets ($ billion)
1	Industrial and Commercial Bank of China	China	4,005.58
2	China Construction Bank Corp.	China	3,397.13
3	Agricultural Bank of China	China	3,232.68
4	Bank of China	China	2,989.16
5	Mitsubishi UFJ Financial Group	Japan	2,773.82
6	JPMorgan Chase & Co.	US	2,533.60
7	HSBC Holdings	UK	2,521.77
8	BNP Paribas	France	2,348.11
9	Bank of America	US	2,281.23
10	China Development Bank	China	2,201.86
11	Credit Agricole Group	France	2,112.04
12	Wells Fargo	US	1,951.76
13	Japan Post Bank	Japan	1,873.50
14	Mizuho Financial Group	Japan	1,850.10
15	Sumitomo Mitsui Financial Group	Japan	1,847.47
16	Citigroup Inc.	US	1,843.06
17	Deutsche Bank	Germany	1,766.85
18	Banco Santander	Spain	1,730.08
19	Barclays PLC	UK	1,528.89
20	Societe Generale	France	1,527.43

Source: 'Top 100 Banks in the World', RelBanks, 2 April 2018, http://www.relbanks.com/worlds-top-banks/assets.

---

[7] 'Top 100 Banks in the World', RelBanks, 02 April 2018, http://www.relbanks.com/worlds-top-banks/assets.

for the Fintech revolution to build a fairer and more equal global banking system and to have a more proportionate allocation of capital and resources across developed countries and emerging economies.

Within each major economy, banking assets are concentrated in the hands of a few leading banks. For example, in China, the Big Four banks (i.e., ICBC, China Construction Bank, Agricultural Bank of China, and Bank of China) plus the Bank of Communication own 41.21% of total banking assets.[8] The US has 5,542 commercial banks and savings institutions whose money is insured by the Federal Deposit Insurance Corporation (FDIC).[9] Despite the large number of banking institutions, top players in the US occupy most of the market share. In New York State, JPMorgan Chase Bank alone accounts for $563,6 billion or 33.3% of all deposits in the state.[10] The UK has the largest banking industry in Europe, which is also the fourth-largest one in the world. The country has more than 300 banks and 45 building societies, with a total of over 9,000 bank branches and 70,000 cash machines.[11] However, the banking industry is dominated by some large British banks. HSBC, Barclays, RBS, and Lloyds manage over 75% of personal current accounts and 85% of business accounts in the UK, and these four banks have over £5 trillion assets and 560,000 employees.[12] Moreover, the top three banks in Finland control 85% of the market, while the top three Norwegian banks occupy 84% of its banking sector.[13] It is clear that there is little space for new players and innovative business models in the highly consolidated global banking industry.

Due to their size and interconnectedness, major banks are frequently referred to as being 'too big to fail' (TBTF), as their failure would be catastrophic for the financial sector and have a ripple impact on the entire economy.[14] As a result, when a banking crisis arrives, the government will have no choice but to intervene and bail out the largest banks and lending institutions. This phenomenon was widely observed in the global financial crisis 2007–2008. Fannie Mae and Freddie Mac, two US mortgage lenders, were

---

[8] PBoC, 'China Financial Stability Report 2015', September 2015, p. 37, http://www.pbc.gov.cn/eportal/fileDir/english/resource/cms/2015/09/20150906616281480816.pdf.
[9] FDIC, 'Quarterly Banking Profile: Second Quarter 2018', p. 1, https://www.fdic.gov/analysis/quarterly-banking-profile/fdic-quarterly/2018-vol12-3/fdic-v12n3-2q2018.pdf.
[10] FDIC, 'Deposit Market Share Report', 30 June 2018, https://www5.fdic.gov/sod/sodMarketRpt.asp?barItem=2.
[11] 'Banks in the UK', RelBanks, accessed 1 June 2023, http://www.relbanks.com/europe/uk.
[12] Ibid.
[13] Thorsten Beck, Asli Demirguc-Kunt, and Ross Levine, 'Bank Concentration and Crises', National Bureau of Economic Research Working Paper, August 2003, https://www.nber.org/papers/w9921.pdf.
[14] Imad Moosa, 'The Myth of Too Big to Fail'. *Journal of Banking Regulation* (2010) 11: 319, 320.

bailed out by the US government in September 2008.[15] In order to support the UK banking industry and save failing institutions like RBS, the UK government implemented a number of financial measures. At their height, these interventions cost £137 billion in cash, which was given to the banks in the form of new capital and loans.[16] More recently, in March 2023, backed by the Swiss government's emergency rescue plan, the largest bank in Switzerland—UBS—was asked to acquire the failing Credit Suisse, which together now hold $1.7 trillion in assets.[17] However, this kind of capital and liquidity support for TBTF banks, funded by taxpayers' money, could have negative impacts on the economy. It not only creates the problem of moral hazards[18], but also results in serious competition issues as smaller banks are unable compete against large lenders owing to lack of resources, economic scales, and government backups. It also leads to inadequate services provided for those who really need banking and finance, causing the problem of financial exclusion. In addition, the higher level of bank market concentration is said to constrain the liquidity position of small businesses which tend to hold less cash, have less access to lines of credit, and are likely to use greater amounts of expensive trade credit.[19]

Financial regulators have been attempting to address the TBTF problem and implementing regulatory changes to better oversee systemically important banks (SIBs), to reduce their negative systemic impacts and moral hazard risk. The FSB states that additional measures will be taken to address issues relating to SIBs, such as reform of the banking resolution regime to reduce the need for state support of failing banks, as well as the need to improve public information disclosure regarding resolution frameworks, actions, and funding mechanisms.[20] Take the UK as an example. As early as 2000, publication of the Cruikshank Report highlighted the lack of a competitive climate in the banking sector for money transmission, services

---

[15] W. Scott Frame et al., 'The Rescue of Fannie Mae and Freddie Mac', Federal Reserve Bank of New York Staff Report No. 719, March 2015, https://www.newyorkfed.org/medialibrary/media/research/staff_reports/sr719.pdf.

[16] Federico Mor, 'Bank Rescues of 2007–09: Outcomes and Cost', House of Commons Library Research Briefing, 8 October 2018, p. 4, https://researchbriefings.files.parliament.uk/documents/SN05748/SN05748.pdf.

[17] Mark Thompson, 'UBS Is Buying Credit Suisse in Bid to Halt Banking Crisis', CNN, 20 March 2023, https://edition.cnn.com/2023/03/19/business/credit-suisse-ubs-rescue/index.html.

[18] The phrase 'moral hazard' in economics describes a circumstance in which a party lacks the motivation to take precautions against a financial risk because it is shielded from any possible repercussions. In the banking scenario, it refers to the situation where senior bankers are incentivised to pursue extra profits by participating in risky business activities, as largest banks are likely to be saved by the governments during a crisis.

[19] Liang Han, Song Zhang, and Francis J Greene, 'Bank Market Concentration, Relationship Banking, and Small Business Liquidity'. International Small Business Journal (2017) 35: 365, 366.

[20] FSB, 'Evaluation of the Effects of Too-Big-To-Fail Reforms: Final Report', 1 April 2021, https://www.fsb.org/wp-content/uploads/P010421-1.pdf.

to individual consumers, and services to SMEs.[21] According to the report, there are significant regulatory barriers to entry in the industry, businesses are represented on the board of the regulatory body, banks' exposure to competition law is diminished, and banks are frequently permitted to enact their own regulations. Accordingly, the UK government has called for reforms to increase competition in the banking industry. After the global financial crisis, politicians have urged for more banks to be built to promote competition and provide more choices of financial products and services for consumers. It was suggested that the largest British banks should be forced to sell their branches to spur competition and create space for challengers.[22] However, according to a study by the UK's Competition and Market Authority, the market shares of personal current accounts have remained stable over time, apart from mergers and acquisitions, which indicates the difficulty of growth and expansion in the banking sector.[23] Additionally, larger banking account providers reportedly received more complaints and a lower customer satisfaction rating than their smaller competitors. It highlights the need to bring more competition to the banking sector.

5.3 Who are digital-based challenger banks?

In the UK, the FCA was established in 2013, with an operational objective to promote competition in the interest of financial consumers.[24] Under the economic and political environment that welcomes more competition, a number of challenger banks have emerged in recent years, together with some more established challengers, to contest dominant banks. Entrepreneurs create new digital banks with no legacy in order to compete with dominant lenders for a larger part of the market by leveraging the most recent advancements in Fintech and consumers' scepticism with current lenders. Most challenger banks have developed a straightforward, low-cost business strategy and reduced the complexity of traditional branch networks. They mainly offer financial products and services targeting customers who are underserved by conventional banks, such as small businesses and ordinary consumers.

---

[21] Don Cruikshank, 'Competition in UK Banking: A Report to the Chancellor of the Exchequer', UK Parliament, 19 June 2000, https://hansard.parliament.uk/commons/2000-06-19/debates/3aa321eb-2cff-4a9a-bef7-c51c31416ef3/CruickshankReport.
[22] Hannah Kuchler and Elaine Moore, 'Miliband Set to up the Ante over Big Banks', The Financial Times, 9 July 2012, p. 21.
[23] Competition and Market Authority, 'Personal Current Accounts: Market Study Update', UK Government, 18 July 2014, p. 9, https://assets.publishing.service.gov.uk/media/53c834c640f0b610aa000009/140717_-_PCA_Review_Full_Report.pdf.
[24] Financial Services and Markets Act 2000 (UK), section 1E.

It should be noted that great differences can be found among challenger banks in the UK. For instance, some are perceived as a smaller version of major lenders as they offer traditional banking services and try to grab market shares from the Big Five, such as Virgin Money and Metro Bank. In January 2011, Virgin Money acquired the nationalised Northern Rock, and it went to float its shares on the LSE in November 2014.[25] Metro Bank, founded in 2010, was the first new bank to open business in the UK in over 100 years. It aims to bring back personal banking services, and opens every store seven days a week, from 8 a.m. to 8 p.m. on weekdays.[26] Customers can walk into any branches of Metro Bank without an appointment. It also offers a same-day account opening service, which differentiates itself from other high-street banks.

Moreover, an increasing number of retailers have entered the financial services industry.[27] Some supermarket chains have joined the competition by offering reward point credit cards, low-cost personal loans, current and saving accounts, and other financial products and services. Examples of supermarket-backed challenger banks are Asda Money, Tesco Bank, Sainsbury's Bank, and M&S Bank. Customers of Sainsbury's Bank can earn points with its Nectar Reward Scheme when they use any of its financial services like credit cards, insurance, savings, and travel money.[28] Tesco Bank, relying on the extensive presence of its grocery and convenience stores across Britain, has already become a main competitor to the largest banks, and has 6.5 million customers for its financial services.[29]

Meanwhile, a new breed of digital-aided challenger banks has been established, so as to provide specialist financial services and products for customers who are ignored or underserved by traditional banks. Digital banks are frequently referred to as neo banks, virtual banks, online-only banks, and app-based banks in the media. As fresh market players, they are said to have clean reputations and attract less public cynicism.[30] Moreover, these new lenders have adopted innovative and low-cost business models, as they carry out most businesses online rather than via traditional branches. They focus on underexploited business areas like buy-to-let property finance, SME

---

[25] Andrew Bolger and Emma Dunkley, 'Branson Makes Pound(s) 70m As Virgin Money Floats', *The Financial Times*, 14 November 2014, p. 26.
[26] 'About Us', Metro Bank, accessed 1 June 2023, https://www.metrobankonline.co.uk/about-us/.
[27] KPMG, 'The Game Changers: Challenger Banking Results', May 2015, p. 2.
[28] Sainsbury's Bank's, accessed 1 June 2023, https://www.sainsburysbank.co.uk/.
[29] Elaine Moore, 'Challengers Line up to Take on the Big Banks', *The Financial Times*, 14 July 2012, p. 3.
[30] Sharlene Goff, 'Challenger Banks Have the Big Four in their Sights', *The Financial Times*, 16 August 2014, p. 8.

lending, and consumer lending. Such digital-based challenger banks are the product of the ongoing Fintech revolution as they have utilised big data, AI, and other technologies to build their unique business model and provide better and more convenient services for customers. Many of them operate purely online without brick-and-mortar stores. Clearly, this chapter focuses on such digital-based challenger banks. Fintech grants these challenger banks significant competitive edges and allows them to survive, compete, and prosper. Many digital banks have achieved instant success, gaining sizeable market shares thanks to their unique market emphasis and customer-centric attitude.

5.4 Why do digital banks rise?

The rapid rise of digital-based challenger banks after the global financial crisis and Covid-19 pandemic can be explained by multiple reasons. Firstly, the public's trust in the banking industry has been greatly eroded due to the financial crisis. According to a survey, only 16% of respondents agree that 'banks generally provide good quality products and services which are sold responsibly', 83% of people believe 'bankers are greedy and get paid too much', and 80% say 'banks aren't doing enough to support the economy'.[31] Take RBS as an example; it was bailed out by taxpayers' money in 2008, but, afterwards, its business posted total losses of £58 billion as a result of troubled takeovers, restructuring charges, bad lending and other poor trading decisions, and fines and legal costs.[32] Moreover, recent scandals in the banking industry, like the Libor manipulation and the mis-selling of payment protection insurances and interest rate swaps, further undermined the public's confidence. It is evident that established lenders suffered severe reputational damages in the post-crisis era, so the challenger banks, by creating new brands, are able to distinguish themselves from existing players, giving them an advantage of having no historical legacy.

Secondly, challenger banks find their markets by accommodating the financing needs of some marginalised customers who are underserved by dominant lenders. For instance, many smaller businesses have been facing a financing dilemma for a long time, as banks have become risk-adverse after the financial crisis and tightened credit provision for risky start-ups.

---

[31] YouGov and Cambridge, 'Public Trust in Banking', April 2013, p. 16, http://cdn.yougov.com/cumulus_uploads/document/ylf7gpof19/Public_Trust_in_Banking_Final.pdf.
[32] Jill Treanor, 'Losses of £58bn Since the 2008 Bailout—How Did RBS Get Here?', *The Guardian*, 24 February 2017, https://www.theguardian.com/business/2017/feb/24/90bn-in-bills-since-2008-how-did-rbs-get-here-financial-crisis-.

Obviously, SMEs play a vital and indispensable role in the British economy. It was reported that the UK has 5,236,390 SMEs, representing 99.9% of the total number of businesses, employing 15.16 million people, and generating a combined revenue of £1.65 trillion.[33] Moreover, SMEs contributed to 49.8% of the UK's GDP.[34] However, it remains difficult for SMEs to secure a loan from banks, as many of them cannot provide valid collaterals or pass banks' strict credit tests. According to the Bank of England (BoE), SMEs only received 37% of total bank credits in the UK, whilst the majority of 63% was granted to large corporations.[35] Therefore, a number of challenger banks tend to focus their businesses on SME financing, which not only helps smaller businesses obtain funding to grow, but also wins themselves numerous clients overlooked by large lenders. Similarly, some challenger lenders target the booming buy-to-let property market, by offering mortgages to all types of property investors. In 2016, Aldermore originated £1 billion buy-to-let loans, with a 25% annual growth.[36] Apparently, as challenger banks attempt to offer differentiated products and services to conquer market shares, they indeed fill the niches of the banking industry. According to Andy Golding, the CEO of OneSavings Bank, challenger banks are 'dancing in the gaps' left by major players.[37] Moreover, most challenger banks claim themselves as customer-centric, as they emphasise the fairness and ethical culture in their banking activities, which clearly contrasts with large incumbent banks which are known for profit-making (or loss-making) and bankers' bonus culture.

Thirdly, digital-based challenger banks have adopted distinctive ways of distribution based on Fintech, which is able to cut their operating expenses significantly. Most of them have been relying on brokers, online platforms, and smartphone apps to reach customers, rather than constructing a large number of physical branches like their larger rivals do. Traditional lenders possessing a branch network have to bear very high operating costs. For example, Barclays has 1,305 branches and 36,000 full-time employees in the

---

[33] Department for Business, Innovation & Skills, 'Business Population Estimates 2014', UK Government, 26 November 2014, p. 4, https://www.gov.uk/government/statistics/business-population-estimates-2014.

[34] Matthew Ward and Chris Rhodes, 'Small Businesses and the UK Economy', UK Parliament, 09 December 2014, p. 7, https://researchbriefings.files.parliament.uk/documents/SN06078/SN06078.pdf.

[35] The percentage is calculated by the author from BoE data, 'BankStats (Monetary & Financial Statistics)', Table A8.1, accessed 1 June 2023, http://www.bankofengland.co.uk/statistics/Pages/bankstats/current/default.aspx.

[36] Aldermore, 'Annual Report and Accounts 2016', https://investors.aldermore.co.uk/sites/default/files/attachments/pdf/strategicreport_aldermore_ar16_web.pdf.

[37] Ashley Armstrong, 'One Savings Bank Targets IPO Valuation of up to £600m', *Telegraph*, 7 May 2014, http://www.telegraph.co.uk/finance/newsbysector/banksandfinance/privateequity/10813002/One-Savings-Bank-targets-IPO-valuation-of-up-to-600m.html.

UK.[38] In contrast, the publicly listed Aldermore Bank does not have a single branch and only employs 569 staff.[39] Aldermore serves its customers online, by phone, and face to face through its network of 12 regional offices across the UK. The low-cost strategy means digital banks do not have geographical boundaries for their businesses, so they can expand explosively in a short time without hefty IT and infrastructure investments. However, while the online-only banking service draws a lot of attention from the younger generations who grew up with personal computers, mobile phones, and the internet, most middle-aged and older people might still prefer to visit a physical branch when receiving financial services.

Last but not least, the Covid-19 pandemic has changed consumer habits significantly. More people are getting used to working from home and shopping online. Both traditional banks and Fintech banks have been offering more services through their websites and smartphone apps. The entire Fintech industry experienced rapid growth during the pandemic, when financial institutions and consumers actively embraced digital financial services.[40] Now 71% of global consumers are using digital banking platforms on a weekly basis.[41] Also, consumers are using more financial services and purchasing virtual assets like NFTs in Metaverse and other virtual settings. Additionally, the recent 'open banking' initiative helps digital banks and Fintech companies grow further. By enabling third-party payment services and other financial service providers to access transactions and other data from banks, open banking promotes secure interoperability in the banking sector. Open banking is trusted by over 6.5 million consumers in the UK, providing precious data for Fintech platforms to design data-driven products and offer personalised financial services.[42] All these factors contribute to the rise of digital banks as consumer behaviours change.

---

[38] Barclays PLC, 'Annual Report 2016', p. 247, https://home.barclays/content/dam/home-barclays/documents/investor-relations/annualreports/ar2016/Barclays%20PLC%20Annual%20Report%202016.pdf.
[39] Shawbrook PLC, 'Annual Report and Accounts 2016', p. 130, https://www.shawbrook.co.uk/media/228610/Shawbrook-Report-and-Accounts-2016.PDF.
[40] Lerong Lu and Alice Lingsheng Zhang, 'Regulating Fintech Corporations Amidst Covid-19 Pandemic: An Analysis of Ant Group (Alipay)'s Suspension of IPO and Business Restructuring'. *Company Lawyer* (2021) 42: 341–343.
[41] Kevin Martin, 'How Banking Will Change After COVID-19', HSBC, 26 November 2020, https://www.hsbc.com/insight/topics/how-banking-will-change-after-covid-19.
[42] 'What Is Open Banking?', Open Banking, accessed 1 June 2023, https://www.openbanking.org.uk/what-is-open-banking/.

5.5 Case study: digital banks in the UK

Digitally focused challenger banks are the latest market players in the UK's banking arena. Most of them had been incorporated in the 2010s and backed by PE firms. Despite the short history, British digital banks have been expanding quickly. According to a report, their return on equity (ROE) ratio reached 17.0%, which outperformed not only the UK's big five banks (4.6%), but also other larger challengers (9.5%).[43] Digital banks also enjoyed relatively low expenses, as they had an average cost-to-income ratio of 48.5%, compared with 80.6% for large banks.[44] This section assesses the business models and evolutionary paths of some successful Fintech-enabled challenger banks in the UK, including Aldermore, Shawbrook, Atom, Monzo, Starling, and Revolut.

5.5.1 Aldermore and Shawbrook

Aldermore Bank describes itself as 'an SME-focused bank which operates with modern, scalable, and legacy-free infrastructure'.[45] Founded in 2009, Aldermore has been growing rapidly since its establishment and is now one of the UK's leading alternative lenders. In March 2015, Aldermore launched a successful IPO in London and raised £75 million from selling new shares to investors.[46] Its business model has been highly endorsed by global investors. Blue-chip, long-term investors from the US and the UK, as well as hedge funds, participated in Aldermore's IPO, which saw demand for the bank's shares five times exceed its supply. Currently, its shares are listed on the main board of the LSE and it is a constituent of the Financial Times Stock Exchange (FTSE) 250. In 2022, its yearly pre-tax profits amounted to £204.7 million, up from £157.8 million in 2021, which indicated its quick expansion and considerable profitability.[47] Aldermore has over 750,000 customers in the UK and it has a net lending amount of £15.5 billion.[48]

---

[43] KPMG, 'Framing New Futures: Challenger Banking Report 2017', October 2017, https://assets.kpmg.com/content/dam/kpmg/uk/pdf/2017/10/challenger-banks-framing-new-futures.pdf.
[44] Ibid.
[45] 'About Us', Aldermore, accessed 1 June 2023, http://www.aldermore.co.uk/about-us/.
[46] 'Aldermore Bank Shares Surge by 12% on London Debut', *The Guardian*, 10 March 2015, https://www.theguardian.com/business/2015/mar/10/aldermore-bank-shares-surge-by-12-on-london-debut.
[47] Aldermore, 'Aldermore Group PLC Report and Accounts for the Year Ended 30 June 2022', p. 13, https://www.investors.aldermore.co.uk/system/files/uploads/financialdocs/aldermore-group-annual-report-and-accounts-fy2022.pdf.
[48] Ibid.

The rapid success of Aldermore resulted from its accurate customer focus and low-cost operating strategy. The centre of its business is to provide commercial finance, mortgage, and saving services for British SMEs, homebuyers, and savers. It attracts deposits from savers and then extends loans in four specialised areas: asset finance, invoice finance, SME commercial mortgage, and residential mortgage. Instead of operating a branch network as most lenders do, Aldermore offers most services online, by phone, or face-to-face in its regional offices, which reduces costs significantly. Besides, it aims to deliver the kind of banking as it is supposed to be, which features good services, full transparency, and community focus.[49] The better and friendly service in combination with more availability of credit for smaller businesses is no doubt a strong selling point. Moreover, Aldermore claims that it is known for customer-focused innovation. For instance, it allows its customer to post comments about its products and services online without any edits, which provides valuable suggestions for other customers. Up to now, the market share occupied by Aldermore is still relatively small compared to that of established lenders. Its asset finance business took up 3% of the £14 billion market in the UK; its invoice finance had a market share of 0.9% of the £19 billion market; and its SME commercial mortgages represented 1% of the £44 billion market.[50] Nonetheless, judging from its strong growth prospect, Aldermore has the potential to become a larger lender in the future.

Similarly, Shawbrook Bank has an objective to serve the financial needs of UK SMEs and individuals. It offers a variety of lending and saving products, and its lending division is divided into five parts: commercial mortgages, asset finance, business credit, secured lending, and commercial lending.[51] It has around 1,000 members of staff and operates in 10 offices throughout the UK, including four principal locations and six smaller ones, whilst serving over 300,000 active customers.[52] In 2011, its primary investor acquired Whiteaway Laidlaw Bank, and then rebranded it as Shawbrook Bank. In the following years, its investors bought several other financial companies like Commercial First, Link Loans, Singers Asset Finance, and Centric Commercial Finance, and then incorporated them into the banking businesses

---

[49] Aldermore aims to support communities where it operates. For example, deposits received by Aldermore are only loaned in the UK; its premises and staff are all located in the UK, which is close to the communities they serve; it greatly supports UK government policies and schemes, such as Help to Buy; its corporate culture mirrors that of other UK SMEs, so it is able to appreciate the real needs of SME communities; and it actively supports young entrepreneurs in UK schools to develop business skills. See 'About Us', Aldermore, accessed 1 June 2023, http://www.aldermore.co.uk/about-us/.
[50] Ibid.
[51] 'About Us', Shawbrook, accessed 1 June 2023, https://www.shawbrook.co.uk/about-us/.
[52] Ibid.

of Shawbrook. In April 2015, Shawbrook raised £90 million in its IPO with admission to the LSE, and later it was admitted to the FTSE 250 index.[53] So far it has made loans to more than 60,000 SMEs across the UK, making it a leading bank of SME financing. The success of Shawbrook within a short period of time has demonstrated the potential market scale of SME financing that has been greatly underestimated by dominant banks.

Generally speaking, SME-focused digital banks, like all other lenders, have a business model of taking deposits from the public and then making loans to potential borrowers. However, in terms of who to make loans to, many challenger banks provide tailored financing services for SMEs, such as asset finance, invoice finance, and SME mortgages. Asset financing, including leasing and hire purchase, refers to the funding for capital (asset) investments in machinery, plant, and equipment.[54] By using asset financing, the business does not need to make one-off and large payments to buy the relevant asset upfront. Instead, it can breakdown the payment into an affordable monthly rent or instalment, while having the right to use the asset. At the end of the asset finance agreement, the business might have the option to purchase the asset at a nominal price (hire purchase). Invoice financing means lending to SMEs against their outstanding invoices, which includes the forms of factoring and invoice discounting.[55] By utilising invoice financing tools, the business will be advanced the value of the invoices they have created. In terms of factoring, the factoring lender will collect the debt instead of the business, but invoice discounting allows the business to maintain the credit control and collection facility to receive the payment from their customers. SME mortgaging means lending to SMEs to fund their purchase of properties.

Another reason explaining the success of Shawbrook and Aldermore is their low-cost strategy empowered by Fintech. Obviously, mainstream banks on high streets have a high level of expenses, as they have to purchase or rent offices in good locations. They also hire a large number of staff and have to maintain complex business structures as well as a massive computer system. On the contrary, challenger banks rely on modern internet technology and have a simple and straightforward business model with limited branches and a small number of employees. The cost-effective operation, in combination with a specialised market target, brings challenger banks obvious competitive

---

[53] Denise Roland and Ashley Armstrong, 'Challenger Bank Shawbrook Fetches £725m Valuation on IPO', *The Telegraph*, 1 April 2015, http://www.telegraph.co.uk/finance/newsbysector/banksandfinance/11508186/Challenger-bank-Shawbrook-fetches-725m-valuation-on-IPO.html.

[54] 'What Is Asset Finance?', Startups, accessed 1 June 2023, http://startups.co.uk/what-is-asset-finance/.

[55] 'Invoice Finance: What Can You Raise?', Startups, accessed 1 June 2023, http://startups.co.uk/invoice-finance-what-can-you-raise/.

advantages over established lenders. For Aldermore and Shawbrook, their ROE ratio reached 18.2%, the highest in the UK's banking industry. Clearly, the success of challenger banks brings more competition to the banking sector and forces mainstream lenders to pay more attention to SME financing and consumer lending.

5.5.2 Atom Bank

Nowadays, more and more people prefer to manage their finance on the go. Atom is a novel digital bank based in Durham, England, which obtained its banking licence from the UK's PRA in June 2015. As of March 2017, it had raised capital of £219 million from institutional investors, including Spanish lender BBVA, fund manager Neil Woodford, and Toscafund.[56] Atom is the first UK bank that is built exclusively for smartphones, which means it can only be accessed via its app on smartphones and tablets, which can be downloaded from Apple Store or Google Play. It is also known for its personal experience, as customers are allowed to design their own logo for their personal banking and give it a name—whatever they like. Customers can log into the Atom app by passcode, fingerprint, face recognition, or voice recognition. Clearly, Fintech not only brings convenience for financial consumers, but also improves the security level by utilising people's biometric data to verify their identities. Moreover, customers of Atom can seek instant help from its support teams by making a call or using the built-in chat service, which is available 24/7/365. Currently, Atom offers competitive rates for its savers, with the annualised interest rate ranging from 3.75% for a six-month fixed-term deposit to 4.45% for a five-year deposit.[57] The bank is also planning to tap into other retail financial services like current accounts. On the other hand, Atom makes loans to small businesses and offers mortgages to first-time home buyers through its brokers. Atom has attracted a lot of attention from the public. During its pilot operation phase in 2016, there were over 40,000 potential users registering interest.[58] As more people turn to mobile banking, it has been suggested that the total number of branch visits in the UK reduced by 50% to 268 million a year in 2020.[59]

---

[56] Emma Dunkley, 'Atom Bank Raises £83m from Shareholders as it Eyes Expansion', *The Financial Times*, 3 March 2017, https://www.ft.com/content/c075542e-fc09-3c27-bb98-7fe5f7d3df34.

[57] 'Fixed Rate Savings', Atom Bank, accessed 1 June 2023, https://www.atombank.co.uk/fixed-saver/.

[58] Lee Boyce, 'Atom Bank Opens its Doors to all Savers with Two Best-Buy Deals—But Fixed Rates Have Been Cut', This Is Money, 6 October 2016, http://www.thisismoney.co.uk/money/saving/article-3824910/Atom-Bank-opens-doors-savers-two-best-buy-deals-fixed-rates-cut.htm.

[59] Emma Dunkley, 'Atom Bank to Offer Residential Mortgages', *The Financial Times*, 6 December 2016, https://www.ft.com/content/1e3cd566-bbb1-11e6-8b45-b8b81dd5d080.

5.5.3 Monzo

Monzo is a mobile-only bank based in London which is operating through its mobile app and is famous for the bank's coral-colour debit cards. Monzo only focuses its business on consumer banking and is praised for good customer experience. In 2015, Monzo was established by Tom Blomfield who previously worked for another challenger bank, Starling. At that time, Monzo (the company was originally named Mondo) received its restricted banking licence, and in April 2017 the restrictions had been lifted, so Monzo became a fully authorised bank which could offer current accounts to customers.[60] Monzo has developed apps for both iOS and Android smartphones, offering a range of personalised services such as real-time transaction notifications and balance sheet updates, personal categorisation of transactions, instant card freezing if the Monzo card is stolen or lost, overview of customers' spending habits, and overseas use of the Monzo card without extra charge. It is extremely fast and convenient for consumers to open an account. New customers only need to download the Monzo app on their smartphones. Then, they are required to upload a photo of a valid identity document such as a passport or driving licence and to record a selfie video to verify the identity. After that, the account will be opened, with their debit cards being posted to the home address.

The Monzo app uses its built-in map function to record the location where a transaction takes place and instantly displays the transaction in bank statements together with the logo of the vendor company. Also, the app automatically categorises the transaction based on the company involved in the payment. For instance, a purchase with Tesco will be put under the 'groceries' category, while a payment to Uber will be categorised under 'transport'. Customers can provide instant feedback within the app to improve the accuracy of categorisation. As of March 2023, Monzo had accumulated 7 million users, and it has a big online community that helps improve the design of mobile banking, like suggesting new features, testing the app, and providing user feedback to the developers.[61] Clearly, Monzo is building the bank with its customers, and has 800 members of staff and three offices in London, Cardiff, and Las Vegas. Monzo's size is still much smaller than the big five banks, as it had £71.2 million of customer deposits, in contrast to £400 billion on Lloyds'

---

[60] Monzo, 'Welcome to Monzo Bank', 5 April 2017, https://monzo.com/blog/2017/04/05/banking-licence.
[61] 'About Monzo', Monzo, accessed 1 June 2023, https://monzo.com/about/.

balance sheet.[62] Nonetheless, Monzo has grown rapidly as it has attracted a large number of loyal users by holding community activities and crowdfunding events. For example, in December 2018, Monzo raised £20,000,000 from 36,006 customers via crowdfunding in 2 days, 2 hours, and 45 minutes.[63] The online-only business model of Monzo also appeals to VC and PE funds. In June 2019, Monzo doubled its valuation to £2 billion after raising £113 million from a group of PE investors led by Y Combinator, a US-based investment firm.[64] Most recently, Monzo plans to expand its business outside the UK and attempt to enter the US market.

5.5.4 Starling Bank

Starling Bank is another mobile-only digital bank headquartered in London. In January 2014, Anne Boden, a former banker and tech entrepreneur, established Starling, and in July 2016, the PRA and FCA granted Starling a banking licence.[65] Similar to Monzo, Starling provides its personal clients with a current account and debit card that is Mastercard-compatible and has contactless capabilities. Moreover, it offers business banking accounts that can be accessed through its banking app. Customers can access a range of financial services beyond a basic bank account through an in-app marketplace, including overdrafts, loans, housing offers, insurance, and savings deals. Customers enjoy extra benefits like receiving immediate notifications whenever they spend or receive payments, insights showing spending patterns, no fees when traveling abroad, and round-the-clock client support.[66] Customers can reach the live customer support staff via the app, email, or phone 24/7 if they need assistance. There are no monthly fees for either personal or business accounts, and Starling provides Euro accounts that let customers send and receive Euros for free.

Other features of the Starling app include 'Goals', a virtual change jar that lets users save for vacations or house furnishings. Users can quickly lock

---

[62] Lionel Laurent, 'Monzo: Can a $2.5 Billion Banking Upstart Really Dislodge JPMorgan?', *Bloomberg*, 26 June 2019, https://www.bloomberg.com/opinion/articles/2019-06-26/monzo-can-a-2-5-billion-banking-upstart-dislodge-jpmorgan.

[63] Monzo, 'You've Invested £20,000,000 in Monzo', 5 December 2018, http://monzo.com/blog/2018/12/05/crowdfunding-closes.

[64] Kalyeena Makortoff, 'Monzo Valued at £2bn After Fresh Funding Round from US', *The Guardian*, 25 June 2019, http://www.theguardian.com/business/2019/jun/25/monzo-digital-bank-doubles-value-2bn-fresh-funding-round-y-combinator.

[65] 'The Road to Starling', Starling Bank, accessed 1 June 2023, https://www.starlingbank.com/about/road-to-starling/.

[66] Ibid.

their Starling cards in-app if they think they've misplaced them and quickly unlock the cards if they locate them again. A tap in the software can also be used to cancel and reorder cards. Customers can toggle the spending caps on everything from ATM payments to gambling activities using the Starling app. Users can also take advantage of additional features like the bill-splitting option called 'Settle Up' by some simple taps without disclosing their sort codes or account numbers to their peers. What's more, the app offers the ability to quickly send money overseas, at market-based rates, to more than 35 countries. A number of digital wallets, including Apple Pay, Google Pay, Samsung Pay, Fitbit Pay, and Garmin Pay, can be linked to the Starling card. Travellers can benefit from extra services that come with the Starling card, including fee-free ATM withdrawals and payment processing anywhere Mastercard is accepted. More recently, Starling has introduced location-based fraud protection for its customers, as transactions will be blocked if they don't match a customer's mobile phone location.[67] In addition, Starling is making its technologies, such as its API, available to other businesses, financial organisations, and even governments so they can use such technologies and Starling's infrastructure to create new Fintech systems. For example, one of Starling's clients, the UK's Department for Work and Pensions, has been using its Banking-as-a-Service and payment systems.[68]

5.5.5 Revolut

Revolut is a UK-based Fintech business that provides multiple types of financial services, including P2P payments, currency exchanges, cryptocurrencies, insurance, and loans. It also offers pre-paid VISA or Mastercard debit cards. Revolut was established in July 2015 at the Level39 tech accelerator in London's Canary Wharf by Nikolay Storonsky and Vlad Yatsenko, and as of November 2022 it had over 25 million retail customers and processed 330 million transactions per month.[69] Revolut has an extensive global operation, with presence in the US, India, Mexico, Brazil, and New Zealand. In the UK, users can get a free standard account which includes a British pound

---

[67] Tom Warren, 'Meet the British Mobile Banks Showing the US How It's Done: Monzo and Starling Are Transforming UK Spending', The Verge, 13 June 2019, https://www.theverge.com/2019/6/13/18663036/monzo-starling-mobile-banks-uk-report.

[68] 'Welcome to Banking-as-a-Service', Starling Bank, accessed 1 June 2023, https://www.starlingbank.com/blog/platformification-of-banking-industry/.

[69] Revolut, 'Revolut Tops 25 Million Retail Customers As Global Expansion Continues', 17 November 2022, https://www.revolut.com/en-GR/news/revolut_tops_25_million_retail_customers_as_global_expansion_continues/.

current account and a Euro IBAN account.[70] In December 2018, Revolut obtained a specialised banking licence from the ECB through the Bank of Lithuania.[71] Therefore, Revolut is permitted to take deposits and provide consumer credit in the EU but not investment services. As of February 2023, Revolut was poised to obtain a banking licence in the UK, as it had been regulated as an electronic money institution for several years.[72]

Most functions and features of Revolut's app are similar to that of Monzo and Starling. However, Revolut appears to be a helpful tool for international travellers and anyone transferring money abroad. For example, Revolut allows card holders to spend abroad in over 150 currencies at the interbank exchange rate, with a fee of 0.5% for anything above £1,000 each month.[73] Each customer is also given a free monthly allowance of £200 to use at international ATMs; any withdrawals made in excess of £200 are subject to a 2% charge.[74] Additionally, it provides travel insurance to protect customers' health and belongings for as little as £1 per day through Revolut Travel Ltd. Users of Revolut can transmit and receive money from one another with a few quick taps. To make transfers more interesting and recognisable, users can also attach notes, images, and GIFs. Apart from overseas travelling and money transfer, users can exchange a number of mainstream cryptocurrencies, including BTC, Litecoin, Ethereum, BTC Cash, and XRP, without visiting crypto exchanges. Revolut is becoming a popular one-stop Fintech platform for smartphone users globally.

5.6 Case study: digital banks in China

We will now look at a group of digital-based challenger banks in China. China's banking industry is known for its strong state influence in the operation of banking and financial institutions. Although the country has been experiencing market-oriented economic reform since the late 1970s, some crucial sectors like banking, telecommunications, and energy have been

---

[70] Mary-Ann Russon, 'What Is Revolut?', *BBC*, 2 April 2019, http://www.bbc.co.uk/news/business-47768661.
[71] Nicholas Megaw, 'Lithuania Licence Lets Revolut Launch Banking Products', *The Financial Times*, 23 December 2018, http://www.ft.com/content/989904f0-fe2c-11e8-aebf-99e208d3e521.
[72] Anna Isaac, 'Fintech Firm Revolut Moves Closer To UK Banking Licence After First Annual Profit', *The Guardian*, 01 March 2023, https://www.theguardian.com/business/2023/mar/01/uk-Fintech-firm-revolut-much-delayed-accounts-reveal-first-annual-profit.
[73] 'Personal Fees (Standard)', Revolut, accessed 1 June 2023, https://www.revolut.com/legal/standard-fees/.
[74] Ibid.

subject to some level of state control.[75] Over 50% of the shares in each of the Big Four Chinese banks are owned by the Chinese State Council through its investment subsidiary, Central Huijin Investment Ltd.[76] The Chairmen and CEOs of the Big Four, who have vice-ministerial administrative rankings, are appointed by the central government. Thus, they are often seen as government officials instead of bankers. As a result, China's state-run banks strongly prefer lending to other state-owned companies and are hesitant to extend credit to privately held businesses, particularly SMEs. A study found that while SMEs now account for the majority of new employment in China and produce close to 60% of the country's economic output, they only receive a fifth of all bank loans.[77] In order to address the financing difficulties of SMEs and boost competition and innovation in the banking industry, the Chinese government has initiated reforms to allow qualified private investors to set up privately funded banks.[78] These banks are considered as Chinese challenger banks though their sizes are incomparable to traditional big lenders. This section focuses on two Chinese digital banks: Tencent's WeBank and Alibaba's E-Commerce Bank (MyBank).

5.6.1 WeBank

In January 2015, WeBank opened its business as the first online-only bank in China which is entirely owned by private investors.[79] WeBank is a joint venture led by China's internet giant Tencent which takes up 30% of the bank's shares. It was named after Tencent's star product WeChat, a popular messaging app having 1.1 billion users. The registered capital of WeBank is CNY3 billion ($483.3 million).[80] It is best described as a portable financial services platform based on the internet and Fintech, targeting individual consumers and small and micro enterprises. It does not have any physical branches. WeBank issues loans based on big data credit scores and face

---

[75] Lerong Lu, 'Private Banks in China: Origin, Challenges and Regulatory Implications'. *Banking and Finance Law Review* (2016) 31: 585, 585–587.
[76] Lerong Lu, *Private Lending in China: Practice, Law, and Regulation of Shadow Banking and Alternative Finance* (Abingdon: Routledge, 2018), p. 28.
[77] Emma Dong and Simon Rabinovitch, 'China's Lending Laboratory', *The Financial Times*, 23 May 2012, p. 11.
[78] Lerong Lu, 'Private Banks in China: Origin, Challenges and Regulatory Implications'. *Banking and Finance Law Review* (2016) 31: 585, 592.
[79] Gabriel Wildau, 'China's First Online-Only Lender Launched', *The Financial Times*, 6 January 2015, p. 16.
[80] 'Tencent Ready to Launch China's First Private Internet Bank, WeBank', *South China Morning Post*, 29 December 2014, http://www.scmp.com/news/china-insider/article/1670474/tencent-ready-launch-chinas-first-private-internet-bank-webank.

recognition technology without requesting collateral. As it has no brick-and-mortar presence, its business model is akin to that of Ally Bank in the US and Atom Bank in the UK which can only be accessed through their websites or mobile apps. The then Chinese Premier Li Keqiang was invited to Shenzhen, where Tencent Group is based, to make a keynote speech for WeBank's opening ceremony when he praised WeBank for pushing forward China's banking reform and stated that 'it's one small step for WeBank, one giant step for financial reform'.[81]

Key products of WeBank include Weili Loan for consumers, which is based on Tencent's QQ and WeChat social networking platforms and known for its 100% online application procedure. Customers only need to provide their names, identity cards, and phone numbers to apply for a line of credit ranging from CNY500 to 200,000, and the product has met the financing demands of most consumers and small businesses.[82] After securing the line of credit, customers can choose to request funds or repay loans anytime, as the money will arrive at their designated bank accounts within one minute of sending requests. Weili Loan service is available 24/7 for a sizable number of middle- and low-income customers underserved by conventional banks thanks to internet technology and Tencent's extensive customer base. Apart from Weili Loan, WeBank offers a portfolio of financial services via its app such as wealth management, Weizhuang Loan (interior decoration finance), and Weiche Loan (used cars purchasing finance). In 2017, WeBank posted a net income of CNY1.45 billion, which was over three times the figure in 2016.[83] It has a relatively low bad loan ratio of under 1%, as it relies on big data and other Fintech to precisely measure the credit risks of borrowers. As of December 2021, WeBank had extended loans worth over CNY1 trillion to corporate clients, and the daily transaction number peaked at 798 million.[84] Clearly, WeBank's extensive social network and cutting-edge technologies have helped it rapidly establish itself as a significant Fintech bank.

5.6.2 Zhejiang E-Commerce Bank (MyBank)

Zhejiang E-Commerce Bank, also known as MyBank, is another prominent online-only digital bank in China, established by the e-commerce giant

---

[81] Gabriel Wildau, 'China's First Online-Only Lender Launched', *The Financial Times*, 6 January 2015, p. 16.
[82] 'Weili Loan Application', WeBank, accessed 1 June 2023, https://w.webank.com/.
[83] Jason Tan, 'Tencent-Backed WeBank Hits $21 Billion Valuation', *Caixin*, 5 November 2018, https://www.caixinglobal.com/2018-11-05/tencent-backed-webank-hits-21-billion-valuation-101343111.html.
[84] 'About Us', WeBank, accessed 1 June 2023, https://www.webank.com/about.

Alibaba. MyBank received its administrative approval from the Chinese banking regulator in June 2015, with a registered capital of CNY4 billion ($645 million).[85] Ant Group holds 30% of shares in MyBank and Fosun International and Wanxiang Group possess 25% and 18% stakes in the bank respectively.[86] Yu Shengfa, the then president of MyBank, commented that 'MyBank is an important milestone for Ant Group's development to provide financial services for small and micro enterprises and individuals'.[87] At the opening ceremony of MyBank, the chairman of Alibaba Jack Ma recalled the hardship of borrowing money when first starting doing business: 'I was setting up a small company and needed 30,000 yuan. It took me three months to collect all the invoices that I had used as collateral for borrowing, but I still failed to secure a loan. At that time, I thought if there were a bank focusing on this kind of thing [lending to small businesses], it would help many entrepreneurs to succeed.'[88]

Therefore, financial inclusion has been the main mission for MyBank. According to the WB, financial inclusion refers to the availability to both individuals and businesses of useful and affordable financial products and services, such as payments, transactions, savings, credit, and insurance, that are provided in a sustainable and accountable manner.[89] Fintech platforms play a crucial role in attaining financial inclusion, which is a necessary step toward reducing poverty and increasing prosperity. In MyBank's case, it has developed a number of specialised loan services for small businesses based on customers' varied financing needs. For instance, it has introduced 'E-Commerce Loan' for merchants on Alibaba's Taobao and Tmall e-commerce sites. Additionally, it provides a 'Wangnong Loan' for farmers and a unique loan for webmasters who operate internet businesses. As of the end of 2018, MyBank had total assets of CNY95.9 billion ($14 billion) and the bank's capital adequacy rate was 12.1%.[90] Over 12 million customers, primarily small companies, have used MyBank services. With 420 technology employees out of an overall workforce of 800, MyBank President Jin Xiaolong asserted that technology is the foundation of his bank.[91] The success of MyBank is undoubtedly attributed to advanced technology and a focused market niche.

---

[85] 'Alibaba-Affiliated Online Bank Get Green Light from China Regulator', *Reuters*, 27 May 2015, http://www.reuters.com/article/us-alibaba-bank-ldUSKBN0OC0SI20150527.
[86] Ibid.
[87] Ibid.
[88] 'The Fourth Anniversary of MyBank', Sohu, 27 June 2019, http://www.sohu.com/a/323432934_413980.
[89] 'Financial Inclusion Overview', WB, accessed 1 June 2023, https://www.worldbank.org/en/topic/financialinclusion/overview.
[90] MyBank, '2018 Financial Report', p. 4, https://gw.alipayobjects.com/os/basement_prod/a0e755ca-07da-494d-97c3-cf322233dcd2.pdf.
[91] 'The Fourth Anniversary of MyBank', Sohu, 27 June 2019, http://www.sohu.com/a/323432934_413980.

5.7 Could digital banks fit into existing regulatory frameworks?

Despite the difference of distributional methods and customer focus, challenger banks' businesses remain similar to that of existing lenders. Therefore, either challenger banks or incumbent banks have to comply with the same set of regulatory rules in most aspects. In the UK, any firms that wish to conduct deposit-taking businesses have to obtain a Part 4A permission from the PRA, which it will only grant with consent from the FCA.[92] After the authorisation process, a bank will be subject to prudential regulation from the PRA and conduct regulation from the FCA, which together forms the twin-peak regulatory model. The PRA and FCA have set up a New Bank Start-up Unit in order to facilitate the process of filing application for becoming a bank.[93] Financial regulators provide detailed information and support for establishing a bank in regard to five steps: early stages, pre-application, application, mobilisation, and after authorisation.

The PRA and FCA were created by the Financial Services Act 2012, as a regulatory response to the global financial crisis. During the crisis, the UK witnessed the failure of Northern Rock in September 2007, the first bank run in the country since Victorian times.[94] Also, HBOS and RBS were nationalised by the UK government to save the industry and prevent further crisis. Therefore, in order to safeguard the soundness of large financial institutions in the post-crisis era, as well as to maintain the UK's financial stability, the PRA was founded to be in charge of prudential regulation of over 1,700 banks, building societies, insurers, and credit unions in the UK. The PRA has a general objective of promoting the safety and soundness of PRA-authorised persons,[95] and it is empowered to make detailed rules, contained in the PRA Rulebook, for its regulated firms. In the past, the regulatory approach of the Financial Services Authority (FSA) was described as light touched. Even though the FSA was once sceptical about the funding model of Northern Rock, it failed to force the bank to make a change.[96] Currently, the PRA plays a more active role than its predecessor in supervising British banks. For instance, along with the BoE and its Financial Policy Committee, the PRA carried out a series of stress testing to examine whether the balance sheets of

---

[92] Financial Services and Markets Act 2000 (UK), section 55A.
[93] BoE, 'New Bank Start-Up Unit: What You Need to Know from the UK's Financial Regulators', March 2017, http://www.bankofengland.co.uk/pra/Documents/authorisations/newfirmauths/nbsuguide.pdf.
[94] 'Britain's Bank Run: The Bank that Failed', *The Economist*, 20 September 2007, p. 1.
[95] Financial Services and Markets Act 2000 (UK), section 2B(2).
[96] UK Parliament, 'The Run on the Rock: Fifth Report of Session 2007–08', 24 January 2008, https://publications.parliament.uk/pa/cm200708/cmselect/cmtreasy/56/5602.htm.

UK lenders could endure hypothetical situations of economic shocks.[97] In the first round of stress testing in 2014, the Co-operative Bank failed the test and was asked to recapitalise, whilst Lloyds Banking Group and RBS were found at risk when facing the worst economic conditions in the test.[98] Thus, by utilising new regulatory techniques, the PRA seems more capable of preventing bank insolvency and preserving financial stability.

On the other hand, the FCA was made to replace the FSA. It is responsible for regulating the conduct of over 26,000 financial firms in the UK, as well as the prudential behaviours of more than 23,000 firms not supervised by the PRA. The FCA has three operation objectives: protect consumers, enhance market integrity, and promote competition.[99] After it took over, it has been using its administrative power to correct the wrongdoings of banks to protect financial consumers. For example, lots of British consumers have been sold financial products they do not really need by several large banks, like payment protection insurance (PPI). Accordingly, in 2015, the FCA imposed a fine of £117 million on Lloyds Banking Group for its unfair practice regarding handling customers' complaints about PPI.[100] Clearly, the FCA plays an important role in protecting the interests of financial consumers and ensuring the high standard of business conduct in the banking industry. Moreover, promoting competition is another priority of FCA's working tasks, as it knows that allowing consumers to have more choices is the key for having effective competition in the financial industry. When customers are able to switch accounts easily between different financial service providers, firms will have strong incentives to improve the quality of their products and services so as to retain and attract customers.[101] Therefore, the Current Account Switching Service (CASS) was introduced, operated by Pay.UK, an interbank payment system, which covers 99% of the UK market and cuts the time of switching current accounts to only seven days.[102] As of March 2023, the simple and free CASS had helped more than 8 million UK customers to switch bank accounts, and the programme already included almost 50 banks and

---

[97] BoE, 'The Bank of England's Approach to Stress Testing the UK Banking System', October 2015, https://www.bankofengland.co.uk/-/media/boe/files/stress-testing/2015/the-boes-approach-to-stress-testing-the-uk-banking-system.

[98] 'Co-Op Bank Fails Bank of England Stress Tests', BBC, 16 December 2014, https://www.bbc.co.uk/news/business-30491161.

[99] Financial Services and Markets Act 2000 (UK), section 1B.

[100] FCA, 'Final Notice to Lloyds Banking Group', 4 June 2015, https://www.fca.org.uk/publication/final-notices/lloyds-banking-group-2015.pdf

[101] FCA, 'Making Current Account Switching Easier: The Effectiveness of the Current Account Switch Service (CASS) and Evidence on Account Number Portability', March 2015, https://www.fca.org.uk/publication/research/making-current-account-switching-easier.pdf.

[102] 'The Current Account Switch Service—Your Guarantee to a Successful Switch', CASS, accessed 1 June 2023, https://www.currentaccountswitch.co.uk/.

building societies.[103] It benefits challenger lenders considerably as they can solicit customers who are fed up with their original banks.

As for Chinese digital-based challenger banks, they will be subject to the same regulatory requirements as any existing commercial banks. In early 2015, the then banking regulator CBRC reorganised its institutional structure and set up a new department responsible for the supervision of private banks, city commercial banks, and city credit cooperatives.[104] Accordingly, the latest digital banks have been included in China's current banking regulatory framework. However, the innovative online-only banks such as WeBank and MyBank have raised some regulatory concerns. In contrast to traditional banks, they have a distinguished business model based on information technologies like big data and the cloud computing system. Since WeBank and MyBank do not operate brick-and-mortar branches, most services including account opening and loan application are executed online. Therefore, the verification of users' identification remains a complicated technical and legal issue. WeBank has developed a facial recognition system to verify users' identities. The bank is working with the National Citizen Identity Card Query Service Centre (affiliated to the PRC Ministry of Public Security), so that it is able to accurately and timely ascertain users' identities online by cross-examining their online video image, the photos on identity cards, and other biological information provided by the Centre.[105] However, Chinese law does require that customers need to personally visit a bank branch to complete an identity check if they plan to borrow a loan, so whether this new identity recognition system can replace the in-person check remains unclear.

In December 2016, the CBRC released the 'Guiding Opinions on Supervising Private Banks' (the 'Opinions'), which outlined the general rules and guidelines for the supervision of newly founded privately owned banks and digital challenger banks. The overall principle is to ensure prudential regulation and innovative development at the same time, as well as the combination of unified regulation and differentiated regulation.[106] Unified regulation means that private banks should comply with any existing prudential regulatory requirements for commercial banks, while differentiated

---

[103] Ibid.
[104] In April 2018, the CBRC ceased operation and was merged into the CBIRC. Then, in March 2023, the government announced the plan to replace the CBIRC with the newly founded National Financial Regulatory Administration (NFRA). See Chinese Government, 'China to Set up National Financial Regulatory Administration', 7 March 2023, https://english.www.gov.cn/news/topnews/202303/07/content_WS6406ffa2c6d0a757729e7d6c.html.
[105] 'Tencent to Work with Authorities to Improve Facial Recognition for Banking Use', *Xinhua*, 15 April 2015, https://www.chinadaily.com.cn/business/tech/2015-04/15/content_20441029.htm.
[106] CBRC, 'CBRC's Guiding Opinions on Supervising Private Banks', YINJIANFA (2016) No. 57, Article 1.

regulation suggests that based on the special characteristics of private banks, the regulator will set separate regulatory arrangements if necessary. There are some key points of the development strategy for private banks: (1) specialised operation—private banks should set the proper development direction, clarify differentiated development strategies and practical business policies, leverage on comparative advantages, and play a complementary role to existing commercial banks; (2) market positioning—private banks should focus on basic banking businesses such as deposit-taking, loan-making, and FXs, serve for the real economy—especially micro, small, and medium-sized enterprises, rural areas, and local communities—and provide more targeted and convenient services for entrepreneurs and innovative businesses; (3) model innovation—the regulator encourages private banks to explore new business models like 'big deposits, small loans' and 'individual deposits, small loans', so as to match the financing demands of the economy; and (4) technological application—the regulatory requirements support private banks to utilise latest technologies including big data, cloud computing, and mobile internet, to achieve the innovations in products, services, and management, to offer inclusive financial services, contributing to the sustainable and innovative growth of the banking industry.[107]

In terms of prudential regulation for new banks, the regulator will focus on certain areas: corporate governance, capital adequacy management, risk management, related party transaction management, and shareholding management.[108] The regulator also aims to strengthen the regulation of the shareholders of private banks. For example, the actual controlling shareholders should be Chinese residents without dual nationalities or foreign permanent residence.[109] It means that the founders of private banks should represent 100% of capital coming from China. In addition, shareholders are asked to report to the local branches of the banking regulator in terms of the following issues: audited annual financial reports; change of registered capital and issues regarding the merger and division of businesses; change of shareholding structure (above 5%) or actual controlling party, and introduction of external strategic investors; change of related parties; large litigations or disputes, significant business risks, and other significant changes of business operation; and other reporting requirements by the CBRC. Finally, the Opinions ask the banking regulator and its local offices to strengthen cooperation and coordination with other authorities and local governments,

---

[107] Ibid., Article 2.
[108] Ibid., Article 3.
[109] Ibid., Article 4(1).

building an information-sharing mechanism for effective regulation.[110] The regulators aim to establish a preventative mechanism to handle emergent accidents and potential risks, as well as setting up a market exit mechanism for private banks that fall into insolvency.

In the 2019 government working report, the then Chinese premier Li Keqiang announced that the government would encourage the development of private banks and community banks in order to serve the real economy and optimise the financial system.[111] So far there have been 18 private banks obtaining regulatory approvals from the banking regulator, among which 17 have already started operation. The vice-chairman of CBIRC, Cao Yu, expressed that, 'there will be no quota or scale limitations on private banks. Any applicants meeting relevant standards will be approved in a normalised way.'[112] As of early 2019, outstanding loans from private banks to small and micro enterprises amounted to CNY50.4 billion and the number of borrowers reached 1.55 million.[113] Based on the financial technologies and massive client resources of funding shareholders, the new digital challenger banks have been providing tailored financial services for e-commerce entrepreneurs, small businesses, and farmers in China, forming a unique business model that is able to achieve a more inclusive financial industry. The British and Chinese regulators' experience in regulating digital banks has provided some insight into the global regulatory reform.

5.8 Further regulatory concerns over digital banks

As discussed, digital-focused challenger banks have to comply with most regulatory standards governing existing commercial banks. However, owing to their distinctive business models and technologies, challenger banks are likely to receive some differentiated treatment from financial regulators, giving them more space to grow and serve the niche market. Since regulators have established the same rules for all lenders, whether they are big banks with a thousand branches or online-only banks with no branches, it is obvious that the small market scale of digital challenger banks has forced them to bear relatively high compliance costs. It is reported that it cost more money for smaller banks to access payment services that are run by dominant

---

[110] Ibid., Article 5(5).
[111] Chinese Government, '2019 Government Working Report', 5 March 2019, http://www.gov.cn/zhuanti/2019qglh/2019lhzfgzbg/index.htm.
[112] 'Close Supervision Over Private Banks', *Caijing*, 11 June 2019, http://finance.caijing.com.cn/20190611/4594723.shtml.
[113] Ibid.

banks.[114] This section analyses four regulatory issues that are of particular relevance to digital banks: deposit insurance, capital requirements, data protection and privacy, and financial innovation.

5.8.1 Deposit insurance

Deposit insurance is an important financial infrastructure that guarantees the savings of depositors to be repaid in the event of bank failure. It has become a prevalent institutional design for most countries having a banking industry. Deposit insurance is perceived as an effective mechanism protecting depositors for, if their banks become insolvent, they do not need to wait for the completion of the liquidation process to get their money back or to worry about getting only a small proportion of their entire savings. Deposit insurance works along with the lender of last resort and the government bailout as one country's financial safety net which can prevent bank runs and maintain financial stability.[115] According to the International Association of Deposit Insurers (IADI), there were 145 jurisdictions that had established explicit deposit insurance schemes as of July 2019, up from 12 in 1974.[116] Obviously, deposit insurance has shown its importance when there is an increasing number of digital challenger banks being established across the world. The new banks with innovative technologies and business models are prone to extra risks and bank failures, which might result in financial losses for savers. With deposit insurance, users of digital banks are protected against potential monetary losses, encouraging more financial consumers to try the services of new banks offering better quality and more convenience. However, it can also lead to the problem of moral hazards, as financial consumers do not need to consider the risks of their service providers since any bad consequences will be undertaken by deposit insurers.

The US was the first country to establish a national deposit insurance scheme, which is currently managed by the FDIC. It was founded in 1934 during the Great Depression when thousands of US banks failed. The US has around 27,000 deposit-taking institutions and bank failures are not rare, as we saw in the run of Silicon Valley Bank in March 2023. It seemed necessary for the federal government to establish such a mechanism to deal with

---

[114] Sharlene Goff, 'Challenger Banks Have the Big Four in their Sights', *The Financial Times*, 16 August 2014, p. 8.
[115] Heidi M. Schooner and Michael W. Taylor, *Global Bank Regulation: Principles and Policies* (Cambridge, MA: Academic Press, 2010), p. 52.
[116] IADI, 'Deposit Insurance Systems', accessed 1 June 2023, https://www.iadi.org/en/deposit-insurance-systems/.

failed banks, to compensate depositors, and to restore financial stability. The coverage of FDIC was $100,000 per depositor per bank before 2008. The compensation standard was raised to $250,000 after the global financial crisis.[117] In the UK, authorised banks are registered under the FSCS, which is the country's deposit insurer. The money of British savers will be reimbursed by the FSCS if their banks encounter financial difficulties. The deposit compensation limit in the UK is £85,000 per person per bank, regardless of how many accounts a customer hold.[118] In case of a joint account, the limit of compensation is doubled to £170,000. In China, its recently established deposit insurance scheme can compensate CNY500,000 per saver per bank, which is able to cover 98% of all deposit accounts in China's commercial banks.[119]

5.8.2 Capital requirements

In most cases, the regulatory rules apply equally to all banks including challenger lenders. However, the current banking regulatory framework is said to favour incumbent banks over challengers, especially the capital requirements.[120] The PRA's regulatory approach to Pillar 2A capital, a regulatory requirement for lenders on the add-ons of capitals that individual companies have to set aside above the sector's minimum standard, is an example of the capital rules that might be disadvantageous for digital banks. In light of Pillar 2A, challenger banks have to calculate their capital requirements based on the riskiness of each loan they have extended, by using the PRA's standardised model. As challenger banks are new to the market, they lack track business data and loan records as well as have a more radical business model, so their businesses are likely to be considered as containing more risks. It results in a higher risk rating and therefore higher capital add-ons. In contrast, established banks, based on their historic lending data, are able to use their own customised models to calculate the riskiness of loans, which normally results in lower capital requirements compared with banks using the standardised model. The variation between two models can be as much as 960% for residential mortgages.[121] It means that more of challenger banks' capitals shall be held in reserve rather than being lent

---

[117] FDIC, 'How Are My Deposit Accounts Insured by the FDIC?', 12 April 2023, http://www.fdic.gov/deposit/covered/categories.html.
[118] FSCS, 'What We Cover', accessed 1 June 2023, https://www.fscs.org.uk/what-we-cover/.
[119] Lerong Lu, 'Private Banks in China: Origin, Challenges and Regulatory Implications'. *Banking and Finance Law Review* (2016) 31: 585, 598.
[120] KPMG, 'The Game Changers: Challenger Banking Results', May 2015, p. 17.
[121] Kathryn Gaw, 'Bank of England Relaxes Regulations for Challenger Banks', FT Adviser, 27 February 2017, https://www.ftadviser.com/Articles/2017/02/24/FTA-Challenger-banks.

out, leading to a major competitive disadvantage. In this regard, the current regulatory practices in the banking sector might prejudice the further development of emerging digital banks. The British Bankers' Association (BBA) has addressed this issue to the regulators by proposing a more flexible risk assessment regime which can reduce the impacts of negative rating on challenger banks.[122] In February 2017, the PRA issued a consultation paper and pledged to alter the Pillar 2A capital requirements to allow challenger banks and small lenders to provide more competitive mortgage services for UK consumers.[123]

5.8.3 Financial security and data protection

Digital-only banks such as Monzo, Starling, and WeBank, whilst offering better user experience and convenience, also raise concerns regarding security issues and personal data protection. In traditional banking, most financial activities, such as opening accounts and applying for loans, have to be done in person at a physical branch. As more and more banking activities are moving online, regulators have to ensure that such practices will be subject to the same level of supervision as they are completed in store, to protect the interests of financial consumers. In particular, the in-app identity verification of mobile users by employing facial recognition, voice recognition, fingerprint sensors, and other bio data needs more regulatory scrutiny to enhance the safety level. Moreover, digital financial service providers have to pay extra attention to safeguard the personal data of their users, as well as combating phishing websites and mobile apps and preventing other fraud mechanisms that might be exploited by financial crimes. Personal data including bio data can only be collected, stored, used, and shared by banks if full consent is obtained from users. Otherwise, digital banks would breach privacy law and data protection regulations in a given jurisdiction and face potential fines or even criminal charges. Moreover, digital banks are recommended to hold regular consumer education activities to raise the risk awareness and good habits of users when accessing financial services online and via smartphone apps.

---

[122] BBA, 'Promoting Competition in the UK Banking Industry Report' (2014).
[123] BoE, 'Refining the PRA's Pillar 2A Capital Framework', Policy Statement 22/17, 3 October 2017, https://www.bankofengland.co.uk/prudential-regulation/publication/2017/refining-the-pra-pillar-2a-capital-framework.

5.8.4 Financial innovation incubator

For global financial regulators working with emerging Fintech platforms, such as digital challenger banks, finding a balance between financial innovation, financial stability, and consumer protection has remained a major challenge. Take the UK's FCA as an example. The FCA puts the competitive objective at the centre of its regulatory work, which stimulates the growth of disrupters in the financial industry to promote innovation and competition. Its regulatory sandbox initiative has caught worldwide attention, and is said to cement the UK's position as a leading Fintech country. The sandbox allows businesses to test novel products, services, business models, and delivery mechanisms under a temporary lighter regulatory environment, which is beneficial for Fintech businesses, including digital challenger banks.[124] Clearly, financial innovation defies conventional business models, services, and products. Thus, it is difficult for challengers to innovate under the existing regulatory standards that have been designed for the existing players. Accordingly, the FCA's sandbox regime can help firms test their products in a safer and more flexible environment without the overhaul of regulatory systems. It is likely to create a win-win situation for Fintech businesses, regulators, and financial consumers. Over 550 applications have been submitted to the regulatory sandbox since it opened, including Fintech platforms for distributed ledger technology (DLT), AI, open banking, API, digital ID, embedded finance, services aimed at facilitating access to finance, and RegTech.[125] It is obvious that digitally focused challenger banks can use the sandbox to conduct Fintech experiments, such as reimagining how banking services are delivered and creating custom financial products for customers, without being restricted by regulatory red tape.

5.9 Conclusion

The chapter has considered the rising digital-focused challenger banks as an example of the Fintech revolution happening in the area of banking services. The global financial crisis, bank failures, and scandals of some large banks have undermined people's confidence in the established institutions.

---

[124] FCA, 'Regulatory Sandbox', November 2015, https://www.fca.org.uk/publication/research/regulatory-sandbox.pdf.
[125] FCA, 'Regulatory Sandbox Accepted Firms', 21 February 2023, https://www.fca.org.uk/firms/innovation/regulatory-sandbox/accepted-firms.

In contrast, digital challenger banks, with no historical legacies, have adopted a simplified and low-cost business model based on the internet and smartphone apps, giving them a strong competitive advantage. At present, digital banks across the world mainly target niche markets, serving marginalised customers such as small businesses, internet entrepreneurs, and personal consumers in rural areas who are overlooked by incumbent banks. The special market focus and customer-centric spirit enable those Fintech disrupters to occupy substantial market shares within a short period of time. Both the UK and China have witnessed the establishment and success of several digital-focused challenger banks, such as Monzo, Starling, Revolut, and WeBank. Some of them were launched by tech entrepreneurs or senior bankers, while others have been backed by BigTech such as Tencent and Alibaba. They have distinctive channels of providing financial services and are known for promoting financial inclusion.

In terms of financial regulation and supervision, challenger banks are no exception. They have to comply with all the existing regulatory rules set for any commercial banks. However, the current banking regulatory system is said to favour mainstream lenders over newcomers. Challenger banks have to hold larger capital buffers than traditional banks do, restricting their lending abilities and potential growth. Competition plays a key role in improving the quality of financial services for consumers. Therefore, financial regulators, such as the FCA and CBIRC, have endeavoured to create a level playing field for both challenger banks and incumbent lenders. The regulatory sandbox regime is a good example of allowing Fintech companies to innovate and experiment novel banking businesses without bearing the burden of existing regulatory duties in full. Moreover, as most digital banks have employed big data, AI, and other information technologies to provide convenient services, regulators should pay extra attention to safeguard the financial security and data safety of financial consumers using app-based banking services. Finally, digital-based challenger banks might pose a threat to consumer protection and financial stability, as there are likely to be more bank runs as a result of intensified competition in the banking industry. Therefore, a well-functioning deposit insurance system is necessary for any countries that are experiencing the Fintech revolution. Deposit insurance can not only compensate the financial losses of savers in the event of bank failures, but also reduce the possibility of bank runs as it boosts the confidence of depositors. Together with other elements of the financial safety net, deposit insurance could help mitigate the systemic risks and promote financial stability.

6
Fintech in Online Lending Marketplaces

6.1 Introduction

This chapter explores the Fintech revolution happening in the field of online lending. The emphasis of the discussion is corporate finance. It asks whether online P2P lending improves the effectiveness of allocating financial resources and if it fosters financial equality among different sizes of corporations. P2P lending is the practice of lending to unrelated individuals or businesses through online platforms without the involvement of traditional banks.[1] Crowdfunding, which refers to the practice of funding a project or business venture by raising small amounts of money from a large number of people via online portals, is a concept similar to P2P lending. In the UK, P2P lending is viewed as loan-based crowdfunding by the financial regulators.[2] It is said to benefit both sides of the lending parties, for it increases the amount of money available for both consumer and business borrowers while giving investors more investment options and higher returns. In 2005, Zopa, the world's first online lending platform, was launched in the UK. The country now has more than 70 active online lending websites, such as Funding Circle, LendInvest, Assetz Capital, and Folk2Folk. The UK P2P lending industry was expected to generate £365 million in revenue in 2023.[3] Other countries like the US, China, Singapore, India, Brazil, Russia, France, and Germany all have sizable online lending markets.

Across the globe, P2P lending has been widely used by SMEs as an alternative financing method in the absence of sufficient bank loans and other traditional credit products. After the Covid-19 pandemic, the financing challenges faced by SMEs have become a pressing concern for policy-makers because they might jeopardise innovation, competition, and economic development. Although SMEs are of critical importance to national economies, they are reported to experience constant financing restraints. For instance,

---

[1] 'Peer-to-Peer Lending: Banking Without Banks', *The Economist*, 1 March 2014, p. 70.
[2] FCA, 'Crowdfunding', 18 April 2016, http://www.fca.org.uk/consumers/financial-services-products/investments/types-of-investment/crowdfunding.
[3] IbisWorld, 'Peer-to-Peer Lending Platforms in the UK—Market Size 2010–2028', 21 March 2022, https://www.ibisworld.com/united-kingdom/market-size/peer-to-lending-platforms/.

SMEs represent 99% of the business population in Europe.[4] They produce 66% of the jobs and 58% of the economic output in the EU, but the total amount of bank credit they received decreased by 35% in the 2010s.[5] Across the Atlantic, the lending amount of the ten biggest US banks to small businesses totalled $44.7 billion in 2014, down 33% from $72.5 billion in 2006.[6] Similar trends can be observed in the Asia-Pacific region, where SMEs take up 96% of the total business number and produce 62% of employment as well as 42% of the region's aggregated GDP.[7] In stark comparison, only 18.7% of all bank loans in the Asia-Pacific region go to SMEs. The SME financing dilemma in the post-crisis period is undoubtedly a worldwide phenomenon that has attracted intense media, policy-making, and academic attention. This has prompted the development of more alternative financing options for SMEs, including the burgeoning online P2P lending market, which is frequently regarded as the most practical financing choice for smaller companies.

In light of this, the goal of this chapter is to analyse the global expansion of online P2P lending marketplaces and its implications for policy-makers and regulators regarding alternative financing for SMEs. Section 6.2 considers the economic importance and financial dilemma of SMEs and illustrates the pressing need for SMEs to have P2P lending as an alternative financing option. Sections 6.3–6.5 present the online P2P lending markets in three countries with the most online lending transactions: the UK, the US, and China. Section 6.6 examines a number of benefits that P2P loans have over bank loans for both borrowers and investors, including more diverse funding sources, higher investment returns, the expedited process, and increased transparency. Section 6.7 investigates the policies and regulatory frameworks governing the P2P lending industry. Section 6.8 makes a tentative conclusion.

6.2 SMEs' financing difficulty and alternative finance

The SME financing puzzle in the post-crisis era has become a global phenomenon, drawing intense attention from the media, policy-makers, and academics. SMEs' limited access to financing resources, to a large extent,

---

[4] European Commission, 'Access to Finance for SMEs', accessed 1 June 2023, http://ec.europa.eu/growth/access-to-finance_en.
[5] 'Financing Europe's Small Firms: Don't Bank on the Banks', *The Economist*, 16 August 2014, p. 57.
[6] Ruth Simon, 'Big Banks Cut Back on Small Business', *The Wall Street Journal*, 27 November 2015, A1.
[7] Asian Development Bank, 'Asia's SMEs Need Growth Capital To Become More Competitive—ADB Report', 2 September 2015, http://www.adb.org/news/asia-s-smes-need-growth-capital-become-more-competitive-adb-report.

results from banks' unwillingness to lend, as the current financial regulatory regime seems to discourage risk-taking. A large number of SMEs lacking credit history or effective collaterals are likely to be refused by mainstream financial institutions. For example, 26% of SMEs in the UK seeking to borrow a bank loan or overdraft have received a rejection letter.[8] Prior to the development of online lending, the majority of people, including policy-makers, thought that the problem of SME funding could only be solved by expanding the availability of bank credit. This is because most SMEs, unlike large businesses and multinational companies which can raise funds from international capital markets, primarily rely on domestic banks to borrow money. In the current economic environment, many banks are hesitant to lend money to what they view as risky start-ups, so government policies to encourage bank lending to SMEs don't seem to be working. As a result, only alternative finance markets, which include financial instruments and distribution channels that are developing outside of the conventional financial industry, can help close the SME financing gap.[9] Among different alternative finance methods, the burgeoning online P2P lending market is likely to be the most feasible financing option for SMEs.

SMEs are independent and non-subsidiary firms having employees no more than a given number. The classification standards of SMEs vary across different jurisdictions. In the UK, SMEs refer to any businesses with 0–250 employees. A small-sized company should satisfy at least two of the following standards: the turnover is no more than £10.2 million; the balance sheet total is no more than £5.1 million; and the number of employees should not exceed 50.[10] Similarly, a medium-sized company should meet at least two of the following standards: the turnover is no more than £36 million; the balance sheet total is no more than £18 million; and the number of employees should not exceed 250.[11] Apart from these criteria, authorities such as the Bank of England have used different methodologies to classify businesses in different sizes. For example, large businesses mean enterprises with an annual debit account turnover over £25 million, while SMEs are those with an annual debit account turnover less than £25 million.[12] SMEs are entitled to extra financial supports and benefits from governments under various policy

---

[8] Martin Arnold, 'Alternative Finance Route for Small Firms', *The Financial Times*, 5 November 2016, p. 2.
[9] University of Cambridge and EY, 'Moving Mainstream: The European Alternative Finance Benchmarking Report', February 2015, p. 9, https://www.jbs.cam.ac.uk/faculty-research/centres/alternative-finance/publications/moving-mainstream/.
[10] Companies Act 2006 (UK), section 382.
[11] Companies Act 2006 (UK), section 465.
[12] BoE, 'Credit Conditions Review 2017 Q1', 13 April 2017, https://www.bankofengland.co.uk/credit-conditions-review/2017/2017-q1.

initiatives, including research funding, competitiveness and innovation funding, lax regulatory requirements, and reduced fees for administrative compliance.[13]

SMEs play an important and indispensable role in the UK's national economy. As Table 6.1 shows, there were approximately 5.5 million businesses in the UK's private sector in 2022. SMEs (5,501,260) stood for 99.9% of the business population, while large corporations (7,675) took up only 0.1% of the total number. The combined annual turnover of all British SMEs amounted to £2.12 trillion (51.1% of the private sector), compared with £2.03 trillion (48.9%) for large businesses. Moreover, SMEs hired 16.4 million people (60.5%) in the private sector, compared with 10.6 million employees (39.5%) working for large businesses in the UK. It is obvious that SMEs offer the majority of working opportunities, which is critical to the government's policies of promoting employment and economic growth. A survey suggested that most university students (86%) in the UK, despite their preference to join household-name companies after graduation, finally ended up working for SMEs and only14% of graduates would be recruited by large corporations.[14] This indicates that helping SMEs will result in more jobs being created for future generations.

In terms of overall economic outputs, SMEs have contributed to 49.8% of GDP in the UK.[15] SMEs have been dominating most business sectors,

Table 6.1 The number of businesses, with employment and turnover figures, in the UK.

	Business number	Employment (thousands)	Turnover (£ millions)
All businesses	5,508,935	27,054	4,156,773
SMEs (0–250 employees)	5,501,260	16,432	2,124,439
Large enterprises (over 250 employees)	7,675	10,622	2,032,334

Source: Department for Business, Energy and Industrial Strategy, 'Business Population Estimates for the UK and the Regions 2022', UK Government, 6 October 2022, https://www.gov.uk/government/statistics/business-population-estimates-2022/business-population-estimates-for-the-uk-and-regions-2022-statistical-release-html.

---

[13] 'What Is an SME?', European Commission, accessed 1 June 2023, http://ec.europa.eu/growth/smes/business-friendly-environment/sme-definition_en.
[14] 'Working for Small Businesses', University of Kent, accessed 1 June 2023, http://www.kent.ac.uk/careers/sme.htm.
[15] Matthew Ward and Chris Rhodes, 'Small Businesses and the UK Economy', UK Parliament, 9 December 2014, p. 7, https://researchbriefings.files.parliament.uk/documents/SN06078/SN06078.pdf.

especially three industries: 'construction' (914,000 or 17% of all SMEs), 'professional, scientific, and technical activities' (762,000 or 14%), and 'wholesale and retail trade and repair' (547,000 or 10%).[16] Owners of SMEs tend to share a more optimistic view about their business prospects, suggesting that they are likely to be the main source of economic growth in any country. According to the British Business Bank (BBB), 46% of SMEs planned to grow turnover, while most large businesses just aimed to maintain their current market shares.[17] After the UK's withdrawal of EU membership (Brexit), small businesses are expected to experience fast growth amidst the overall economic slowdown.[18]

Moreover, the employees of SMEs generally feel more satisfied with their jobs than those serving large corporations. A survey conducted by the Trades Union Congress indicated that SME employees had the highest job satisfaction rate (21% strongly agreeing and 41% tending to agree) compared with people employed elsewhere.[19] The survey also suggested that SME employees were most committed (64%) and loyal (58%) to their employers.[20] Moreover, SME employees have been given more freedom to choose personal working patterns. They encountered fewer cases of bullying at work and lower stress level, as well as had fewer complaints about overtime working. In a nutshell, SME employees are considered as the happiest employees who enjoy a better work–life balance, encouraging more people to start their own businesses or join smaller firms from large corporations. SMEs seem to be an ideal working place for people who value flexible working styles, which are the trend after the Covid-19 pandemic.

Theoretically speaking, SMEs are able to draw upon a variety of financing methods to obtain credit or capital to fund their business operation. Bank loans play a principal role in SME financing, but there also exist multiple non-bank financing channels.[21] Corporate financing methods can be divided into internal funding and external funding.[22] Internal financing means an

---

[16] Department for Business, Energy and Industrial Strategy, 'Business Population Estimates for the UK and the Regions 2022', UK Government, 6 October 2022, p. 14, https://www.gov.uk/government/statistics/business-population-estimates-2022/business-population-estimates-for-the-uk-and-regions-2022-statistical-release-html.

[17] BBB, 'Small Business Finance Markets 2014', p. 4, https://www.british-business-bank.co.uk/research/small-business-finance-markets-2014/.

[18] Tim Wallace, 'SMEs Expect to Grow Faster Next Year Despite Brexit Vote', *The Telegraph*, 1 October 2016, http://www.telegraph.co.uk/business/2016/10/01/smes-expect-to-grow-faster-next-year-despite-brexit-vote/.

[19] Federation of Small Businesses, 'Happiest Employees Work for Small Businesses', 2 September 2008, http://www.fsb.org.uk/news.aspx?rec=4749.

[20] Ibid.

[21] BIS, 'SME Access to External Finance', BIS Economics Paper No.16, January 2012, p. 6.

[22] R. Glenn Hubbard, Anil K. Kashyap, and Toni M. Whited, 'Internal Finance and Firm Investment'. *Journal of Money, Credit and Banking* (1995) 27: 683–701.

enterprise acquiring financing sources inside the business itself, such as raising capital from existing shareholders or using retained profits in previous financial years. In contrast, external financing allows entrepreneurs to gain funds from sources outside the business, such as bank loans, P2P loans, asset financing, and VC.

Further, corporate finance theories have categorised financing approaches into debt financing and equity financing.[23] In debt financing, a company borrows money from a person, a company, or a bank with the agreement to return the principal and interest at a later date. Bank loans, overdrafts, and private lending are typical examples of debt financing which has certain advantages over equity financing. Bounded by loan agreements, lenders are unable to intervene or control borrowers' business. Also, the costs of financing are more predictable and could be spread through a fixed period of time. The disadvantage of debt financing, however, is that borrowers are obliged to repay funds on a regular basis, even if the economic environment or business condition deteriorate. On the other hand, corporates can make use of equity financing to raise capital by selling shares to existing or new investors through PE, VC, or public share offering. PE funds target established businesses as they seek acquisition or full control of companies with a mature business model, while VC funds tend to limit their investment decisions to early-stage companies and have a strong preference for businesses in the technology sector.[24] Public share issuance, such as IPO, is the process of selling shares to public investors and listing shares on the regulated stock exchanges. The IPO procedure is complicated, costly, and time-consuming, and involves the work of a group of financial and legal advisors.[25] As a result, accessing capital markets to raise funds has been a preserve for large companies rather than SMEs. Equity financing has some substantial benefits. For instance, equity investors, who become shareholders of the businesses that raise funds, will undertake and share any risks of business operation with existing shareholders. The money invested is not allowed to be returned to shareholders in most circumstances. The downside of equity financing is that entrepreneurs have to distribute business profits to any new investors (shareholders), who have voting rights and can participate in the corporate decision-making process.

Despite having various financing approaches, SMEs find it difficult to obtain sufficient credits from the banking sector. The situation has gotten

---

[23] David Hillier et al., *Corporate Finance*, 2nd ed. (New York: McGraw-Hill Higher Education, 2013), p. 527.
[24] Small Business Service, 'A Mapping Study of Venture Capital Provision to SMEs in England', October 2015, p. 5.
[25] Alan Dignam and John Lowry, *Company Law*, 12th ed. (Oxford: Oxford University Press, 2022), p. 61.

worse after the global financial crisis, the Covid-19 pandemic, and the subsequent economic slowdowns, when most businesses, big or small, have encountered weakening consumer demand and plummeting sales and profits. As the UK has been keeping a close trading relationship with the rest of the world, its businesses have suffered significant financial losses owing to the worldwide economic recessions through trade, finance, and other channels.[26] In particular, SMEs have been heavily hit by the crises, as they not only faced squeezed revenues and profit margins but also encountered a reducing amount of bank credit. As a response to the deteriorating macroeconomic environment, the financial industry has become more risk-averse, so banks feel more reluctant to extend loans to SME borrowers. There has been a continuous decline in the amount of bank loans available for SMEs, as banks tightened their lending criteria amidst risk concerns.[27] Prior to the crises, the financial industry observed intense competition as banks competed to lend out money to win greater market share. Thus, at that time, banks had less stringent loan requirements for SME borrowers. Nowadays, however, banks have become cautious about excessive risk-taking owing to stricter regulatory standards imposed by the international organisations and national financial authorities, such as Basel III which requires banks to hold extra capital buffers against risky assets.[28] As a consequence, a great number of SMEs not having credit data and valid collaterals have been denied their bank loan applications. In 2007, 90% of SMEs seeking external finance managed to secure funding, but the figure fell sharply to 74% in the 2010s. Access to finance has become a top challenge for European SMEs, along with other urgent issues like customer-finding, the cost of production or labour, and the availability of skilled staff.[29]

From the BoE's official lending data, we can observe the great inequality regarding the allocation of bank credits towards business borrowers in different magnitude. In February 2023, UK financial institutions lent a total of £21.01 billion to all businesses.[30] Loans worth £5.08 billion (24.2%) were granted to SMEs, while £15.93 billion (75.8%) was given to large businesses.[31]

---

[26] Shiv Chowla, Lucia Quaglietti, and Lukasz Rachel, 'How Have World Shocks Affected the UK Economy?', Bank of England Quarterly Bulletin 2014 Q2, p. 167, https://www.bankofengland.co.uk/-/media/boe/files/quarterly-bulletin/2014/how-have-world-shocks-affected-the-uk-economy.pdf.
[27] BIS, 'SME Access to External Finance', BIS Economics Paper No.16, January 2012.
[28] BIS, 'Basel III: A Global Regulatory Framework for More Resilient Banks and Banking Systems', June 2011, https://www.bis.org/publ/bcbs189.pdf.
[29] European Commission, 'Annual Report on European SMEs 2015/2016', November 2016, p. 20, https://op.europa.eu/en/publication-detail/-/publication/4872cbee-aa5a-11e6-aab7-01aa75ed71a1.
[30] BoE, 'Bankstats Tables—Table A8.1', accessed 1 June 2023, https://www.bankofengland.co.uk/statistics/tables.
[31] Ibid.

As discussed previously, UK SMEs account for 99.9% of private businesses, 60% of employment, and half of the national GDP. By contrast, they only obtain less than a quarter of total business loans in the country. Evidently, the amount of bank loans given to SMEs is not commensurate with their economic status or actual demand, giving rise to the financing dilemma of SMEs. The problem has been further compounded by other factors. In terms of the approval rate of bank loan applications, it was 79% for small-sized businesses and 88% for medium-sized businesses.[32] It means that larger businesses have a better chance of securing bank loans. This is because most lending managers assume that the level of credit risk will go down with the increase of business size. Each year, around 100,000 small businesses in the UK have about £4 billion loan applications rejected by major banks.[33] Evidently, SMEs need sufficient funding to grow and prosper; otherwise they would lose business opportunities to large corporations or even foreign competitors. The unequal credit provision towards different businesses leads to the SME financing puzzle, which could possibly be mitigated by alternative finance methods.

6.3 P2P lending in the UK

The UK is the birthplace for online P2P lending markets, as the world's first P2P lending platform Zopa was launched in London in 2005, and since then the UK's P2P lending industry has experienced fast expansion. Through online platforms, British P2P lenders have been matching individual and business borrowers with investors who have spare money and capital, skipping traditional banks as credit intermediaries in the lending chain. According to the UK's P2P Finance Association (now the 36H Group under Innovate Finance), P2P lending refers to a debt-based funding arrangement made possible by an electronic network that consists of direct one-to-one contracts between a single recipient and a number of fund providers.[34] Whereas borrowers of P2P loans are typically small businesses or retail consumers, a significant proportion of lenders are retail consumers. P2P lending is also called 'loan-based crowdfunding' in the UK, and the concept of which

---

[32] BBA, 'Bank Support for SMEs—4th Quarter 2016', http://www.bba.org.uk/news/statistics/sme-statistics/bank-support-for-smes-4th-quarter-2016/.

[33] Martin Arnold, 'Alternative Finance Route for Small Firms', *The Financial Times*, 5 November 2016, p. 2.

[34] The Peer-to-Peer Finance Association, 'Rules of the Peer-to-Peer Finance Association', May 2015, Para. 2.1.

Table 6.2 The five largest P2P lending platforms in the UK by loan volume.

Rank	1	2	3	4	5
P2P lending platform	Funding Circle	Zopa	LendInvest	Assetz Capital	Folk2Folk
Founding year	2010	2005	2013	2012	2013
Total loan volume	£8.3 billion	£5.66 billion	£3 billion	£1.4 billion	£460 million

Source: The table is compiled based on Kathryn Gaw, 'The Five Largest P2P Platforms by Lending Volumes', P2P Finance News, 27 August 2021, https://p2pfinancenews.co.uk/2021/08/27/revealed-the-five-largest-p2p-platforms-by-lending-volumes/.

was invented by the FCA.[35] It belongs to the booming alternative finance markets which include financial instruments and distributive channels operating outside of the traditional financial industry.[36] Moreover, it is dubbed as 'banking without banks', which brings a better deal for participants in any online lending agreement.[37] It reduces transactional costs for borrowers and offers more investment opportunities at better rates for ordinary savers. Most borrowers of P2P loans in the UK are consumers and small businesses having restricted access to banks. When making P2P loan applications, borrowers have to submit relevant documents online, and then lending platforms will carry out the identity check, credit risk evaluation, and other due diligence work. If borrowers satisfy relevant lending criteria, their prospective loans will be listed on an electronic marketplace and would soon be funded by registered investors.

The UK owns the largest alternative finance market in Europe, representing 74.3% of total market share.[38] At present, the UK holds over 80 P2P lending platforms underwriting P2P loans in billions of pounds each year. Table 6.2 lists the five largest P2P lending platforms in the UK by the total amount of loans they have extended. Funding Circle and Zopa are the top players in the industry, as they have made loans worth £8.3 and £5.66 billion respectively since their inception. Other platforms are also growing quickly. There are currently four P2P lending platforms with loan values over

---

[35] FCA, 'Crowdfunding', 18 April 2016, https://www.fca.org.uk/consumers/crowdfunding.
[36] University of Cambridge and EY, 'Moving Mainstream: The European Alternative Finance Benchmarking Report', February 2015, https://www.jbs.cam.ac.uk/faculty-research/centres/alternative-finance/publications/moving-mainstream/.
[37] 'Peer-to-Peer Lending: Banking Without Banks', The Economist, 1 March 2014, p. 70.
[38] University of Cambridge and EY, 'Moving Mainstream: The European Alternative Finance Benchmarking Report', February 2015, p. 13, https://www.jbs.cam.ac.uk/faculty-research/centres/alternative-finance/publications/moving-mainstream/.

£1 billion and at least seven platforms with lending volumes over £100 million. Some of them have specialised market targets. Nearly £0.5 billion was lent by Folk2Folk to company owners, farmers, and real-estate developers in the UK. Assetz Capital was among the few alternative lenders chosen by the government to offer the Coronavirus Business Interruption Loan Scheme (CBILS) during the Covid-19 pandemic.[39] The CBILS allows P2P lenders to offer facilities of up to £5 million to smaller businesses in the UK that are suffering disruptions in their cash flow due to lost or delayed revenues. It offers a large selection of commercial finance products, such as term loans, overdrafts, invoice financing, and asset financing options. Clearly, the P2P lending industry has evolved into a relatively mature market which plays a vital role in the UK's economy. P2P lenders have gradually moved towards mainstream and form a key component of the financial industry. According to one estimate, the lending capacity of all P2P platforms was equivalent to 2% of banks in 2014, and the figure is expected to exceed 10% in the 2020s.[40] Despite the fact that P2P lending constitutes a small proportion of total lending in the financial industry, its growth potential should not be underestimated. In addition, Table 6.2 shows a high level of market concentration in the UK's online lending market. The top three platforms (Zopa, Funding Circle, and LendInvest) account for almost 60% of total loans. This could have a negative impact on the industry's growth owing to the lack of effective competition.

P2P lending platforms in the UK can be grouped into different categories depending on various standards, such as the way that interest rates are calculated. Some platforms allow investors to propose a predefined interest rate, upon agreement with potential borrowers. Other P2P websites adopt the so-called reverse auction model, under which lenders have to take a bid to make loans and those who offer the lowest interest rate will win the bid. Apart from that, P2P platforms can be broadly divided into P2P consumer lending and P2P business lending. While many platforms (e.g., Zopa and RateSetter) principally target consumer borrowers, there are increasing P2P portals like Funding Circle which focus on SME lending, property development loans, and other business financing options. The latter is referred to as peer-to-business (P2B) lending), which enables SMEs to borrow funds from a large

---

[39] Assetz Capital, 'SME Lender Assetz Capital Approved for Accreditation as Lender under Coronavirus Business Interruption Loan Scheme (CBILS)', 6 May 2020, https://www.assetzcapital.co.uk/press-releases/sme-lender-assetz-capital-approved-for-accreditation-as-lender-under-coronavirus-business-interruption-loan-scheme-cbils/.

[40] BBB, 'Small Business Finance Markets 2014', p. 5, https://www.british-business-bank.co.uk/research/small-business-finance-markets-2014/.

pool of retail and institutional investors.[41] P2B lending has been praised for its quick processing times, flexible terms, transparency, and user-friendliness when compared to bank loans. Take Funding Circle as an example, as it has a vision to revolutionise the outdated banking system. Since its establishment in 2010, Funding Circle has assisted 135,000 businesses in financing their business plans and helped them borrow £15.2 billion.[42] Now it has a presence in the US, Germany, Spain, and the Netherlands. Investors in Funding Circle include the UK government, local councils, universities, and other financial organisations. Under the Business Finance Partnership, the UK government lent £20 million to SMEs through Funding Circle. Also, the government-backed BBB advanced £40 million to smaller business borrowers via the same platform. Apparently, P2B lending portals work as a conduit between prospective investors and money-strapped SMEs, which contributes to sustainable economic growth.

6.4 P2P lending in the US

P2P lending marketplaces have quickly expanded in the US. In 2021, the P2P lending industry in North America reached a value of over $31.3 billion.[43] Online lending can be a helpful tool for both lenders and borrowers in the US. However, it is important to consider the risks and disadvantages that could arise, such as the lack of FDIC protection and the potential for default.[44] Based on the nature of borrowers, the US's P2P lending marketplaces could be divided into subcategories like student loans, real-estate loans, consumer credit loans, and small business loans. LendingClub and Prosper Marketplace are currently the two titans of the online lending sector in the US.[45] Both platforms link lenders directly with borrowers, who can be either individuals or enterprises. This eliminates the need for borrowers to deal with high-interest banks and credit card companies. As a result of the loan transactions being disintermediated, everyone concerned benefits. The investors

---

[41] University of Cambridge, 'Moving Mainstream: The European Alternative Finance Benchmarking Report', February 2015, p. 18, https://www.jbs.cam.ac.uk/faculty-research/centres/alternative-finance/publications/moving-mainstream/.

[42] 'Fast, Flexible Business Loans', Funding Circle, accessed 1 June 2023, http://www.fundingcircle.com/uk/.

[43] Acumen Research and Consulting, 'P2P Lending Market Size to Hit USD 804.2 Billion by 2030', January 2023, https://www.acumenresearchandconsulting.com/p2p-lending-market.

[44] The FDIC is a government-run organisation that offers deposit protection to customers of American commercial banks and savings institutions. The Banking Act of 1933, passed during the Great Depression to rebuild confidence in the US financial system, established the FDIC.

[45] Peter Rudegeair, 'Layoffs Mount at Online Lenders', *The Wall Street Journal*, 8 July 2016, C1.

receive a better return, borrowers can get reduced interest rates, and the online lending platforms make money by offering their services.

Prosper was launched in 2006 as the first online P2P lending platform in the US. As of the end of 2022, Prosper had helped 1.3 million individuals receive more than $21 billion in loans.[46] The P2P lending site does not take part in the transactions; it merely acts as a meeting venue for investors and borrowers. To enable borrowers to acquire loans at the most affordable rates, Prosper initially employed the reverse auction model. In reality, a transaction under this model took a very long time to complete. This strategy had a high default rate because it solely relied on the FICO credit score to determine a borrower's creditworthiness. In November 2008, the SEC decided that the sale of P2P loans would be considered as securities and ordered Prosper to stop operation.[47] Back in 2009, investors were given the option by Prosper to select between two pricing models: the reverse bidding model or the differentiated pricing model, in which the platform bases the rate on the investor's credit rating. Later, Prosper discovered that more than half of customers had selected the latter model, so it discontinued the use of dual models. It currently only permits the differentiated model, in which the applicant publishes their credit information online and Prosper then evaluates and assesses their credit history based on that information. Prosper charges a 1–3% commission on loan transactions and needs an FICO score over 640 to consider application for a personal loan.[48] Inspired by Facebook, Prosper incorporated social networking features into its lending platforms, enabling users to create smaller communities with people who have things in common like their employment. Users, however, started losing interest in this function, as more institutional investors joined the platform and began to focus solely on the credit rating number rather than the characteristics of the users.

LendingClub was established in 2007 in San Francisco. It has become the largest online lending platform in the US, and it is a digital marketplace that provides personal loans of between $1,000 and $40,000 and a completely branchless banking experience.[49] It assists members in consolidating high-interest debt, achieving financial independence, and saving money. It was the

---

[46] 'Smart, Simple Tools for Borrowing, Saving & Earning', Prosper, accessed 1 June 2023, https://www.prosper.com/.
[47] SEC, 'Order Instituting Cease-and-Desist Proceedings Pursuant to Section 8A of the Securities Act of 1933, Making Findings, and Imposing a Cease-and-Desist Order', 24 November 2008, https://www.sec.gov/litigation/admin/2008/33-8984.pdf.
[48] Bankrate, 'Prosper Personal Loans: 2023 Review', 13 January 2023, https://www.bankrate.com/loans/personal-loans/reviews/prosper/.
[49] 'Personal Loans', LendingClub, accessed 1 June 2023, https://www.lendingclub.com/loans/personal-loans.

first P2P lender in the US to offer loan trading on a secondary market and file its offerings as securities with the SEC. LendingClub's business strategy is to accept loan requests and authorisations from its users while determining the interest rate based on credit score. Following that, users will receive LendingClub receipts, which investors can then acquire. A separate banking institution will hold the funds before transferring them to debtors. LendingClub charges commission over deals to provide these services. Through its IPO in 2014, it raised $870 million from global investors.[50] Depending on the need for funding, there are four distinct loan types: loans for small businesses, loans for credit card debt, loans for debt repayment, and loans for the purchase of furniture or a home. The growth rate for the small business loan was 92.85%, while the growth rate for other loans was 181.32%. Each loan will be assigned a level between 1 and 25 based on the rating algorithm used by LendingClub. In order to give institutional investors another option to access the consumer credit asset class, LendingClub collaborates with WeBank, which will securitise the loans issued through its platform.[51] However, the securitisation of P2P loans does carry some potential risks, and it is thought to have contributed significantly to the previous financial crisis.

6.5 P2P lending in China

China holds one of the largest online lending industries in the world. In 2018, it had 6,063 P2P lending platforms with a total lending volume of CNY7.69 trillion ($1.12 trillion).[52] However, it had gone through a series of crises as a large number of platforms collapsed or faced investigations regarding fraud or illegal deposit-taking activities in the late 2010s. Tang Ning, the founder of CreditEase, one of China's top Fintech firms, introduced P2P lending to the country in 2006.[53] With 6 million users and CNY8 billion in annual lending, Yirendai.com, the online lending division of CreditEase, successfully launched an IPO in New York in December 2015. Another well-known P2P lending platform in China is Paipaidai, which was the first P2P firm to obtain government permission for its operations. Over 12 million

---

[50] Leslie Picker and Noah Buhayar, 'LendingClub Surges in Debut After $870 Million U.S IPO', Bloomberg, 11 December 2014, https://www.bloomberg.com/news/articles/2014-12-11/lendingclub-surges-in-debut-after-870-million-u-s-ipo.
[51] 'LendingClub Securitization Program', LendingClub, accessed 1 June 2023, https://www.lendingclub.com/investing/institutional/securitization.
[52] Lingyi Finance, 'P2P Lending Industry Annual Report 2018', 3 January 2019, https://www.01caijing.com/article/34230.htm.
[53] CreditEase, accessed 1 June 2023, http://english.creditease.cn/about/Overview.html.

users in 98% of Chinese cities have been served by Paipaidai.[54] Other top P2P lending platforms are Lufax, Hongling Capital, and PPMoney.

P2P lending transactions increased dramatically in the 2010s as a consequence of the thousands of Chinese online lending platforms that had been matching the financing requests from lenders with the investment needs of borrowers. With an average loan amount of CNY129,000, 12.52 million borrowers participated in P2P financing in 2018; on the other end, there were 11.14 million investors and their average investment was CNY145,300.[55] In 2018, the average lending duration increased to 315 days from 251 days in 2017 and 253 days in 2016, with an average yearly interest rate of 9.57% for P2P loans.[56]

The P2P lending sector in China has grown quickly for several reasons. Strong financing demands from Chinese SMEs and individual borrowers, who are underserved by the state banks, have largely propelled the market. In contrast to the US and the UK, where P2P consumer lending has dominated online lending markets, over 40% of lending volume in China is made up of P2B transactions.[57] Private business owners frequently use P2P lending as an alternative form of funding. Many well-known P2P networks in China, including Paipaidai, Dianrong, and Jimubox, started their business ventures by making loans to SMEs. Some P2P portals even emerged from previous underground money houses. While the majority of P2P lending platforms were upgraded from informal lending businesses and wealth management firms, a tiny percentage of them began as professional online lending websites.

P2P lending is also seen as a dynamic part of China's internet finance industry. Internet finance combines the latest information technologies with innovative financial services.[58] The three main areas of internet finance—payment and settlement services, online lending, and the selling of investment products—can be considered as the prototypes of financial technology in China.[59] By utilising their sizable clients and big data, Chinese internet giants like Baidu, Alibaba, and Tencent have recently extended their

---

[54] 'About Us—Paipaidai', Paipaidai, accessed 1 June 2023, http://www.ppdai.com/help/aboutus.
[55] Lingyi Finance, 'P2P Lending Industry Annual Report 2018', 3 January 2019, https://www.01caijing.com/article/34230.htm.
[56] Ibid.
[57] Luke Deer, Jackson Mi, and Yuxin Yu, 'The Rise of Peer-to-Peer Lending in China: An Overview and Survey Case Study', Association of Chartered Certified Accountants, October 2015, p. 7, https://www.accaglobal.com/content/dam/ACCA_Global/Technical/manage/ea-china-p2p-lending.pdf.
[58] Jing Bian, 'Internet Finance in China: Half Lava? Half Ocean?'. *Journal of International Banking Law and Regulation* (2014) 29: 743.
[59] Takeshi Jingu, 'Internet Finance Growing Rapidly in China', Nomura Research Institute, 10 March 2014, p. 1, https://www.nri.com/-/media/Corporate/en/Files/PDF/knowledge/publication/lakyara/2014/03/lakyaravol189.pdf.

businesses into the financial sector. The information can be used to assess a consumer's credit standing in order to provide financial services that are tailored to their specific requirements. Also, to create mobile banking, online securities broking, and online wealth management services, Chinese conventional banks, securities firms, insurance firms, and investment funds gradually moved their existing services online. There are some clear benefits of internet finance over traditional finance. Due to the minimal service threshold and simple online access, internet finance is accessible to regular consumers and small businesses, unlike conventional financial organisations that favour big clients. Also, internet financial portals can offer their customers round-the-clock support because of their online operations.

Despite the popularity of P2P lending in China, the industry is often associated with illegal operations and financial frauds, due to the lack of effective regulation for a long period of time. For example, some online lending platforms solicit funds from investors and form a large capital pool before lending out the money, making them de facto underground banks without a licence. This violates the principle that P2P platforms should only be information intermediaries rather than credit intermediaries.[60] Only 19.5% (1,185) of Chinese P2P lending platforms were in normal operation in 2018, while 77.1% (4,672) of them were in an abnormal state, such as being involved in litigation or declaring bankruptcy.[61] Many P2P networks have experienced operational issues like frozen withdrawals, runaway bosses, and ceased operations.[62] Ezubao, formerly China's largest P2P lending platform, ceased operations in 2015 after the claim that it had solicited CNY59.8 billion from investors through fictitious investment projects promoted on its website and had failed to repay CNY38 billion of those funds.[63] The company's executives acknowledged that Ezubao was a fully Ponzi scheme that used investors' money to support their luxurious lifestyles. According to some research, fraud played a significant role in China's P2P online lending crisis, and a number of structural factors enabled financial crimes that led to the market's collapse.[64] It indicates that a proactive system of compliance

---

[60] International Organization of Securities Commissions, 'IOSCO Research Report on Financial Technologies (Fintech)', February 2017, https://www.iosco.org/library/pubdocs/pdf/IOSCOPD554.pdf.
[61] Lingyi Finance, 'P2P Lending Industry Annual Report 2018', 3 January 2019, https://www.01caijing.com/article/34230.htm.
[62] Lerong Lu, *Private Lending in China: Practice, Law, and Regulation of Shadow Banking and Alternative Finance* (Abingdon: Routledge, 2018), p. 44.
[63] 'China's $8.6 Billion P2P Fraud Trial Starts: Xinhua', *Reuters*, 16 December 2016, https://www.reuters.com/article/us-china-fraud-ezubao-idUSKBN145012.
[64] Li Huang and Henry N. Pontell, 'Crime and Crisis in China's P2P Online Lending Market: A Comparative Analysis of Fraud'. *Crime, Law and Social Change* (2023) 79: 369–393, https://doi.org/10.1007/s10611-022-10053-y.

that includes more thorough and transparent financial supervision is likely to be more effective than a mainly reactive approach to combating financial crime.

6.6 P2P lending vs bank lending: can financial disintermediation win?

This section examines some benefits of P2P loans over conventional bank loans, especially for SME borrowers. As financial intermediaries, banking institutions play a crucial part in the economy by accepting public deposits and disbursing loans to individuals, companies, and governments.[65] Banks, however, have been struggling with the issue of information asymmetry because it is challenging for them to fully understand the financial conditions of borrowers. A large number of small companies are unable to provide adequate information, such as trading and credit histories, so their chances of passing banks' stringent credit tests have decreased. This has made the problem of information asymmetry extremely serious in the field of SME lending. As banks have tightened lending standards in response to the global financial crisis and the Covid-19 pandemic to reduce credit risk, the situation of SME financing is growing worse. However, it is claimed that the booming P2P lending sector will help finance SMEs and offset the decline in bank loans.

Financial disintermediation refers to the process of eradicating different forms of financial intermediaries from lending and investment transactions.[66] The prevalence of intermediaries in financial markets is one of the topics that has persisted in the research on corporate finance.[67] However, an increasing number of investors, in particular institutional investors, manage to get rid of intermediaries and participate in direct corporate investments through multiple channels such as PE. The phenomenon of financial disintermediation has been observed in debt financing as well, such as private lending and online P2P lending. The conventional banking model, where banks give loans to individuals and corporates by leveraging on their vast reserve of deposits, has both advantages and weaknesses. For example, the participation of banks in the lending chain pushes up the lending costs significantly, for banks are expensive businesses requiring substantial investments in branch

---

[65] Federal Reserve Bank of San Francisco, 'What Is the Economic Function of a Bank?', July 2001, http://www.frbsf.org/education/publications/doctor-econ/2001/july/bank-economic-function.
[66] Paul Taylor, 'Middle Men Deleted as the Word Spreads', *The Financial Times*, 27 October 1998, p. 15.
[67] Lily Fang, Victoria Ivashina, and Josh Lerner, 'The Disintermediation of Financial Markets: Direct Investing in Private Equity'. *Journal of Financial Economics* (2015) 116: 160–178.

networks, properties, and complex IT systems.[68] Ultimately, all expenditures will be borne by banks' customers, namely savers and borrowers. The bureaucratic loan-making procedures used by banks also make the lending process time-consuming for prospective borrowers. However, financial intermediaries do bring some benefits to lending parties and to the economy as a whole. Banks are professional institutions and they are more experienced in assessing credit risks of potential borrowers, which could hardly be done by individual investors. Banks make good use of spare money in society owing to their economies of scale, as they are able to conduct due diligence over borrowers on behalf of millions of depositors, saving time and money for individuals.[69] Additionally, banks run a uniform financing platform for people looking for credit, so borrowers do not need to look for lenders separately.

P2P lending, however, is likely to make conventional financial intermediaries less attractive. Legally, banks have a debtor–creditor relationship with both their depositors and their borrowers, acting as intermediaries for credit.[70] In practice, P2P lending platforms achieve a similar economic function as banks, but actually they are working as pure information intermediaries instead of credit intermediaries. The principal function of P2P lending websites is to assist the information exchange between investors and borrowers. In doing so, P2P platforms allow investors to find unrelated borrowers online, or vice versa. Prospective borrowers list their funding requests online, including the amount of money, purpose of borrowing, term time, and interest rate. Such information will be viewed by thousands of investors. By eliminating banks in the loan-making process, P2P platforms still perform the same money-matching activities (i.e., the function of banking to a large extent). P2P portals, as information intermediaries, do not constitute a party of relevant lending contracts that they help to conclude.

P2P lending has some notable advantages because of its straightforward and effective business model. The first advantage is in providing more financing opportunities at affordable costs for SMEs. Compared with banks, P2P lending websites are able to utilise different funding sources to arrange loans for potential borrowers. The primary source of funding for domestic banks

---

[68] Martin Arnold, 'Big Lenders Criticised for Slow Take-up of Technology', *The Financial Times*, 14 September 2017, p. 14.

[69] Economies of scale are factors that cause the average cost of producing something to fall as the volume of its output increases. See 'Economies of Scale and Scope', *The Economist*, 20 October 2008, http://www.economist.com/node/12446567.

[70] Ross Cranston et al., *Principles of Banking Law*, 3rd ed. (Oxford: Oxford University Press, 2018), p. 190.

is deposits, though more banks have lately turned to money market funds and interbank markets for capital.[71] P2P platforms, in comparison, have a wider range of funding options and no geographical restrictions. They can ask private investors, institutional investors, and governmental organisations for funding. For instance, through Funding Circle, 72,000 individual investors have loaned £2.8 billion while receiving interest payments totalling £135 million.[72] Most P2P investors have been depositors who feel unsatisfied with the interest rates offered by banks and thus move their money to P2P platforms. Besides, P2P lending is becoming more and more popular among institutional investors, hedge funds, and asset management firms. In the US, almost 80% of funding in P2P platforms has come from institutional investors.[73] In the UK, the government plays a proactive role in P2P business lending. In 2017, the BBB agreed to lend £40 million to small businesses registered with Funding Circle.[74] The European Investment Bank also promised to advance £100 million to smaller companies in the UK through the P2P platform.[75] P2P lending platforms undoubtedly draw money from a variety of private and public investors worldwide. They expand funding for SMEs and eliminate the geographic restrictions on conventional banking operations. In the meantime, the cost of borrowing P2P loans has been kept at a moderate level. In P2P lending markets there is no financial intermediary extracting value from lending parties. P2P lending platforms adopt a cost-saving organisational model with fewer employees and offices, in contrast to traditional banks, which have generated enormous profits from lending money. The financial benefit will be distributed to end customers. For instance, Funding Circle only charges 1% of the loan amount as administrative fees.[76] It is likely to cause a sharp fall in interest rates for borrowers as well as bring higher returns for investors, creating a win-win situation for all parties involved. Small companies in the UK can take out loans up to £500,000 for a maximum of five years at 4.50%.[77] In reality, obtaining a P2P loan will cost no more than getting a bank loan. Small businesses can repay business loans in one lump sum and only pay interest based on the actual time

---

[71] John Carney, 'Basics of Banking: Loans Create a Lot More Than Deposits', *CNBC*, 26 February 2013, https://www.cnbc.com/id/100497710.
[72] 'Lending to UK Businesses', Funding Circle, accessed 1 June 2023, http://www.fundingcircle.com/uk/investors/.
[73] Amy Cortese, 'Loans that Avoid Banks? Maybe Not', *The New York Times*, 4 May 2014, https://www.nytimes.com/2014/05/04/business/loans-that-avoid-banks-maybe-not.html.
[74] Emma Dunkley, 'Funding Circle: Small Business Backing', *The Financial Times*, 6 January 2017, p. 17.
[75] Emma Dunkley, 'Funding Circle to Allocate £100m of EU Loans', *The Financial Times*, 21 June 2016, p. 21.
[76] 'Lending to UK Businesses', Funding Circle, accessed 1 June 2023, http://www.fundingcircle.com/uk/investors/.
[77] 'Business Loans & Funding in the UK', Funding Circle, accessed 1 June 2023, http://www.fundingcircle.com/uk/businesses/.

of borrowing, since P2P borrowers are exempt from early repayment fees in most cases.

The second benefit of P2P lending is that it gives lenders, most of whom are regular savers, excellent investment chances with higher returns. The majority of people only have limited investment choices, such as savings accounts, mutual funds, and pension funds, due to their limited financial resources and lack of investment knowledge. Average savers are unable to purchase most wealth management products because of the high requirements for customers who must be high-net-worth individuals (HNWIs).[78] However, the rise of P2P lending has given people more investment opportunities. The threshold for purchasing Zopa's classic P2P lending products is only £10, and more sophisticated products like Zopa Plus and Zopa Core require a minimum capital of £1,000.[79] The fact that P2P lending is a form of crowdfunding accounts for the low investment barrier. P2P loans are funded by a collection of investors who will split the loan amount. For example, if there are 1,000 investors and the total loan amount is as large as £1 million, each investor will only need to contribute £1,000 to the pool of funds. Thus, the P2P investment threshold is lowered by the sharing function. In addition, the safety of any P2P transaction has been guaranteed by both technical methods and regulatory requirements. The money of an investor will be automatically divided into small portions being allocated to different loan projects. The diversification procedure lessens the impact of a potential default and lowers the risk exposure to specific borrowers. Moreover, P2P lending platforms like Lending Works and Landbay have established special reserve funds to recover investors' money in the event of debtors' default, which adds extra protection for investors.[80] Obviously, P2P investors enjoy good monetary returns on their funds. After the global financial crisis, interest rates were kept extremely low by central banks around the world in the 2010s.[81] In some countries, it even led to a negative interest rate for bank savings—that is, lower than the inflation rate. Disappointed by ultra-low interest rates offered by banks, savers have been actively seeking investments that could generate better yields, such as P2P lending and crypto assets. Funding Circle predicts that P2P users in the UK will earn annual returns of 5–8%.[82] Without

---

[78] HNWIs refer to people with over $1 million in liquid financial assets.
[79] Zopa, 'What Is the Minimum Amount that I Can Lend in Each Product?', accessed 1 June 2023, https://www.zopa.com/help.
[80] Tara Evans, 'Peer-to-Peer Lending: Everything You Need to Know About the Leading Websites', *The Telegraph*, 18 July 2016, http://www.telegraph.co.uk/personal-banking/savings/peer-to-peer-lending-everything-you-need-to-know-about-the-leadi/.
[81] Jon Cunliffe, 'Why Are Interest Rates Low?', BoE, 16 November 2016, http://www.bankofengland.co.uk/publications/Documents/speeches/2016/speech935.pdf.
[82] 'Lending to UK Businesses', Funding Circle, accessed 1 June 2023, http://www.fundingcircle.com/uk/investors/.

doubt, P2P lending is attractive to a large number of savers owing to the decent financial returns, making it an alternative to bank savings and mutual funds. P2P investors should be aware that they are not protected by deposit insurance like the FSCS in the UK. As a consequence, investors will suffer financial losses when borrowers make defaults. During the financial crisis, Zopa experienced its highest default rate of 5.54% of total loans. Frauds and other financial risks may also be present to investors. Fortunately, there has never been a major P2P lending platform failure in the UK.

The third advantage of P2P lending over bank lending is its quick financing process. P2P lending is regarded as hassle-free and efficient compared to the lengthy complicated process of applying for a bank loan. Funding Circle has a straightforward and transparent loan application process as business borrowers just need to file applications online and upload relevant materials in an electronic format.[83] It takes 10 minutes for borrowers to create an application, which will be allocated a dedicated loan manager immediately. Within the next 24 hours, borrowers will be informed of a decision of whether their loan application is approved or not. Then, it takes no more than seven days for Funding Circle to advertise the loans on its proprietary e-marketplace where such loans are going to be financed by registered investors. After receiving funds from investors, Funding Circle will deposit the money in a bank account nominated by borrowers without any delay. The seven-day lending procedure is unthinkable in the traditional banking industry, where it takes several weeks, if not months, to process a loan application.

The fourth advantage of P2P lending is that it reduces information asymmetry and fosters market transparency and openness. P2P lending networks can actually do a better job of resolving the persistent information asymmetry issue that banks run into. Equipped with big data and AI, P2P platforms are able to accurately measure the size and location of credit risks relating to borrowers in a few seconds. Some online lenders have hired financial engineers to create cutting-edge risk models to assess a variety of factors related to borrowers, such as gender, age, marital status, level of education, years of employment, company size, monthly payment, loan amount, debt to income ratio, and delinquency history.[84] When assessing the credit risks of small businesses, big data usage gives P2P lending platforms a distinct edge over

---

[83] 'Business Loans & Funding in the UK', Funding Circle, accessed 1 June 2023, http://www.fundingcircle.com/uk/businesses/.

[84] Xuchen Lin, Xiaolong Li, and Zhong Zheng, 'Evaluating Borrower's Default Risk in Peer-to-Peer Lending: Evidence from a Lending Platform in China'. *Applied Economics* (2017) 49: 3538–3554.

banks. In contrast, it remains difficult for banks to evaluate the creditworthiness of SME borrowers under the traditional analytical methods. In the old days, community banks kept a close relationship with businesses operating in the same district, so when it came to loan-making, community banks would have abundant informal materials to assess the credit backgrounds of local borrowers.[85] Nowadays, the majority of community banks have been combined into large banking institutions, which frequently base their loan decisions on financial modelling and credit scores. However, many smaller companies find it difficult to provide enough information about their operations. As a result, they are unable to clear the rigorous credit test and obtain a bank loan. P2P lending platforms, on the other hand, have been creating predictive models based on various types of data. Some of them have developed algorithms that take into consideration the social media activity of business owners, their cash flow and deposit amounts, as well as the general industry trend. To assess SMEs' creditworthiness, all pertinent information will be taken into account, improving their chances of receiving a loan. However, this has sparked debates over personal privacy and data security because P2P portals can only gather, process, and disseminate pertinent data with the complete consent of the information owners.[86] Apart from the enhanced tool to assess credit risks, most online lending platforms conduct lending activities with a high level of business transparency, thanks to the strict disclosure requirements.[87] The FCA has made detailed disclosure guidelines, which will be looked at in the following section, that apply to both P2P lending platforms and potential borrowers. Investors can use a wealth of information as a result to make wise investment decisions. For the regulatory purpose, the information can also be used by financial authorities to track the sector and anticipate financial risks.

6.7 Regulation of P2P lending platforms

This section assesses the policies and regulations of online P2P lending markets in the US, China, and the UK. A sound legal and regulatory framework is a prerequisite for developing the financial industry. Online P2P

---

[85] Karen Mills, 'Use Data to Fix the Small Business Lending Gap', *Harvard Business Review*, 16 September 2014, https://hbr.org/2014/09/use-data-to-fix-the-small-business-lending-gap.
[86] Information Commissioner's Office, 'Big Data, Artificial Intelligence, Machine Learning And Data Protection', 4 September 2017, http://ico.org.uk/media/for-organisations/documents/2013559/big-data-ai-ml-and-data-protection.pdf.
[87] Laura Noonan, 'P2P Lenders to Be Asked to Reveal Defaults', *The Financial Times*, 12 August 2017, p. 2.

lending markets, which have brought tremendous benefits to market participants, clearly need government support and well-designed regulatory rules to maximise their economic and social value.

6.7.1 International regulatory practices in the US and China

The P2P lending sector in the US does not have a particular regulatory framework. It complies with the country's current financial laws, which safeguard both the lending and investment sides of the economy. The securities regulation, e-commerce regulation, and consumer protection regulation all have jurisdiction over the US P2P lending industry. For instance, the Securities Exchange Act of 1934 created the SEC. The SEC is headquartered in Washington, DC, and it is in charge of overseeing securities-related businesses in the US.[88] The SEC has a broad range of authority, including the ability to make rules and law enforcements, and bring legal actions against companies and individuals who break rules. Securities issuers must adhere to stringent guidelines for information disclosure and are forbidden from disseminating false information. Prosper and LendingClub were added to the SEC's regulatory framework in 2008, and all P2P lending platforms in the US are now required to register and submit relevant information.[89] The notes issued by P2P lending platforms are regarded as unregistered securities. However, the SEC's strict regulatory requirements are likely to prevent new players from entering the industry. Also, there are several layers of consumer safety regulation overseen by the CFPB.[90] The Federal Trade Commission is responsible for monitoring unfair practices and frauds in the P2P lending sector and ensuring market competitiveness. Moreover, in order to ensure that banks making use of P2P lending networks safeguard depositors' money, the FIDC also oversees relevant activities.

China has created a thorough regulatory framework for its P2P lending industry. There are two sources of rules. Firstly, the existing civil laws and regulations that govern traditional private lending activities are applied to online lending transactions. For example, P2P loan agreements are subject to provisions under the Part III Contract of China's Civil Code, in particular, Chapter 12 on Loan Contract, which sets out detailed rules regarding any

---

[88] 'What We Do', SEC, accessed 1 June 2023, https://www.sec.gov/about/what-we-do.
[89] Benjamin Lo, 'It Ain't Broke: The Case for Continued SEC Regulation of P2P Lending'. *Harvard Business Law Review* (2016) 6: 87, 88–90.
[90] There is a debate on whether the SEC or the CFPB should be given the power to regulate P2P lending activities in the US. See Paul Slattery, 'Square Pegs in a Round Hole: SEC Regulation of Online Peer-to-Peer Lending and the CFPB Alternative'. *Yale Journal on Regulation* (2013) 30: 233, 261.

lending agreements' format, the interest rate, loan purpose, default, loan inspection, and extension.[91] Secondly, there exist specialised regulations for the online P2P lending platforms. In 2016, four Chinese authorities—the China Banking Regulatory Commission (CBRC), Ministry of Industry and Information Technology, Ministry of Public Security, and State Internet Information Office—jointly issued a set of interim measures for online lending businesses, which has provided an overall regulatory regime for P2P lending websites.[92] It contains rules regarding the definition of P2P loans, the registration requirement for P2P lending platforms, the duties and prohibited activities for platforms, the protection of lenders and borrowers, the information disclosure regime, and online lending supervision and administration.[93] Online lending platforms must register with their local financial regulatory body under the measures.[94] The temporary measures limit the platforms' commercial functions to serving as simple information intermediaries.[95] In order to lower the risk that platform owners will steal money, it also required all platforms to set up custody accounts with commercial banks for investor and borrower funds kept by the platforms.[96] In order to support the implementation of interim measures, the CBRC and other governmental departments have promulgated extra official guidance on registration of the P2P lending platform, the custodian rules, and the information disclosure rules in 2016 and 2017.

6.7.2 Government policies to promote P2P lending in the UK

The financing difficulty of SMEs stops entrepreneurs from starting new businesses and impedes the further growth of existing businesses. To address this problem, the UK government has issued several policies to increase SME financing. It has been working closely with the BoE to operate the Funding for Lending Scheme (FLS).[97] The FLS, supported by the central bank's liquidity, enables banks and building societies to borrow funds from the central bank at

---

[91] Civil Code of the People's Republic of China 2020, Articles 667–680.
[92] CBRC et al., 'Interim Measures for the Administration of the Business Activities of Online Lending Information Intermediary Institutions', 2016, Order No. 1.
[93] Penalties may be administrative or even criminal if one of its provisions is violated. See ibid., Chapter 7 'Legal Liability'.
[94] Ibid., Article 5.
[95] Ibid., Articles 2–3.
[96] Ibid., Article 28.
[97] BoE, 'Funding for Lending and Other Market Operations', accessed 1 June 2023, http://www.bankofengland.co.uk/markets/funding-for-lending-and-other-market-operations.

a discounted rate and these will then extend loans to SMEs at an interest rate below the market level. Moreover, the BBB was set up by the government to bring capital from both public and private sectors to establish an effective financing market for smaller businesses.[98] The BBB is not a real bank for it does not lend money by itself, but, instead, it has been given the mandate to manage government-related programmes concerning SME finance. Partnering with 80 financial institutions, including banks, leasing companies, VC funds, and online lending platforms, the BBB provides extensive funding support for entrepreneurs in the UK. In 2015, it collected £2.3 billion to finance 40,000 smaller businesses and it planned to offer an extra £2.9 billion to SMEs in the upcoming years.[99] The Recovery Loan Scheme (RLS), which the BBB introduced during the Covid-19 pandemic, provides financing facilities of up to £2 million per business group and is intended to support UK companies' access to capital as they seek to expand and invest.[100]

The government has introduced a series of initiatives to encourage private investments to SMEs, such as the Business Finance Partnership (BFP) and the Start-Up Loans Scheme (SLS). Under the BFP, the government has invested £1.2 billion in smaller businesses through non-bank financing channels including investment funds and P2P lenders.[101] Aside from the government's input, at least an equal amount of money will be contributed by private investors to top up the budget. The SLS started in September 2012 with a proposal to offer £82.5 million to young entrepreneurs aged 18–30.[102] It is run by a state-owned organisation which plans to give £2,500 to each young entrepreneur starting a new business. Furthermore, the government has launched some tax-advantaged VC schemes to support SME finance, such as the Enterprise Investment Scheme, the Venture Capital Trust Scheme, and the Seed Enterprise Investment Scheme.[103] Such schemes are likely to incentivise PE investors and venture capitalists to divert more capital to

---

[98] 'What We Do?', BBB, accessed 1 June 2023, http://british-business-bank.co.uk/what-the-british-business-bank-does/.

[99] BBB, 'Annual Report and Accounts 2015', July 2015, https://www.british-business-bank.co.uk/wp-content/uploads/2015/07/British-Business-Bank-Annual-Report-and-Accounts-20151.pdf.

[100] BBB, 'Recovery Loan Scheme', accessed 1 June 2023, https://www.british-business-bank.co.uk/ourpartners/recovery-loan-scheme/.

[101] Kylie MacLellan, 'UK Channels Business Lending Via Alternative Financiers', *Reuters*, 12 December 2012, http://uk.reuters.com/article/uk-britain-lending/uk-channels-business-lending-via-alternative-financiers-idUKBRE8BB0E920121212.

[102] BBB, 'Start Up Loans', accessed 1 June 2023, http://www.startuploans.co.uk.

[103] HM Treasury, 'Tax-Advantaged Venture Capital Schemes: Ensuring Continued Support for Small and Growing Businesses', UK Government, 10 July 2014, https://www.gov.uk/government/consultations/tax-advantaged-venture-capital-schemes-ensuring-continued-support-for-small-and-growing-businesses.

SMEs, as the tax relief compensates for the extra financial risks associated with investments in early-stage businesses.

In addition, the government has spent a lot of effort helping business borrowers to acquire funds from P2P lending platforms and other novel Fintech channels. For example, it urges banks to inform small businesses that if they are rejected, there are possible alternative finance methods, and to pass the information of their clients to certain alternative finance platforms (e.g., Funding Options, Business Finance Compared, and Funding Xchange).[104] In April 2016, the government announced the Innovative Finance ISA which promises tax-free returns for British savers who invest their money in P2P loans.[105] The Innovative Finance ISA has an investment limit of £20,000 per tax year. The inclusion of P2P lending investments in official tax-free ISA schemes clearly benefits the P2P lending industry, as increasing numbers of savers are expected to join P2P lending as they are entitled to the same tax-free policies as those who save money under a cash ISA or purchase securities under an investment ISA. The Innovative Finance ISA seems to level the playing field between P2P lending platforms and traditional banks and securities brokers.

6.7.3 P2P lending industry self-regulation in the UK

In 2011, Zopa, Funding Circle, and Rate Setter co-founded the Peer-to-Peer Finance Association (P2PFA) as the industry self-regulatory body for the UK's online lending sector. Despite the P2PFA's dissolution in 2020 and replacement by the 36H Group as part of Innovate Finance, it serves as a useful case study for researching self-regulatory bodies for P2P networks.[106] The P2PFA's goals are to raise the bar for ethical business practices in the online loan sector and to better safeguard investors who use online platforms. The association has three main goals: (1) to seek to secure public policy and regulatory and fiscal conditions that enable the UK-based P2P finance sector

---

[104] Martin Arnold, 'Alternative Finance Route for Small Firms', *The Financial Times*, 5 November 2016, p. 2.
[105] Emma Dunkley, 'Peer-to-Peer Lending Isa Brings Fresh Set of Risks, Say Experts', *The Financial Times*, 11 July 2015, p. 4.
[106] The 36H Group was named after the Financial Services and Markets Act 2000 (UK)'s Article 36H, which serves as the legislative foundation for retail investment through lending platforms. The 36H Group offers lending platforms a unified and powerful voice. The Group, which is part of Innovate Finance, collaborates closely with regulators, policy-makers, and other stakeholders. All lending platforms authorised and governed by the FCA under Article 36H are eligible to join the Group. See '36H Group', Innovate Finance, 1 June 2023, https://www.innovatefinance.com/36hgroup/.

to compete fairly and grow responsibly; (2) to ensure that members demonstrate high standards of business conduct, to demonstrate leadership, and to promote confidence in the sector; and (3) to raise awareness and understanding of the benefits and risks of P2P finance.[107] The P2PFA plays an important role in the UK's online lending industry. Most P2P lending platforms have been a member of the P2PFA, which represents over 90% of market shares.

To achieve its objectives, the P2PFA promulgated operating principles for its members to follow, including a series of high-level principles and specific rules relating to transparency, risk management, and governance and control.[108] For instance, P2P platforms are obliged to provide adequate information for investors to make informed investment decisions. Such information shall include but not be limited to the expected return, details of fees and surcharges, a clear warning of capital risk, where the money is lent, and any automatic functions (e.g., auto-lend, auto-bid, or auto-reinvest).[109] The P2PFA also requires its members to segregate the money of their customers from the P2P companies' own assets, in line with the FCA's client money rules.[110] Further, it has imposed an obligation on its members to submit data about lending volumes and customer complaints on a quarterly basis.[111] Evidently, relevant operating principles are crucial to ensure a high standard of business conduct and a proper level of consumer protection in the P2P lending industry. However, these industry guidelines have been playing a more supplementary role after the introduction of the FCA's official regulatory rules in 2014.

6.7.4 The FCA's official regulation of P2P lending platforms

The UK is the first country to have established an official regulatory regime for online P2P lending. The regulation of P2P lending falls within the FCA's existing regulatory framework, as the FCA has included P2P lending (loan-based crowdfunding) in the regulated activities under Article 36H of the

---

[107] P2PFA, 'Rules of the Peer-to-Peer Finance Association', May 2015, para. 3.1.
[108] P2PFA, 'Peer-to-Peer Finance Association Operating Principles', June 2015, Article 3. P2PFA members must comply with the following high-level principles in all their undertakings: (1) operate their business with technical and professional competence; (2) run their business with integrity; (3) transact with customers in an honest and fair way; (4) be transparent about how their platform works; (5) promote and maintain high standards of business practice; and (6) commit to provide good-value financial service products to retail consumers.
[109] Ibid., Article 7.
[110] Ibid., Article 13.
[111] Ibid., Articles 26–27.

Regulatory Activities Order.[112] Therefore, anyone operating P2P lending platforms has to obtain the FCA's authorisation. In October 2012, the FCA issued a consultation paper (CP13/13) which proposed a set of rules to protect investors accessing P2P lending and other crowdfunding platforms.[113] In March 2014, the FCA released a policy statement (PS14/4) outlining detailed rules for regulating P2P lending platforms.[114] The PS14/4 came into force on 1 April 2014 and marked the establishment of a formal regulatory framework over P2P lending activities. Generally speaking, it is a disclosure-based regulatory system which protects P2P investors by promoting the level of information transparency of lending platforms and lending transactions. It contains rules in seven areas for any P2P lending platform operating in the UK, which are summarised below.

(1) Prudential capital requirement: the capital adequacy requirement refers to a certain amount of capital that financial institutions are asked to hold. A financial firm has to maintain a certain level of capital against its assets, which can prevent the firm from undertaking excessive risks and reduces the possibility of falling into insolvency. For example, banks and other deposit-taking institutions are subject to strict capital requirements under the Basel Accords.[115] Similarly, the FCA requires P2P lending platforms to hold compulsory regulatory capital in order to withstand potential financial shocks and cover operating losses. The requirement for any UK-based P2P platforms will be the higher of the following two standards: a fixed minimum amount of £20,000 (transitional arrangement between 1 April 2014 and 31 March 2017) or £50,000 (from 1 April 2017); or the combination of 0.2% of the first £50 million of total value of loaned funds outstanding + 0.15% of the next £200 million of total value of loaned funds outstanding + 0.1% of the next £250 million of total value of loaned funds outstanding + 0.05% of any remaining balance of total value of loaned funds outstanding above £500 million.[116] The amount

---

[112] Financial Services and Markets Act 2000 (Regulated Activities) (Amendment) (No. 2) Order 2013, Article 36H.

[113] FCA, 'The FCA's Regulatory Approach to Crowdfunding (and Similar Activities)' FCA CP13/13, October 2013, https://www.fca.org.uk/publication/consultation/cp13-13.pdf.

[114] FCA, 'The FCA's Regulatory Approach to Crowdfunding over the Internet, and the Promotion of Non-Readily Realisable Securities by Other Media: Feedback to CP13/13 and Final Rules', PS14/4, March 2014, https://www.fca.org.uk/publication/policy/ps14-04.pdf.

[115] BIS, 'Basel III: A Global Regulatory Framework for More Resilient Banks and Banking Systems', June 2011, https://www.bis.org/publ/bcbs189.pdf.

[116] FCA, 'The FCA's Regulatory Approach to Crowdfunding Over the Internet, and the Promotion of Non-Readily Realisable Securities by Other Media: Feedback to CP13/13 and Final Rules', PS14/4, March 2014, p. 20, https://www.fca.org.uk/publication/policy/ps14-04.pdf.

of required capital depends on the amount of client money that a P2P platform is holding. As a micro-prudential regulatory tool, the capital requirement is able to safeguard the safety and soundness of individual P2P lending platforms. Moreover, the requirement can protect the benefits of investors to some extent, as their platforms have to possess enough prudential capital to cope with potential financial difficulties. The differentiated standard for platforms with different sizes of loans also encourages competition in the online lending industry, reflecting the principle of proportionality.

(2) Client money rule: financial firms holding money for their clients relating to investment business are subject to client money rules contained in the FCA's Client Assets Sourcebook.[117] It asks relevant firms to have sufficient protective mechanisms in place for the clients' money that they are looking after. As the P2P lending market has become an important part of the UK's financial industry, the FCA requires P2P lending platforms, when designing their lending and repayment procedures, to comply with the Client Assets Sourcebook rules, such as the segregation of client money, statutory trusts in terms of client money, and retrieving information in the event of insolvency in order to achieve a timely return of client money.[118] All of these rules should be taken into consideration when P2P lending platforms design their lending and repayment procedures.

(3) Cancellation right: it generally requires that if any financial contracts are made at a distance, customers should be able to withdraw their money within the first 14 calendar days, without incurring a penalty or needing to give any explanations. This applies to the P2P lending market, as most P2P loan agreements are concluded online, which fits into the definition of distance financial contracts. P2P platforms that do not have a secondary market have to satisfy one of the following two standards: a P2P firm may allow consumers to invest in loan agreements immediately, but when requested it should repay consumers with their money within the first 14 days; or consumers will not be able to invest money in loan agreements within the first 14 days after they register with any P2P platform.[119] If the platform has a secondary market and allows investors to sell their loans to other investors at

---

[117] 'FCA Handbook', FCA, accessed 1 June 2023, https://www.handbook.fca.org.uk/handbook/CASS.
[118] FCA, 'The FCA's Regulatory Approach to Crowdfunding Over the Internet, and the Promotion of Non-Readily Realisable Securities by Other Media: Feedback to CP13/13 and Final Rules', PS14/4, March 2014, p. 22, https://www.fca.org.uk/publication/policy/ps14-04.pdf.
[119] FCA, 'The FCA's Regulatory Approach to Crowdfunding (and Similar Activities)' FCA CP13/13, October 2013, p. 28, https://www.fca.org.uk/publication/consultation/cp13-13.pdf.

market price, it would be unreasonable to give investors the extra withdraw right.

(4) Information disclosure rule: information disclosure is critical to protect financial consumers, as financial firms are supposed to provide accurate and adequate information for their consumers to make informed decisions. Firms have to illustrate both benefits and risks of an investment and, in particular, they should not downplay the possibility of potential losses. Investors on P2P platforms are susceptible to different types of financial risks including credit risk, market risk, operation risk, and systemic risk. Investors could suffer financial losses if their borrowers default or their platforms encounter any financial or operational problems. Thus, investors should be given sufficient information and risk warning before contributing their money to the investments. The FCA asks P2P lending platforms to disclose relevant information to investors, including but not limited to information about the firm, information about the service, financial promotion rules, performance information, guarantees, protections and security mechanisms, comparative information, and periodic reporting information.[120]

(5) FCA reporting requirement: the FCA has imposed a mandatory reporting obligation on P2P lending platforms to submit information such as financial position reports, client money reports, regular reports on investments, and complaints reports.[121] It enables the regulator to monitor lending trends and detect potential risks, as well as ensure that consumers are treated fairly. Apparently, having sufficient industry data lays a sound foundation for effective financial regulation. The FCA has been conducting a consultation process with major P2P lenders, discussing potential new reporting obligations regarding the past performance of loans and the amount of due diligence work that P2P platforms are supposed to do over the borrower's past performance.[122]

(6) Administration in the event of platform failure: the insolvency of certain P2P platforms will be inevitable in a highly competitive market, and therefore it is necessary to have an administration procedure in place to protect investors as well as to reduce the negative impacts on the economy. P2P loan agreements are entered into by lenders

---

[120] Ibid., p. 29.
[121] Ibid., p. 34.
[122] Laura Noonan, 'P2P Lenders to Be Asked to Reveal Defaults', *The Financial Times*, 12 August 2017, p. 2.

(investors) and borrowers, while P2P platforms only serve as information intermediaries who are not considered as a contractual party. Accordingly, the failure of a P2P lending platform will not cause direct economic losses to investors using that platform. But it will be difficult for individual investors to administer their loans on an individual basis if their online platforms no longer exist. As all contracts have been made in an electronic form stored in the systems of P2P platforms, investors do not even know the identity of their debtors. It is common that one investor only owns a small percentage of a P2P loan which has been crowdfunded by hundreds of investors. Therefore, in order to protect investors' interests when a platform goes bust, the FCA requires P2P lenders to set up the following arrangements in advance: client money should be distributed to investors under the client money rules; a new client bank account should be set up to receive ongoing payments for existing loans under the client money rules; no new loans should be made and existing loans will remain valid under their original terms; and the firm's arrangements to manage those existing loans, apportioning repayments to the right investors and following up late repayments or borrower defaults, should come into effect.[123]

(7) Dispute resolution process: it is imperative to have a complaints procedure for financial consumers who feel prejudiced or unsatisfied about the financial services they are receiving. Thus, the FCA requires P2P firms to establish a complaint handling process for investors. After the internal procedure, investors are entitled to take their complaints further to the FOS.[124] In the UK, any dispute between customers and companies that offer financial services could be resolved through the FOS, which is a free and simple-to-use tool.

In July 2018, the FCA issued a consultation paper (CP18/20) proposing some changes to the regulatory framework over loan-based crowdfunding.[125] Then in June 2019, the FCA confirmed the latest regulatory rules for P2P platforms in its policy statement (PS19/14).[126] For retail customers who are fresh

---

[123] FCA, 'The FCA's Regulatory Approach to Crowdfunding (and Similar Activities)' FCA CP13/13, October 2013, p. 26, https://www.fca.org.uk/publication/consultation/cp13-13.pdf.
[124] Ibid., p. 33.
[125] FCA, 'Consultation Paper: Loan-Based ("Peer-to-Peer") and Investment-Based Crowdfunding Platforms: Feedback on Our Post-Implementation Review and Proposed Changes to the Regulatory Framework', FCA CP18/20, July 2018, https://www.fca.org.uk/publication/consultation/cp18-20.pdf.
[126] FCA, 'Policy Statement: Loan-Based ("Peer-to-Peer") and Investment-Based Crowdfunding Platforms: Feedback to CP18/20 and Final Rules', FCA PS19/14, June 2019, https://www.fca.org.uk/publication/policy/ps19-14.pdf.

to the P2P lending industry, the FCA is limiting investments in P2P agreements to 10% of their investable assets.[127] This is a crucial way to make sure investors don't expose themselves to unnecessary risk. For new retail customers who received regulated financial guidance, the investment restriction will not be applicable. With a focus on credit risk assessment, risk management, and fair valuation practices, there are also more specific requirements to specify what kind of governance arrangements, systems, and controls P2P lending platforms must have in place to support the outcomes they intend to achieve. Additionally, it established the minimal information that P2P platforms must give investors and introduced a requirement that lending platforms evaluate investors' knowledge and experience of P2P investments when no professional guidance has been provided to them. Finally, in some cases, the regulation applies the FCA's Mortgage and Home Finance Conduct of Business (MCOB) Sourcebook and other FCA Handbook requirements to P2P platforms that sell home finance products to investors.[128]

6.8 Conclusion

This chapter has discussed how the Fintech revolution has led to an increase in online lending markets. Online P2P lending enhances the distribution of capital to areas that need it the most, furthering financial equality between small companies and large corporations. As discussed, SMEs are of paramount importance to the global economy. In the UK, they account for 99.9% of the business population, 60% of private sector employment, and half of the national GDP. Nonetheless, they only obtain a quarter of total business loans from banks, as financial institutions have been hesitant to lend to smaller businesses after the global financial crisis. Obvious, the amount of financial credit allocated to SMEs does not match their economic contributions and actual demands, resulting in the longstanding SME financing dilemma.

The chapter then assessed the rising online P2P lending markets in the US, China, and the UK. Through analysis from a functional perspective, it concludes that P2P lending can be utilised by SMEs as an effective alternative finance method to close the financing gap. In practice, P2P lending has multiple advantages over bank lending, as financial disintermediation creates extra value for both investors and borrowers. The chapter has also

---

[127] Ibid.
[128] FCA, 'FCA Confirms New Rules for P2P Platforms', 4 June 2019, https://www.fca.org.uk/news/press-releases/fca-confirms-new-rules-p2p-platforms.

examined policies and regulatory rules relating to P2P lending sectors across the world. The UK government has launched several projects to promote SME finance like the FLS, BFP, and Innovative Finance ISA. In a nutshell, governments have tried to reduce SMEs' reliance on traditional banks and to build a multilevel financing system for smaller businesses. The current regulatory framework in the UK is comprised of the industry self-regulation and the FCA's official regulation. Since 2014, the P2P lending market has entered into a new era as loan-based crowdfunding has been included in the FCA's regulated activities. P2P lending platforms have to comply with a series of regulatory requirements ranging from prudential capital requirements to business conduct rules. Arguably, the online P2P lending industry, under effective regulation, will continue to experience fast growth in the future, supplying more funds to SMEs.

7
Fintech in Monetary and Payment Systems

7.1 Introduction

This chapter discusses the Fintech revolution in relation to monetary and payment systems, which have the most far-reaching impact on people's life and work. Fintech also affects the way in which most commercial transactions are conducted. Since the invention of BTC in 2008, as the first generation of blockchain-based cryptocurrencies, we have seen the emergence of over 10,000 digital coins across the world.[1] Most cryptocurrencies are launched by private entrepreneurs and corporations, challenging the dominant position of central banks and monetary authorities who used to preserve the power of making money. Cryptocurrencies have certain advantages like decentralisation and anonymity, but they are also criticised for aiding illicit activities and money laundering. One significant disadvantage of crypto coins is the price instability, making them a less desirable option for serving as the medium of exchange. Accordingly, stablecoins, such as Tether and Diem, have been created to address the problem of price volatility as their value is pegged to mainstream currencies, commodities, and financial instruments. To counter the rise of privately issued digital coins, central banks began to create official or sovereign digital currencies, known as CBDCs.[2] Meanwhile, the time has witnessed the digital transformation of payment methods, as people and businesses are embracing contactless and mobile payment instruments like Apple Pay, Google Pay, Alipay, and WeChat Pay.[3] Thanks to the prevalence of digital money and payment systems, a number of countries and cities are quickly becoming a cashless society.

After this introduction, Section 7.2 presents the fast evolution of digital money and payment systems, as governments and financial authorities

---

[1] 'Number of Cryptocurrencies Worldwide from 2013 to February 2023', Statista, accessed 1 June 2023, https://www.statista.com/statistics/863917/number-crypto-coins-tokens/.
[2] Lerong Lu and Hang Chen, 'Digital Yuan: The Practice and Regulation of China's Central Bank Digital Currency'. *Butterworths Journal of International Banking and Financial Law* (2021) 36: 601–603.
[3] Lerong Lu, 'Decoding Alipay: Mobile Payments, a Cashless Society and Regulatory Challenges'. *Butterworths Journal of International Banking and Financial Law* (2018) 33: 40–43.

have made policy initiatives to go cashless in the 21st century. Section 7.3 focuses on the blockchain-based cryptocurrencies, such as BTC and Ethereum, explaining their operating mechanisms and what accounts for the investment mania. It also considers regulatory issues in relation to financial stability, money laundering, and initial coin offerings (ICOs). Section 7.4 examines the advantages and limitations of stablecoins, which are perceived as a more advanced version of cryptocurrencies, invented to solve the price volatility issue. Section 7.5 considers CBDCs as global central banks proactively promote official digital money in order to enhance public trust and maintain their economic influence. Section 7.6 discusses the popular mobile payment networks around the world, including Fintech payment systems based on NFC technology and QR code. Section 7.7 draws a conclusion.

7.2 Towards a cashless society: the evolving digital money and payment network

Currency and payment systems make up a nation's fundamental financial infrastructure, which underpins the operation of modern businesses. Money is at the centre of any financial system. It has evolved throughout history from actual commercial commodities like grains and shells, to precious metals like gold and silver, and finally to paper notes that are issued by central banks. The explosive growth of digital money in various forms has been observed in the global financial system since the turn of the 21st century. There are several explanations for this phenomenon. Firstly, after the global financial crisis of 2007–2008, businesses and consumers have been actively looking for alternatives to traditional fiat money (i.e., banknotes and coins). This is because people are losing trust in the current banking and monetary institutions. Fiat money has dominated the world's economy for a long time, as notes and coins are issued by one country's central bank or financial authority, such as the US dollar, European Euro, British pound, and Chinese yuan.[4] Secondly, growth of the digital economy has been facilitated by recent technological advancements in the areas of AI, big data, cloud computing, and blockchain. It causes cutting-edge financial technology to emerge. Due to the widespread use of personal computers, smartphones, and the internet, digital currency and payments are now technologically ready. Thirdly, the Covid-19

---

[4] Robert J. Barro, 'Money and the Price Level under the Gold Standard'. *The Economic Journal* (1979) 89: 13–33.

pandemic has sped up society's shift to a virtual economy because a large portion of people have been conducting business, relaxing, and shopping from home. This has led to a rise in demand for Fintech and digital money services that can be easily accessed online, through mobile apps, or in the Metaverse.[5]

As a result, numerous types of digital currency have emerged, as both private and public sectors propose to create their own digital currency for the economy of the future. So far, we have seen three waves of digital money creation. The first wave is the rise of blockchain-based cryptocurrencies. Privately created cryptocoins like BTC and Ethereum, which challenge the status quo of the global financial system and central banks' dominant role in money production and circulation, have swiftly become prevalent as both a new asset class and a payment method.[6] In 2008, the concept of BTC was invented by Satoshi Nakamoto who published an online paper advocating a new form of electronic cash that people can send to each other without going through disgraced banks.[7] Various types of digital tokens, including Dogecoin, Cardano, and Ethereum, have since grown in popularity. There were 10,397 types of digital currency being traded globally as of February 2022.[8] A few benefits of cryptocurrencies are decentralisation, cost-effective transactions, and anonymity. However, cryptocurrencies are less suited to become the medium of exchange and the store of wealth over the long term due to their severe price volatility. For instance, the price of BTC dropped below $30,000 in May 2022, which is 50% less than the peak it reached in November 2021.[9]

The second wave of digital money innovation is the growth of stablecoins, which have been created to address the concern of price instability as observed in most cryptocurrencies. The price of stablecoins, such as Tether (USDT) and Meta-backed Diem, is pegged to mainstream currencies, physical commodities, or financial instrument.[10] They are viewed as a safer alternative by consumers and investors who can actually track the value of the assets that support stablecoins. Due to their linkage to recognised

---

[5] Lerong Lu and Alice Lingsheng Zhang, 'Regulating Fintech Corporations Amidst Covid-19 Pandemic: An Analysis of Ant Group (Alipay)'s Suspension of IPO and Business Restructuring'. *Company Lawyer* (2021) 42: 341–343.
[6] Lerong Lu, 'Bitcoin: Speculative Bubble, Financial Risk and Regulatory Response'. *Butterworths Journal of International Banking and Financial Law* (2018) 33: 178–182.
[7] 'Financial Technology: Friends or Foes?', *The Economist*, 6 May 2017, p. 12.
[8] 'Number of Cryptocurrencies Worldwide from 2013 to February 2023', Statista, accessed 1 June 2023, https://www.statista.com/statistics/863917/number-crypto-coins-tokens/.
[9] Scott Chipolina, 'Bitcoin Falls Below $30,000 for First Time Since July 2021', *The Financial Times*, 10 May 2022, https://www.ft.com/content/d2a9df43-1ea0-4fb2-9b02-4944589fd909.
[10] Gary B. Gorton and Jeffery Y. Zhang, 'Taming Wildcat Stablecoins'. *The University of Chicago Law Review* (2023) 90: 909–971.

official currencies issued by central banks, fiat-based stablecoins have partially addressed the issue of weak public trust. Depending on whether they have a centralised or decentralised design, stablecoins can use a variety of price stabilising strategies. The majority of cryptocurrencies and stablecoins have been created by private companies, such as tech firms, investment funds, and entrepreneurs, and their lack of government support appears to limit their ability to gain wider adoption.

The third wave of digital money invention is the occurrence of CBDCs. Global monetary authorities and central banks have started to design their own versions of digital currencies, known as CBDCs or sovereign digital money, so as to maintain their prestigious status and influence over the economy. The BIS reports that 86% of central banks surveyed have been actively involved in CBDC-related research projects, proofs of concept, and pilot programmes.[11] In the 2020s, CBDC is likely to be the most important undertaking for central banks around the world. Some well-known CBDC pilot projects include the European Central Bank's digital euro, the PBoC's digital yuan, and, more recently, the US Federal Reserve's digital dollar.[12] Countries like China intend to use CBDCs to support the implementation of their national strategy of currency internationalisation by encouraging the wider use of sovereign digital money in cross-border, retail, and wholesale transactions.[13] We can anticipate the coexistence of both private and public digital money in the near future, which will present several technical obstacles and regulatory issues.

Apart from the three waves of Fintech innovations in money, payment methods have gone through tremendous digital transformation in the 2010s. The rapid adoption of mobile payment over more established payment methods like cash, cheques, and bank cards is mostly attributable to the rise in use of smartphones and the introduction of high-speed mobile networks like 4G and 5G. According to estimates, 5G mobile networks could boost the global economy by $565 billion by 2034, as nations compete in developing 5G

---

[11] Codruta Boar, Henry Holden, and Amber Wadsworth, 'Impending Arrival—a Sequel to the Survey on Central Bank Digital Currency', BIS Papers No. 107, January 2020, https://www.bis.org/publ/bppdf/bispap107.pdf.
[12] The US Federal Reserve, 'Federal Reserve Board Releases Discussion Paper that Examines Pros and Cons of a Potential U.S. Central Bank Digital Currency (CBDC)', 20 January 2022, https://www.federalreserve.gov/newsevents/pressreleases/other20220120a.htm.
[13] Lerong Lu and Alice Lingsheng Zhang, 'China Experiments with Cross-Border Payments of Central Bank Digital Currencies', Columbia Law School's Blog on Corporations and Capital Markets, 17 December 2021, https://clsbluesky.law.columbia.edu/2021/12/17/china-experiments-with-cross-border-payments-of-central-bank-digital-currencies/.

information highways.[14] Manufacturers of smartphones sold 314.4 million devices in the first quarter of 2022, with Samsung (which holds a 23.7% market share), Apple (18.0%), Xiaomi (12.7%), OPPO (8.7%), and Vivo (8.0%) dominating the industry.[15] The popularity of smartphone use and the 5G network is the prerequisite for digital mobile payments. Additionally, more retailers and customers have chosen mobile payments during the Covid-19 pandemic as physical contact of buying with cash could spread the virus. As a result, the majority of traditional brick-and-mortar businesses, including restaurants, grocery stores, clothing stores, and online-to-offline (O2O) services like bike sharing, food delivery, and taxi services now accept mobile payments. With partnerships with more than 2,700 banks, Apple Pay has 127 million users, while the largest mobile payment system in the world, Alipay, has 450 million users.[16] The US mobile payment market is worth about $112 billion, whereas the Chinese mobile payment business is worth CNY38 trillion ($5.7 trillion).[17]

Many countries and cities have declared their intention to promote a cashless society in the 2020s as a result of the widespread use of digital currency and mobile payment options. In 2023, Sweden claimed that it would completely adopt digital currency and eliminate cash in the very near future.[18] In the UK, the use of cash has declined rapidly. Cash accounted for 60% of all payments made in the UK in 2008, while the figure quickly dropped to 28% in 2018.[19] Due to its world-class telecom infrastructure and extremely high smartphosine adoption rate, China has promoted a cashless society and over 1 billion of its citizens are familiar with e-money and mobile payment services provided by Alipay and WeChat Pay.[20] A survey suggests that 14% of Chinese residents no longer carry any cash when going out, while 26%

---

[14] Justin McCurry, 'US Dismisses South Korea's Launch of World-First 5G Network as "Stunt"', *The Guardian*, 4 April 2019, https://www.theguardian.com/technology/2019/apr/04/us-dismisses-south-koreas-launch-of-world-first-5g-network-as-stunt.
[15] International Data Corporation, 'Smartphone Market Share', 17 May 2021, https://www.idc.com/promo/smartphone-market-share/vendor.
[16] Helen H. Wang, 'Alipay Takes on Apple Pay and PayPal on their Home Turf', *Forbes*, 30 October 2016, https://www.forbes.com/sites/helenwang/2016/10/30/will-alipay-dominate-global-mobile-payments/.
[17] Leslie Hook and Gabriel Wildau, 'China Mobile Payments Soar as US Clings to Plastic', *The Financial Times*, 14 February 2017, p. 12.
[18] The Wharton School of the University of Pennsylvania, 'Going Cashless: What Can We Learn from Sweden's Experience?', 31 August 2018, https://knowledge.wharton.upenn.edu/article/going-cashless-can-learn-swedens-experience/.
[19] UK Finance, 'UK Payment Markets Reports 2019 Summary', June 2019, p. 3, https://www.ukfinance.org.uk/sites/default/files/uploads/pdf/UK-Finance-UK-Payment-Markets-Report-2019-SUMMARY.pdf.
[20] Lerong Lu, 'Decoding Alipay: Mobile Payments, a Cashless Society and Regulatory Challenges'. *Butterworths Journal of International Banking and Financial Law* (2018) 33: 40–43.

carry less than CNY100 ($15).[21] The cashless or even cardless way of life has not only made shopping, dining, and using public transportation much more convenient for consumers, but also raised the standard for hygiene in these establishments. It is expected that more global cities and countries will go cashless in the near future, because building a cashless society is likely to be an appealing policy objective for governments and financial authorities.

7.3 Cryptocurrencies

7.3.1 Definition and operating mechanism

Cryptocurrency, commonly referred to as crypto, virtual currency, or blockchain-based digital currency, is a type of digital money that operates as a medium of exchange over a network of computers independent of any centralised authority like a central bank or governmental agency. Blockchain, a distributed public ledger that is updated and maintained by the coin holders, is the technology that underlies cryptocurrencies.[22] Through a process known as mining, when investors employ computer power to solve complex mathematical issues, new units of BTC are being created. Additionally, users have the option of purchasing the currencies from brokers, then storing and spending them in digital wallets. The holds of cryptocurrencies do not possess any tangible assets. Instead, they possess a digital key that enables owners of cryptocurrencies to transfer a record or a unit of measurement between individuals without the use of a dependable third party. That is why cryptocurrencies are called virtual currencies in many cases, which is opposite to physical currencies like banknotes and coins. The creation of the latter lies in the monopolised power of central banks, and their operation would require the involvement of third parties like commercial banks and payment systems.

We have witnessed an unprecedented rise in blockchain-based digital currencies including BTC, Ethereum, BNB, XRP, Cardano, Solana, and Dogecoin since the debut of BTC as the first cryptocurrency in 2008. Over 10,000 different coins are currently listed in cryptocurrency exchanges. Due to the fact that two cryptocurrencies—BTC, with a market cap of

---

[21] 'About 14% People Carry No Cash in China', *China Daily*, 6 September 2017, http://www.chinadaily.com.cn/bizchina/tech/2017-09/06/content_31633683.htm.
[22] See Chapter 2, Section 2.3 for a more thorough explanation of blockchain technology.

$580.27 billion, and Ethereum, with a market cap of $250.21 billion—represent over 70% of the market value of all cryptocurrencies, the market is very concentrated.[23] Due to its popularity and substantial market share, BTC will therefore be used as our primary example while addressing cryptocurrencies in this chapter. The system of BTC is P2P in its essence, for transactions occur among users directly without the involvement of traditional financial intermediaries. Each user is a tiny fraction of the whole BTC universe. The creation and exchange of BTCs takes place in a blockchain as a decentralised public record system. Clearly, BTC and the underlying blockchain technology not only represent the very frontier of the ongoing Fintech revolution, but also echo the spirit of Adam Smith's free-market ideology.

This section intends to analyse the BTC trading and mining mania. It explores relevant legal and regulatory issues relating to AML, evasion of FX controls, and the illegal fundraising activities of start-ups by ICOs, as well as the financial meltdown and platform collapse in global cryptocurrency markets. It also considers the latest regulatory changes around the world, including various approaches to determining the legitimacy of ICOs, the restructuring of top BTC exchanges, and the forthcoming state-backed digital currencies.

7.3.2 What accounts for the popularity of BTC?

The rise of BTC and other virtual currencies is partly because of the global financial crisis 2007–2008 that has made many ordinary people and investors partly lose confidence in the existing financial system and rethink the possible future forms of money. During the Covid-19 pandemic, more people tend to use digital currencies or invest in crypto assets as they work from home and shop online, resulting in a sharp increase in non-physical commercial and financial transactions taking place every second.[24] Moreover, government measures to support the digital or virtual economy typically coincide with the rise in popularity of cryptocurrencies. Most nations, including Australia, China, Denmark, Germany, India, Japan, the Netherlands, Norway, Singapore, the UK, and the US, have seen a considerable decline in the quantity of

---

[23] 'Cryptocurrency Prices by Market Cap', CoinMarketCap, accessed 1 June 2023, https://coinmarketcap.com/.
[24] Lerong Lu and Alice L.S. Zhang, 'Regulating Fintech Corporations Amidst Covid-19 Pandemic: An Analysis of Ant Group (Alipay)'s Suspension of IPO and Business Restructuring'. *The Company Lawyer* (2021) 42: 341–343.

cash and cash-like transactions, which decreased at an average annual rate of 6% from 2006 to 2016.[25]

In recent years, the demand for virtual currencies has taken off for a multiplicity of reasons. Firstly, an increasing number of start-up companies are choosing to raise money through ICOs. An ICO is, to some extent, akin to an IPO when a private business sells shares on a stock exchange for the first time and thus becomes a publicly traded company. Issuers sell digital coins or tokens to investors who, for fiat or virtual currency, obtain a stake in the start-up, such as a right to use the service or software provided by the start-up.[26] More companies and individuals are thinking about using ICOs to raise money or take part in investment opportunities.[27] The marketplaces for these digital assets are less regulated than traditional capital markets. Even if they may offer a novel and effective way to conduct financial transactions, they also increase the danger of fraud and market manipulation. Unlike global capital markets, the price of digital coins largely depends on the valuation of their issuers and a small community of investors. Thus, for many newly launched digital currencies, the price hike has been considered as self-dictated, as the limited number of potential buyers means low market liquidity. The price of the cryptocoins is likely to face a sudden fall at any time.

Secondly, the BTC bubble is a speculation carnival for investors and traders across the world. For global investors, BTC seems to be a perfect object on which they could take a bet on its ever-growing intrinsic value. This is because there is a theoretical maximum number of all BTCs circulated, which is around 21 million (20,999,999.9769 BTCs). Therefore, as time lapses, it will cost more and more time and money to mine new BTCs, leading to their skyrocketing price. As stated, the market capitalisation of all BTCs was estimated at $580.27 billion as of March 2022, making it an increasingly important asset class for retail and institutional investors like hedge funds and family offices. Globally, there are predicted to be over 300 crypto-focused hedge funds, with an expected 150% market growth in 2021 and an average fund size of US$58.6 million.[28] Moreover, as a result of the growth of Fintech trading platforms like Trading 212 and Robinhood during the Covid-19 epidemic, more retail investors began participating in cryptocurrency investing.

---

[25] Tanai Khiaonarong and David Humphrey, 'Cash Use Across Countries and the Demand for Central Bank Digital Currency'. *Journal of Payments Strategy and Systems* (2019) 13: 32–46.

[26] Izabella Kaminska and Alice Woodhouse, 'Bitcoin Rises Above $4,000 in Record Run for Digital Currency', *The Financial Times*, 14 August 2017, https://www.ft.com/content/e2d3fcb8-80cf-11e7-94e2-c5b903247afd.

[27] 'Spotlight on Initial Coin Offerings (ICOs)', SEC, accessed 1 June 2023, https://www.sec.gov/securities-topic/ICO.

[28] PwC, '4th Annual Global Crypto Hedge Fund Report 2022', June 2022, https://www.pwc.com/gx/en/financial-services/pdf/4th-annual-global-crypto-hedge-fund-report-june-2022.pdf.

Thirdly, the rapid rise of the BTC price is partly due to strict FX controls in some countries. For example, the Chinese government in 2016 introduced several exchange control methods to curb capital outflows, including complex approval procedures for sending money out of the country.[29] Due to the difficulty of transferring money between countries through official banking channels, some businesses and individuals in the affected countries try to convert local currencies into BTCs first, and then exchange BTCs into the currencies of destination. This seems to be a feasible and convenient way of moving large amounts of money outside the border of any country without being caught by law enforcers, despite the potential market risks (i.e., the price fluctuation of BTCs). However, that is partly why BTC is criticised for assisting in contravening national laws and financial regulations, leading to more stringent regulatory rules to be imposed or even a total ban in certain jurisdictions.

Last but not least, BTC has attracted a large number of so-called digital 'miners' to dig new coins and seek fortune. The process of creating new BTCs is called mining, for miners use special software to solve maths problems (the difficulty of which increases over time) in exchange for new coins. In the early days, miners solved maths problems by using their personal computers and processors. Later, miners tried to employ graphics cards for gaming and making 3D animation which are more efficient in running advanced algorithms to produce BTCs. Most recently, application-specific integrated circuits have been used for BTC mining which have a stronger computing power but consume less electricity. It was estimated, in 2014, that at least $1 billion was invested in mining equipment.[30] As more and more miners joined the BTC network, the likelihood for individuals to solve the maths problems decreased, so miners started to collaborate through mining pools. Each member of the pool will be rewarded a certain number of BTCs in proportion to their workload. Mining plays an important and indispensable role in the BTC world, contributing to the system's efficiency, stability, and security.

Numerous miners and investors have become multimillionaires overnight, as a result of the bullish market. The wealth effect, in turn, has drawn more entrepreneurs, professional investors, and tech talents into the BTC arena. For example, some IT programmers in the US have turned the basements of their houses into BTC mining fields, equipped with sophisticated computer

---

[29] Charles Clover, 'China's Capital Curbs Hit EU Companies', *The Financial Times*, 7 December 2016, p. 6.
[30] Stephen Foley and Izabella Kaminska, 'Bitcoin "Miners" Caught in Arms Race', *The Financial Times*, 23 August 2014, p. 14.

hardware and monitors with scrolling lists of seemingly random numbers and letters.[31] Some Chinese investors have set up BTC mines with complex computing systems in small towns high up in the mountains where visitors have to bring their own cans of oxygen.[32] This is because of the Chinese government's negative attitude towards the legitimacy of BTC mining, as the large amount of money flowing from such mines is beyond state control. A 24-hour mine like this can produce around 50 BTCs per day, which equal approximately $1.4 million based on the current market price. Clearly, China has become the centre of the cryptocurrency universe, for at its peak BTC trading in the country accounted for 90% of the world's total transactions.[33]

7.3.3 The nature of BTC: is it real money?

We have not reached a consensus on the precise nature of BTC and other crypto assets, including whether they should be regarded as money in the conventional sense, despite the feverish investing activities in these assets. Money has changed over the course of human history, from commodities like cowrie shells, to precious metals like gold and silver, to officially issued coins and paper notes. The creation of fiat money and related payment methods like cheques and bank cards in the 20th century considerably increased economic efficiency and decreased transaction costs.

In the eyes of the general public, the term money mostly refers to physical coins and banknotes. Economists believe that money has to fulfil three basic functions—as a medium of exchange, a unit of account, and a store of value.[34] Legal scholars define money as any item that is generally being treated as payment for goods and services or repayment of debts by community.[35] Clearly, money is essential to any modern commercial transactions as it solves the trust problem between transacting parties. Otherwise, any transaction would need a double coincidence of wants, which is the foundation of a bartering economy. Governments regard money as legal tender or fiat,

---

[31] Sarah O'Brien, 'Bitcoin "Miners" Dig More than Just the Money', *CNBC*, 15 August 2017, https://www.cnbc.com/2017/08/15/Bitcoin-miners-dig-more-than-just-the-money.html.

[32] Danny Vincent, 'We Looked Inside a Secret Chinese Bitcoin Mine', *BBC*, 4 May 2016, http://www.bbc.com/future/story/20160504-we-looked-inside-a-secret-chinese-Bitcoin-mine.

[33] Peng Qinqin, Wu Yujian, and Han Wei, 'China Steps up Curbs on Virtual Currency Trading', *Caixin*, 8 September 2017, https://www.caixinglobal.com/2017-09-09/101142821.html.

[34] Paul Davidson, 'Money and the Real World'. *The Economic Journal* (1972) 82: 101–115.

[35] Ross Cranston et al., *Principles of Banking Law*, 3rd ed. (Oxford: Oxford University Press, 2018), p. 363.

as their acceptance by the public is prescribed by law. Fiat money derives its value from state endorsement, as it does not have the intrinsic value or use value as commodity money has.

When BTC is being examined against the aforementioned criteria to define money, we find that it could fit into the characterisation of money to some extent. For instance, cryptocurrencies can be used as a medium of exchange. An increasing number of companies, restaurants, and charities have started to accept certain digital tokens, so consumers could exchange BTC for goods and services that they want. Tesla allows consumers to purchase its brand merchandise using Dogecoin, and there has been a circulating rumour that the electric car maker would accept BTC for its cars.[36] However, most large corporations like Amazon and Walmart still do not take cryptocurrencies for payment, so the primary use of digital tokens has remained a tool for financial investment or speculation.

In the future, if cryptocurrencies are becoming more widely accepted by businesses and governments, there will be more products and services coming with a price label in BTC. This will make BTC a unit of account similar to mainstream currencies like the USD, GBP, Euro, JPY, and CNY. In September 2021, El Salvador adopted BTC as its legal tender, as the world's first country to give cryptocurrencies an official endorsement.[37] Vendors could not refuse to accept this form of money if they represent legal tender. Thus, BTC and other crypto tokens are likely to welcome more official backing, especially from some smaller countries that are experiencing a falling exchange rate and seeking alternatives to their own currencies.

Finally, whether BTC can be viewed as a store of value is still controversial. We have witnessed the spectacular rise of the BTC price since its invention, as 1 BTC was only worth $0.06 in July 2010 and its price stood over $50,000 in February 2024.[38] Therefore, any long-term investors or savers who have purchased BTC would enjoy handsome profits compared with most financial instruments like shares, bonds, unit funds, or saving products. However, in practice, most holders of BTC are short-term investors or speculators who trade crypto assets frequently within a very short time frame, like day trading. Such trading activities could expose investors to enormous market risks, as the price of BTC once lost over 30% overnight.

---

[36] 'Tesla Starts Accepting Once-Joke Cryptocurrency Dogecoin', *BBC*, 15 January 2022, https://www.bbc.co.uk/news/business-60001144.

[37] Christine Murray, 'El Salvador Endures Bumpy First Week with Bitcoin as Legal Tender', *The Financial Times*, 10 September 2021, https://www.ft.com/content/842415ec-06cb-437b-932f-f868d4f55fc4.

[38] The real-time price of BTC can be viewed at 'Bitcoin Price', CoinDesk, accessed 1 June 2023, https://www.coindesk.com/price/bitcoin/.

7.3.4 Risks of BTC and regulatory concerns

The rapid rise of BTC and other virtual currencies increasingly raises legal and regulatory concerns. At present, it is difficult to ascertain how large the BTC bubble is, when it will burst, and what forms of governmental responses are actually needed. Clearly, overoptimism about the future of blockchain technology, BTC, and any other cryptocurrencies should be avoided, as irrational exacerbation often leads to financial disaster. In an ever-changing financial world, we should bear in mind the proverb 'Caution is the parent of safety'. Therefore, policy-makers and financial regulators need to pay attention to various risks presented by BTCs. For example, BTCs have been widely used as a practical method to transfer money internationally, so as to evade national FX regulations. It has resulted in capital flight in some jurisdictions and thus violated financial regulatory rules. This section discusses four primary regulatory concerns relating to cryptocurrencies: AML, ICO, financial stability, and the direction in which cryptocurrency will develop in the future.

The first regulatory concern is about the AML dilemma. Aside from circumventing FX regulations, BTCs have been criticised for aiding global money laundering activities. For instance, in July 2017, Alexander Vinnik, a Russian citizen who operates the BTC exchange BTC-e, was accused by the US authority of laundering over $4 billion for criminal activities ranging from computer hacking to drug trafficking.[39] Larry Fink, the CEO of BlackRock, the largest asset management firm in the world, commented that, 'Bitcoin just shows you how much demand for money laundering there is in the world. That's all it is.'[40] BTCs seem to be a perfect tool for laundering criminal proceeds as all transactions bypass the regulated banking system, making the tracking of money movement difficult for public authorities. In contrast to the traditional financial industry bounded by disclosure and transparency rules, the BTC market allows 100% anonymity (or pseudonymity). The purchasing or selling of BTCs does not require user identification, and BTC exchanges do not need to keep proper documentation of their users and transactions. Moreover, BTC transactions can be executed through the so-called dark web by using 'The Onion Router (TOR)' network, which hides the

---

[39] Samuel Gibbs, '"Criminal Mastermind" of $4bn Bitcoin Laundering Scheme Arrested', *The Guardian*, 27 July 2017, https://www.theguardian.com/technology/2017/jul/27/russian-criminal-mastermind-4bn-Bitcoin-laundering-scheme-arrested-mt-gox-exchange-alexander-vinnik.

[40] Fred Imbert, 'Blackrock CEO Larry Fink Calls Bitcoin an "Index of Money Laundering"', *CNBC*, 13 October 2017, https://www.cnbc.com/2017/10/13/blackrock-ceo-larry-fink-calls-Bitcoin-an-index-of-money-laundering.html.

real IP address of users. What makes criminal investigations more difficult is the decentralised feature of BTC. A transaction typically spreads across multiple jurisdictions, creating uncertainty about which country's authority has the power to launch a criminal investigation. It also causes difficulty in terms of which country's AML laws and regulations should be applied.

The second regulatory concern pertaining to BTC is whether the ICOs are legitimate under securities regulation. The answer varies across different countries. The Howey Test is used in the US to determine whether cryptocurrencies or ICOs are considered as securities.[41] When deciding whether a transaction meets the criteria for an investment contract, it alludes to a case decided by the US Supreme Court. If it is determined to be an investment contract, the transaction will be regarded as a security, and then the registration requirements under the Securities Act of 1933 and the Securities Exchange Act of 1934 will apply. Judged by the Howey Test, some cryptocurrencies and ICOs do satisfy the criteria for being investment contracts, making them subject to US securities laws. In September 2017, the SEC charged a businessman and two companies running ICOs with fraud and selling unregistered securities (around $300,000).[42] However, in cases where large ICOs are backed by major law firms and Silicon Valley tycoons, the regulator tends to interpret such practices in favour of the fundraisers. Across the Pacific, the Chinese authorities have taken a tough stand on ICOs. On 4 September 2017, the PBoC together with six government departments jointly issued 'The Notice of Preventing Financial Risks Relating to Initial Coin Offerings' (the Notice).[43] This piece of regulation plays a vital role in determining the legal status of ICOs in the world's largest market for BTCs and other cryptocurrencies. The Notice describes ICOs as unregistered and illegal public fundraising activities, which could result in criminal offences under PRC Criminal Law, including offences for illegal selling of tokens, illegal securities issuance, and illegal fundraising, and for financial fraud and pyramid schemes.[44] In addition, it has imposed an immediate ban on any new ICOs.[45] Organisers of completed ICOs are required to set up repaying arrangements, so as to protect the interest of existing investors and to manage financial risks. As ICOs have been deemed illegal

---

[41] SEC v W.J. Howey Co, 328 US 293 (1946).
[42] SEC, 'SEC Exposes Two Initial Coin Offerings Purportedly Backed by Real Estate and Diamonds', 29 September 2017, https://www.sec.gov/news/press-release/2017-185-0.
[43] PBoC, 'The Notice of Preventing Financial Risks Relating to Initial Coin Offerings', 4 September 2017, http://www.pbc.gov.cn/goutongjiaoliu/113456/113469/3374222/index.html.
[44] Ibid., Article 1.
[45] Ibid., Article 2.

in China, the BTC price immediately fell by 9% to $4,437 following the release of the Notice.[46]

Thirdly, when dealing with the booming virtual currency market, global financial regulators have placed a high priority on the protection of financial stability. Although the $150-billion cryptocurrency market only takes up a small proportion of the entire financial industry, the rapid growth suggests its increasing importance. The recent price hike likely indicates the formation of an asset bubble. Clearly, investors who entered the BTC market at an early stage have profited handsomely from the massive rally, but for new investors there seem to be more risks than prospective benefits. The continuing bullish market is, to a large extent, driven by pure speculation rather than the fundamentals of virtual currencies. A further price correction is expected in the near future. In 2008, the burst of the US subprime housing bubble triggered the global financial crisis and subsequent economic recessions. The destructive power of a financial bubble is self-evident as it undermines people's confidence in the capitalist economy and liberal democracy. The Chinese central bank and securities regulator are particularly wary of any signs of a speculative bubble, for the country encountered a devastating stock market crash in 2015.[47] The burst of the BTC bubble could have a negative impact on the global economy and even cause social unrest, as relevant investments are not covered by official financial protection schemes, like deposit insurance. As a result, when a crisis hits, BTC investors will have to bear all financial losses themselves. Thus, in September 2017, the Chinese authorities ordered some top BTC exchanges (including OKCoin, Huobi, and BTCC) to close down and submit plans for liquidating their businesses, so as to cool speculative activities and prevent the next financial crisis.[48] The market responded fiercely to the announcement, as the BTC price slumped by over 20%.[49] However, over-the-counter (OTC) transactions are still allowed, and mining activities have not been affected so far. Accordingly, whether such extreme regulatory methods are effective or not remains unclear. These methods could force investors to trade directly with each other or trade through foreign platforms, leading to extra financial risk and greater difficulty

---

[46] Nan Ma, 'China Halts Virtual Coin-Based Fundraising After Declaring Offerings Illegal', *The Financial Times*, 5 September 2017, p. 18.

[47] Lerong Lu and Longjie Lu, 'Unveiling China's Stock Market Bubble: Margin Financing, the Leveraged Bull and Governmental Responses'. *Journal of International Banking Law and Regulation* (2017) 32: 146, 149.

[48] 'China Orders Bitcoin Exchanges in Capital City to Close', *BBC*, 19 September 2017, http://www.bbc.co.uk/news/business-41320568.

[49] Ben Chapman, 'Bitcoin Plummets More Than 20% After China Vows to Close Cryptocurrency Exchanges', *Independent*, 15 September 2017, http://www.independent.co.uk/news/business/news/Bitcoin-latest-updates-drops-china-close-crypto-currency-exchanges-btccchina-a7947826.html.

in monitoring and supervision. In November 2022, FTX, the world's third-largest cryptocurrency exchange based in the Bahamas, suddenly collapsed due to a liquidity crisis.[50] The bankruptcy of FTX resulted in billions of investor losses, and its senior executives have faced fraud and other charges in the US, as more than $8 billion in FTX's customer funds is missing. The failure of a significant cryptocurrency exchange can have effects on investors and the overall economy that are equivalent to those of previous financial crises, as demonstrated by the case of FTX.

Fourthly, policy-makers and financial authorities are concerned about the direction of cryptocurrency development going forward. As mentioned, one distinctive feature of cryptocurrencies is decentralisation and non-authority intervention. However, this is about to change as governments in several countries have been testing state-backed cryptocurrencies. The issuance of notes and the creation of new money had been the preserve of central banks for centuries until the recent invention of P2P virtual currencies, so it is unsurprising that monetary authorities feel reluctant to hand over this great power to individuals and companies which can easily create a new virtual currency simply with personal computers connected to the internet. An official cryptocurrency seems to be a compromise between financial innovation and state control. State-backed virtual currencies will make it easier for central banks and financial regulators to oversee the money flow and detect underlying financial risks. In addition, it could facilitate the making, implementation, and adjustment of monetary policies in particular jurisdictions. Since 2014, the PBoC has carried out several trial runs of its prototype digital currency.[51] The PBoC could be the first major central bank to issue virtual money endorsed by the state. The Bank of Canada is also examining the possibility of introducing a government-issued digital currency.[52] A consortium of Japanese commercial banks has obtained regulatory approval from the central bank and financial regulator to launch the 'J-Coin', a quasi-official cryptocurrency which can be used to pay for goods and services as well as transfer money via smartphones.[53]

---

[50] Dietrich Knauth and Tom Hals 'Failed Crypto Exchange FTX Has Recovered Over $5 Bln, Attorney Says', *Reuters*, 11 January 2023, https://www.reuters.com/business/finance/ftx-seeks-court-rulings-asset-sales-customer-privacy-2023-01-11/.

[51] 'China Is Developing its Own Digital Currency', *Bloomberg*, 23 February 2017, https://www.bloomberg.com/news/articles/2017-02-23/pboc-is-going-digital-as-mobile-payments-boom-transforms-economy.

[52] Ben Fung, Scott Hendry, and Warren E. Weber, 'Canadian Bank Notes and Dominion Notes: Lessons for Digital Currencies', Bank of Canada Staff Working Paper 2017-5, http://www.bankofcanada.ca/wp-content/uploads/2017/02/swp2017-5.pdf.

[53] Martin Arnold and Leo Lewis, 'Japan's Big Banks Plan Digital Currency Launch', *The Financial Times*, 26 September 2017, https://www.ft.com/content/ca0b3892-a201-11e7-9e4f-7f5e6a7c98a2.

7.4 Stablecoins

7.4.1 Definition and operating mechanism

The second generation of digital money is often referred to as stablecoins, such as Tether (USDT), CACHE Gold, and Meta's Diem. They have been created by corporations and other private entities to resolve certain shortcomings of the first-generation cryptocurrencies, especially their extreme price fluctuation and value instability.[54] As their name suggests, stablecoins have been designed to possess value that is relatively stable, as they will be backed by real assets like traditional currencies and commodities in most scenarios. Stablecoins are intended to trade at part with a benchmark asset, usually the US dollar or gold. As a result, stablecoins can be utilised better as the unit of account or store of value, as well as in other situations where it might be less advantageous to employ volatile cryptocurrencies. While preserving stability in relation to their reference assets is a key goal shared by all stablecoins, there are significant differences between them in terms of their economic structure, backing quality, stability assumptions, and legal safeguards for coin owners.[55] Stablecoins are most commonly acquired by traders and investors through exchange platforms. Moreover, by putting down the necessary collateral with the issuing company, such as US dollars with Tether or actual gold with CACHE, it is possible to create brand-new stablecoins.

Since 2020, stablecoins have attracted lots of media attention, when Facebook attempted to launch Libra (later renamed as Diem) as the social media giant's own cryptocurrency and payment system. The Diem has nonetheless later come under harsh criticism and opposition from central banks, academia, and the general public over issues related to monetary sovereignty, financial stability, data privacy, and anti-competitive issues.[56] As of April 2023, the total market capitalisation of stablecoins amounted to $132.62 billion, representing 12.8% of the overall value of all cryptocurrencies.[57] Since the majority of stablecoins are backed by US dollars in a 1:1 ratio, they have often been traded at a price of near $1 per coin. From Table 7.1 we can see that the most popular stablecoins are Tether (USDT) and USD

---

[54] Gary B. Gorton and Jeffery Y. Zhang, 'Taming Wildcat Stablecoins'. *The University of Chicago Law Review* (2023) 90: 909–971.
[55] Christian Catalini and Alonso de Gortari, 'On the Economic Design of Stablecoins', SSRN, 6 August 2021, http://dx.doi.org/10.2139/ssrn.3899499.
[56] Hannah Murphy, 'Facebook's Libra Currency to Launch Next Year in Limited Format', *The Financial Times*, 27 November 2020, https://www.ft.com/content/cfe4ca11-139a-4d4e-8a65-b3be3a0166be.
[57] 'Top Stablecoin Tokens by Market Capitalization', CoinMarketCap, accessed 1 June 2023, https://coinmarketcap.com/view/stablecoin/.

Table 7.1 The top five stablecoins by market capitalisation.

Rank	Name	Price	Market capitalisation	Circulating supply
1	Tether (USDT)	$1.00	$80,427,905,969	80,351,588,890 USDT
2	USD Coin (USDC)	$0.9999	$32,378,960,875	32,377,344,130 USDC
3	Binance USD (BUSD)	$1.00	$6,957,890,908	6,956,739,385 BUSD
4	Dai (DAI)	$0.9996	$5,251,364,278	5,252,802,018 DAI
5	TrueUSD (TUSD)	$1.00	$2,115,219,413	2,112,950,272 TUSD

Source: Based on information from 'Top Stablecoin Tokens by Market Capitalization', CoinMarketCap, accessed 1 June 2023, https://coinmarketcap.com/view/stablecoin/.

Coin (USDC) as they have a market capitalisation of $80.43 and $32.38 billion respectively. Other leading dollar-backed stablecoins are Binance USD (BUSD), Dai (DAI), and TrueUSD (TUSD) which all have a collective value of over $1 billion. Clearly, stablecoins are viewed as one of the most feasible options for future digital money, given their price stability mechanism and close link with mainstream currencies, commodities, and other real assets.

In practice, stablecoins are reliant on a collection of technologies akin to those powering more well-known cryptocurrencies like BTC and Ethereum. Therefore, the users of stablecoins could enjoy the same benefits offered by any cryptocurrencies, like transparency, transaction security, anonymity, and privacy, as we have discussed in the previous section. Stablecoins, on the other hand, are less susceptible to price fluctuations, which are thought to be the biggest problem for most digital coins and which prevents them from being widely used as a major currency. To reduce their price volatility, the majority of stablecoins have their value pegged to one or more mainstream world currencies or to other tangible assets like gold and silver. Stablecoins are therefore a special category of cryptocurrency whose price is supported by the value of their underlying assets. To maintain public confidence and price stability, the company or other entities that produce and operate stablecoins would need to maintain a reserve of underlying assets equivalent to the total quantity of stablecoins in circulation. Stablecoin owners have the option to redeem their coins for the underlying assets.

The popularity of stablecoins is partly attributed to the growing trend of DeFi, which refers to the provision of financial services and products by using smart contracts and blockchain-based protocols. DeFi allows consumers to access basic financial services like saving, lending, borrowing, and investments without the involvement of banks or other financial institutions.[58] Stablecoins are the application of DeFi in money and payment systems, which forms the foundation and key infrastructure of a DeFi world.

Investors, by purchasing stablecoins and depositing them in decentralised lending protocols, could achieve a better return than traditional fixed-income investments like savings, bonds, and money market funds. For instance, TerraUSD holders have been provided with a 20% annual return on investment, which is the primary reason for stablecoins' rising popularity.[59] The higher return and potentially safer design make stablecoins appeal to many risk-taking investors of cryptocurrencies or traditional investors holding financial assets such as shares and bonds.

7.4.2 Main categories of stablecoins

Based on how they function, particularly the type of underlying assets, there are four distinct types of stablecoins. Firstly, there are fiat-backed stablecoins, which are the most common stablecoins, as their value is backed by US dollars, Euros, Chinese yuan, or other major fiat currencies at a fixed ratio like 1:1. Examples are TUSD, USDT, USDC, and Diem. Most of them have been created by issuers who hold off-chain (i.e., not on the blockchain) collateral through regulated banks which serve as the depositary of fiat currencies to support the value of such stablecoins. The creation of fiat-based stablecoins is intended to promote wider use of cryptocurrencies. As a result, cryptocurrency users can utilise fiat-pegged stablecoins to make online purchases just like they would with any other kind of virtual money. Fiat-pegged stablecoins have another noteworthy feature in that their value is correlated to that of the fiat currency that serves as their underlying asset. Accordingly, they don't fully base their value on the short-term effects of supply and demand, so they are typically seen as a more trustworthy type of cryptocurrency.

Secondly, there are commodity-backed stablecoins, which are pegged to the price of commodities and physical assets including precious metals, oil, and real estate. Gold has been the most common commodity to be used as collateral for such stablecoins. Traditional commodity investors are particularly drawn to these stablecoins. It is because the stablecoins enable them to invest in gold without having to source and store real gold, which could be expensive and time-consuming. Examples are Tether Gold (XAUT) and Paxos Gold (PAXG). The stablecoins can typically be redeemed by their holders at a conversion rate to obtain the real assets. However, the cost of holding and safeguarding the commodity backing is part of the stablecoins' operation.

---

[59] Zeke Faux and Muyao Shen, 'A $60 Billion Crypto Collapse Reveals a New Kind of Bank Run', *Bloomberg*, 19 May 2022, https://www.bloomberg.com/news/articles/2022-05-19/luna-terra-collapse-reveal-crypto-price-volatility.

Thirdly, there are crypto-backed stablecoins, which have their price collateralised by one or a portfolio of cryptocurrencies and the peg is executed on-chain (i.e., on the blockchain) via smart contracts. Stablecoins backed by crypto function essentially the same as stablecoins backed by fiat. It maintains the value of a pegged asset. However, the cryptocurrency-backed stablecoin uses reserved cryptocurrency instead of money as collateral. In most cases, Ethereum is used. One of the most well-known stablecoins with a cryptocurrency backing is MakerDAO. It pools enough ether (ETH) on the Ethereum blockchain in a self-executing smart contract to serve as collateral for its stablecoin. Users can then mint DAI, the MakerDAO stablecoin, once the amount of collateral in the smart contract hits a specific threshold.

Fourthly, there are algorithmic stablecoins, such as TerraUSD, which are not backed by any currencies, commodities, or virtual assets. Instead, they rely on computer algorithms to adjust the supply of stablecoins in an intelligent manner. At any time, the algorithms will automatically mint (create) new coins or burn (remove) existing coins from circulation, according to real-time data regarding the fluctuating demand for such digital tokens. A typical algorithmic stablecoin structure, known as a two-coin system, uses one coin to buffer market volatility while the other tries to maintain the peg. The former token is widely traded on secondary decentralised markets and is also identified as a balancer or sharing token. Algorithmic stablecoins rely on independent investors engaging in price stabilising arbitrage in order to get market incentives to sustain a supposedly stable ecosystem. However, it is dangerous to rely on independent, market-driven people to carry out discretionary arbitrage without being bound by the laws or any financial regulations.

7.4.3 Advantages and limitations of stablecoins

Since the first wave of cryptocurrencies, including BTC and Ethereum, are entirely virtual, there is no reliable process for setting their prices because they have no intrinsic value. Thus, the value of BTC and most cryptocurrencies is basically determined by the overall market supply and demand of relevant digital tokens, which has rendered their price incredibly unstable. Also, as cryptocurrencies have been issued by private entities, they do not have the endorsement from governments. Therefore, it is less likely for BTC to become a common means of exchange due to the price fluctuation, the lack of underlying assets, and the lack of state credit. In contrast, stablecoins have been created to address these limitations associated with cryptocurrencies.

They are considered as a safer option for investors and consumers who could actually observe the value of assets underpinning stablecoins. In particular, fiat-based stablecoins, which are pegged to official currencies issued by central banks, have partially solved the issue of a lack of public trust.

There are various price stabilisation mechanisms for stablecoins, depending on whether they have adopted a centralised or decentralised design. Take Tether as an example of centralised stablecoins. They would need a central custodian to manage and hold the underlying assets. Tether, as it is backed by US dollars, has a bank account to hold the currency reserves in an amount equivalent to the number of Tethers being circulated. Therefore, the price fluctuation of Tether could be minimised. On the other hand, there exist other decentralised stablecoins which could also achieve the function of price stability without resorting to a centralised authority. For instance, Dai, as a cryptocurrency-backed stablecoin, is operating on Ethereum blockchain. It employs a smart contract to manage collaterals and maintain a value of $1.00 without actually holding any US dollars in a bank account. This is done through the automatic adjustment of the number of digital coins in circulation to prevent price fluctuation.

It is debatable if stablecoins will actually be able to attain long-term price stability, which is a requirement for developing a widely used type of digital currency. Clearly, the price of stablecoins' underlying assets could still undergo fierce price change. In recent years, we have experienced the Covid-19 pandemic, the war in Ukraine, and many other economic and geo-political incidents, leading to enormous price fluctuation of major currencies and commodities like oil and wheat. A lot of 'black swan' events expose investors to highly unexpected financial risks, and it is unlikely that investors will have fully safe or stable assets in the current macroeconomic environment.[60] Therefore, if the underlying assets of stablecoins start to lose value or become illiquid during any economic turmoil, the price of stablecoins, correspondingly, will be likely to experience high volatility. In this sense, the price of stablecoins is not always stable, so its name might be a misleading label. It is simply that inventors and operators of stablecoins try to use their names to attract more risk-averse investors.

The US Federal Reserve, in its '2022 Financial Stability Report', pointed out that stablecoins are susceptible to runs, when investors rush to convert their holding of stablecoins to underlying assets.[61] In May 2022, the price of

---

[60] Lerong Lu, 'Black Swans and Grey Rhinos: Demystifying China's Financial Risks and the Financial Regulatory Reform'. *Butterworths Journal of International Banking and Financial Law* (2018) 33: 594–597.
[61] The US Federal Reserve Board, 'Financial Stability Report', May 2022, p. 42, https://www.federalreserve.gov/publications/files/financial-stability-report-20220509.pdf.

TerraUSD fell below $1.00, which is the value figure that most dollar-backed stablecoins would like to maintain.[62] It's because Luna, a sister cryptocurrency to TerraUSD that uses the same operating system, underwent a price crash and dropped from over $100 to under a penny. Moreover, many investors of Tether, as the world's largest stablecoin, have often raised the concern whether Tether has sufficient US dollars or other dollar equivalents in its bank account to support their token value. In February 2021, Tether settled a legal dispute with the New York Attorney General's Office, as the corporation and a crypto firm Bitfinex agreed to pay a total fine of $18.5 million for making false statements about the backing of Tether. According to Attorney General Letitia James, 'Tether's claims that its virtual currency was fully backed by U.S. dollars at all times was a lie'.[63] Moreover, a senior regulator from the US warned Tether investors about the lack of interoperability because stablecoins based on dollars cannot be exchanged for one another directly.[64] Not all stablecoins operate in the same way across multiple blockchains. For stablecoins to be widely utilised in daily payment rather than investing, this could be a significant barrier.

7.5 Central bank digital currencies (CBDCs)

There is no denying that the global economy has been embracing Fintech-enabled digital money. However, it is less certain about which form of digital currencies will dominate tomorrow's financial world. As discussed, cryptocurrencies are prone to significant price fluctuation, and their lack of public authority and ineffective regulation often cause regulatory challenges like money laundering and financial instability. Similarly, the value of stablecoins is not always stable as their operators have claimed, due to the insufficient reserve of underlying assets. So far, it doesn't seem like traditional fiat currencies could be replaced by either the first-generation cryptocurrencies or the more current stablecoins. Therefore, as an official response to the crypto age, central banks and monetary authorities around the world have started

---

[62] The collapse of both Luna and TerraUSD wiped out $60 billion market value for investors. See Zeke Faux and Muyao Shen, 'A $60 Billion Crypto Collapse Reveals a New Kind of Bank Run', *Bloomberg*, 19 May 2022, https://www.bloomberg.com/news/articles/2022-05-19/luna-terra-collapse-reveal-crypto-price-volatility.
[63] New York State Attorney General, 'Attorney General James Ends Virtual Currency Trading Platform Bitfinex's Illegal Activities in New York', 23 February 2021, https://ag.ny.gov/press-release/2021/attorney-general-james-ends-virtual-currency-trading-platform-bitfinexs-illegal.
[64] Jesse Hamilton, 'Top US Bank Watchdog Warns of Stablecoins' Lack of Interoperability', CoinDesk, 8 April 2022, https://www.coindesk.com/policy/2022/04/08/top-us-bank-watchdog-warns-of-stablecoins-lack-of-interoperability/.

investigating and testing CBDCs. This section considers the incentives for central banks to introduce official digital currencies and the various design options of CBDCs.

7.5.1 Definition and operating mechanism

Aside from cryptocurrencies and stablecoins, the third type of digital money is state-backed CBDCs or sovereign digital currencies. They denote the official solution to the rise of digital money and Fintech payment networks. Central banks aim to exploit CBDCs to join the currency competition, having addressed certain limitations of privately issued digital tokens. CBDCs have certain advantages that are typically found in central bank-issued money (i.e., banknotes) such as settlement finality, liquidity, and integrity. Such features make them more widely acceptable for the digital economy. CBDCs are the digital representation of sovereign currency made by one jurisdiction's monetary authority that will appear on the liability side of their balance sheets.[65] Contrary to decentralised money like BTCs and stablecoins, CBDCs are governed by a centralised system similar to that for conventional currencies, like US dollars, Euros, British pounds, and Japanese yen. Since governments are pushing for digital payment and a cashless society, all transaction records and stored data of CBDCs will therefore be accessible to authorities. CBDCs also contribute to more effective monetary policy solutions, as they not only act as official money and payment systems but also work as an interest leverage tool. In practice, they could even be charged with extra regulatory functions like the AML tool or fraud prevention procedure, as well as cross-border applications to accelerate currency internationalisation.[66]

CBDCs have drawn a lot of interest recently as a potential digital substitute for conventional fiat currencies. They are issued and backed by central banks, which are in charge of preserving the integrity and stability of the financial system. CBDCs are a new type of money being issued digitally by central banks as legal tender, which is genuine money in the legal and economic

---

[65] John Kiff et al., 'A Survey of Research on Retail Central Bank Digital Currency', IMF Working Paper No. 20/104, June 2020, https://www.imf.org/en/Publications/WP/Issues/2020/06/26/A-Survey-of-Research-on-Retail-Central-Bank-Digital-Currency-49517.

[66] Lerong Lu and Alice Lingsheng Zhang, 'China Experiments with Cross-Border Payments of Central Bank Digital Currencies', Columbia Law School's Blog on Corporations and Capital Markets, 17 December 2021, https://clsbluesky.law.columbia.edu/2021/12/17/china-experiments-with-cross-border-payments-of-central-bank-digital-currencies/.

sense.[67] This makes them distinct from privately issued cryptocurrencies like BTC. CBDCs represent cash-like direct claims on the central bank. The BoE perceives CBDCs as a financial innovation in terms of both the form of money provided to the public and the financial infrastructure on which payments can be made.[68] They have the potential to develop into a regulatory toolset if used widely. Initially, they are utilised as an official cash alternative to compete with other digital currencies. Different technological standards, such as distributed ledger technology or a more centralised strategy, can be used to build and deploy CBDCs. Regardless of their design features, CBDCs are expected to be subject to regulatory requirements that are comparable to those that apply to conventional fiat currencies as well as extra regulatory rules because of their digital character, such as cybersecurity and data privacy laws.

According to the BIS, 86% of 65 surveyed central banks have been engaging in some form of CBDC work, with 60% of them having progressed from conceptual research to experiences or proofs-of concepts and 14% moving forward to development and pilot arrangements.[69] Since 2014, the PBoC has carried out several trial runs of its prototype cryptocurrency, and it could be the first major central bank to issue virtual money endorsed by the state.[70] In 2018, the BoE explored the design mode of freely trading bank deposits against CBDCs by elaborating a set of core principles of CBDC issuance.[71] In January 2022, the US Federal Reserve expressed potential interest in developing its digital currency (digital dollars) and issued a discussion paper examining the pros and cons of the adoption of CBDCs.[72] At present, CBDCs seem to be the most viable non-physical currency option for the digital economy thanks to their advanced regulatory functions, stable value, and,

---

[67] Tommaso Mancini Griffoli et al., 'Casting Light on Central Bank Digital Currency', IMF Staff Discussion Notes No. 18/08, 13 November 2018, https://www.imf.org/en/Publications/Staff-Discussion-Notes/Issues/2018/11/13/Casting-Light-on-Central-Bank-Digital-Currencies-46233.

[68] BoE, 'Central Bank Digital Currency Opportunities, Challenges and Design', BoE Discussion Paper, 12 March 2020, https://www.bankofengland.co.uk/-/media/boe/files/paper/2020/central-bank-digital-currency-opportunities-challenges-and-design.pdf.

[69] Codruta Boar, Henry Holden, and Amber Wadsworth, 'Impending Arrival—a Sequel to the Survey on Central Bank Digital Currency', BIS Papers No. 107, January 2020, https://www.bis.org/publ/bppdf/bispap107.pdf.

[70] Lerong Lu and Hang Chen, 'Digital Yuan: The Practice and Regulation of China's Central Bank Digital Currency'. *Butterworths Journal of International Banking and Financial Law* (2021) 36: 601–603.

[71] Michael Kumhof and Clare Noone, 'Central Bank Digital Currencies—Design Principles and Balance Sheet Implications', BoE Staff Working Paper No. 725, May 2018, https://www.bankofengland.co.uk/-/media/boe/files/working-paper/2018/central-bank-digital-currencies-design-principles-and-balance-sheet-implications.

[72] The US Federal Reserve Board, 'Federal Reserve Board Releases Discussion Paper that Examines Pros and Cons of a Potential U.S. Central Bank Digital Currency (CBDC)', 20 January 2022, https://www.federalreserve.gov/newsevents/pressreleases/other20220120a.htm.

most importantly, official endorsement and wide acceptability. However, it is argued that CBDCs may increase the risk of bank runs because a significant quantity of savings will likely be moved away from commercial banks. In addition, they could result in the rise of the surveillance state, whereby governments are able to collect more transaction data from citizens and restrict their financial freedom.

7.5.2 Market vs state: currency competition

The decentralisation and lack of interference from governments are two distinguishing characteristics of cryptocurrencies. This is set to change, though, as a large number of countries have been experimenting with state-backed digital currency. Up until the recent invention of P2P virtual currencies, the issuance of notes and the creation of new money had been the exclusive preserve of central banks for centuries. As a result, it is not surprising that monetary authorities are reluctant to transfer this great power to individuals or organisations, since anyone with access to the internet can now easily create a new virtual currency. An official cryptocurrency appears to be a compromise between governmental control and financial innovation. At present, a hundred nations are presently studying CBDCs in some capacity, with some testing and possibly giving them to the general population. Evidently, one possible turning point in the history of money is the introduction of CBDCs. With CBDCs, central banks and financial regulators will find it simpler to monitor the money flow and identify underlying risks associated with state-backed virtual currencies. Other benefits of CBDCs include settlement finality, liquidity, and integrity, which are often present in central bank-issued money. These advantages make CBDCs a more commonly accepted form of payment for digital trade.

So far, the digitisation of money has raised the mounting issue of currency competition, as both private and public sectors compete to create new forms of digital tokens, making their own monetary standards for the future economy. CBDCs seem to be an effective solution in the eyes of monetary authorities because they help to restrict the use of privately produced digital currencies, which could endanger monetary sovereignty and financial stability. It is also challenging to monitor and regulate privately issued digital money operating outside the realm of a country's financial regulatory architecture. In contrast, CBDCs are a sort of centrally controlled cryptocurrency that central banks can use to counteract the market dominance of private payment systems. Central banks are able to monitor almost all transactions made by CBDCs. The regulatory powers against criminal and illegal activities may be expanded for CBDCs. In the event that a large amount of data is gathered through their use, CBDCs could also serve as a future regulatory toolkit for financial authorities.

Evidently, CBDCs compete more favourably than other digital currencies thanks to the strong backing of the national credit and the requirement of compulsory circulation. CBDCs could assist central banks in increasing the efficiency of monetary policy. Due to their digital nature, they can be used as a payment method as well as an interest-leverage instrument to improve the way monetary policies are transmitted. It is clear that CBDCs make it more straightforward for central banks to develop, implement, and adjust monetary policies in most jurisdictions. Since they are the fiat currency issued by a central bank, they benefit from the attribute of having unlimited legal credit. They are subject to the same legal indemnity framework as banknotes and coins due to the fact they are considered as legal tender. If the requirements for acceptance are met, neither individuals nor businesses may refuse to accept CBDCs when they are being used to pay any public or private debts. Being legal tender is the ultimate goal for any digital currency if it is going to be used on an expansive basis, so this is a significant competitive advantage for any CBDCs.

7.5.3 Design options and characteristics

This section will examine five essential design elements of CBDCs. Firstly, CBDCs are likely to substitute cash in circulation, which is known as M0 in economics.[73] In practical terms, CBDCs often function as M0 to replace cash as the fundamental unit of money. M0 is the term used to describe the currency used by people in daily transactions, as opposed to the reserve currency kept in banks. It is classified as money in the strictest sense, since it is monopolistically issued by the central bank of a sovereign state and because there are alternative commonly used payment methods like cheques and credit cards. Currency is divided into layers according to its liquidity: M0 is the direct claim on the central bank with the highest liquidity; M1 contains both currency in circulation and tradable deposits, which represents the direct purchasing power of society as a whole; M2 typically consists of M1 and other non-tradable deposits like the time deposit; and M3 is made up of M2 and other current assets like government bonds, bank acceptances, and

---

[73] Lerong Lu and Hang Chen, 'Digital Yuan: The Practice and Regulation of China's Central Bank Digital Currency'. *Butterworths Journal of International Banking and Financial Law* (2021) 36: 601–603.

commercial paper. When calculating the inflation rate and making monetary policies, central banks should classify CBDCs as cash (rather than deposits or other current assets) if they are to be considered M0, which would give them immediate purchasing power on the commodity market. On the other hand, the fundamental idea behind issuing CBDCs is the digitisation of currency, whose inherent value is just as secure as that of legal tender.

Secondly, CBDCs can be used in three different application contexts: retail, wholesale, and cross-border.[74] Retail CBDCs, often referred to as general-purpose CBDCs, are virtual currencies designed for use by individuals and small businesses. They can be applied to a range of transactions, including in-person, online, and P2P payments. They are easier to use and marketed towards the general public. Most existing CBDC projects, such as China's digital yuan and Sweden's e-krona, are targeted at retail transactions.[75] At the retail level, direct cash payment without any settlement activities through banks or other financial institutions is the most straightforward and popular option for concluding transactions. The benefits of cash payments in this situation are evident, including their adaptability, rapidity, and widespread acceptance. Cash becomes the best payment mechanism for retail purchases, which is also what CBDCs want to do. Furthermore, CBDCs can lower clients' storage expenses and the danger associated with carrying cash. They lessen the time lag and lower the cost of transfers among commercial banks. They can also reduce a nation's maintenance costs for its currency. Wholesale CBDCs, on the contrary, are digital currencies made for use in high-value interbank settlements and other financial transactions conducted by banks and other major financial organisations. They are designed for usage within the financial sector and are not often available to the general public. The design aspects of CBDC applications vary in real-world use. While Dinero Electronico in Ecuador and Petro in Venezuela are primarily focused on retail CBDCs, Project Jasper in Canada adopts a hybrid approach with an emphasis on wholesale CBDCs. Apart from retail and wholesale applications, by enhancing CBDCs' cross-border applicability, central banks can encourage the further development and widespread adoption of sovereign digital money.[76] According to the FSB, there is a consensus among major economies, such as the G20, to enhance cross-border

---

[74] Andrew Usher et al., 'The Positive Case for a CBDC', Bank of Canada Staff Discussion Paper, 20 July 2021, https://www.bankofcanada.ca/wp-content/uploads/2021/07/sdp2021-11.pdf.
[75] Lerong Lu and Hang Chen, 'Digital Yuan: The Practice and Regulation of China's Central Bank Digital Currency'. *Butterworths Journal of International Banking and Financial Law* (2021) 36: 601–603.
[76] Lerong Lu and Alice Lingsheng Zhang, 'Could the Dragon Now Fly Beyond Borders? Contextualizing Regulatory Aspects and Risks for China's CBDC Cross-Border Use'. 1 September 2021. https://ssrn.com/abstract=3935854.

payments.[77] It is evident that national economies would benefit if CBDCs offered cross-border payment services that were less expensive, faster, more transparent, and inclusive.

Thirdly, CBDCs could be offered in either token-based or account-based formats.[78] Despite being a purely technical issue, the division of CBDCs has significant effects on their design, expense, identity verification, and access management. Account-based CBDCs are digital currencies that may be accessed using a digital wallet or other electronic devices and are kept in a central bank account.[79] They can be used for a number of transactions, including P2P payments, online purchases, and in-person payments. They can be held by individuals, companies, and financial institutions. A trusted third party is often used in an account-based method to confirm a user's identification as the account holder. It is also used to check a user's account balance before allowing them to make a payment. The accounts are then appropriately debited and credited. Account-based CBDCs could result in unnecessary expenses, and the requirement for additional verification stages could incur similar costs and deficiencies in current financial systems. For wholesale CBDC and interbank payments, where the compromise between accessibility and identity proof seems to be more clear-cut, an account-based solution might be more appropriate. In contrast, token-based CBDCs are digital money represented by digital tokens or other tokenised assets.[80] They are transferable between users and can be kept in a digital wallet or other technological device. CBDCs built on tokens may offer further features or capabilities, like compatibility with smart contracts or other programmable forms of currency. In practice, the verification of token-based CBDCs employing blockchain technology removes the requirement to check a customer's balance before approving a transaction. A transaction will be automatically executed as long as users can prove their identity as the token holder, such as providing a private key and signing the transaction, and meet the necessary level of identity criteria. Although there is a danger involved when a private key is lost, there are ways to maintain the control of ownership in such situations. Without the requirement for an account, token-based systems can offer a more direct, cash-like approach. Multifactor authentication

---

[77] FSB, 'Enhancing Cross-Border Payments: Stage 3 Roadmap', 13 October 2020, https://www.fsb.org/wp-content/uploads/P131020-1.pdf.

[78] Alexander Lee, Brendan Malone, and Paul Wong, 'Tokens and Accounts in the Context of Digital Currencies', US Federal Reserve Board Feds Notes, 23 December 2020, https://www.federalreserve.gov/econres/notes/feds-notes/tokens-and-accounts-in-the-context-of-digital-currencies-122320.html.

[79] BIS, 'Central Bank Digital Currencies: System Design and Interoperability', September 2021, p. 4, https://www.bis.org/publ/othp42_system_design.pdf.

[80] Ibid.

is used to stop double-spending, which is the practice of simultaneously spending or spending the same cash more than once.

Fourthly, CBDCs' operating models can be categorised as centralised, decentralised, or hybrid.[81] A central authority, such as a central bank, which has the authority to control the flow of currency and keep an eye on transactions involving it, issues and regulates centralised CBDCs. This is the most common design option for global central banks. However, CBDCs that function in a decentralised manner are supported by distributed ledger technology, such as blockchain. Transactions with decentralised CBDCs are documented on a public, decentralised network and are often protected by cryptographic methods. The additional design option could produce a hybrid CBDC, where decentralised and centralised components of CBDCs are combined. They operate similarly to a centralised CBDC in the way that they are issued and managed by a central bank. However, they are also supported by a decentralised ledger system, making them comparable to a decentralised CBDC or other first-generation cryptocurrencies like BTC and Ethereum. Compounding the advantages of both centralised and decentralised digital currencies is the ultimate aim of creating any hybrid CBDC. For instance, a hybrid CBDC can provide transaction efficiency and transparency that typically belong to a decentralised digital currency, whilst possessing the beneficial features of a centralised digital currency, such as state credit, security, and stability. As a result, this might make hybrid CBDCs a more appealing choice to governments and a broader range of users, such as individuals, corporations, and financial institutions.

Fifthly, the anonymity design is likely to be another crucial feature of CBDCs. When creating CBDCs, central banks must strike a fine balance between the requirements for AML compliance and the protection of personal data privacy, so the anonymity feature should be carefully considered.[82] In the EU, the proportionality test is a requirement for member states to ensure that the regulatory power given to any government under a particular law does not improperly restrict other fundamental rights.[83] The Court of Justice of the European Union (CJEU) may review the AML transaction monitoring procedure to determine whether a case requiring banks to

---

[81] Wouter Bossu et al., 'Legal Aspects of Central Bank Digital Currency: Central Bank and Monetary Law Considerations', IMF Working Paper No. 2020/254, 20 November 2020, https://www.imf.org/en/Publications/WP/Issues/2020/11/20/Legal-Aspects-of-Central-Bank-Digital-Currency-Central-Bank-and-Monetary-Law-Considerations-49827.

[82] Lerong Lu and Alice Lingsheng Zhang, 'Could the Dragon Now Fly Beyond Borders? Contextualizing Regulatory Aspects and Risks for China's CBDC Cross-Border Use'. 1 September 2021. https://ssrn.com/abstract=3935854.

[83] The Charter of Fundamental Rights of the European Union, Article 52(1).

implement the detection and reporting of suspicious customer activity complies with the GDPR.[84] Future outcomes of AML legislation enforcement may be subject to extrajudicial assessments because the protection of data privacy as a fundamental human right must first be respected. Thus, EU member states are most likely to adopt the anonymity mechanism when designing their CBDCs. They will then gradually improve the design features for containing AML risks in order to balance the fundamental rights of individuals with the protection of public interest and reducing compliance costs. This viewpoint has been strengthened by the latest study conducted by the ECB on the anonymity of CBDCs.[85] However, when personal data are used to identify and prevent crimes, Chinese authorities tend to believe that such data are exempt from data protection laws. In mainland China, there are no special provisions that address the issue of AML compliance with respect to the collection of personal data, but the country's PIPL does mandate that administrative officials and regulators should only collect personal data to the extent necessary to meet legal requirements.[86] As a result, creating a token-based CBDC system with complete anonymity is seen as a risky endeavour and is unlikely to be approved by Chinese regulators in the future. China's digital currency is probably going to follow the controlled anonymity approach.[87] The authentication of digital yuan users' identities relies on a controlled anonymity system that fully utilises the particular features of the digital currency—'front-end voluntary' and 'back-end real-name'—in order to preserve privacy and personal data protection. When users transact with one another, it is anonymous; however, the central bank will keep all transaction data under the real names of the users.

It is clear that individual countries have distinctive political, economic, and legal systems, and thus they might adopt different strategies to make their current financial and legal frameworks more compatible with the CBDC experiments. The importance of carefully weighing the benefits and limitations of various CBDC solutions is paramount, as central banks and financial regulators need to adjust their policy initiatives to meet their unique local circumstances. The practical requirements and policy goals of a country

---

[84] GDPR, Article 23.
[85] Anonymity voucher is a new concept introduced by the ECB to create flexibility for users who want to transfer CBDCs without revealing information to the AML authority if they have enough vouchers to spend (a ratio of one voucher per CBDC unit transferred). See ECB, 'Exploring Anonymity in Central Bank Digital Currencies', December 2019, https://www.ecb.europa.eu/paym/intro/publications/pdf/ecb.mipinfocus191217.en.pdf.
[86] PIPL, Article 34.
[87] Lerong Lu and Hang Chen, 'Digital Yuan: The Practice and Regulation of China's Central Bank Digital Currency'. *Butterworths Journal of International Banking and Financial Law* (2021) 36: 601–603.

will ultimately dictate how a CBDC project is designed and implemented within its border.

7.6 Mobile payment systems

7.6.1 Historical development of payment methods

The payment industry has witnessed significant changes in the 2000s and 2010s. People can now make payments using a variety of methods, including cash, cheques, credit cards, debit cards, mobile banking, direct debit, and standing orders. A total of 39.3 billion payments were made in the UK in 2018, with approximately 90% of those coming from consumers and the rest coming from businesses, the government, and not-for-profit organisations.[88] There exist traditional methods of making payments such as paying by cash (banknotes or coins) and paying by cheques. Cash payments once dominated all payment methods, but they have been in steady decline. In early 2010s, cash accounted for 60% of all payments made in the UK, but now it has fallen to only 28%.[89] In the US, as people use cash less frequently, the number of ATMs has decreased annually over the previous few years to 451,500.[90] It is because smartphone payments and card payments, particularly those with the contactless payment function, have grown quickly. Following the Covid-19 outbreak, a growing percentage of consumers never use cash at all and are now using cards and other payment options to manage their expenditure. Digital payments have become more common as a result of the fact that 95% of internet users now access the internet through a mobile device.[91]

Although paying by cheques seems old-fashioned, it is still a standard payment method, especially among the older generation. Due to the growth of card payments and internet payments since the early 1990s, the use of cheques has drastically reduced. In the UK, there were 1.32 billion cheque payments issued in 2008, but 10 years later, that number had significantly

---

[88] UK Finance, 'UK Payment Markets Reports 2019 Summary', June 2019, p. 2. https://www.ukfinance.org.uk/sites/default/files/uploads/pdf/UK-Finance-UK-Payment-Markets-Report-2019-SUMMARY.pdf.
[89] Ibid., p. 3.
[90] Jim Carlton, 'The Number of ATMs Has Declined as People Rely Less on Cash', *The Wall Street Journal*, 3 March 2023, https://www.wsj.com/articles/the-number-of-atms-has-declined-as-people-rely-less-on-cash-81268fa2.
[91] 'The Age of the Appacus: Fintech in China', *The Economist*, 25 February 2017, p. 65.

decreased to 342 million.[92] However, when payers are unaware of the recipient's bank account information, cheque payments are still a preferred payment option that is practical and secure. People who receive cheques must take them to a bank branch and ask the staff members to deposit the funds into their own accounts. However, there are several drawbacks to using cheques for payment. Given that cheques do not always clear immediately, it could take longer than other methods of payment. Cheque recipients may need to wait a specific amount of time before the funds appear in their accounts. Furthermore, using cheques requires caution because they are vulnerable to fraud. There are three basic types of cheque fraud: counterfeit, forgery, and fraudulently altered cheques.[93] A cheque is counterfeit if it was made on a non-bank paper in order to look real. Although it refers to an actual account, it was actually authored by a fraudster with the intent to commit fraud. A valid cheque that has a different account holder's signature on it is referred to as a forgery. The cheque was signed by the fraudster to create a fake signature. A fraudulently altered cheque has been made out by a legitimate customer but has had some part of it changed before it has been cashed, such as changing the amount or the recipient's name. The cheque is no longer valid because it has been modified.

Card payments are likely among the most used forms of payment, especially for routine supermarket and retail purchasing, aside from cash and cheques. Debit cards and credit cards are the two primary categories of plastic payment cards. Instead of using cash, debit card users make purchases and the funds are immediately debited from their bank accounts. The money will then be instantly transferred from the payers to the payees. In many countries, debit cards have surpassed cash as the preferred mode of payment. With credit cards, users can make purchases using a line of credit provided by the institutions that issue the cards. In fact, cardholders borrow money to make payments with a pledge to reimburse the issuers later, along with interest and other fees if they do not pay off the amount in full. The evolution of bank cards has been seen over time. Magnetic stripe or swipe cards are the traditional types of bank cards. On the reverse of the cards there is a real stripe that stores data using modified iron-based magnetic particles. When making a purchase, the cardholder must first swipe the card against the terminal

---

[92] UK Finance, 'UK Payment Markets Reports 2019 Summary', June 2019, p. 5. https://www.ukfinance.org.uk/sites/default/files/uploads/pdf/UK-Finance-UK-Payment-Markets-Report-2019-SUMMARY.pdf.

[93] 'Types of Cheque Fraud', Cheque and Credit Clearing Company, accessed 1 June 2023, http://www.chequeandcredit.co.uk/information-hub/cheque-fraud-advice/types-cheque-fraud.

device and then authorise the transaction with their PIN or signature. Magnetic stripe cards are not very secure since fraudsters can easily copy the information on the strip to create a new card and use it to make purchases to steal money from bank accounts. Due to this, card issuers have been switching over to Europay, Mastercard, and VISA (EMV) chip cards in the 2010s, replacing magnetic stripe cards.[94]

So far, the majority of bank cards have undergone an update to chip and PIN cards, which increases the level of complexity and security of financial transactions. On the top side of chip cards, there is a real computer chip implanted. The cardholder must first insert their card into the terminal before entering their PIN or signing their name. To validate and authorise the transaction, the terminal will get in touch with the issuer using the data from the chip and PIN. Compared to magnetic strip cards, chip cards offer far better security against fraud. The complicated technical standard makes it more difficult to counterfeit chips than stripes. Chips have the ability to generate a constantly changing, one-of-a-kind code each time a payment needs to be made, unlike magnetic strips that can only store static information about cardholders. It is impossible for thieves to read the information on the card because of the dynamic number. In the US, 88% of Mastercard credit cards use chip technology presently.[95] Additionally, more bank cards now include the contactless payment feature. It enables cardholders to conduct payment transactions by just tapping their cards over the device without entering additional information. The contactless cards' integrated circuits store the data that the terminal will wirelessly read using NFC technology. In the UK, Australia, and Canada, over 60% of bank cards now have contactless capability; however, the technology is still not commonly used in the US and Japan.[96]

In addition, direct debits and standing orders are favoured when it comes to regular bill payment. Most consumers choose standing orders or direct debits when paying regular bills to local authorities like utility companies or tax authorities. The distinction between these two payment methods is a source of much confusion. Both of these are requests for your banking institution to regularly pay a third party. When consumers create a standing order, they instruct the banks to make a payment to a certain recipient on a regular basis—for example, a utility company or a broadband service

---

[94] EMV refers to 'Europay, Mastercard, and VISA' which are the three companies that originally developed the technological standard of chip cards.

[95] Charisse Jones, 'Chip-Enabled Credit Cards Mark a Bittersweet 1-Year Anniversary', *USA Today*, 3 October 2016, http://eu.usatoday.com/story/money/personalfinance/2016/10/03/chip-credit-cards-anniversary-pin/91237606/.

[96] Robert Armstrong, 'At Last, US Banks Are Introducing Contactless Cards', *The Financial Times*, 7 January 2019, http://www.ft.com/content/445a308c-02f3-11e9-9d01-cd4d49afbbe3.

provider. Only the consumers are authorised to modify the standing order's specifics, including the recipient and amount. It takes up to three days before the money is transferred. With a direct debit, consumers grant a third-party permission to take a specific sum of money out of their account. The funds will then be instantly sent to the account of the third party, such as the credit card provider. Standing orders are slower and more expensive than direct debits; hence direct debits have taken over as the preferred mode of payment for many businesses.

7.6.2 NFC vs QR code: the technical battle

Nowadays there have been two competing sets of technologies frequently used in the mobile payment industry across the world: NFC and QR code. Both technologies have attracted a large number of IT companies and smartphone makers, as they serve as the technological foundations for smartphone networks. NFC has been employed by notable mobile payment systems like Apple Pay, Samsung Pay, and Android Pay. In contrast, QR code has been mainly used by Chinese mobile payment providers, such as Alipay and WeChat Pay.

NFC is a simple but versatile low-power interface between two devices, supported by some international standards and an independent certification process.[97] The NFC technology originated from radio frequency identification (RFID), and it was jointly developed by Philips and Sony as a new standard for digital devices to establish a P2P network to exchange information and data. An electronic device can gather and analyse data from another device or anything with an NFC tag, thanks to this short-range wireless technology. NFC tags are passive devices since they store information that active NFC devices can access and read. Without an internet connection, power and data will be delivered through linked inductive circuits in close proximity of a few centimetres. In practical terms, a number of major contactless payment systems employ NFC extensively. Additionally, it offers a condensed and adaptable method to convey information for advertisements and social media features like sharing contacts, images, videos, music, and files. With Android Beam, for instance, two Android phones may be held together to share webpages, pictures, contacts, and instructions.[98]

---

[97] Mike Hendry, *Near Field Communications Technology and Applications* (Cambridge: Cambridge University Press, 2014), p. 3.
[98] 'Share Content by NFC with Android Beam', Google, accessed 1 June 2023, https://support.google.com/nexus/answer/2781895.

So far, NFC has been adopted by smartphone operating systems devised by Alphabet (Google), Apple, and Microsoft. Although NFC chips have been built inside credit cards for the purpose of making contactless payments for a long time, the latest change is to incorporate such technology into smartphones and wearables like fitness trackers and smartwatches. When NFC is applied into any contactless payment system, smartphones need to be swiped at an NFC reader, which is normally installed near the cashier machines, so as to complete a contactless payment. NFC is said to digitalise people's wallets as we only need to take a smartphone with NFC chips to buy groceries, take a taxi, or buy a cup of coffee. Users have to hold their smartphones or smartwatches close to contactless payment terminals. Then, relevant payments will complete automatically within a few seconds, as the NFC devices transmit information regarding the smartphone users' debit and credit cards. Since NFC occurs within very short distance, the payment transactions are considered secure and hard to tamper. NFC is also energy-efficient compared with other wireless communication methods.[99] In the future, it is possible that we could store and use any plastic cards (e.g., loyalty card, transportation card, library card, or business card) on our smart devices via NFC. The potential of NFC should not be underestimated for it can be applied in various commercial scenarios. For instance, passive NFC tags can be built into printed advertisements, posters, and informational kiosks to transmit additional information that enables smartphone users to open a web address, get a discount voucher, or view a map.

QR code is a two-dimensional barcode (or matrix barcode) with small black-and-write squares representing data in grid form which can be deciphered by a computer or mobile device.[100] The barcode is a type of machine-readable optical label comprising information regarding the item where it is attached. In order to store data in a more efficient manner, QR code utilises four standardised encoding modes: numeric, alphanumeric, binary, and kanji. QR code can be scanned by electronic devices like the built-in cameras of any smartphone, and then the information will be processed by the devices using Reed–Solomon error correction until the image is finally interpreted.[101] Finally, the data will be extracted from the visual patterns that are present in both horizontal and vertical components of the QR code. QR

---

[99] ST Microelectronics, 'NFC: A World of Opportunities', July 2022, https://www.st.com/content/ccc/resource/sales_and_marketing/promotional_material/brochure/group0/89/ac/b1/59/22/41/4f/47/NFC_a_World_of_Opportunities/files/NFC_Solutions_from_ST.pdf/jcr:content/translations/en.NFC_Solutions_from_ST.pdf.

[100] 'Why QR Codes Are on the Rise', *The Economist*, 2 November 2017, http://www.economist.com/the-economist-explains/2017/11/02/why-qr-codes-are-on-the-rise.

[101] For more information about 'Reed–Solomon codes' see Susan Loepp and William K. Wootters, *Protecting Information: From Classical Error Correction to Quantum Cryptography* (Cambridge: Cambridge University Press 2006), p. 193.

codes often encompass information for a locator, identifier, or tracker pointing to a specific website or smartphone application. In 1994, QR code was firstly invented by Denso, a Japanese automotive manufacturer.[102] It was originally used to track vehicle components during the manufacturing process as QR code allows workers and machines to scan a large number of components at an ultra-high speed. After QR code was invented, it became popular outside the car industry owing to its speediness of reading and great capacity of storing data. Nowadays, QR code has been utilised in a much broader context ranging from commercial tracking applications to consumer smartphone applications. Its popularity has been growing rapidly with the arrival of the smartphone age, as over 5 billion people in the world now own at latest one mobile device.[103]

However, QR codes have received a mixed reaction around the world.[104] In China and some Asian countries, QR codes have become a common and everyday way of connecting the offline life with smartphone apps and websites. However, in the US and Europe, QR codes are less favourable due to the low penetration rate. Clearly, QR codes have multiple advantages over other information technologies. They are versatile and convenient in terms of marketing products and services as they can be printed on product packaging, newspapers, magazines, posters, and billboards. They can be easily added to TV or online advertisements at no extra costs while adding great value to the products and services. As a result, viewers are able to interact with content creators as QR code bridges the offline world with the online one seamlessly. Apart from that, QR codes can be created with images, logos, and other artworks to improve their visual attractiveness and enhance branding and marketing effects.

7.6.3 Case study: Alipay and WeChat Pay

With an estimated user penetration rate of 40.4% and an average annual transaction value of $3,940 per user, China has the largest mobile payment market in the world.[105] The user penetration rates are 27.5% for South Korea, 26.7% for the UK, 26.6% for India, 25.6% for the US, and 24.3% for Germany.

---

[102] 'QR Code Development Story', Denso, accessed 1 June 2023, http://www.denso-wave.com/en/technology/vol1.html.
[103] Kyle Taylor and Laura Silver, 'Smartphone Ownership Is Growing Rapidly Around the World, but Not Always Equally', Pew Research Center, 5 February 2019, http://www.pewresearch.org/global/2019/02/05/smartphone-ownership-is-growing-rapidly-around-the-world-but-not-always-equally/.
[104] Rebecca Sentence, 'The Pros and Cons of QR Codes', Econsultancy, 18 April 2019, http://www.econsultancy.com/the-pros-and-cons-of-qr-codes/.
[105] Katharina Buchholz, 'China's Mobile Payment Adoption Beats All Others', Statista, 8 July 2022, https://www.statista.com/chart/17909/pos-mobile-payment-user-penetration-rates/.

Alipay and WeChat Pay, two major providers of mobile payment who have been widely embraced by retailers, restaurateurs, and e-commerce platforms, control the burgeoning industry for payment apps in China. The development of mobile payment systems in China is unique in a sense that payment options used to be fairly limited just 10 years ago. Cash had been the dominant form of payment for several decades prior to the rise of smartphone payment methods. Credit card use was never broadly adopted in a nation with a large number of small businesses that serve consumers, leading to a leapfrog effect where businesses and consumers moved straight from cash to digital payment applications.

Alipay had a very humble beginning. It was launched in 2003 as a simple built-in payment tool of Taobao.com. Thanks to the rapid development of the online shopping industry in the 2000s and 2010s, Taobao has become one of the most popular online shopping portals in China. In 2010, it occupied 80% of China's e-commerce market, with 170 million registered shoppers. It defeated eBay to become the market leader in the country.[106] Accordingly, Alipay enjoyed an exponential growth as most transactions on Taobao were settled via Alipay. In May 2011, the PBoC granted third-party online payment licences to Alipay along with another 26 internet finance companies.[107] Thus, Alipay was among the first group of Fintech companies to obtain official authorisation to operate an online payment system. Until then, it had been largely regarded as an e-payment facility for online shopping.

2011 marked a new era for Alipay, as it expanded its payment service from online to offline. It launched its smartphone app on both Apple IOS and Google Android platforms, allowing smartphone users to pay for purchases and services in high-street retailers, cafes, and restaurants. In contrast to mobile payment systems which adopt the NFC technology, such as Apple Pay and Samsung Pay, Alipay and most Chinese Fintech companies have chosen QR code to carry out the mobile payment function. Alipay uses QR code because it has a lower infrastructure threshold, making it cheaper and easier to popularise the country in a short time. When making mobile payments in-store, shoppers will use the Alipay app on their smartphone to generate a one-off QR code, and then the retailers' staff will hold a specially designed barcode reading gun to scan the QR code and complete the transaction. An alternative way of receiving payment is for some retailers to print out their

---

[106] Mark Greeven et al., 'The Case Study: How Taobao Bested eBay in China: Dealing with a Powerful New Rival', *The Financial* Times, 13 March 2012, p. 10.

[107] Hogan Lovells, 'Third Party Payment Licences in China—Are They Within the Grasp of Foreign Investors?', 16 June 2014, https://www.hoganlovells.com/en/publications/third-party-payment-licences-in-china-are-they-within-the-grasp-of-foreign-investors.

Alipay accounts which are presented in QR code and then stick the printed QR code near the counter. Consumers can use their smartphone cameras to scan QR code and make immediate transfers. The latter method does not even require any investment in payment hardware, rendering the mobile payment facility available for everyone, including small shops, street vendors, and street artists.

WeChat Pay is one of the leading third-party payment platforms and it is affiliated to the Tencent Group. Established in 1998, Tencent is an internet-based technology and cultural enterprise headquartered in Shenzhen, which has the mission to 'improve the quality of life through internet value-added services'.[108] Through its user-oriented business philosophy, it delivers various integrated internet solutions to billions of netizens across the world. The key products of Tencent include popular social networking software QQ and WeChat, Tencent Games, Tencent Literature, QQ Music, QQ Mail, Tencent News, and Tencent Video. By adopting 'WeChat Pay is more than payment' as its slogan, WeChat Pay is committed to provide safe, convenient, and professional online payment services for its users and enterprises.[109] As of August 2018, the number of WeChat Pay's active monthly users was around 1.058 billion.[110] WeChat Pay has been accepted by millions of stores in over 30 industries. Users are able to use it when seeing doctors, shopping, dining, travelling, and paying utility bills, as the mobile payment network offers smartlife solutions. It is particularly well recognised for its red envelope feature, which is based on the Chinese custom of giving money to family and friends in red envelopes (*hongbao*) for special occasions.

WeChat Pay has been extensively used by Chinese residents when making payments, transferring money, and giving red envelopes. With the increasing number of Chinese residents travelling overseas, WeChat Pay has also been accepted by thousands of stores across the world. However, the payment options might vary depending on whether the users have a bank card issued in China or not.[111] If users have a China-issued bank card, they will be able to use the full functions of WeChat Pay without any restrictions. Users have to verify their accounts by providing identity documents such as a mainland resident ID card, Chinese passport, Mainland Travel Permit for Hong Kong and Macao Residents, or Mainland Travel Permit for Taiwan Residents. Then they can link WeChat Pay with savings cards and credit cards from

---

[108] Tencent, accessed 1 June 2023, https://www.tencent.com/en-us/.
[109] 'About WeChat Pay', QQ, accessed 1 June 2023, https://kf.qq.com/faq/181012y6bUNR181012nMFnMr.html.
[110] Ibid.
[111] 'How Can Foreigners Use WeChat Pay?', *China Daily*, 9 January 2019, http://www.chinadaily.com.cn/m/beijing/zhongguancun/2019-01/09/content_37425026.htm.

over 70 Chinese banks. With the above documents verified and bank cards linked, users are able to use WeChat Pay for most online and in-store purchases. On the other hand, if users do not have a China-issued bank card, they will face certain restrictions when using WeChat Pay. It supports most VISA and Mastercard credit cards issued by any global banks. Users just need to link the cards to WeChat Wallet and then could enjoy the payment services when accessing e-commerce websites or use mobile apps such as JD, Ctrip, Qunar, Didi, Air China, and China Railway Corporation. However, the latter type of WeChat Pay (restricted account) can only be used to make payments; users are not allowed to transfer money or send red envelopes. According to a survey, 64.4% of foreigners who live in China use WeChat Pay for multiple purposes including transportation, group buying, take-aways, dining, convenience stores, supermarkets, and online supermarkets.[112]

Alipay and WeChat Pay, as a cost-effective payment option, have brought great benefits and convenience for both retailers and consumers. They also have had a profound impact on the operation of banks and traditional payment networks. QR codes automatically generated by smartphone apps are one-off, constantly changing to enhance the level of security. Users have to set up a passcode or use biometric information, such as the fingerprint censor and facial recognition function on their smartphones, to verify their identities before initiating payments. Alipay and WeChat Pay can be linked to debit and credit cards issued by most banks, so as to function as a mobile e-wallet.

In China, the swift shift from traditional payment methods (cash and cards) to mobile payment is due to the popularisation of smartphones in the 2010s. Ninety-five per cent of internet users in the country now go online through mobile equipment.[113] At present, most brick-and-mortar stores like supermarkets, restaurants, and clothes shops, as well as O2O services such as taxi hailing, food delivering, and bike sharing will accept mobile payment options including Alipay and its main rivals like WeChat Pay.[114] Alibaba and Tencent have teamed up with millions of retailers across the country to build a cashless society. For instance, the US cafe chain Starbucks decided to accept WeChat Pay at its 2,600 outlets in China, except for one located at Alibaba's Hangzhou headquarters.[115] Outside China, Alipay and WeChat Pay have been expanding fast to promote their innovative payment services to consumers

---

[112] Ibid.
[113] 'The Age of the Appacus: Fintech in China', *The Economist*, 25 February 2017, p. 65.
[114] Leslie Hook and Gabriel Wildau, 'China Mobile Payments Soar as US Clings to Plastic', *The Financial Times*, 14 February 2017, p. 12.
[115] Louise Lucas, 'Tencent Grabs Mobile Pay Share from Alibaba', *The Financial Times*, 2 May 2017, p. 14.

in Asia, Europe, and the US. In the UK, some department stores, including Harrods and Selfridges, accept Alipay.[116] Alipay now has 450 million users all over the world, making it the largest mobile payment system, contesting fiercely with its US competitors like PayPal and Apple Pay.[117]

Making payment by smartphones has become a default option for many Chinese people. Even beggars on the streets are presenting QR codes to receive donations instead of receiving banknotes and coins.[118] The market scale of China's mobile payment sector amounts to CNY38 trillion ($5.7 trillion), which is 50 times that of the US market ($112 billion).[119] Alipay is extremely streamlined and convenient, allowing consumers to complete transactions in a few seconds without taking out their wallets. During the Chinese New Year, people tend to hand out virtual red envelopes to their relatives and friends, which is a built-in function of Alipay and WeChat Pay, leading to the digitalisation of the millennium-old tradition.[120] As a result of the proliferation of mobile payment facilities, many Chinese cities have become cashless and cardless. Seventy-four per cent of participants in a survey said they can survive for over one month with only CNY100 in their pockets.[121] Clearly, smartphones installed with Alipay or WeChat Pay apps have become the only essential thing for people to carry when going out shopping, dining, and for entertainment.

As Fintech service providers rewrite the rules of the financial industry, the businesses of traditional banks and card payment systems have taken a beating. In the past, China UnionPay was the principal payment system in the country as most bank cards issued in China use UnionPay's payment and clearing network. Even VISA and MasterCard found it difficult to compete with it. However, Alipay has surpassed UnionPay in terms of the daily number of processing payments, underscoring Alipay's dominant position in the entire payment industry.[122] Alipay earned CNY139 billion ($20.84 billion)

---

[116] Justina Crabtree, 'How Alipay Is Helping London Stores Cash in on China's Golden Week', *CNBC*, 6 October 2016, http://www.cnbc.com/2016/10/06/how-alipay-is-helping-london-stores-cash-in-on-chinas-golden-week.html.

[117] Helen H. Wang, 'Alipay Takes on Apple Pay and PayPal on Their Home Turf', *Forbes*, 30 October 2016, https://www.forbes.com/sites/helenwang/2016/10/30/will-alipay-dominate-global-mobile-payments/.

[118] Guo Kai, 'China's Mobile Payment Era: Costs and Benefits', *China Daily*, 11 May 2017, http://www.chinadaily.com.cn/china/2017-05/11/content_29295024.htm.

[119] Leslie Hook and Gabriel Wildau, 'China Mobile Payments Soar as US Clings to Plastic', *The Financial Times*, 14 February 2017, p. 12.

[120] Yuan Yang, 'Alibaba and Tencent Open New Front in Red Envelope War', *The Financial Times*, 30 January 2017, p. 16.

[121] 'About 14% People Carry No Cash in China', *China Daily*, 6 September 2017, http://www.chinadaily.com.cn/bizchina/tech/2017-09/06/content_31633683.htm.

[122] Gabriel Wildau, 'Alipay Bypasses China UnionPay on Fees', *The Financial Times*, 1 August 2016, p. 14.

from its payment services, which would otherwise have been channelled to UnionPay and major card issuers like the ICBC and Bank of China.[123] Moreover, Alipay also poses a major threat to retail banking, as an increasing number of savers have moved their money from their bank accounts to Alipay e-wallets. Within the Alipay app, various financial services are provided such as wealth management, securities investment, insurance, and loan facilities. In practice, Alipay is serving as a de facto gateway to Ant Group's Fintech business empire. To many consumers, what makes Alipay's e-wallet particularly attractive is an add-on service called Yu'E Bao, which invests consumers' money in money-market funds but permits them to use and withdraw the money on demand like a current account. Yu'E Bao offers an annualised return higher than bank saving rates, and interest is paid on a daily basis into consumers' Alipay accounts. Attracted by the decent return and convenience, millions of savers have opted for Alipay as their default banking account, leading to a sharp drop in deposits for major Chinese banks. As of July 2017, Yu'E Bao had around 260 million users, with the market volume of money-market funds in China reaching a record-breaking CNY5.11 trillion ($770 billion).[124] Apparently, the fast expansion of Alipay and WeChat Pay has eroded the deposit base, revenue, and profitability of China's banking industry. It shows the competitive relationship between traditional financial institutions and Fintech platforms. Global Fintech businesses and their regulators could learn a lesson from these Chinese practices.

7.7 Conclusion

Any financial system revolves around money. This chapter has assessed the rapid development of digital money in its many forms since the turn of the 21st century. For the economy of the future, both the private and public sectors advocate creating their own digital currencies. Blockchain-based cryptocurrencies, stablecoins, and CBDCs are the three rounds of digital currency innovation that have so far occurred. They all have advantages and disadvantages. This book suggests that, due to the state backing, constant value, and solid technological infrastructure, CBDCs have been viewed as the most viable form of money for the future. In contrast, privately issued crypto assets and stablecoins are more geared towards financial speculation and investments. Finally, thanks to the growing usage of digital currency and

---

[123] Ibid.
[124] 'Outstanding Balance of Yu'E Bao Surpassed Merchant Bank's Personal Deposits', *Xinhua*, 5 July 2017, http://news.xinhuanet.com/finance/2017-07/05/c_1121264650.htm.

mobile payment methods, many nations and cities have declared their aim to create a cashless society in the near future. The widespread use of smartphones and the launch of high-speed mobile networks like 5G are largely accountable for the quick uptake of mobile payment over traditional payment methods like cash, cheques, and bank cards. As a result of growing Fintech, it is expected that cash will soon disappear in many parts of the world.

8
Conclusion

The global Fintech revolution has brought significant changes to the financial services industry. This book, by applying Lu's Analysis Model as an original analytical framework, has identified the main achievements of Fintech innovations for both consumers and Fintech corporations. The integration of modern financial services with advanced technologies like blockchain, big data, cloud computing, and AI has greatly improved business efficiency and productivity in the financial sector. It results in greater profit margins for existing financial institutions and creates more business opportunities for entrepreneurs. The interests of investors and shareholders of Fintech corporations, large or small, would be firstly satisfied in this sense. Moreover, Fintech innovations are beneficial for other stakeholders in the financial services industry. It has brought better, more convenient, personalised, and low-cost customer experience with improved access to banking and finance. The book has identified that innovation, disintermediation, automation, virtualisation, accessibility, customer centricity, and scalability are the seven characteristics shared by the majority of Fintech companies. The examples of virtual currencies, P2P lending platforms, and digital banks have showcased that Fintech is indeed conducive to the building of a more equal, democratic, and inclusive financial system that is working for everyone. With more shared financial infrastructure and facilities empowered by cloud computing and VR, Fintech inventions contribute to a greener and more sustainable financial industry in line with the ESG standard. Clearly, the global Fintech revolution has arrived. This book presents detailed case studies of Fintech innovations and regulatory approaches in countries such as China, Singapore, Australia, the UK, and the US. However, the scope of the discussion can never be exhaustive, as we have witnessed the rise of Fintech in most parts of the world with the potential to change the geography of finance, similar to what is happening in India.[1]

The book has critically assessed the concept of Fintech in Chapter 2. There is still some debate regarding the exact definition of Fintech and the

---

[1] Julien Migozzi, Michael Urban, and Dariusz Wojcik, '"You Should Do What India Does": FinTech Ecosystems in India Reshaping the Geography of Finance', *Geoforum* (2023), https://doi.org/10.1016/j.geoforum.2023.103720.

categories of financial services, institutions, markets, and activities that the term actually covers. From the functional perspective, the nature of finance (i.e., the 'fin' component of Fintech) has never changed. In our economy, Fintech is carrying out tasks that traditional finance used to do, like matching the supply and demand for capital, evaluating credit risks, and making investment decisions. Fintech, however, often executes the same tasks in a more intelligent, effective, and economical manner since it widely uses data analytics and AI. As today's financial innovations will soon become the standard in tomorrow's financial industry, the book concludes that Fintech is an ever-evolving and relative concept. Researchers, practitioners, and policy-makers need to bear this in mind. Then, Chapter 2 has evaluated the major technological innovations that have been transforming the financial sector (i.e., the 'tech' component of Fintech), especially the 'ABCDE' acronym which stands for artificial intelligence, blockchain, cloud computing, data (big data), and e-commerce. Such technological breakthroughs are the real driving force behind most Fintech innovations, setting them apart from traditional finance. Therefore, it is safe to say that technology is the key to understanding the essence of Fintech. Without the creation and broad application of disruptive technologies, the global Fintech revolution would not have been accomplished.

The book has examined important elements in the complex, multidimensional, and dynamic Fintech ecosystem and how they interact with each other to reshape the financial service industry in Chapters 3 and 4. Discussions on the Fintech ecosystem cover three aspects: Fintech venues (e.g., physical venues like global Fintech hubs and virtual venues like Metaverse), Fintech regulators (e.g., regulatory toolkits, objectives, and strategies), and Fintech businesses (e.g., the established financial institutions, Fintech startups, FHCs, and BigTech). The book has evaluated a number of thriving global Fintech hubs in six continents, including San Francisco, New York, Sydney, Beijing, Shanghai, Shenzhen, Mumbai, Singapore, Paris, Frankfurt, London, Dubai, and Nairobi. Their successes can be attributed to multiple economic, political, and social factors, such as the sound regulatory framework, supportive policies, skilled workforce, favourable tax structure, local technology industries, strong financial investments, and education. The book has discussed some effective regulatory toolkits and strategies for financial authorities, including RegTech and regulatory sandbox regimes. In short, policy-makers and regulators have to strike a delicate balance between promoting financial innovation on the one hand, and protecting consumer interests and safeguarding financial stability on the other. Then, the book has analysed distinctive Fintech business models. Fintech corporations exist in different forms. They could be incumbent banks and other financial institutions that actively embrace technology to upgrade their businesses and infrastructure, or newly launched start-ups that leverage on Fintech to fill market gaps. Some Fintech companies have grown into large and complex FHCs, like Ant Group, which presents unique regulatory challenges such as financial stability and competition issues. In addition, BigTech, such as Apple, Amazon, Alibaba, Meta, Alphabet, and Tencent, have started to offer financial services, meriting extra regulatory scrutiny due to their substantial market influence and possession of enormous data. The relationship between Fintech corporations and incumbent banks is both competitive and cooperative, as they are like the frenemy. The book has discussed corporate finance (e.g., SPAC, VC, PE, and IPO) and corporate governance (e.g., DCSS) issues regarding Fintech corporations, with a focus on innovations in business organisation and listing options. The book concludes that a sound corporate legal framework is necessary for the further growth of Fintech. It predicts that those Fintech corporations complying with the ESG principle will attract most investments and customers in the future.

The Fintech revolution is happening across most financial sectors, such as banking, lending, payments, insurance, investments, and currency. The book has carried out detailed case studies of Fintech revolutions in three areas—digital banking, online P2P lending, and virtual money and payment—in Chapters 5–7. The first case study has assessed the global rise of digitally focused challenger banks. The global financial crisis and continuous scandals of the largest banks, known as TBTF, have undermined people's confidence in the banking industry. This has been further demonstrated in the recent crises of Credit Suisse in Europe and Silicon Valley Bank in the US in 2023. Conversely, Fintech-enabled challenger banks have no historical legacy and adopt a simplified and low-cost business model based on the internet and smartphone applications. Digital banks have strong competitive advantages in distribution channels and bespoke services. Many of them target niche markets by serving customers like small businesses and personal consumers ignored by current banks. Apparently, the special market focus and customer-centric spirit have contributed to the rapid success of Fintech disrupters such as Monzo, Starling, Revolut, N26, and WeBank. However, it seems difficult for challenger banks to completely shake up the banking industry dominated by large players. The book suggests that the current banking regulatory system has been designed for mainstream banks rather than newcomers. Due to the limited trading histories and differentiated risk assessment models, challenger banks have to hold more capital buffers than their larger rivals, limiting their growth potential to some extent. The regulators have attempted to design a more suitable capital regime to minimise the negative impacts of existing regulations on the development of neo banks. The book urges that financial regulators and policy-makers need to create a level playing field for both challenger banks and incumbent lenders. The launch of regulatory sandbox initiatives that facilitate the innovation of banking services is a good practice. Also, regulators need to spare more efforts in protecting the financial security and data safety of financial consumers using app-based banking services. Deposit insurance is increasingly important, as it could compensate the financial losses of savers in the event of bank runs, as well as maintain financial stability, helping more consumers choose the services offered by digital banks. Hopefully, in the upcoming years, we will witness some digital challenger banks becoming mainstream players in the banking system.

The second case study has explored the Fintech revolution happening in the field of online lending marketplaces. The book suggests that online P2P lending increases the efficiency of financial resource allocation, promoting financial equality among various sizes of companies. In particular, SMEs can use P2P lending as an alternative financing approach to fill the funding deficit. The book has recognised multiple advantages of P2P lending over bank lending, as financial disintermediation creates extra value for both investors and borrowers. P2P lending can increase the number of financing options available to SMEs at reasonable costs, since online lenders can use a variety of funding sources, including private investors, institutional investors, and governmental organisations, to prepare loans for potential borrowers. When compared to bank savings, P2P lending offers its investors, the majority of whom are regular savers, excellent investment opportunities with higher yields. P2P lending is known for its quick financing process, as it takes 10 minutes to get a loan decision and 7 days to receive the full funding in most cases. It also better addresses the problem of information asymmetry and promotes market transparency. The book suggests that more policy support from the government is needed for maximising online lending markets' economic and social functions. The time has witnessed P2P platform bankruptcy crises and fraudulent cases happening in some countries, which calls for the establishment of a sound regulatory system for online lending marketplaces. The combination of industry self-regulation and official regulation seems to be the most effective approach in promoting the market growth while ensuring an adequate level of consumer protection. This approach is well exemplified by the FCA's regulation of online P2P lending platforms, with comprehensive rules covering capital adequacy, client money, cancellation right, information disclosure, data reporting, platform insolvency, and dispute resolution.

The third case study has presented the Fintech revolution in global monetary and payment systems. Money is at the centre of any financial system and fulfils three basic economic functions—as the medium of exchange, a unit of account, and a store of value. We have seen the explosive growth of digital money in various forms since the turn of the 21st century. Both the private and public sectors compete to offer digital currencies for the economy of the future. The book has discussed the three waves of digital money creation—cryptocurrencies, stablecoins, and CBDCs. Each form of digital currency has its advantages and limitations. Crypto coins like BTC and Ethereum are known for decentralisation, cost-effective transactions, and anonymity. However, they are less suited to become the medium of exchange and store of wealth in the long term due to their severe price volatility. Stablecoins have been created to address the price instability issue, as their value is pegged to mainstream currencies, commodities, or financial instruments. However, the price stabilisation mechanism is not always effective because of the insufficient backing of underlying assets like gold or US dollars. Stablecoins are also susceptible to runs when investors rush to convert their holdings to underlying assets. The book concludes that privately issued crypto assets and stablecoins are more for the purpose of financial investment and speculation. Monetary authorities are proactively testing CBDCs or sovereign digital money, as they feel reluctant to hand over the power of making money to private entities. In this sense, official digital money seems to be a compromise between financial innovation and state control. The book suggests that CBDCs could be the most feasible money option for tomorrow's economy, owing to the state backing, stable value, and sound technical infrastructure. Moreover, countries and global cities have declared their ambition of building a cashless society in the near future, as a result of the widespread use of digital currency and mobile payment based on smartphones and the 5G network. It is predictable that cash will soon vanish in many parts of the world. The book recognises the advantages of a cashless society, while pointing out the potential problems such as data misuse, the surveillance state, and financial exclusion.

Fintech has undergone a worldwide revolution. This book has showcased the transformative force of technological innovations in the modern economy, where Fintech delivers better customer experience while assisting financial institutions improve business efficiency and profitability. Nonetheless, this book has demonstrated the unchanged nature of finance that finds the best way to match money supply and demand in our society, which is the key for readers to understand any complex financial innovations. This book has advocated that global policy-makers and regulators should adopt the best international practices discussed in the previous chapters, so as to fulfil Fintech's economic potential and social value, while avoiding unwanted risks and problems. Fintech, if properly regulated, is capable of creating a more efficient, democratic, and inclusive financial industry. Fintech has become an essential part of any sustainable economy in the 21st century.

Bibliography

A&E Television Networks. 'Thomas Edison: Facts. House & Inventions—History'. 9 November 2009. http://www.history.com/topics/inventions/thomas-edison.

ACA Group. 'AML Compliance Software: ComplianceAlpha RegTech Solution'. Accessed 1 June 2023. https://www.acaglobal.com/our-solutions/compliancealpha/aml-kyc-cip.

Academy of Internet Finance, Zhejiang University, Zhejiang University International Business School (ZIBS), et al. 'Global Fintech Hub Report 2020'. September 2020. https://www.cnfin.com/upload-xh08/2020/0911/1599789407455.pdf.

Accelerator Frankfurt. 'Accelerator Frankfurt Program'. Accessed 1 June 2023. https://www.acceleratorfrankfurt.com/the-program/.

Acemoglu, Daron, and Pascual Restrepo. 'Robots and Jobs: Evidence from US Labor Markets'. *Journal of Political Economy* vol. 128 (2020): p. 2188.

Acumen Research & Consulting. 'P2P Lending Market Size to Hit USD 804.2 Billion by 2030'. January 2023. https://www.acumenresearchandconsulting.com/p2p-lending-market.

Adrian, Tobias. 'BigTech in Financial Services'. International Monetary Fund. 16 June 2021. https://www.imf.org/en/News/Articles/2021/06/16/sp061721-bigtech-in-financial-services.

Aldermore. 'About Us'. Accessed 1 June 2023. http://www.aldermore.co.uk/about-us/.

Aldermore. 'Aldermore Group PLC Report and Accounts for the Year Ended 30 June 2022'. Published in 2022. https://www.aldermore.co.uk/media/f2cbo453/aldermore-group-annual-report-and-accounts-fy2022.pdf.

Aldermore. 'Annual Report and Accounts 2016'. Published in 2017. https://www.aldermore.co.uk/media/binozguo/20557_aldermore_ar16_web.pdf.

Aliaj, Ortenca, Sujeet Indap, and Miles Kruppa. 'The SPAC Sponsor Bonanza'. *The Financial Times*, 13 November 2020. https://www.ft.com/content/9b481c63-f9b4-4226-a639-238f9fae4dfc.

Alibaba. 'Alibaba Group Announces December Quarter 2018 Results'. 30 January 2019. http://www.alibabagroup.com/en/news/press_pdf/p190130.pdf.

Alibaba. 'ICBC. Alibaba and Ant Financial Form Comprehensive Strategic Partnership Bringing Enhanced Fintech and Financial Services to Users'. 16 December 2019. https://www.alibabagroup.com/en/news/press_pdf/p191216.pdf.

Alibaba Cloud. 'What Is the Difference Among Public Cloud, Private Cloud and Hybrid Cloud?'. Accessed 1 June 2023. http://www.alibabacloud.com/knowledge/public-cloud-private-cloud-hybrid-cloud.

Alipay. 'About Alipay'. Accessed 1 June 2023. https://about.alipay.com/.

Allen & Overy. 'The Role of Private Investment in Public Equity (PIPE) in Financing SPACs Business Combinations'. 1 June 2021. https://www.allenovery.com/en-gb/global/news-and-insights/publications/the-role-of-private-investment-in-public-equity-pipe-in-financing-spacs-business-combinations.

Alqubali, Rayana. 'Saudi Arabia Will See More Fintech Unicorns Soon. Head of Kingdom's Top Fintech Body Says'. *Arab News*, 23 August 2021. https://www.arabnews.com/node/1915866/business-economy.

Apple. 'Apple Card'. Accessed 1 June 2023. https://www.apple.com/uk/apple-card/.

Bibliography

Armour, John, Dan Awrey, Paul Davies, et al. *Principles of Financial Regulation* (Oxford: Oxford University Press, 2016).

Armstrong, Ashley. 'One Savings Bank Targets IPO Valuation of Up to £600m'. *Telegraph*, 7 May 2014. http://www.telegraph.co.uk/finance/newsbysector/banksandfinance/privateequity/10813002/One-Savings-Bank-targets-IPO-valuation-of-up-to-600m.html.

Armstrong, Robert. 'At Last, US Banks Are Introducing Contactless Cards'. *The Financial Times*, 7 January 2019. http://www.ft.com/content/445a308c-02f3-11e9-9d01-cd4d49afbbe3.

Arner, Douglas W., Janos Barberis, and Ross P. Buckley. 'The Evolution of Fintech: A New Post-Crisis Paradigm?'. *Georgetown Journal of International Law* vol. 47 (2016): p. 1271.

Arnold, Martin. 'Alternative Finance Route for Small Firms'. *The Financial Times*, 5 November 2016.

Arnold, Martin. 'Big Lenders Criticised for Slow Take-up of Technology'. *The Financial Times*, 14 September 2017.

Arnold, Martin, and Emma Dunkley. 'BBVA Enters UK with Atom Deal'. *The Financial Times*, 24 November 2015.

Arnold, Martin, and Leo Lewis. 'Japan's Big Banks Plan Digital Currency Launch'. *The Financial Times*, 26 September 2017. https://www.ft.com/content/ca0b3892-a201-11e7-9e4f-7f5e6a7c98a2.

Asian Development Bank. 'Asia's SMEs Need Growth Capital to Become More Competitive—ADB Report'. 2 September 2015. http://www.adb.org/news/asia-s-smes-need-growth-capital-become-more-competitive-adb-report.

Assetz Capital. 'SME Lender Assetz Capital Approved for Accreditation as Lender under Coronavirus Business Interruption Loan Scheme (CBILS)'. 6 May 2020. https://www.assetzcapital.co.uk/press-releases/sme-lender-assetz-capital-approved-for-accreditation-as-lender-under-coronavirus-business-interruption-loan-scheme-cbils/.

Atom Bank. 'Fixed Rate Savings'. Accessed 1 June 2023. https://www.atombank.co.uk/fixed-saver/.

Australian Securities and Investments Commission. 'Enhanced Regulatory Sandbox'. Accessed 1 June 2023. https://asic.gov.au/for-business/innovation-hub/enhanced-regulatory-sandbox/.

Australian Securities and Investments Commission. 'Innovation Hub'. Accessed 1 June 2023. https://asic.gov.au/for-business/innovation-hub/.

Awrey, Dan, and Kathryn Judge. 'Why Financial Regulation Keeps Falling Short'. Columbia Law School's Blog on Corporations and the Capital Markets. 25 February 2020. https://clsbluesky.law.columbia.edu/2020/02/25/why-financial-regulation-keeps-falling-short/.

AXA. 'AXA UK Retail Launches Moja—its New Digital-Only Insurance Brand'. 22 September 2022. https://www.axa.co.uk/newsroom/media-releases/2022/axa-uk-retail-launches-moja-its-new-digital-only-insurance-brand/.

Back, Aaron. 'LendingClub: Where's the Growth?'. *The Wall Street Journal*, 5 May 2017. http://www.wsj.com/articles/lendingclub-wheres-the-growth-1494000744.

Bains, Parma, Nobuyasu Sugimoto, and Christopher Wilson. 'BigTech in Financial Services: Regulatory Approaches and Architecture'. International Monetary Fund. January 2022. https://www.imf.org/-/media/Files/Publications/FTN063/2022/English/FTNEA2022002.ashx.

Bank for International Settlements. 'Basel III: A Global Regulatory Framework for More Resilient Banks and Banking Systems'. June 2011. https://www.bis.org/publ/bcbs189.pdf.

Bank for International Settlements. 'SME Access to External Finance'. BIS Economics Paper No. 16. January 2012.

244 Bibliography

Bank for International Settlements. 'BIS Annual Economic Report'. June 2019. https://www.bis.org/publ/arpdf/ar2019e.pdf.

Bank for International Settlements. 'Central Bank Digital Currencies: System Design and Interoperability'. September 2021. https://www.bis.org/publ/othp42_system_design.pdf.

Bank for International Settlements. 'BIS Innovation Hub Work on Suptech and RegTech'. Accessed 1 June 2023. https://www.bis.org/about/bisih/topics/suptech_RegTech.htm.

Bank of America. 'Bank of America Is First in Industry to Launch Virtual Reality Training Program in Nearly 4.300 Financial Centers'. 7 October 2021. https://newsroom.bankofamerica.com/content/newsroom/press-releases/2021/10/bank-of-america-is-first-in-industry-to-launch-virtual-reality-t.html.

Bank of Canada. 'Digital Currencies and Fintech: Research'. Accessed 1 June 2023. https://www.bankofcanada.ca/research/digital-currencies-and-Fintech/research/.

Bank of Communications. 'Bank of Communications News'. 29 September 2015. http://www.bocomgroup.com/BankCommSite/shtml/jyjr/cn/7158/7162/39814.shtml.

Bank of England. 'The Bank of England's Approach to Stress Testing the UK Banking System'. October 2015. https://www.bankofengland.co.uk/-/media/boe/files/stress-testing/2015/the-boes-approach-to-stress-testing-the-uk-banking-system.

Bank of England. 'New Bank Start-up Unit: What You Need to Know from the UK's Financial Regulators'. March 2017. http://www.bankofengland.co.uk/pra/Documents/authorisations/newfirmauths/nbsuguide.pdf.

Bank of England. 'Credit Conditions Review 2017 Q1'. 13 April 2017. https://www.bankofengland.co.uk/credit-conditions-review/2017/2017-q1.

Bank of England. 'Refining the PRA's Pillar 2A Capital Framework'. Policy Statement 22/17 Consultation Paper 3/17. 3 October 2017. https://www.bankofengland.co.uk/prudential-regulation/publication/2017/refining-the-pra-pillar-2a-capital-framework.

Bank of England. 'Central Bank Digital Currency Opportunities. Challenges and Design'. Bank of England Discussion Paper. 12 March 2020. https://www.bankofengland.co.uk/-/media/boe/files/paper/2020/central-bank-digital-currency-opportunities-challenges-and-design.pdf.

Bank of England. 'What Are Cryptoassets (Cryptocurrencies)?'. 19 May 2020. http://www.bankofengland.co.uk/knowledgebank/what-are-cryptocurrencies.

Bank of England. 'PS20/21 CP12/21—Financial Holding Companies: Further Implementation'. September 2021. https://www.bankofengland.co.uk/prudential-regulation/publication/2021/june/financial-holding-companies-further-implementation.

Bank of England. 'Funding for Lending and Other Market Operations'. Accessed 1 June 2023. http://www.bankofengland.co.uk/markets/funding-for-lending-and-other-market-operations.

Bank of England. 'BankStats (Monetary & Financial Statistics)'. Accessed 1 June 2023. http://www.bankofengland.co.uk/statistics/Pages/bankstats/current/default.aspx.

Bankrate. 'Prosper Personal Loans: 2023 Review'. 13 January 2023. https://www.bankrate.com/loans/personal-loans/reviews/prosper/.

Barclays. 'From the Archives: The ATM Is 50'. 27 June 2017. https://home.barclays/news/2017/06/from-the-archives-the-atm-is-50/.

Barclays. 'Annual Report 2016'. Published in 2017. https://home.barclays/content/dam/home-barclays/documents/investor-relations/annualreports/ar2016/Barclays%20PLC%20Annual%20Report%202016.pdf.

Barclays. 'Insights by Barclays'. Accessed 1 June 2023. http://insights.uk.barclays/.

Barro, Robert J. 'Money and the Price Level under the Gold Standard'. *The Economic Journal* vol. 89 (1979): p. 13.

BBC. 'Co-Op Bank Fails Bank of England Stress Tests'. 16 December 2014. https://www.bbc.co.uk/news/business-30491161.
BBC. 'Beijing Overtakes New York as New "Billionaire Capital"'. 25 February 2016. http://www.bbc.co.uk/news/world-asia-china-35657107.
BBC. 'Google AI Defeats Human Go Champion'. 25 May 2017. http://www.bbc.com/news/technology-40042581.
BBC. 'China Orders Bitcoin Exchanges in Capital City to Close'. 19 September 2017. http://www.bbc.co.uk/news/business-41320568.
BBC. 'Greater Bay Area: China's Ambitious but Vague Economic Plan'. 26 February 2019. http://www.bbc.co.uk/news/business-47287387.
BBC. 'AI Steps Up in Battle Against Covid-19'. 18 April 2020. http://www.bbc.com/news/technology-52120747.
BBC. 'Tesla Overtakes Toyota to Become World's Most Valuable Carmaker'. 1 July 2020. https://www.bbc.com/news/business-53257933.
BBC. 'China's Tech Giants Fall under Regulator's Pressure'. 16 March 2021. https://www.bbc.co.uk/news/business-56410769.
BBC. 'Facebook Changes Its Name to Meta in Major Rebrand'. 28 October 2021. https://www.bbc.co.uk/news/technology-59083601.
BBC. 'Tesla Starts Accepting Once-Joke Cryptocurrency Dogecoin'. 15 January 2022. https://www.bbc.co.uk/news/business-60001144.
Beck, Thorsten, Asli Demirguc-Kunt, and Ross Levine. 'Bank Concentration and Crises'. National Bureau of Economic Research Working Paper. August 2003. https://www.nber.org/papers/w9921.pdf.
Beijing Government. '2018 Beijing Higher Education Graduates Employment Report'. December 2018. http://jw.beijing.gov.cn/xxgk/zxxxgk/201812/t20181229_66964.html.
Beijing Times. 'Over 300.000 Businesses Accepted Alipay'. 1 February 2007. http://tech.sina.com.cn/i/2007-02-01/03591363850.shtml.
Bian, Jing. 'Internet Finance in China: Half Lava? Half Ocean?'. *Journal of International Banking Law and Regulation* vol. 29 (2014): p. 743.
Binham, Caroline. 'UK Regulators Are the Most Fintech Friendly'. *The Financial Times*, 12 September 2016. https://www.ft.com/content/ff5b0be4-7381-11e6-bf48-b372cdb1043a.
Bloomberg. 'China Is Developing Its Own Digital Currency'. 23 February 2017. https://www.bloomberg.com/news/articles/2017-02-23/pboc-is-going-digital-as-mobile-payments-boom-transforms-economy.
Boar, Codruta, Henry Holden, and Amber Wadsworth. 'Impending Arrival—a Sequel to the Survey on Central Bank Digital Currency'. BIS Paper No. 107. January 2020. https://www.bis.org/publ/bppdf/bispap107.pdf.
Boghani, Priyanka. 'Tencent Poised to Lead China's Charge into the Metaverse'. S&P Global. 17 March 2022. https://www.spglobal.com/marketintelligence/en/news-insights/latest-news-headlines/tencent-poised-to-lead-china-s-charge-into-the-Metaverse-69311462.
Bolger, Andrew, and Emma Dunkley. 'Branson Makes Pound(s) 70m as Virgin Money Floats'. *The Financial Times*, 14 November 2014.
Bossu, Wouter, Masaru Itatani, Catalina Margulis, et al. 'Legal Aspects of Central Bank Digital Currency: Central Bank and Monetary Law Considerations'. International Monetary Fund Working Paper No. 2020/254. 20 November 2020. https://www.imf.org/en/Publications/WP/Issues/2020/11/20/Legal-Aspects-of-Central-Bank-Digital-Currency-Central-Bank-and-Monetary-Law-Considerations-49827.
Boyce, Lee. 'Atom Bank Opens Its Doors to All Savers with Two Best-Buy Deals—But Fixed Rates Have Been Cut'. Thisismoney. 6 October 2016. http://www.thisismoney.

co.uk/money/saving/article-3824910/Atom-Bank-opens-doors-savers-two-best-buy-deals-fixed-rates-cut.htm.

Bradshaw, Tim, and Attracta Mooney. 'Disaster Strikes as Deliveroo Becomes "Worst IPO in London's History"'. *The Financial Times*, 1 April 2021. https://www.ft.com/content/bdf6ac6b-46b5-4f7a-90db-291d7fd2898d.

British Bankers' Association. 'Promoting Competition in the UK Banking Industry Report'. Published in 2014.

British Bankers' Association. 'Bank Support for SMEs—4th Quarter 2016'. http://www.bba.org.uk/news/statistics/sme-statistics/bank-support-for-smes-4th-quarter-2016/.

British Business Bank. 'Small Business Finance Markets 2014'. Published in 2014. https://www.british-business-bank.co.uk/wp-content/uploads/2020/09/BBB_Small-Business-Finance-Markets-2014_Online_Interactive-tagged.pdf.

British Business Bank. 'Annual Report and Accounts 2015'. July 2015. https://www.british-business-bank.co.uk/wp-content/uploads/2015/07/British-Business-Bank-Annual-Report-and-Accounts-20151.pdf.

British Business Bank. 'Recovery Loan Scheme'. Accessed 1 June 2023. https://www.british-business-bank.co.uk/ourpartners/recovery-loan-scheme/.British Business Bank. 'What We Do?'. Accessed 1 June 2023. http://british-business-bank.co.uk/what-the-british-business-bank-does/.

British Council. 'Should Robots Be Citizens?'. Accessed 1 June 2023. http://www.britishcouncil.org/anyone-anywhere/explore/digital-identities/robots-citizens.

Buchholz, Katharina. 'China's Mobile Payment Adoption Beats All Others'. Statista. 8 July 2022. https://www.statista.com/chart/17909/pos-mobile-payment-user-penetration-rates/.

Built in NYC. 'Top Tech Companies in NYC'. Accessed 1 June 2023. https://www.builtinnyc.com/companies/type/Fintech-companies-nyc.

Bullock, Nicole, and Jennifer Hughes. 'Hong Kong Wrestles with New York for Listings Laurels'. *The Financial Times*, 29 December 2016.

Caijing. 'Close Supervision Over Private Banks'. 11 June 2019. http://finance.caijing.com.cn/20190611/4594723.shtml.

Cambridge Centre for Alternative Finance. '2018 Global Fintech Hub Report—the Future of Finance Is Emerging: New Hubs, New Landscapes'. 14 November 2018. https://www.jbs.cam.ac.uk/wp-content/uploads/2020/08/2018-ccaf-global-fintech-hub-report-eng.pdf.

Cambridge English Dictionary. 'Financial Technology (Fintech)'. Accessed 1 June 2023. https://dictionary.cambridge.org/dictionary/english/financial-technology.

Campbell, Peter. 'Osborne Wants London to Be Global Centre for Fintech'. *The Financial Times*, 11 November 2015. https://www.ft.com/content/1f24a25e-886f-11e5-90de-f44762bf9896.

Cao, Minjie. '2005: A Key Year for China's E-Commerce Industry'. *Oriental Morning Post*, 7 May 2005. http://tech.sina.com.cn/i/2005-05-07/0948600190.shtml.

Cappitech. 'Transaction Reporting with Cappitech'. Accessed 1 June 2023. https://www.cappitech.com/regulation/ppc-brand/.

Carlton, Jim. 'The Number of ATMs Has Declined as People Rely Less on Cash'. *The Wall Street Journal*, 3 March 2023. https://www.wsj.com/articles/the-number-of-atms-has-declined-as-people-rely-less-on-cash-81268fa2.

Carney, John. 'Basics of Banking: Loans Create a Lot More Than Deposits'. *CNBC*, 26 February 2013. https://www.cnbc.com/id/100497710.

Carstens, Agustin. 'Big Techs in Finance: Forging a New Regulatory Path'. Bank for International Settlements. 8 February 2023. https://www.bis.org/speeches/sp230208.pdf.

Catalini, Christian, and Alonso de Gortari. 'On the Economic Design of Stablecoins'. *SSRN*. 6 August 2021. http://dx.doi.org/10.2139/ssrn.3899499.

CB Insights. 'The Complete List of Unicorn Companies'. Accessed 1 June 2023. http://www.cbinsights.com/research-unicorn-companies.

Cellan-Jones, Rory. 'Facebook's Libra Pitches to Be the Future of Money'. *BBC*, 18 June 2019. http://www.bbc.co.uk/news/technology-48667525.

CFA Institute. 'ESG Investing and Analysis'. Accessed 1 June 2023. https://www.cfainstitute.org/en/research/esg-investing.

Chaffey, Dave. *Digital Business and E-Commerce Management*. 7th ed. (London: Pearson, 2019).

Chapman, Ben. 'Bitcoin Plummets More Than 20% After China Vows to Close Cryptocurrency Exchanges'. *Independent*, 15 September 2017. http://www.independent.co.uk/news/business/news/Bitcoin-latest-updates-drops-china-close-crypto-currency-exchanges-btccchina-a7947826.html.

Chavan, Ishwari. 'India's Fintech Market Size at $31 Billion in 2021. Third Largest In World'. *India Times*, 10 January 2022. https://bfsi.economictimes.indiatimes.com/news/Fintech/indias-Fintech-market-size-at-31-billion-in-2021-third-largest-in-world-report/88794336.

Chen, Wenjie, Mico Mrkaic, and Malhar Nabar. 'Lasting Effects: The Global Economic Recovery 10 Years After the Crisis'. International Monetary Fund. 3 October 2018. https://www.imf.org/en/Blogs/Articles/2018/10/03/blog-lasting-effects-the-global-economic-recovery-10-years-after-the-crisis.

Cheque and Credit Clearing Company. 'Types of Cheque Fraud'. Accessed 1 June 2023. http://www.chequeandcredit.co.uk/information-hub/cheque-fraud-advice/types-cheque-fraud.

China Daily. 'Taobao to See Transactions Top 100bn Yuan in 2008'. 16 June 2008. http://www.chinadaily.com.cn/bizchina/2008-06/16/content_6764882.htm.

China Daily. 'Alibaba Unit to Start Credit-Based Visa Application Services for Luxembourg'. 16 July 2015. http://usa.chinadaily.com.cn/epaper/2015-07/16/content_21301110.htm.

China Daily. 'About 14% People Carry No Cash in China'. 6 September 2017. http://www.chinadaily.com.cn/bizchina/tech/2017-09/06/content_31633683.htm.

China Daily. 'How Can Foreigners Use WeChat Pay?'. 9 January 2019. http://www.chinadaily.com.cn/m/beijing/zhongguancun/2019-01/09/content_37425026.htm.

China Finance. 'MyBank Jin XiaoLong: SME Finance Is No Longer Difficult'. 9 July 2017. http://finance.china.com.cn/news/special/wtfh/20170709/4281638.shtml.

China News. 'Beijing Financial Street Financial Institutions Asset Scale Is Approaching RMB100 Trillion'. 29 April 2018. http://www.chinanews.com/fortune/2018/04-29/8503009.shtml.

China Securities Regulatory Commission. 'Press Conference for Deputy Governor of PBOC Mr. Pan Gongsheng Commenting on the Meeting between Financial Regulators and Ant Group'.12 April 2021. http://www.csrc.gov.cn/pub/newsite/zjhxwfb/xwdd/202104/t20210412_395827.html.

Chinese Government. '2019 Government Working Report'. 5 March 2019. http://www.gov.cn/zhuanti/2019qglh/2019lhzfgzbg/index.htm.

Chinese Government. 'China to Set Up National Financial Regulatory Administration'. 7 March 2023. https://english.www.gov.cn/news/topnews/202303/07/content_WS6406ffa2c6d0a757729e7d6c.html.

Chipolina, Scott. 'Bitcoin Falls Below $30.000 for First Time Since July 2021'. *The Financial Times*, 10 May 2022. https://www.ft.com/content/d2a9df43-1ea0-4fb2-9b02-4944589fd909.

Chiu, Iris H.-Y., and Joanna Wilson. *Banking Law and Regulation* (Oxford: Oxford University Press, 2019).

Chohan, Usman W. 'Non-Fungible Tokens: Blockchains, Scarcity, and Value'. Critical Blockchain Research Initiative Working Papers. 24 March 2021. http://dx.doi.org/10.2139/ssrn.3822743.

Chowla, Shiv, Lucia Quaglietti, and Lukasz Rachel. 'How Have World Shocks Affected the UK Economy?'. Bank of England Quarterly Bulletin 2014 2. https://www.bankofengland.co.uk/-/media/boe/files/quarterly-bulletin/2014/how-have-world-shocks-affected-the-uk-economy.pdf.

Christoffersen, Peter. *Elements of Financial Risk*. 2nd ed. (Cambridge, MA: Academic Press, 2012).

Citrix. 'What Is Access Control?'. Accessed 1 June 2023. https://www.citrix.com/solutions/secure-access/what-is-access-control.html.

Clover, Charles. 'China's Capital Curbs Hit EU Companies'. *The Financial Times*, 7 December 2016.

Coinbase. 'About—Coinbase'. Accessed 1 June 2023. https://www.coinbase.com/about.

Coinbase. 'What Is DeFi?'. Accessed 1 June 2023. https://www.coinbase.com/learn/crypto-basics/what-is-defi.

CoinDesk. 'Bitcoin Price'. Accessed 1 June 2023. https://www.coindesk.com/price/bitcoin/.

CoinMarketCap. 'Cryptocurrency Prices by Market Cap'. Accessed 1 June 2023. https://coinmarketcap.com/.

CoinMarketCap. 'Top Stablecoin Tokens by Market Capitalization'. Accessed 1 June 2023. https://coinmarketcap.com/view/stablecoin/.

Coinstar. 'Coinstar Teams with Amazon to Provide Amazon Cash Reload Sites'. 15 May 2018. https://www.coinstar.com/press-releases/coinstar-teams-with-amazon-to-provide-amazon-cash-reload-sites.

Competition and Market Authority. 'Personal Current Accounts: Market Study Update'. UK Government. 18 July 2014. https://assets.publishing.service.gov.uk/media/53c834c640f0b610aa000009/140717_-_PCA_Review_Full_Report.pdf.

Consumer Financial Protection Bureau (US). 'Policy on No-Action Letters'. 16 October 2014. https://www.federalregister.gov/articles/2014/10/16/2014-24645/policy-on-no-action-letters.

Cornelli, Giulio, Sebastian Doerr, Lavinia Franco, and Jon Frost. 'Funding for Fintechs: Patterns and Drivers'. Bank for International Settlements Quarterly Review. September 2021. https://www.bis.org/publ/qtrpdf/r_qt2109c.pdf.

Cortese, Amy. 'Loans that Avoid Banks? Maybe Not'. *The New York Times*, 4 May 2014. https://www.nytimes.com/2014/05/04/business/loans-that-avoid-banks-maybe-not.html.

Coughlan, Sean. 'Oxford Top of Global University Rankings'. *BBC*, 11 September 2019. http://www.bbc.co.uk/news/education-49666979.

Cowley, Stacy. 'Block Says Cash App Breach Affected 8 Million Users'. *The New York Times*, 6 April 2022. https://www.nytimes.com/2022/04/06/business/block-cash-app-data-breach.html.

Crabtree, Justina. 'How Alipay Is Helping London Stores Cash in on China's Golden Week'. *CNBC*, 6 October 2016. http://www.cnbc.com/2016/10/06/how-alipay-is-helping-london-stores-cash-in-on-chinas-golden-week.html.

Cranston, Ross, Emilios Avgouleas, Kristin van Zwieten, Christopher Hare, and Theodor van Sante. *Principles of Banking Law*. 3rd ed. (Oxford: Oxford University Press, 2018).

Cruikshank, Don. 'Competition in UK Banking: A Report to the Chancellor of the Exchequer'. UK Parliament. 19 June 2000. https://hansard.parliament.uk/commons/2000-06-19/debates/3aa321eb-2cff-4a9a-bef7-c51c31416ef3/CruickshankReport.

Cunliffe, Jon. 'Why Are Interest Rates Low?'. Bank of England. 16 November 2016. http://www.bankofengland.co.uk/publications/Documents/speeches/2016/speech935.pdf.

Current Account Switch Service. 'The Current Account Switch Service—Your Guarantee to a Successful Switch'. Accessed 1 June 2023. https://www.currentaccountswitch.co.uk/.
Curtis, Sophie. 'Bill Gates: A History at Microsoft'. *Telegraph*, 4 February 2014. http://www.telegraph.co.uk/technology/bill-gates/10616991/Bill-Gates-a-history-at-Microsoft.html.
Darrow, Barb. 'How These Fortune 500 Companies Are Moving to the Cloud?'. *Fortune*, 19 July 2016. http://fortune.com/2016/07/19/big-companies-many-clouds/.
Davidson, Paul. 'Money and the Real World'. *The Economic Journal* vol. 82 (1972): p. 101.
Davis, Andrew. 'How Square Became a $26 Billion Company'. *CNBC*, 10 October 2019. http://www.cnbc.com/2019/10/10/how-square-became-26-billion-dollar-company.html.
Deer, Luke, Mi Jackson, and Yu Yuxin. 'The Rise of Peer-to-Peer Lending in China: An Overview and Survey Case Study'. Association of Chartered Certified Accountants. October 2015. https://www.accaglobal.com/content/dam/ACCA_Global/Technical/manage/ea-china-p2p-lending.pdf.
de Jong, Marc, Nathan Marston, and Erik Roth. 'The Eight Essentials of Innovation'. McKinsey Quarterly. 1 April 2015. https://www.mckinsey.com/business-functions/strategy-and-corporate-finance/our-insights/the-eight-essentials-of-innovation.
Deloitte. 'Blockchain Technology: A Game-Changer in Accounting?'. March 2016. https://www2.deloitte.com/content/dam/Deloitte/de/Documents/Innovation/Blockchain_A%20game-changer%20in%20accounting.pdf.
Deloitte. 'RegTech Is the New Fintech'. 2016. https://www2.deloitte.com/content/dam/Deloitte/tw/Documents/financial-services/tw-fsi-regtech-new-fintech.pdf.
Deloitte. 'Connecting Global Fintech: Interim Hub Review 2017'. April 2017. https://www2.deloitte.com/tr/en/pages/finance/articles/a-tale-of-44-cities-global-fintech-hub-federation-gfhf-connecting-global-fintech-hub-report.html.
Deloitte. 'The Future of Regulatory Productivity. Powered by RegTech'. 2017. https://www2.deloitte.com/content/dam/Deloitte/us/Documents/regulatory/us-regulatory-future-of-regulatory-productivity-powered-by-regtech.pdf.
Deloitte. 'AI Leaders in Financial Services: Common Traits of Frontrunners in the Artificial Intelligence Race'. 2019. https://www2.deloitte.com/content/dam/insights/us/articles/4687_traits-of-ai-frontrunners/DI_AI-leaders-in-financial-services.pdf.
Deloitte. 'Cloud Computing: More Than Just a CIO Conversation'. 2019. https://www2.deloitte.com/content/dam/Deloitte/ar/Documents/financial-services/Cloud-Banking-2030-Julio-2019.pdf.
Deloitte. 'The Fintech Dilemma: When to Scale Up Your Business?'. Accessed 1 June 2023. https://www2.deloitte.com/uk/en/pages/financial-services/articles/fintech-dilemma-when-to-scale-up-your-business.html.
Deloitte. 'Financial Services Regulatory Timeline Tool'. Accessed 1 June 2023. https://www2.deloitte.com/uk/en/pages/financial-services/articles/financial-services-regulatory-timeline-tool.html.
Demos, Telis. 'As Industry Evolves, PayPal, Peers Rise Up'. *The Wall Street Journal*, 2 June 2016.
Denso. 'QR Code Development Story'. Accessed 1 June 2023. http://www.denso-wave.com/en/technology/vol1.html.
Department for Business, Energy and Industrial Strategy. 'Business Population Estimates for the UK and the Regions 2022'. UK Government. 6 October 2022. https://www.gov.uk/government/statistics/business-population-estimates-2022/business-population-estimates-for-the-uk-and-regions-2022-statistical-release-html.
Department for Business. Innovation and Skills. 'Business Population Estimates 2014'. UK Government. 26 November 2014. https://www.gov.uk/government/statistics/business-population-estimates-2014.

Dignam, Alan, and John Lowry. *Company Law*. 12th ed. (Oxford: Oxford University Press, 2022).

Dimock, Michael. 'Defining Generations: Where Millennials End and Generation Z Begins'. Pew Research Center. 17 January 2019. https://www.pewresearch.org/fact-tank/2019/01/17/where-millennials-end-and-generation-z-begins/.

Diners Club. 'Diners Club Credit Card History'. Accessed 1 June 2023. https://www.dinersclub.com/about-us/history.

Dong, Emma, and Simon Rabinovitch. 'China's Lending Laboratory'. *The Financial Times*, 23 May 2012.

Douglas, Jacob. 'These American Workers Are the Most Afraid of AI Taking Their Jobs'. *CNBC*, 7 November 2019. http://www.cnbc.com/2019/11/07/these-american-workers-are-the-most-afraid-of-ai-taking-their-jobs.html.

Dow, James, and Gary Gorton. 'Stock Market Efficiency and Economic Efficiency: Is There a Connection?'. *Journal of Finance* vol. 52 (1997): p. 1087.

Dubai Financial Services Authority. 'DFSA Innovation and Crypto'. Accessed 1 June 2023. https://www.dfsa.ae/innovation.

Dublin City Council. 'Financial Services in Dublin'. Accessed 1 June 2023. https://dublin.ie/invest/key-sectors/financial-services/.

Dunkley, Emma. 'A Tech Take on Wealth Management: Entrepreneurship: Nick Hungerford. Nutmeg'. *The Financial Times*, 3 December 2014.

Dunkley, Emma. 'Peer-to-Peer Lending Isa Brings Fresh Set of Risks. Say Experts'. *The Financial Times*, 11 July 2015.

Dunkley, Emma. 'Challengers Prise Open Grip of Larger Rivals'. *The Financial Times*, 4 May 2016.

Dunkley, Emma. 'Funding Circle to Allocate £100m of EU Loans'. *The Financial Times*, 21 June 2016.

Dunkley, Emma. 'Fintech Start-Ups Put Banks under Pressure'. *The Financial Times*, 12 September 2016. https://www.ft.com/content/ce8fa350-737f-11e6-bf48-b372cdb1043a.

Dunkley, Emma. 'Atom Bank to Offer Residential Mortgages'. *The Financial Times*, 6 December 2016. https://www.ft.com/content/1e3cd566-bbb1-11e6-8b45-b8b81dd5d080.

Dunkley, Emma. 'Funding Circle: Small Business Backing'. *The Financial Times*, 6 January 2017.

Dunkley, Emma. 'Atom Bank Raises £83m from Shareholders as It Eyes Expansion'. *The Financial Times*, 3 March 2017. https://www.ft.com/content/c075542e-fc09-3c27-bb98-7fe5f7d3df34.

Dunkley, Emma, and Nicolle Liu. 'Lufax Holds Off on Listing While Beijing Scrutinises Online Lenders'. *The Financial Times*, 21 March 2018. http://www.ft.com/content/8a7bf706-2cbd-11e8-a34a-7e7563b0b0f4.

Egan, Matt. 'Celebs Including A-Rod and Ciara Are Getting into SPACs: What Could Go Wrong?'. *CNN*, 23 February 2021. https://edition.cnn.com/2021/02/23/investing/spac-arod-kaepernick-celebrities/index.html.

eToro. 'Invest in Virtual Worlds at MetaverseLife CopyPortfolio'. Accessed 1 June 2023. https://www.etoro.com/smartportfolios/Metaverselife.

Euronext. 'Euronext Paris'. Accessed 1 June 2023. https://www.euronext.com/en/markets/paris.

European Banking Authority. 'EBA Analysis of RegTech in the EU Financial Sector'. June 2021. https://www.eba.europa.eu/eba-assesses-benefits-challenges-and-risks-RegTech-use-eu-and-puts-forward-steps-be-taken-support.

European Banking Authority. 'Financial Innovation and Fintech'. Accessed 1 June 2023. https://www.eba.europa.eu/financial-innovation-and-Fintech.

European Business Review. 'Ecommerce: Online Banking and Payments'. 21 February 2022. https://www.europeanbusinessreview.com/ecommerce-online-banking-and-payments/.

European Central Bank. 'Exploring Anonymity in Central Bank Digital Currencies'. December 2019. https://www.ecb.europa.eu/paym/intro/publications/pdf/ecb.mipinfocus191217.en.pdf.

European Commission. 'Annual Report on European SMEs 2015/2016'. November 2016. https://op.europa.eu/en/publication-detail/-/publication/4872cbee-aa5a-11e6-aab7-01aa75ed71a1.

European Commission. 'Access to Finance for SMEs'. Accessed 1 June 2023. http://ec.europa.eu/growth/access-to-finance_en.

European Commission. 'What Is an SME?'. Accessed 1 June 2023. http://ec.europa.eu/growth/smes/business-friendly-environment/sme-definition_en.

European Parliament. 'The Ethics of Artificial Intelligence: Issues and Initiatives'. 11 March 2020. https://www.europarl.europa.eu/thinktank/en/document/EPRS_STU(2020)634452.

European Parliament. 'EU Digital Markets Act and Digital Services Act Explained'. 14 December 2021. https://www.europarl.europa.eu/news/en/headlines/society/20211209STO19124/eu-digital-markets-act-and-digital-services-act-explained.

European Securities and Markets Authority. 'Report to the European Commission: Use of Fintech by CSDs'. 2 August 2021. https://www.esma.europa.eu/sites/default/files/library/esma70-156-4576_report_to_ec_on_use_of_fintech_by_csds.pdf.

Evans, Tara. 'Peer-to-Peer Lending: Everything You Need to Know About the Leading Websites'. *The Telegraph*, 18 July 2016. http://www.telegraph.co.uk/personal-banking/savings/peer-to-peer-lending-everything-you-need-to-know-about-the-leadi/.

EY. 'Landscaping UK Fintech: Commissioned by UK Trade & Investment'. 6 August 2014. http://www.ey.com/Publication/vwLUAssets/Landscaping_UK_Fintech/$FILE/EY-Landscaping-UK-Fintech.pdf.

EY. 'Fintech and Ecosystems'. Accessed 1 June 2023. https://www.ey.com/en_gl/banking-capital-markets/Fintech-ecosystems.

Fang, Lily, Victoria Ivashina, and Josh Lerner. 'The Disintermediation of Financial Markets: Direct Investing in Private Equity'. *Journal of Financial Economics* vol. 116 (2015): p. 160.

Faux, Zeke, and Muyao Shen. 'A $60 Billion Crypto Collapse Reveals a New Kind of Bank Run'. *Bloomberg*, 19 May 2022. https://www.bloomberg.com/news/articles/2022-05-19/luna-terra-collapse-reveal-crypto-price-volatility.

Federal Deposit Insurance Corporation. 'Deposit Market Share Report'. 30 June 2018. https://www5.fdic.gov/sod/sodMarketRpt.asp?barItem=2.

Federal Deposit Insurance Corporation. 'Quarterly Banking Profile: Second Quarter 2018'. 30 June 2018. https://www.fdic.gov/analysis/quarterly-banking-profile/fdic-quarterly/2018-vol12-3/fdic-v12n3-2q2018.pdf.

Federal Deposit Insurance Corporation. 'How Are My Deposit Accounts Insured by the FDIC?'. 12 April 2023. http://www.fdic.gov/deposit/covered/categories.html.

Federal Financial Supervisory Authority. 'Fintech Innovation Hub'. Accessed 1 June 2023. https://www.bafin.de/EN/Aufsicht/Fintech/Fintech_node_en.html.

Federal Reserve Board. 'Federal Reserve Board Releases Discussion Paper that Examines Pros and Cons of a Potential U.S. Central Bank Digital Currency (CBDC)'. 20 January 2022. https://www.federalreserve.gov/newsevents/pressreleases/other20220120a.htm.

Federal Reserve Board. 'Financial Stability Report'. May 2022. https://www.federalreserve.gov/publications/files/financial-stability-report-20220509.pdf.

Federal Reserve Board. 'Financial Holding Companies'. Accessed 1 June 2023. https://www.federalreserve.gov/supervisionreg/fhc.htm.

252 Bibliography

Federal Reserve Bank of San Francisco. 'What Is the Economic Function of a Bank?'. July 2001. http://www.frbsf.org/education/publications/doctor-econ/2001/july/bank-economic-function.

Federation of Small Businesses. 'Happiest Employees Work for Small Businesses'. 2 September 2008. http://www.fsb.org.uk/news.aspx?rec=4749.

Ferran, Eilis, and Ho Look Chan. *Principles of Corporate Finance Law*. 2nd ed. (Oxford: Oxford University Press, 2014).

Financial Conduct Authority. 'The FCA's Regulatory Approach to Crowdfunding (and Similar Activities)'. FCA Consultation Paper 13/13. October 2013. https://www.fca.org.uk/publication/consultation/cp13-13.pdf.

Financial Conduct Authority. 'The FCA's Regulatory Approach to Crowdfunding Over the Internet. And the Promotion of Non-Readily Realisable Securities by Other Media: Feedback to CP13/13 and Final Rules'. FCA Policy Statement 14/4. March 2014. https://www.fca.org.uk/publication/policy/ps14-04.pdf.

Financial Conduct Authority. 'Making Current Account Switching Easier: The Effectiveness of the Current Account Switch Service (CASS) and Evidence on Account Number Portability'. March 2015. https://www.fca.org.uk/publication/research/making-current-account-switching-easier.pdf.

Financial Conduct Authority. 'Final Notice to Lloyds Banking Group'. 4 June 2015. https://www.fca.org.uk/publication/final-notices/lloyds-banking-group-2015.pdf.

Financial Conduct Authority. 'Regulatory Sandbox'. November 2015. https://www.fca.org.uk/publication/research/regulatory-sandbox.pdf.

Financial Conduct Authority. 'Crowdfunding'. 18 April 2016. https://www.fca.org.uk/consumers/crowdfunding.

Financial Conduct Authority. 'Consultation Paper: Loan-Based ('Peer-to-Peer') and Investment-Based Crowdfunding Platforms: Feedback on Our Post-Implementation Review and Proposed Changes to the Regulatory Framework'. FCA Consultation Paper 18/20. July 2018. https://www.fca.org.uk/publication/consultation/cp18-20.pdf.

Financial Conduct Authority. 'FCA Confirms New Rules for P2P Platforms'. 4 June 2019. https://www.fca.org.uk/news/press-releases/fca-confirms-new-rules-p2p-platforms.

Financial Conduct Authority. 'Policy Statement: Loan-Based ('Peer-to-Peer') and Investment-Based Crowdfunding Platforms: Feedback to CP18/20 and Final Rules'. FCA Policy Statement 19/14. June 2019. https://www.fca.org.uk/publication/policy/ps19-14.pdf.

Financial Conduct Authority. 'Investor Protection Measures for Special Purpose Acquisition Companies: Changes to the Listing Rules (PS21/10)'. July 2021. https://www.fca.org.uk/publication/policy/ps21-10.pdf.

Financial Conduct Authority. 'Regulatory Sandbox Accepted Firms'. 21 February 2023. https://www.fca.org.uk/firms/innovation/regulatory-sandbox/accepted-firms.

Financial Conduct Authority. 'FCA Handbook—CASS'. Accessed 1 June 2023. https://www.handbook.fca.org.uk/handbook/CASS.

Financial Conduct Authority. 'RegTech'. Accessed 1 June 2023. https://www.fca.org.uk/firms/innovation/RegTech.

Financial Ombudsman Service. 'Our Homepage'. Accessed 1 June 2023. https://www.financial-ombudsman.org.uk/.

Financial Services Compensation Scheme. 'What We Cover'. Accessed 1 June 2023. https://www.fscs.org.uk/what-we-cover/.

Financial Stability Board. 'BigTech in Finance: Market Developments and Potential Financial Stability Implications'. 9 December 2019. https://www.fsb.org/wp-content/uploads/P091219-1.pdf.

Bibliography

Financial Stability Board. 'Enhancing Cross-Border Payments: Stage 3 Roadmap'. 13 October 2020. https://www.fsb.org/wp-content/uploads/P131020-1.pdf.

Financial Stability Board. 'Evaluation of the Effects of Too-Big-To-Fail Reforms: Final Report'. 1 April 2021. https://www.fsb.org/wp-content/uploads/P010421-1.pdf.

Financial Stability Board. 'Fintech and Market Structure in the COVID-19 Pandemic: Implications for Financial Stability'. 21 March 2022. https://www.fsb.org/wp-content/uploads/P210322.pdf.

Financial Stability Board. 'Fintech'. 5 May 2022. https://www.fsb.org/work-of-the-fsb/financial-innovation-and-structural-change/Fintech/.

Findexable. 'Global Fintech Rankings Report: Bridging the Gap'. June 2021. https://findexable.com/wp-content/uploads/2021/06/Global-Fintech-Rankings-2021-v1-23-June-21.pdf.

Fintech Australia. 'What Is Fintech?'. Accessed 1 June 2023. https://www.fintechaustralia.org.au/what-is-fintech.

FintechHK. 'Fact Sheet: Hong Kong Fintech Landscape'. 13 January 2023. https://www.hongkong-fintech.hk/en/insights/news/news-2023/fact-sheet-hong-kong-fintech-landscape/.

Fintech Saudi. 'About Us'. Accessed 1 June 2023. https://Fintechsaudi.com/about/.

Fleming, Sean. 'Minister Fleming Publishes Ireland for Finance Action Plan 2021'. Government of Ireland. 11 February 2021. https://www.gov.ie/en/press-release/101ac-minister-fleming-publishes-ireland-for-finance-action-plan-2021/.

Flood, Chris. 'China Tightens Money Market Regulation'. *The Financial Times*, 1 February 2016.

Flototto, Max, Eitan Gold, Uzayr Jeenah, Mayowa Kuyoro, and Tunde Olanrewaju. 'Fintech n Africa: The End of the Beginning'. McKinsey. 30 August 2022. https://www.mckinsey.com/industries/financial-services/our-insights/Fintech-in-africa-the-end-of-the-beginning.

Foley, Stephen, and Izabella Kaminska. 'Bitcoin "Miners" Caught in Arms Race'. The Financial Times, 23 August 2014.

Fontanella-Khan, James, Hannah Murphy, and Miles Kruppa. 'Facebook Gives Up on Crypto Ambitions with Diem Asset Sale'. *The Financial Times*, 27 January 2022. https://www.ft.com/content/e237df96-7cc1-44e5-a92f-96170d34a9bb.

Fortune. 'Global 500'. Accessed 1 June 2023. https://fortune.com/global500/2019/.

Frame, W. Scott, Andreas Fuster, Joseph Tracy, and James Vickery. 'The Rescue of Fannie Mae and Freddie Mac'. Federal Reserve Bank of New York Staff Report No. 719. March 2015. https://www.newyorkfed.org/medialibrary/media/research/staff_reports/sr719.pdf.

Freshfields. 'EU Fintech Regulation: Key Themes and Trends'. Accessed 1 June 2023. https://www.freshfields.com/en-gb/our-thinking/campaigns/technology-quotient/Fintech/eu-Fintech-regulation-key-themes-and-trends/.

Frost, Jon, Leonardo Gambacorta, Yi Huang, Hyun Song Shin, and Pablo Zbinden. 'BigTech and the Changing Structure of Financial Intermediation'. *Economic Policy* vol. 34 (2019): p. 761.

FundApps. 'About Us'. Accessed 1 June 2023. https://www.fundapps.co/about-us.

Funding Circle. 'Business Loans & Funding in the UK'. Accessed 1 June 2023. http://www.fundingcircle.com/uk/businesses/.

Funding Circle. 'Fast, Flexible Business Loans'. Accessed 1 June 2023. http://www.fundingcircle.com/uk/.

Funding Circle. 'Lending to UK Businesses'. Accessed 1 June 2023. http://www.fundingcircle.com/uk/investors/.

Fung, Ben, Scott Hendry, and Warren E. Weber. 'Canadian Bank Notes and Dominion Notes: Lessons for Digital Currencies'. Bank of Canada Staff Working Paper 2017-5. February 2017. http://www.bankofcanada.ca/wp-content/uploads/2017/02/swp2017-5.pdf.

Garon, Jon M. 'Legal Implications of a Ubiquitous Metaverse and a Web3 Future'. *Marquette Law Review* vol. 106 (2022): p. 163.

Gaw, Kathryn. 'Bank of England Relaxes Regulations for Challenger Banks'. *FT Adviser*. 27 February 2017. https://www.ftadviser.com/Articles/2017/02/24/FTA-Challenger-banks.

Gaw, Kathryn. 'The Five Largest P2P Platforms by Lending Volumes'. P2P Finance News. 27 August 2021. https://p2pfinancenews.co.uk/2021/08/27/revealed-the-five-largest-p2p-platforms-by-lending-volumes/.

Gibbs, Samuel. '"Criminal Mastermind" of $4bn Bitcoin Laundering Scheme Arrested'. *The Guardian*, 27 July 2017. https://www.theguardian.com/technology/2017/jul/27/russian-criminal-mastermind-4bn-Bitcoin-laundering-scheme-arrested-mt-gox-exchange-alexander-vinnik.

GigCapital. 'Process—Shareholder Approval, Founder Vote Requirements, and Redemption Offer'. 27 December 2019. https://www.gigcapitalglobal.com/de-spac-process-shareholder-approval-founder-vote-requirements-and-redemption-offer/.

Goff, Sharlene. 'Challenger Banks Have the Big Four in Their Sights'. *The Financial Times*, 16 August 2014.

Goldman Sachs. 'Office Locations'. Accessed 1 June 2023. https://www.goldmansachs.com/our-firm/locations.html.

Google. 'Share Content by NFC with Android Beam'. Accessed 1 June 2023. https://support.google.com/nexus/answer/2781895.

Gorton, Gary B., and Jeffery Y. Zhang. 'Taming Wildcat Stablecoins'. *The University of Chicago Law Review* vol. 90 (2023): p. 909.

Government of India. 'Digital India Programme'. Accessed 1 June 2023. https://digitalindia.gov.in/.

Government of Maharashtra (India). 'Mumbai Fintech Hub'. Accessed 1 June 2023. https://Fintech.maharashtra.gov.in/.

Greeven, Mark, Shengyun Yang, Tao Yue, Eric van Heck, and Barbara Krug. 'The Case Study: How Taobao Bested eBay in China: Dealing with a Powerful New Rival'. *The Financial Times*, 13 March 2012.

Griffoli, Tommaso Mancini, Maria Soledad Martinez Peria, Itai Agur, et al. 'Casting Light on Central Bank Digital Currency'. International Monetary Fund Staff Discussion Notes No. 18/08. 13 November 2018. https://www.imf.org/en/Publications/Staff-Discussion-Notes/Issues/2018/11/13/Casting-Light-on-Central-Bank-Digital-Currencies-46833.

Grossman, Sanford J., and Oliver D. Hart. 'One Share-One Vote and the Market for Corporate Control'. *Journal of Financial Economics* vol. 20 (1988): p. 175.

Hale, Thomas. 'How Big Data Really Fits into Lending'. *The Financial Times*, 13 March 2019. https://ftalphaville.ft.com/2019/03/13/1552488421000/How-big-data-really-fits-into-lending/.

Hamilton, Jesse. 'Top US Bank Watchdog Warns of Stablecoins' Lack of Interoperability'. CoinDesk. 8 April 2022. https://www.coindesk.com/policy/2022/04/08/top-us-bank-watchdog-warns-of-stablecoins-lack-of-interoperability/.

Han, Liang, Song Zhang, and Francis J. Greene. 'Bank Market Concentration, Relationship Banking, and Small Business Liquidity'. *International Small Business Journal* vol. 35 (2017): p. 365.

Hangzhou Net. 'The Latest Valuation Ranking of Internet Enterprises in China'. 29 January 2019. http://appm.hangzhou.com.cn/article_pc.php?id=261153.

Harvey, Campbell R., Ashwin Ramachandran, and Joey Santoro. *DeFi and the Future of Finance* (Hoboken, NJ: Wiley, 2021).

Hearst Digital Media. 'Henry Ford—Biography. Founder of Ford Motor Company'. 5 September 2019. http://www.biography.com/business-figure/henry-ford.

Hendry, Mike. *Near Field Communications Technology and Applications* (Cambridge: Cambridge University Press, 2014).
Herbert Smith Freehills. 'Hong Kong Launches Regulatory Sandbox in Wake of Developments in Australia, Malaysia, Singapore, and the UK'. 5 October 2016. https://hsfnotes.com/fsrandcorpcrime/2016/10/05/hong-kong-launches-regulatory-sandbox-in-wake-of-developments-in-australia-malaysia-singapore-and-the-uk/.
Hillier, David, Stephen A. Ross, Randolph W. Westerfield, Jeffrey Jaffe, Bradford D. Jordan. *Corporate Finance*. 2nd ed. (New York: McGraw-Hill Higher Education, 2013).
HM Treasury. 'Tax-Advantaged Venture Capital Schemes: Ensuring Continued Support for Small and Growing Businesses'. UK Government. 10 July 2014. https://www.gov.uk/government/consultations/tax-advantaged-venture-capital-schemes-ensuring-continued-support-for-small-and-growing-businesses.
HM Treasury. 'UK Listings Review'. UK Government. 19 November 2020. https://www.gov.uk/government/publications/uk-listings-review.
HM Treasury. 'The Kalifa Review of UK Fintech'. UK Government. 26 February 2021. https://www.gov.uk/government/publications/the-kalifa-review-of-uk-fintech.
Hogan Lovells. 'Third Party Payment Licences in China—Are They Within the Grasp of Foreign Investors?'. 16 June 2014. https://www.hoganlovells.com/en/publications/third-party-payment-licences-in-china-are-they-within-the-grasp-of-foreign-investors.
Hong Kong Exchanges and Clearing Limited. 'Consultation Paper: Special Purpose Acquisition Companies'. 17 September 2021. https://www.hkex.com.hk/News/Regulatory-Announcements/2021/210917news?sc_lang=en.
Hong Kong Monetary Authority. 'Fintech 2025: Our Fintech Vision'. Accessed 1 June 2023. https://www.hkma.gov.hk/media/eng/doc/key-functions/ifc/fintech/HK_Fintech_2025_eng.pdf.
Hong Kong Monetary Authority. 'Fintech Supervisory Sandbox (FSS)'. Accessed 1 June 2023. https://www.hkma.gov.hk/eng/key-functions/international-financial-centre/Fintech/Fintech-supervisory-sandbox-fss/.
Hong Kong Securities and Futures Commission. 'Market Capitalisation of the World's Top Stock Exchanges'. September 2019. http://www.sfc.hk/web/EN/files/SOM/Market Statistics/a01.pdf.
Hook, Leslie, and Gabriel Wildau. 'China Mobile Payments Soar as US Clings to Plastic'. *The Financial Times*, 14 February 2017.
Howell, Bo. 'Weighing the Pros and Cons of RegTech'. Nasdaq. 26 April 2022. https://www.nasdaq.com/articles/weighing-the-pros-and-cons-of-RegTech.
Hu, Feijun. 'Securities Brokerage Financial Technology Competition'. *Securities Times*, 20 June 2022. https://news.stcn.com/sd/202206/t20220620_4662547.html.
Huang, Li, and Henry N. Pontell. 'Crime and Crisis in China's P2P Online Lending Market: A Comparative Analysis of Fraud'. *Crime, Law and Social Change* vol. 79 (2023): p. 369.
Hubbard, R. Glenn, Anil K. Kashyap, and Toni M. Whited. 'Internal Finance and Firm Investment'. *Journal of Money, Credit and Banking* vol. 27 (1995): p. 683.
Hughes, Jennifer, and Michael Hunter. 'Offshore Renminbi Rises from Record Low'. *The Financial Times*, 5 January 2017.
Hurun Research Institute. 'Hurun Global Unicorn List 2019'. 21 October 2019. https://www.hurun.net/en-US/Info/Detail?num=A38B8285034B.
IbisWorld. 'Peer-to-Peer Lending Platforms in the UK—Market Size 2010–2028'. 21 March 2022. https://www.ibisworld.com/united-kingdom/market-size/peer-to-lending-platforms/.
IBM. 'IaaS, PaaS and SaaS Cloud Service Models'. Accessed 1 June 2023. https://www.ibm.com/cloud/learn/iaas-paas-saas.

IBM. 'SDK vs. API: What's the Difference?'. Accessed 1 June 2023. https://www.ibm.com/cloud/blog/sdk-vs-api.
IBM. 'What Is a Single Point of Failure?'. Accessed 1 June 2023. https://www.ibm.com/docs/en/zos/2.4.0?topic=data-what-is-single-point-failure.
IBM. 'What Is Cloud Computing?'. Accessed 1 June 2023. http://www.ibm.com/uk-en/cloud/learn/what-is-cloud-computing.
IG. 'Algorithmic Trading'. Accessed 1 June 2023. https://www.ig.com/uk/trading-platforms/algorithmic-trading.
Imbert, Fred. 'Blackrock CEO Larry Fink Calls Bitcoin an "Index of Money Laundering"'. *CNBC*, 13 October 2017. https://www.cnbc.com/2017/10/13/blackrock-ceo-larry-fink-calls-Bitcoin-an-index-of-money-laundering.html.
India Times. 'India Has Second-Largest Unbanked Population in the World'. 15 June 2018. https://timesofindia.indiatimes.com/business/india-has-second-largest-unbanked-population-in-the-world/articleshow/64570254.cms.
Information Commissioner's Office. 'Big Data, Artificial Intelligence, Machine Learning and Data Protection'. 4 September 2017. http://ico.org.uk/media/for-organisations/documents/2013559/big-data-ai-ml-and-data-protection.pdf.
Ingves, Stefan. 'Restoring Confidence in Banks'. BIS Basel Committee on Banking Supervision. 4 March 2014. https://www.bis.org/speeches/sp140304.htm.
Innovate Finance. 'Fintech Investment Landscape 2022'. January 2023. https://www.innovatefinance.com/wp-content/uploads/2023/01/innovate-finance-Fintech-investment-landscape-2022.pdf.
Innovate Finance. '36H Group'. 1 June 2023. https://www.innovatefinance.com/36hgroup/.
Institute of International Finance. 'Cloud Computing in the Financial Sector'. August 2018. https://www.iif.com/portals/0/Files/private/32370132_cloud_computing_in_the_financial_sector_20180803_0.pdf.
Inter-American Development Bank. 'Study: Fintech Industry Doubles in Size in Three Years in Latin America and the Caribbean'. 26 April 2022. https://www.iadb.org/en/news/study-Fintech-industry-doubles-size-three-years-latin-america-and-caribbean.
International Association of Deposit Insurers. 'Deposit Insurance Systems'. Accessed 1 June 2023. https://www.iadi.org/en/deposit-insurance-systems/.
International Data Corporation. 'Smartphone Market Share'. 17 May 2021. https://www.idc.com/promo/smartphone-market-share/vendor.
International Organization of Securities Commissions. 'Principles for Ongoing Disclosure and Material Development Reporting by Listed Entities'. October 2002. https://www.sec.gov/about/offices/oia/oia_corpfin/princdisclos.pdf.
International Organization of Securities Commissions. 'IOSCO Research Report on Financial Technologies (Fintech)'. February 2017. https://www.iosco.org/library/pubdocs/pdf/IOSCOPD554.pdf.
Isaac, Anna. 'Fintech Firm Revolut Moves Closer to UK Banking Licence After First Annual Profit'. *The Guardian*, 1 March 2023. https://www.theguardian.com/business/2023/mar/01/uk-Fintech-firm-revolut-much-delayed-accounts-reveal-first-annual-profit.
Jackson, Kevin L. 'The Economic Benefit of Cloud Computing'. *Forbes*, 17 September 2011. http://www.forbes.com/sites/kevinjackson/2011/09/17/the-economic-benefit-of-cloud-computing/.
Jing, Meng. 'Ant Financial Gears Up for More Wealth Management'. *China Daily*, 9 September 2016. http://europe.chinadaily.com.cn/business/2016-09/09/content_26748999.htm.
Jingu, Takeshi. 'Internet Finance Growing Rapidly in China'. Nomura Research Institute. 10 March 2014. https://www.nri.com/-/media/Corporate/en/Files/PDF/knowledge/publication/lakyara/2014/03/lakyaravol189.pdf.

Jones, Adam, and Jennifer Thompson. 'RBS Prepares for Libor Settlement Talks'. *The Financial Times*, 3 November 2012.

Jones, Charisse. 'Chip-Enabled Credit Cards Mark a Bittersweet 1-Year Anniversary'. USA Today. 3 October 2016. http://eu.usatoday.com/story/money/personalfinance/2016/10/03/chip-credit-cards-anniversary-pin/91237606/.

Jones, Rupert. 'The Digital Upstarts Offering App-Only Banking for Smartphone Users'. *The Guardian*, 14 May 2016. https://www.theguardian.com/money/2016/may/14/digital-app-only-banking-smartphone.

JPMorgan. 'Artificial Intelligence Research'. Accessed 1 June 2023. http://www.jpmorgan.com/global/technology/artificial-intelligence.

JPMorgan Chase. 'JPMorgan Chase to Launch Digital Consumer Banking in the U.K.'. 27 January 2021. https://www.jpmorganchase.com/news-stories/jpmorgan-chase-to-launch-digital-consumer-banking-in-the-uk.

Kai, Guo. 'China's Mobile Payment Era: Costs and Benefits'. *China Daily*, 11 May 2017. http://www.chinadaily.com.cn/china/2017-05/11/content_29295024.htm.

Kaminska, Izabella, and Alice Woodhouse. 'Bitcoin Rises Above $4.000 in Record Run for Digital Currency'. *The Financial Times*, 14 August 2017. https://www.ft.com/content/e2d3fcb8-80cf-11e7-94e2-c5b903247afd.

Khan, Zia, Harry Terris, Ben Meggeson, and Mohammad Taqi. 'The World's 100 Largest Banks 2023'. S&P Global. 26 April 2023. https://www.spglobal.com/marketintelligence/en/news-insights/research/the-world-s-100-largest-banks-2023.

Kharpal, Arjun. 'Exclusive: Ant Financial Close to Closing a Bigger-Than-Expected $3.5 Billion Debt Round for International Expansion'. *CNBC*, 17 May 2017. http://www.cnbc.com/2017/05/17/ant-financial-debt-financing-round.html.

Khiaonarong, Tanai, and David Humphrey. 'Cash Use Across Countries and the Demand for Central Bank Digital Currency'. *Journal of Payments Strategy and Systems* vol. 13 (2019): p. 32.

Kiff, John, Jihad Alwazir, Sonja Davidovic, et al. 'A Survey of Research on Retail Central Bank Digital Currency'. International Monetary Fund Working Paper No. 20/104. June 2020. https://www.imf.org/en/Publications/WP/Issues/2020/06/26/A-Survey-of-Research-on-Retail-Central-Bank-Digital-Currency-49517.

Kingdom of Saudi Arabia. 'Homepage: The Progress & Achievements of Saudi Arabia—Vision 2030'. Accessed 1 June 2023. https://www.vision2030.gov.sa/.

Klarna International. 'About Us'. Accessed 1 June 2023. https://www.klarna.com/international/about-us/.

Knauth, Dietrich, and Tom Hals. 'Failed Crypto Exchange FTX Has Recovered Over $5 Bln, Attorney Says'. *Reuters*, 11 January 2023. https://www.reuters.com/business/finance/ftx-seeks-court-rulings-asset-sales-customer-privacy-2023-01-11/.

Kola-Oyeneyin, Topsy, Mayowa Kuyoro, and Tunde Olanrewaju. 'Harnessing Nigeria's Fintech Potential'. McKinsey. 23 September 2020. https://www.mckinsey.com/featured-insights/middle-east-and-africa/harnessing-nigerias-Fintech-potential.

Kolb, Johannes, and Tereza Tykvova. 'Going Public Via Special Purpose Acquisition Companies: Frogs Do Not Turn into Princes'. *Journal of Corporate Finance* vol. 40 (2016): p. 80.

Kollmeyer, Barbara. 'Bitcoin Surges to New High Above $64.000 as Investors Wait for Coinbase IPO'. MarketWatch. 14 April 2021. https://www.marketwatch.com/story/bitcoin-surges-to-new-high-above-64-000-as-investors-wait-for-coinbase-ipo-11618381133.

Korinek, Anton, and Joseph E. Stiglitz. 'Artificial Intelligence and Its Implications for Income Distribution and Unemployment'. National Bureau of Economic Research. December 2017. http://www.nber.org/papers/w24174.

KPMG. 'The Game Changers: Challenger Banking Results'. May 2015.
KPMG. 'Framing New Futures: Challenger Banking Report 2017'. October 2017. https://assets.kpmg.com/content/dam/kpmg/uk/pdf/2017/10/challenger-banks-framing-new-futures.pdf.
KPMG. 'Pulse of Fintech H2 2019'. February 2020. https://assets.kpmg.com/content/dam/kpmg/xx/pdf/2020/02/pulse-of-fintech-h2-2019.pdf.
KPMG. 'Total Fintech Investment Tops US$210 Billion'. February 2022. https://kpmg.com/xx/en/home/media/press-releases/2022/02/total-fintech-investment-tops-us-210-billion.html.
KPMG. 'Pulse of Fintech H1 2022—ASPAC'. August 2022. https://kpmg.com/xx/en/home/insights/2022/08/pulse-of-Fintech-h1-22-aspac.html.
Kuchler, Hannah, and Elaine Moore. 'Miliband Set to Up the Ante Over Big Banks'. *The Financial Times*, 9 July 2012.
Kumhof, Michael, and Clare Noone. 'Central Bank Digital Currencies—Design Principles and Balance Sheet Implications'. Bank of England Staff Working Paper No. 725. May 2018. https://www.bankofengland.co.uk/-/media/boe/files/working-paper/2018/central-bank-digital-currencies-design-principles-and-balance-sheet-implications.
Lambert, Richard A., Christian Leuz, and Robert E. Verrecchia. 'Information Asymmetry, Information Precision, and the Cost of Capital'. *Review of Finance* vol. 16 (2012): p. 1.
Landry, Lauren. 'What Are Alternative Investments?'. Harvard Business School. 8 July 2021. https://online.hbs.edu/blog/post/what-are-alternative-investments.
Laurent, Lionel. 'Monzo: Can a $2.5 Billion Banking Upstart Really Dislodge JPMorgan?'. *Bloomberg*, 26 June 2019. https://www.bloomberg.com/opinion/articles/2019-06-26/monzo-can-a-2-5-billion-banking-upstart-dislodge-jpmorgan.
Layne, Ramey, and Brenda Lenahan. 'Special Purpose Acquisition Companies: An Introduction'. Harvard Law School Forum on Corporate Governance. 6 July 2018. https://corpgov.law.harvard.edu/2018/07/06/special-purpose-acquisition-companies-an-introduction/.
Layne, Ramey, Brenda Lenahan, and Sarah Morgan. 'Update on Special Purpose Acquisition Companies'. Harvard Law School Forum on Corporate Governance. 17 August 2020. https://corpgov.law.harvard.edu/2020/08/17/update-on-special-purpose-acquisition-companies/.
Lee, Aileen. 'Welcome to the Unicorn Club: Learning from Billion-Dollar Start-Ups'. TechCrunch. 2 November 2013. http://techcrunch.com/2013/11/02/welcome-to-the-unicorn-club/.
Lee, Alexander, Brendan Malone, and Paul Wong. 'Tokens and Accounts in the Context of Digital Currencies'. The US Federal Reserve Board Feds Notes. 23 December 2020. https://www.federalreserve.gov/econres/notes/feds-notes/tokens-and-accounts-in-the-context-of-digital-currencies-122320.html.
LendingClub. 'LendingClub Securitization Program'. Accessed 1 June 2023. https://www.lendingclub.com/investing/institutional/securitization.
LendingClub. 'Personal Loans'. Accessed 1 June 2023. https://www.lendingclub.com/loans/personal-loans.
LexisNexis. 'Global Spend on Financial Crime Compliance at Financial Institutions Reaches $213.9 Billion USD According to LexisNexis Risk Solutions Study'. 9 June 2021. https://risk.lexisnexis.com/global/en/about-us/press-room/press-release/20210609-tcoc-global-study.
Lin, Xuchen, Li Xiaolong, and Zhong Zheng. 'Evaluating Borrower's Default Risk in Peer-to-Peer Lending: Evidence from a Lending Platform in China'. *Applied Economics* vol. 49 (2017): p. 3538.
Lingyi Finance. 'P2P Lending Industry Annual Report 2018'. 3 January 2019. https://www.01caijing.com/article/34230.htm.

Lo, Benjamin. 'It Ain't Broke: The Case for Continued SEC Regulation of P2P Lending'. *Harvard Business Law Review* vol. 6 (2016): p. 87.
Lockett, Hudson, and Primrose Riordan. 'Ant Group IPO Faces at Least 6-Month Delay After Beijing Intervention'. *The Financial Times*, 5 November 2020. http://www.ft.com/content/35a95455-338a-4ede-bab3-fd0f098ac268.
Loepp, Susan, and William K. Wootters. *Protecting Information: From Classical Error Correction to Quantum Cryptography* (Cambridge: Cambridge University Press, 2006).
Lu, Lerong. 'Private Banks in China: Origin, Challenges and Regulatory Implications'. *Banking and Finance Law Review* vol. 31 (2016): p. 585.
Lu, Lerong. 'Financial Technology and Challenger Banks in the UK: Gap Fillers or Real Challengers?'. *Journal of International Banking Law and Regulation* vol. 32 (2017): p. 273.
Lu, Lerong. 'How a Little Ant Challenges Giant Banks? The Rise of Ant Financial (Alipay)'s Fintech Empire and Relevant Regulatory Concerns'. *International Company and Commercial Law Review* vol. 28 (2018): p. 12.
Lu, Lerong. 'Decoding Alipay: Mobile Payments, a Cashless Society and Regulatory Challenges'. *Butterworths Journal of International Banking and Financial Law* vol. 33 (2018): p. 40.
Lu, Lerong. 'Bitcoin: Speculative Bubble, Financial Risk and Regulatory Response'. *Butterworths Journal of International Banking and Financial Law* vol. 33 (2018): p. 178.
Lu, Lerong. 'Promoting SME Finance in the Context of Fintech Revolution: A Case Study of the UK's Practice and Regulation'. *Banking and Finance Law Review* vol. 33 (2018): p. 317.
Lu, Lerong. 'Solving the SME Financing Puzzle in the UK: Has Online P2P Lending Got the Midas Touch?'. *Journal of International Banking Law and Regulation* vol. 33 (2018), p. 449.
Lu, Lerong. 'Black Swans and Grey Rhinos: Demystifying China's Financial Risks and the Financial Regulatory Reform'. *Butterworths Journal of International Banking and Financial Law* vol. 33 (2018): p. 594.
Lu, Lerong. *Private Lending in China: Practice, Law, and Regulation of Shadow Banking and Alternative Finance* (Abingdon: Routledge 2018).
Lu, Lerong. 'The Rising Star in the East: Unveiling China's Star Market, the Registration-Based IPO Regime and Capital Markets Law Reform'. *International Company and Commercial Law Review* vol. 31 (2020): p. 394.
Lu, Lerong, and Hang Chen. 'Digital Yuan: The Practice and Regulation of China's Central Bank Digital Currency'. *Butterworths Journal of International Banking and Financial Law* vol. 36 (2021): p. 601.
Lu, Lerong, and Shunqi Yang. 'Do Investors Vote with Their Feet? Commenting on Deliveroo's IPO on London Stock Exchange and the Dual-Class Share Structure'. *Company Lawyer* vol. 42 (2021): p. 332.
Lu, Lerong, and Ningyao Ye. 'Shanghai–London Stock Connect: Operating Mechanism, Opportunities and Challenges'. *Journal of International Banking Law and Finance* vol. 34 (2019): p. 684.
Lu, Lerong, and Alice Lingsheng Zhang. 'Could the Dragon Now Fly Beyond Borders? Contextualizing Regulatory Aspects and Risks for China's CBDC Cross-Border Use'. 1 September 2021. https://ssrn.com/abstract=3935854.
Lu, Lerong, and Alice Lingsheng Zhang. 'China Experiments with Cross-Border Payments of Central Bank Digital Currencies'. Columbia Law School's Blog on Corporations and Capital Markets. 17 December 2021. https://clsbluesky.law.columbia.edu/2021/12/17/china-experiments-with-cross-border-payments-of-central-bank-digital-currencies/.
Lu, Lerong, and Alice Lingsheng Zhang. 'Regulating Fintech Corporations Amidst Covid-19 Pandemic: An Analysis of Ant Group (Alipay)'s Suspension of IPO and Business Restructuring'. *The Company Lawyer* vol. 42 (2021): p. 341.

Lu, Lerong, and Alice Lingsheng Zhang. 'Singapore's SPAC Listing Regime: A Game Changer or a Gap Filler?'. *Securities Regulation Law Review* vol. 50 (2022): p. 25.

Lucas, Louise. 'Chinese Money Market Fund Becomes World's Biggest'. *The Financial Times*, 26 April 2017. https://www.ft.com/content/28d4e100-2a6d-11e7-bc4b-5528796fe35c.

Lucas, Louise. 'Tencent Grabs Mobile Pay Share from Alibaba'. *The Financial Times*, 2 May 2017.

Lucas, Louise. 'Alibaba Restructuring Paves Way for Ant Financial IPO'. *The Financial Times*, 24 September 2019. https://www.ft.com/content/267c395c-de94-11e9-9743-db5a370481bc.

Lucas, Louise, and Don Weinland. 'Alibaba's $60bn Payments Arm Stalls Planned IPO'. *The Financial Times*, 16 May 2017. https://www.ft.com/content/25780a7c-3702-11e7-bce4-9023f8c0fd2e.

Luu, Loi. 'With Blockchain, Knowing Your Customer Is More Important Than Ever'. *Forbes*, 17 May 2018. http://www.forbes.com/sites/luuloi/2018/05/17/with-blockchain-knowing-your-customer-is-more-important-than-ever/.

Ma, Nan. 'China Halts Virtual Coin-Based Fundraising After Declaring Offerings Illegal'. *The Financial Times*, 5 September 2017.

Mackintosh, Phil. 'Nasdaq: 50 Years of Market Innovation'. Nasdaq. 11 February 2021. https://www.nasdaq.com/articles/nasdaq%3A-50-years-of-market-innovation-2021-02-11.

MacLellan, Kylie. 'UK Channels Business Lending Via Alternative Financiers'. *Reuters*, 12 December 2012. http://uk.reuters.com/article/uk-britain-lending/uk-channels-business-lending-via-alternative-financiers-idUKBRE8BB0E920121212.

Makortoff, Kalyeena. 'Monzo Valued at £2bn After Fresh Funding Round from US'. *The Guardian*, 25 June 2019. http://www.theguardian.com/business/2019/jun/25/monzo-digital-bank-doubles-value-2bn-fresh-funding-round-y-combinator.

Margolis, Jonathan. 'Chinese Drone Pioneer DJI Is Still Gaining Altitude'. *The Financial Times*, 13 October 2015. https://www.ft.com/content/a0cfd67a-6dda-11e5-8171-ba1968cf791a.

Martin, Kevin. 'How Banking Will Change After COVID-19'. HSBC. 26 November 2020. https://www.hsbc.com/insight/topics/how-banking-will-change-after-covid-19.

McCamy, Laura. '11 Mind-Blowing Facts About New York's Economy'. *Business Insider*, 24 April 2019. http://markets.businessinsider.com/news/stocks/11-mind-blowing-facts-about-new-yorks-economy-2019-4-1028134328.

McCurry, Justin. 'US Dismisses South Korea's Launch of World-First 5G Network as "Stunt"'. *The Guardian*, 4 April 2019. https://www.theguardian.com/technology/2019/apr/04/us-dismisses-south-koreas-launch-of-world-first-5g-network-as-stunt.

McGinty, Andrew, and Mark Parsons. 'Third Party Payment Licences in China—Are They within the Grasp of Foreign Investors?'. Hogan Lovells. 16 June 2014. https://www.hoganlovells.com/en/publications/third-party-payment-licences-in-china-are-they-within-the-grasp-of-foreign-investors.

McKinsey. 'Value Creation in the Metaverse: The Real Business of the Virtual World'. June 2022. https://www.mckinsey.com/~/media/mckinsey/business%20functions/marketing%20and%20sales/our%20insights/value%20creation%20in%20the%20metaverse/Value-creation-in-the-metaverse.pdf.

McKinsey. 'Europe's Fintech Opportunity'. 26 October 2022. https://www.mckinsey.com/industries/financial-services/our-insights/europes-Fintech-opportunity.

Megaw, Nicholas. 'Lithuania Licence Lets Revolut Launch Banking Products'. *The Financial Times*, 23 December 2018. http://www.ft.com/content/989904f0-fe2c-11e8-aebf-99e208d3e521.

Megaw, Nicholas. 'Germany's N26 Becomes Europe's Top Fintech with $2.7bn Valuation'. *The Financial Times*, 10 January 2019. http://www.ft.com/content/d945cfa8-1419-11e9-a581-4ff78404524e.
Meta. 'What Is the Metaverse?'. Accessed 1 June 2023. https://about.meta.com/what-is-the-Metaverse/.
Metro Bank. 'About Us'. Accessed 1 June 2023. https://www.metrobankonline.co.uk/about-us/.
Microsoft. 'What Is Augmented Reality or AR?'. Accessed 1 June 2023. https://dynamics.microsoft.com/en-us/mixed-reality/guides/what-is-augmented-reality-ar/.
Microsoft. 'What Is Cloud Computing? A Beginner's Guide'. Accessed 1 June 2023. http://azure.microsoft.com/en-gb/overview/what-is-cloud-computing/.
Mills, Karen. 'Use Data to Fix the Small Business Lending Gap'. *Harvard Business Review*, 16 September 2014. https://hbr.org/2014/09/use-data-to-fix-the-small-business-lending-gap.
Millward, Steven. 'Alipay Invades China's High Streets with Mobile Barcode Payments'. Tech in Asia. 1 July 2011. https://www.techinasia.com/alipay-mobile-payments.
Milmo, Dan. 'ChatGPT Reaches 100 Million Users Two Months After Launch'. *The Guardian*, 2 February 2023. https://www.theguardian.com/technology/2023/feb/02/chatgpt-100-million-users-open-ai-fastest-growing-app.
Ming, Cheang. 'FICO with Chinese Characteristics: Nice Rewards, But Punishing Penalties'. *CNBC*, 16 March 2017. http://www.cnbc.com/2017/03/16/china-social-credit-system-ant-financials-sesame-credit-and-others-give-scores-that-go-beyond-fico.html.
Mitchell, Tom. 'Chinese Ponzi scheme sparks calls for protests'. *The Financial Times*. 2 February 2016. https://www.ft.com/content/ade11b08-c9a1-11e5-a8ef-ea66e967dd44.
Mitchell, Tom, and George Parker. 'G20 Takes Up Global Inequality Challenge'. *The Financial Times*, 4 September 2016. https://www.ft.com/content/cc70de98-72aa-11e6-b60a-de4532d5ea35.
Monetary Authority of Singapore. 'Singapore Cements Position as Third Largest Global FX Centre'. 28 October 2022. https://www.mas.gov.sg/news/media-releases/2022/singapore-cements-position-as-third-largest-global-fx-centre.
Monetary Authority of Singapore. 'Fintech and Innovation'. Accessed 1 June 2023. https://www.mas.gov.sg/development/Fintech.
Monetary Authority of Singapore. 'Overview of Regulatory Sandbox'. Accessed 1 June 2023. https://www.mas.gov.sg/development/Fintech/regulatory-sandbox.
Monetary Authority of Singapore. 'Regulation—Banking'. Accessed 1 June 2023. https://www.mas.gov.sg/regulation/Banking.
MoneyLion. 'What Is MoneyLion?'. Accessed 1 June 2023. http://www.moneylion.com/about.
Monzo. 'Welcome to Monzo Bank'. 5 April 2017. https://monzo.com/blog/2017/04/05/banking-licence.
Monzo. 'You've Invested £20.000.000 in Monzo'. 5 December 2018. http://monzo.com/blog/2018/12/05/crowdfunding-closes.
Monzo. 'About Monzo'. Accessed 1 June 2023. https://monzo.com/about/.
Moore, Elaine. 'Challengers Line Up to Take on the Big Banks'. *The Financial Times*, 14 July 2012.
Moosa, Imad. 'The Myth of Too Big To Fail'. *Journal of Banking Regulation* vol. 11 (2010): p. 319.
Mor, Federico. 'Bank Rescues of 2007–09: Outcomes and Cost'. House of Commons Library Research Briefing. 8 October 2018. https://researchbriefings.files.parliament.uk/documents/SN05748/SN05748.pdf.

Morris, Stephen, James Fontanella-Khan, and Arash Massoudi. 'How the Swiss "Trinity" Forced UBS to Save Credit Suisse'. *The Financial Times*, 20 March 2023. https://www.ft.com/content/3080d368-d5aa-4125-a210-714e37087017.

Mueller, Jackson, and Michael S. Piwowar. 'The Rise of Fintech in the Middle East'. Milken Institute. September 2019. https://milkeninstitute.org/sites/default/files/reports-pdf/Fintech%20in%20the%20Middle%20East-FINAL-121119.pdf.

Murphy, Flynn, and Qian Tong. 'China Tech Giants Accused of "Bullying" Consumers with Algorithms'. *Nikkei*, 16 January 2021. https://asia.nikkei.com/Spotlight/Caixin/China-tech-giants-accused-of-bullying-consumers-with-algorithms.

Murphy, Hannah. 'Facebook's Libra Currency to Launch Next Year in Limited Format'. *The Financial Times*, 27 November 2020. https://www.ft.com/content/cfe4ca11-139a-4d4e-8a65-b3be3a0166be.

Murray, Christine. 'El Salvador Endures Bumpy First Week with Bitcoin as Legal Tender'. *The Financial Times*, 10 September 2021. https://www.ft.com/content/842415ec-06cb-437b-932f-f868d4f55fc4.

Murugaboopathy, Patturaja. 'Global SPAC Deal Volumes this Year Surpass Total for 2020'. *Reuters*, 9 March 2021. https://www.reuters.com/article/uk-usa-markets-spac-idUKKBN2B11WG.

MyBank. '2018 Financial Report'. Published in 2019. https://gw.alipayobjects.com/os/basement_prod/a0e755ca-07da-494d-97c3-cf322233dcd2.pdf.

National Payments Corporation of India. 'Unified Payments Interface (UPI) Product Overview'. 1 June 2023. https://www.npci.org.in/what-we-do/upi/product-overview.

NetEase. 'MyBank Earned 315bn Net Profit Last Year. Lower Than Tencent's WeBank'. 8 July 2017. http://tech.163.com/17/0708/13/COR0623V00097U7R.html.

New York State Attorney General. 'Attorney General James Ends Virtual Currency Trading Platform Bitfinex's Illegal Activities in New York'. 23 February 2021. https://ag.ny.gov/press-release/2021/attorney-general-james-ends-virtual-currency-trading-platform-bitfinexs-illegal.

Ng, Rosabel, Jeffrey Lim, Tian Sion Yoong, and Hannah Ng. 'Inside and Outside Singapore's Proposed Fintech Regulatory Sandbox: Balancing Supervision and Innovation'. *Butterworths Journal of International Banking and Financial Law* vol. 31 (2016): p. 596.

Nilsson, Nils J. *Principles of Artificial Intelligence* (Burlington: Morgan Kaufmann, 2014).

Noonan, Laura. 'P2P Lenders to Be Asked to Reveal Defaults'. *The Financial Times*, 12 August 2017.

Norton Rose Fulbright. 'SPACs: The London Alternative'. May 2021. https://www.nortonrosefulbright.com/en-gb/knowledge/publications/94734f5e/spacs-the-london-alternative.

Novet, Jordan. 'Zoom Rocketed 72% on First Day of Trading'. *CNBC*, 18 April 2019. https://www.cnbc.com/2019/04/18/zoom-ipo-stock-begins-trading-on-nasdaq.html.

O'Brien, Sarah. 'Bitcoin "Miners" Dig More Than Just the Money'. *CNBC*, 15 August 2017. https://www.cnbc.com/2017/08/15/Bitcoin-miners-dig-more-than-just-the-money.html.

OECD. 'OECD Science, Technology and Innovation Outlook 2023: Enabling Transitions in Times of Disruption'. 16 March 2023. https://www.oecd.org/sti/oecd-science-technology-and-innovation-outlook-25186167.htm.

OpenAI. 'GPT-4'. Accessed 1 June 2023. https://openai.com/research/gpt-4.

Open Banking. 'What Is Open Banking?'. Accessed 1 June 2023. https://www.openbanking.org.uk/what-is-open-banking/.

Oracle. 'Cloud Computing in Financial Services: A Banker's Guide'. November 2015.

Oracle. 'The Era I Enterprise: Ready for Anything'. April 2016. http://www.oracle.com/us/industries/oracle-era-ready-anything-2969053.pdf.

Osipovich, Alexander. 'Blockchain Makes Inroads into the Stock Market's $1 Trillion Plumbing System'. *The Wall Street Journal*, 7 November 2019. http://www.wsj.com/articles/blockchain-makes-inroads-into-the-stock-markets-1-trillion-plumbing-system-11573131600.

Page, Carly. 'Revolut Confirms Cyberattack Exposed Personal Data of Tens of Thousands of Users'. TechCrunch. 20 September 2022. https://techcrunch.com/2022/09/20/revolut-cyberattack-thousands-exposed/.

Paipaidai. 'About Us—Paipaidai'. Accessed 1 June 2023. http://www.ppdai.com/help/aboutus.

Palma, Stefania. 'Singapore Expands Fintech to Stay Ahead of Other Financial Centres'. *The Financial Times*, 24 September 2019. https://www.ft.com/content/e7000952-b8fa-11e9-8a88-aa6628ac896c.

Paris Fintech Forum. 'Paris Fintech Forum Communities'. Accessed 1 June 2023. https://members.parisFintechforum.com/.

Patel, Freny. 'SPAC Invaders'. Asia Business Law Journal. 2 June 2021. https://law.asia/spac-invaders-asia/.

Patel, Manisha. 'Banks Have a Responsibility to Fix the Financial Education Gap'. The Fintech Times. 14 January 2020. https://theFintechtimes.com/banks-have-a-responsibility-to-fix-the-financial-education-gap/.

PayPal. 'Who We Are——History & Facts'. Accessed 1 June 2023. https://about.pypl.com/who-we-are/history-and-facts/default.aspx.

Peer-to-Peer Finance Association. 'Rules of the Peer-to-Peer Finance Association'. May 2015.

Peer-to-Peer Finance Association. 'Peer-to-Peer Finance Association Operating Principles'. June 2015.

Peng, Qinqin, Wu Yujian, and Han Wei. 'China Steps Up Curbs on Virtual Currency Trading'. *Caixin*, 8 September 2017. https://www.caixinglobal.com/2017-09-09/101142821.html.

People.cn. 'The Ministry of Science and Technology Officially Releases the 2017 Unicorn List: Who Is the New Big Winner?'. 24 March 2018. http://it.people.com.cn/n1/2018/0324/c1009-29886916.html.

People's Bank of China. 'China Financial Stability Report 2015'. September 2015. http://www.pbc.gov.cn/eportal/fileDir/english/resource/cms/2015/09/2015090616281480816.pdf.

People's Bank of China. 'The Notice of Preventing Financial Risks Relating to Initial Coin Offerings'. 4 September 2017. http://www.pbc.gov.cn/goutongjiaoliu/113456/113469/3374222/index.html.

People's Bank of China. 'The Action Plan on Building Shanghai International Financial Centre (2018–2020)', 16 November 2018, https://jrj.sh.gov.cn/jcgk-ghjh/20220922/3ad0412a0a484a1797af008ec01bcd37.html.

People's Bank of China. 'Fintech Development Plan (2019–2021)'. August 2019, http://www.pbc.gov.cn/en/3688110/3688172/4048311/3880801/index.html.

People's Bank of China. 'Trial Measures on Regulation of Financial Holding Companies'. Order No. 4. 11 September 2020.

People's Bank of China. 'Fintech Development Plan (2022–2025)'. 4 January 2022. http://www.pbc.gov.cn/en/3688110/3688172/4437084/4441980/index.html.

Picker, Leslie, and Noah Buhayar. 'LendingClub Surges in Debut After $870 Million U.S IPO'. *Bloomberg*, 11 December 2014. https://www.bloomberg.com/news/articles/2014-12-11/lendingclub-surges-in-debut-after-870-million-u-s-ipo.

Pinsent Masons, 'Banking on Cloud: A Discussion Paper by Pinsent Masons and the BBA (Now UK Finance)', December 2016, https://www.pinsentmasons.com/thinking/special-reports/banking-on-cloud.

Pooley, Cat Rutter. 'London Slips Further Behind New York in Financial Centre Rankings'. *The Financial Times*, 19 September 2019. https://www.ft.com/content/b8ab7f22-daac-11e9-8f9b-77216ebe1f17.

264 Bibliography

PPDai. 'Company Profile'. Accessed 1 June 2023. http://ir.ppdai.com/company-profile.

Prosper. 'Smart. Simple Tools for Borrowing, Saving & Earning'. Accessed 1 June 2023. https://www.prosper.com/.

PwC. 'Where Have You Been All My Life? How the Financial Services Industry Can Unlock the Value in Big Data'. October 2013. http://www.pwc.com/us/en/financial-services/publications/viewpoints/assets/pwc-unlocking-big-data-value.pdf.

PwC. '2018 Annual APEC CEO Survey: Singapore Findings'. 15 November 2018. https://www.pwc.com/sg/en/publications/apec-ceo-survey-sg-2018.html.

PwC. '4th Annual Global Crypto Hedge Fund Report 2022'. June 2022. https://www.pwc.com/gx/en/financial-services/pdf/4th-annual-global-crypto-hedge-fund-report-june-2022.pdf.

PwC. 'Considering an IPO? First, Understand the Costs'. Accessed 1 June 2023. https://wwwhttps://www.pwc.com/us/en/services/deals/library/cost-of-an-ipo.html.pwc.com/us/en/services/deals/library/cost-of-an-ipo.html.

PwC. 'Hong Kong SAR. Individual—Taxes on Personal Income'. Accessed 1 June 2023. https://taxsummaries.pwc.com/hong-kong-sar/individual/taxes-on-personal-income.

PwC. 'How Special Purpose Acquisition Companies (SPACs) Work'. Accessed 1 June 2023. https://www.pwc.com/us/en/services/audit-assurance/accounting-advisory/spac-merger.html.

PwC. 'The 2019 Canadian Fintech Market Map'. Accessed 1 June 2023. https://www.pwc.com/ca/en/industries/technology/canadian-Fintech-market-map.html.

QQ. 'About WeChat Pay'. Accessed 1 June 2023. https://kf.qq.com/faq/181012y6bUNR181012nMFnMr.html.

Rabinovitch, Simon. 'Alibaba's Treasure Draws in Depositors'. *The Financial Times*, 21 December 2013.

Ralph, Oliver. 'Lemonade Aims Takes Its Digital Fizz to German Insurance'. *The Financial Times*, 11 June 2019. https://www.ft.com/content/6533b0ce-8c39-11e9-a1c1-51bf8f989972.

Ramkumar, Amrith. '2020 SPAC Boom Lifted Wall Street Biggest Banks'. *The Wall Street Journal*, 5 January 2021. https://www.wsj.com/articles/2020-spac-boom-lifted-wall-streets-biggest-banks-11609842601.

Raskin, Max. 'The Law and Legality of Smart Contracts'. *Georgetown Law Technology Review* vol. 1 (2017): p. 304.

Reddy, Bobby V. 'Finding the British Google: Relaxing the Prohibition of Dual-Class Stock from the Premium-Tier of the London Stock Exchange'. *Cambridge Law Journal* vol. 79 (2020): p. 315.

RelBanks. 'Top 100 Banks in the World'. 2 April 2018. http://www.relbanks.com/worlds-top-banks/assets.

RelBanks. 'Banks in the UK'. Accessed 1 June 2023. http://www.relbanks.com/europe/uk.

Ren, Ci, and Lerong Lu. 'Special Purpose Acquisition Companies (SPACs): The Global Investment Mania, Corporate Practices, and Regulatory Responses'. *Journal of Business Law*, Issue 1 (2023): p. 22.

Ren, Daniel. 'China Regulators Warn that 90 Pc of Peer-to-Peer Lenders Could Fail in 2017'. *South China Morning Post*, 19 February 2017. http://www.scmp.com/business/china-business/article/2072177/china-regulators-warns-90-pc-peer-peer-lenders-could-fail.

Reserve Bank of India. 'Enabling Framework for Regulatory Sandbox'. 8 February 2018. https://rbidocs.rbi.org.in/rdocs/PublicationReport/Pdfs/ENABLING79D8EBD31FED47A0BE21158C337123BF.PDF.

Restoy, Fernando. 'Regulating Fintech: Is an Activity-Based Approach the Solution?'. Bank for International Settlements. 16 June 2021. https://www.bis.org/speeches/sp210616.htm.

Reuters. 'Alibaba-Affiliated Online Bank Get Green Light from China Regulator'. 27 May 2015. http://www.reuters.com/article/us-alibaba-bank-idUSKBN0OC0-SI20150527.

Reuters. 'China's $8.6 Billion P2P Fraud Trial Starts: Xinhua'. 16 December 2016. https://www.reuters.com/article/us-china-fraud-ezubao-idUSKBN1450I2.

Reuters. 'Fitch: Chinese Banks' Profitability Is Likely to Decline Further'. 7 April 2017. http://www.reuters.com/article/fitch-chinese-banks-profitability-is-lik-idUSFit995515.

Reuters. 'No More Loan Rangers? Beijing's Waning Support for Private Credit Scores'. 4 July 2017. https://uk.reuters.com/article/ant-financial-credit-idUKL3N1JO05W.

Revolut. 'Revolut Tops 25 Million Retail Customers as Global Expansion Continues'. 17 November 2022. https://www.revolut.com/en-GR/news/revolut_tops_25_million_retail_customers_as_global_expansion_continues/.

Revolut. 'Personal Fees (Standard)'. Accessed 1 June 2023. https://www.revolut.com/legal/standard-fees/.

Riemer, Daniel S. 'Special Purpose Acquisition Companies: SPAC and SPAN, or Blank Check Redux'. *Washington University Law Review* vol. 85 (2007): p. 931.

Robertson, Benjamin, and Andrea Tan. 'Why Dual-Class Shares Catch On, Over Investor Worries'. *Bloomberg*, 5 March 2021. https://www.bloomberg.com/news/articles/2021-03-04/why-dual-class-shares-catch-on-over-investor-worries-quicktake-klwbtryg.

Robertson, Harry. 'Wall Street Is Pumped About the Metaverse, But Critics Say It's Massively Overhyped and Will Be a Regulatory Minefield'. *Business Insider*, 25 December 2021. https://markets.businessinsider.com/news/stocks/Metaverse-outlook-overhyped-regulations-facebook-meta-virtual-worlds-genz-2021-12.

Roland, Denise, and Ashley Armstrong. 'Challenger Bank Shawbrook Fetches £725m Valuation on IPO'. *The Telegraph*, 1 April 2015. http://www.telegraph.co.uk/finance/newsbysector/banksandfinance/11508186/Challenger-bank-Shawbrook-fetches-725m-valuation-on-IPO.html.

Rudegeair, Peter. 'Layoffs Mount at Online Lenders'. *The Wall Street Journal*, 8 July 2016.

Ruehll, Mercedes, Primrose Riordan, and Tabby Kinder. 'Global Investors in Limbo After Ant IPO Torpedoed by Beijing'. *The Financial Times*, 15 January 2021. http://www.ft.com/content/f0950778-450e-4ef2-804d-7e16946ac4c0.

Russell, Stuart, and Peter Norvig. *Artificial Intelligence: A Modern Approach*. 4th ed. (London: Pearson, 2021).

Russon, Mary-Ann. 'What Is Revolut?'. *BBC*, 2 April 2019. http://www.bbc.co.uk/news/business-47768661.

Salvage, Peter. 'Artificial Intelligence Sweeps Hedge Funds'. BNY Mellon. March 2019. http://www.bnymellon.com/us/en/what-we-do/business-insights/artificial-intelligence-sweeps-hedge-funds.jsp.

Santander. 'Santander Launches the First Blockchain-Based International Money Transfer Service Across Four Countries'. 12 April 2018. https://www.santander.com/content/dam/santander-com/en/documentos/historico-notas-de-prensa/2018/04/NP-2018-04-12-Santander%20launches%20the%20first%20blockchain-based%20international%20money%20transfer%20service%20across%20-en.pdf.

Schooner, Heidi M., and Michael W. Taylor. *Global Bank Regulation: Principles and Policies* (Cambridge, MA: Academic Press, 2010).

Schwarcz, Steven L. 'Systemic Risk'. *Georgetown Law Journal* vol. 97 (2008): p. 193.

Scurria, Andrew, and Soma Biswas. 'FTX Collapses into Bankruptcy System that Still Hasn't Figured Out Crypto'. *The Wall Street Journal*, 16 November 2022. https://www.wsj.com/articles/ftx-collapses-into-bankruptcy-system-that-still-hasnt-figured-out-crypto-11668550688.

Securities and Exchange Commission. 'Order Instituting Cease-and-Desist Proceedings Pursuant to Section 8A of the Securities Act of 1933, Making Findings, and Imposing a Cease-and-Desist Order'. 24 November 2008. https://www.sec.gov/litigation/admin/2008/33-8984.pdf.

Securities and Exchange Commission. 'JD.com Inc., Prospectus'. 2 December 2014. https://www.sec.gov/Archives/edgar/data/1549802/000104746914009683/a2222411z424b4.htm.

Securities and Exchange Commission. 'SEC Exposes Two Initial Coin Offerings Purportedly Backed by Real Estate and Diamonds'. 29 September 2017. https://www.sec.gov/news/press-release/2017-185-0.

Securities and Exchange Commission. 'What You Need to Know About SPACs—Investor Bulletin'. 25 May 2021. https://www.sec.gov/oiea/investor-alerts-and-bulletins/what-you-need-know-about-spacs-investor-bulletin.

Securities and Exchange Commission. 'Celebrity Involvement with SPACs—Investor Alert'. 10 March 2022. https://www.sec.gov/oiea/investor-alerts-and-bulletins/celebrity-involvement-spacs-investor-alert.

Securities and Exchange Commission. 'Spotlight on Initial Coin Offerings (ICOs)'. Accessed 1 June 2023. https://www.sec.gov/securities-topic/ICO.

Securities and Exchange Commission. 'Strategic Hub for Innovation and Financial Technology (FinHub)'. Accessed 1 June 2023. https://www.sec.gov/finhub.

Securities and Exchange Commission. 'What We Do'. Accessed 1 June 2023. https://www.sec.gov/about/what-we-do.

Sentence, Rebecca. 'The Pros and Cons of QR Codes'. Econsultancy. 18 April 2019. http://www.econsultancy.com/the-pros-and-cons-of-qr-codes/.

Shanahan, Murray. *The Technological Singularity* (Cambridge, MA: MIT Press, 2015).

Shaw, Elise. 'Fintech Investment Likely to Stay Subdued; M&A Could Pick Up Investing'. Forbes Australia. 23 February 2023. https://www.forbes.com.au/news/investing/Fintech-investment-likely-to-stay-subdued-ma-could-pick-up/.

Shawbrook. 'Annual Report and Accounts 2016'. Published in 2017. https://www.shawbrook.co.uk/media/ybyfih3x/shawbrook_ar16.pdf.

Shawbrook. 'About Us'. Accessed 1 June 2023. https://www.shawbrook.co.uk/about-us/.

Shin, Hyun Song. 'Big Tech in Finance: Opportunities and Risks'. Bank for International Settlements. 30 June 2019. https://www.bis.org/speeches/sp190630b.pdf.

Shivdasani, Anil. 'Board Composition, Ownership Structure, and Hostile Takeovers'. *Journal of Accounting and Economics* vol. 16 (1993): p. 167.

Shubber, Kadhim. 'UAE States Put Fintech Sector First'. *The Financial Times*, 7 October 2016.

Simon, Ruth. 'Big Banks Cut Back on Small Business'. *The Wall Street Journal*, 27 November 2015.

Sina. 'Ant Financial Completed A-Round Finance with Valuation Over $45bn'. 6 July 2015. http://finance.sina.com.cn/roll/20150706/030722596271.shtml.

Sina. 'Yu'E Bao Reached 1.43 Trillion Yuan, Near to the Deposit Amount of Big Four'. 1 July 2017. http://finance.sina.com.cn/roll/2017-07-01/doc-ifyhrttz1913643.shtml.

Sina. 'Sesame Credit Hired Chief Privacy Officer'. 18 July 2017. http://tech.sina.com.cn/i/2017-07-18/doc-ifyiakwa4502600.shtml.

Singapore Exchange. 'SGX Introduces SPAC Listing Framework'. 2 September 2021. https://www.sgx.com/media-centre/20210902-sgx-introduces-spac-listing-framework.

Singapore Exchange. 'Why List on SGX'. Accessed 1 June 2023. https://www.sgx.com/securities/why-list-sgx.

Slattery, Paul. 'Square Pegs in a Round Hole: SEC Regulation of Online Peer-to-Peer Lending and the CFPB Alternative'. *Yale Journal on Regulation* vol. 30 (2013): p. 233.

Small Business Administration. 'SBA Authorized Fintech Lenders'. 26 May 2020. https://www.sba.gov/document/report--sba-authorized-fintech-lenders.

Small Business Service. 'A Mapping Study of Venture Capital Provision to SMEs in England'. Small Business Investment Taskforce (UK). October 2015.

Smith, Adam. 'Woman Says She Was Virtually "Raped" in the Metaverse While Others "Passed Around a Bottle of Vodka"'. *The Independent*, 30 May 2022. https://www.independent.co.uk/tech/rape-Metaverse-woman-oculus-facebook-b2090491.html.

Smith, Kirby. 'How Dual-Class Share Structures Create Agency Costs'. Columbia Law School's Blog on Corporations and the Capital Markets. 5 January 2018. https://clsbluesky.law.columbia.edu/2018/01/05/how-dual-class-share-structures-create-agency-costs/.

Sohu. 'Borrow a Loan Up to CNY300.000 Using Sesame Credit'. 1 September 2016. http://www.sohu.com/a/113129483_444830.

Sohu. 'Senior Managers of China's Fintech Giants'. 12 April 2017. http://www.sohu.com/a/133541889_465942.

Sohu. 'The Fourth Anniversary of MyBank'. 27 June 2019. http://www.sohu.com/a/323432934_413980.

Sotheby. 'NFTs: Redefining Digital Ownership and Scarcity'. 6 April 2021. https://www.sothebys.com/en/articles/nfts-redefining-digital-ownership-and-scarcity.

South China Morning Post. 'Tencent Ready to Launch China's First Private Internet Bank, WeBank'. 29 December 2014. http://www.scmp.com/news/china-insider/article/1670474/tencent-ready-launch-chinas-first-private-internet-bank-webank.

Stanford Encyclopedia of Philosophy. 'Artificial Intelligence'. 12 July 2018. http://plato.stanford.edu/entries/artificial-intelligence/.

Starling Bank. 'The Road to Starling'. Accessed 1 June 2023. https://www.starlingbank.com/about/road-to-starling/.

Starling Bank. 'Welcome to Banking-as-a-Service'. Accessed 1 June 2023. https://www.starlingbank.com/blog/platformification-of-banking-industry/.

Startups. 'Invoice Finance: What Can You Raise?'. Accessed 1 June 2023. http://startups.co.uk/invoice-finance-what-can-you-raise/.

Startups. 'What Is Asset Finance?'. Accessed 1 June 2023. http://startups.co.uk/what-is-asset-finance/.

Statista. 'Apple Pay—Statistics & Facts'. December 2021. https://www.statista.com/topics/4322/apple-pay/.

Statista. 'E-commerce Worldwide'. Accessed 1 June 2023. https://www.statista.com/topics/871/online-shopping/.

Statista. 'Number of Cryptocurrencies Worldwide from 2013 to February 2023'. Accessed 1 June 2023. https://www.statista.com/statistics/863917/number-crypto-coins-tokens/.

Statista. 'Number of Monthly Active Facebook Users Worldwide as of 1st Quarter 2023'. Accessed 1 June 2023. https://www.statista.com/statistics/264810/number-of-monthly-active-facebook-users-worldwide/.

Statista. 'Total Value of Investments into Fintech Companies Worldwide from 2010 to 2021'. Accessed 1 June 2023. https://www.statista.com/statistics/719385/investments-into-Fintech-companies-globally/.

ST Microelectronics. 'NFC: A World of Opportunities'. July 2022. https://www.st.com/content/ccc/resource/sales_and_marketing/promotional_material/brochure/group0/89/ac/b1/59/22/41/4f/47/NFC_a_World_of_Opportunities/files/NFC_Solutions_from_ST.pdf/jcr:content/translations/en.NFC_Solutions_from_ST.pdf.

Stevenson, Neal. *Snow Crash* (London: Penguin, 2011).

Stewart, James B. 'Facebook Time: 50 Minutes a Day'. *The New York Times*, 6 May 2016.

Swan, Melanie. *Blockchain: Blueprint for a New Economy* (Sebastopol, CA: O'Reilly. 2015).

Sykes, Jay B. 'The Big Tech Antitrust Bills'. US Congressional Research Service. 13 August 2021. https://crsreports.congress.gov/product/pdf/R/R46875.

Tan, Jason. 'Tencent-Backed WeBank Hits $21 Billion Valuation'. *Caixin*, 5 November 2018. https://www.caixinglobal.com/2018-11-05/tencent-backed-webank-hits-21-billion-valuation-101343111.html.

Taylor, Kyle, and Laura Silver. 'Smartphone Ownership Is Growing Rapidly Around the World, But Not Always Equally'. *Pew Research Center*. 5 February 2019. http://www.pewresearch.org/global/2019/02/05/smartphone-ownership-is-growing-rapidly-around-the-world-but-not-always-equally/.

Taylor, Paul. 'Middle Men Deleted as the Word Spreads'. *The Financial Times*, 27 October 1998.

Testa, Giuseppina, Ramon Compano, Ana Correia, and Eva Ruckert. 'In Search of EU Unicorns—What Do We Know About Them?'. European Commission. 25 February 2022, https://publications.jrc.ec.europa.eu/repository/bitstream/JRC127712/JRC127712_01.pdf.

The Economist. 'Britain's Bank Run: The Bank that Failed'. 20 September 2007.

The Economist. 'Economies of Scale and Scope'. 20 October 2008. http://www.economist.com/node/12446567.

The Economist. 'Foe or Frenemy? Internet Finance in China'. 1 March 2014.

The Economist. 'Peer-to-Peer Lending: Banking Without Banks'. 1 March 2014.

The Economist. 'Financing Europe's Small Firms: Don't Bank on the Banks'. 16 August 2014.

The Economist. 'The Fintech Revolution'. 9 May 2015.

The Economist. 'Technology Companies: The Rise and Fall of the Unicorns'. 28 November 2015.

The Economist. 'The Age of the Appacus: Fintech in China'. 25 February 2017.

The Economist. 'Financial Technology: Friends or Foes?'. 6 May 2017.

The Economist. 'Why QR Codes Are on the Rise'. 2 November 2017. http://www.economist.com/the-economist-explains/2017/11/02/why-qr-codes-are-on-the-rise.

The Economist. 'State of Play: Fintech in Nigeria'. Intelligence Unit Report. 10 June 2020.

The Fintech Times. 'The Rise of Fintech in Canada: Home to a Vibrant Innovation Ecosystem'. 30 March 2022. https://theFintechtimes.com/rise-of-Fintech-in-canada-innovation-ecosystem/.

The Guardian. 'Aldermore Bank Shares Surge by 12% on London Debut'. 10 March 2015. https://www.theguardian.com/business/2015/mar/10/aldermore-bank-shares-surge-by-12-on-london-debut.

Thompson, Mark. 'UBS Is Buying Credit Suisse in Bid to Halt Banking Crisis'. *CNN*, 20 March 2023. https://edition.cnn.com/2023/03/19/business/credit-suisse-ubs-rescue/index.html.

TianHong Fund Management Company. 'Yu'E Bao'. Accessed 1 June 2023. http://www.thfund.com.cn/fundinfo/000198.

Treanor, Jill. 'Losses of £58bn Since the 2008 Bailout—How Did RBS Get Here?'. *The Guardian*, 24 February 2017. https://www.theguardian.com/business/2017/feb/24/90bn-in-bills-since-2008-how-did-rbs-get-here-financial-crisis-.

Tse, Candice. 'GSAM Connect: Into the Metaverse'. Goldman Sachs. 25 August 2022. https://www.gsam.com/content/gsam/us/en/institutions/market-insights/gsam-connect/2022/into-the-Metaverse.html.

UK Department for International Trade. 'UK Fintech: State of the Nation'. April 2019. https://assets.publishing.service.gov.uk/government/uploads/system/uploads/attachment_data/file/801277/UK-fintech-state-of-the-nation.pdf.

UK Finance. 'UK Payment Markets Reports 2019 Summary'. June 2019. https://www.ukfinance.org.uk/sites/default/files/uploads/pdf/UK-Finance-UK-Payment-Markets-Report-2019-SUMMARY.pdf.

UK Parliament. 'The Run on the Rock: Fifth Report of Session 2007–08'. 24 January 2008. https://publications.parliament.uk/pa/cm200708/cmselect/cmtreasy/56/5602.htm.

United Nations. 'Let's Learn Blockchain: Blockchain 101'. 11 April 2018. https://unite.un.org/sites/unite.un.org/files/technovation/1_blockchain_101_ariana_fowler_consensys.pdf.

United Nations. 'The Race to Zero Emissions, and Why the World Depends on It'. 2 December 2020. https://news.un.org/en/story/2020/12/1078612.

United Nations. 'Digital Financing Task Force'. Accessed 1 June 2023. https://www.un.org/en/digital-financing-taskforce.

University of Cambridge. 'Moving Mainstream: The European Alternative Finance Benchmarking Report'. February 2015. https://www.jbs.cam.ac.uk/faculty-research/centres/alternative-finance/publications/moving-mainstream/.

University of Kent. 'Working for Small Businesses'. Accessed 1 June 2023. http://www.kent.ac.uk/careers/sme.htm.

University of Missouri–St. Louis. 'Hashing Functions and Their Uses in Cryptography'. Accessed 1 June 2023. http://www.umsl.edu/~siegelj/information_theory/projects/HashingFunctionsInCryptography.html.

University of Washington. 'The History of Artificial Intelligence'. December 2016. http://courses.cs.washington.edu/courses/csep590/06au/projects/history-ai.pdf.

US Census Bureau. 'Annual Retail Trade Survey Shows Impact of Online Shopping on Retail Sales During COVID-19 Pandemic'. 27 April 2022. https://www.census.gov/library/stories/2022/04/ecommerce-sales-surged-during-pandemic.html.

Usher, Andrew, Edona Reshidi, Francisco Rivadeneyra, and Scott Hendry. 'The Positive Case for a CBDC'. Bank of Canada Staff Discussion Paper. 20 July 2021. https://www.bankofcanada.ca/wp-content/uploads/2021/07/sdp2021-11.pdf.

van Duuren, Emiel, Auke Plantinga, and Bert Scholtens. 'ESG Integration and the Investment Management Process: Fundamental Investing Reinvented'. *Journal of Business Ethics* vol. 138 (2016): p. 525.

Vasagar, Jeevan. 'Singapore Fund Adds to UK Portfolio with Pound(s) 48.5m Deal'. *The Financial Times*, 31 December 2016.

Veal, Angela. 'SPAC Warrants: 8 Frequently Asked Questions'. Eisner Amper. 17 May 2021. https://www.eisneramper.com/spac-warrants-faqs-0421/.

Vincent, Danny. 'We Looked Inside a Secret Chinese Bitcoin Mine'. *BBC*, 4 May 2016. http://www.bbc.com/future/story/20160504-we-looked-inside-a-secret-chinese-Bitcoin-mine.

Virtual Reality Society. 'What Is Virtual Reality?'. Accessed 1 June 2023. https://www.vrs.org.uk/virtual-reality/what-is-virtual-reality.html.

Vodafone. 'M-PESA'. Accessed 1 June 2023. https://www.vodafone.com/about-vodafone/what-we-do/consumer-products-and-services/m-pesa.

Wallace, Tim. 'SMEs Expect to Grow Faster Next Year Despite Brexit Vote'. *The Telegraph*, 1 October 2016. http://www.telegraph.co.uk/business/2016/10/01/smes-expect-to-grow-faster-next-year-despite-brexit-vote/.

Wang, Helen H. 'Alipay Takes on Apple Pay and PayPal on Their Home Turf'. *Forbes*, 30 October 2016. https://www.forbes.com/sites/helenwang/2016/10/30/will-alipay-dominate-global-mobile-payments/.

Wang, Yue. 'Alibaba Finance Affiliate Launches Fund Investment Smartphone App'. *Forbes*, 18 August 2015. https://www.forbes.com/sites/ywang/2015/08/18/alibaba-finance-affiliate-launches-fund-investment-smartphone-app/#115f657f6301.

Ward, Matthew, and Chris Rhodes. 'Small Businesses and the UK Economy'. UK Parliament. 9 December 2014. https://researchbriefings.files.parliament.uk/documents/SN06078/SN06078.pdf.

Warner, Bernhard. 'Why Wall Street Thinks the Metaverse Will Be Worth Trillions'. *Fortune*, 27 January 2022. https://fortune.com/longform/wall-street-Metaverse-web3-investors-roblox-meta-platforms-microsoft/.

Warren, Tom. 'Meet the British Mobile Banks Showing the US How It's Done: Monzo and Starling Are Transforming UK Spending'. The Verge. 13 June 2019. https://www.theverge.com/2019/6/13/18663036/monzo-starling-mobile-banks-uk-report.
Waters, Richard. 'Counter-Terrorism Tools Used to Spot Fraud'. *The Financial Times*, 13 December 2012. https://www.ft.com/content/796b412a-4513-11e2-838f-00144feabdc0.
Watts, Jake Maxwell. 'In Singapore. Making Law a Business'. *The Wall Street Journal*, 3 January 2015.
WeBank. 'About Us'. Accessed 1 June 2023. https://www.webank.com/about.
WeBank. 'WeBank: Leading Digital Bank'. Accessed 1 June 2023. https://res.webank.com/s/hj/www/assets/eng-5b9c186679.pdf.
WeBank. 'Weili Loan Application'. Accessed 1 June 2023. https://w.webank.com/.
Weinland, Don. 'Chinese VC Funds Pour $2.4bn into Silicon Valley Start-Ups'. *The Financial Times*, 18 July 2018. http://www.ft.com/content/463b162a-8a3d-11e8-b18d-0181731a0340.
Weinland, Don. 'Hong Kong to Create Fintech "Sandbox" Allowing Bank Experiments'. *The Financial Times*, 6 September 2016. https://www.ft.com/content/38a662ee-740f-11e6-bf48-b372cdb1043a.
Weinland, Don, and Oliver Ralph. 'Zhongan Launches Insurtech Concept to World'. *The Financial Times*, 25 September 2017. https://www.ft.com/content/c9d10ada-9eb1-11e7-8cd4-932067fbf946.
West, Darrell M., and John R. Allen. 'How Artificial Intelligence Is Transforming the World'. Brookings Institution. 24 April 2018. https://www.brookings.edu/research/how-artificial-intelligence-is-transforming-the-world/.
Wharton School of the University of Pennsylvania. 'Going Cashless: What Can We Learn from Sweden's Experience?'. 31 August 2018. https://knowledge.wharton.upenn.edu/article/going-cashless-can-learn-swedens-experience/.
White & Case. 'US De-SPAC & SPAC Data & Statistics Roundup 2022'. February 2023. https://www.whitecase.com/sites/default/files/2023-02/us-spac-de-spac-data-statistics-round-up-v2.pdf.
Wildau, Gabriel. 'China's First Online-Only Lender Launched'. *The Financial Times*, 6 January 2015.
Wildau, Gabriel. 'Alibaba Eyes Small Business Loans'. *The Financial Times*, 29 January 2015.
Wildau, Gabriel. 'Ant Financial Raises $4.5bn in Record Fintech Private Placement'. *The Financial Times*, 26 April 2016. https://www.ft.com/content/366490b4-0b7d-11e6-9cd4-2be898308be3.
Wildau, Gabriel. 'Alipay Bypasses China UnionPay on Fees'. *The Financial Times*, 1 August 2016.
Wildau, Gabriel. 'China Curbs "Wild West" Loan Sector'. *The Financial Times*, 5 April 2017.
World Bank. 'Financial Inclusion Overview'. Accessed 1 June 2023. https://www.worldbank.org/en/topic/financialinclusion/overview.
World Economic Forum and Deloitte. 'Beneath the Surface: Technology-Driven Systemic Risks and the Continued Need for Innovation'. 28 October 2021. https://www3.weforum.org/docs/WEF_Technology_Innovation_and_Systemic_Risk_2021.pdf.
World Fintech Show. 'DATE Fintech Show. Digital Acceleration & Transformation Expo'. Accessed 1 June 2023. https://worldFintechshow.com/.
Xinhua. 'Online Payment Entered into Instant Pay Age'. 28 July 2011. http://news.xinhuanet.com/newmedia/2011-07/28/c_121733865.htm.
Xinhua. 'Tencent to Work with Authorities to Improve Facial Recognition for Banking Use'. 15 April 2015. https://www.chinadaily.com.cn/business/tech/2015-04/15/content_20441029.htm.

Xinhua. 'Outstanding Balance of Yu'E Bao Surpassed Merchant Bank's Personal Deposits'. 5 July 2017. http://news.xinhuanet.com/finance/2017-07/05/c_1121264650.htm.

Xinhua. 'Ant Group Summoned to Meeting with Regulators: What Signal Did It Send?'. 12 April 2021. http://www.xinhuanet.com/fortune/2021-04/12/c_1127321535.htm.

Yang, Jing. 'Jack Ma's Ant Group Bows to Beijing with Company Overhaul'. *The Wall Street Journal*, 12 April 2021. https://www.wsj.com/articles/ant-group-to-become-a-financial-holding-company-overseen-by-central-bank-11618223482.

Yang, Yuan. 'Alibaba and Tencent Open New Front in Red Envelope War'. *The Financial Times*, 30 January 2017.

Ye, Ningyao, and Lerong Lu. 'How to Harness a Unicorn? Demystifying China's Reform of Share Listing Rules and Chinese Depositary Receipts (CDRs)'. *International Company and Commercial Law Review* vol. 30 (2019): p. 454.

Yicai. 'From 1.0 to 4.0 Era, Ping An Bank Detailed the Transformation Path of AI Bank', *Yicai*, 27 June 2019, https://www.yicai.com/news/100240136.html.

Yohn, Denise Lee. '6 Ways to Build a Customer-Centric Culture'. *Harvard Business Review*, 2 October 2018. https://hbr.org/2018/10/6-ways-to-build-a-customer-centric-culture.

YouGov. 'Public Trust in Banking'. April 2013. http://cdn.yougov.com/cumulus_uploads/document/ylf7gpof19/Public_Trust_in_Banking_Final.pdf.Zopa. 'Our Story'. Accessed 1 June 2023. http://www.zopa.com/about/our-story.

Z/Yen Group. 'The Global Financial Centres Index 32'. 22 September 2022. https://www.longfinance.net/media/documents/GFCI_32_Report_2022.09.22_v1.0_.pdf.

Index

For the benefit of digital users, indexed terms that span two pages (e.g., 52–53) may, on occasion, appear on only one of those pages.

ACA Group 69–70
Accelerator Frankfurt 62
Africa 39–40, 43, 66–67
AI (Artificial Intelligence) 1–2, 16–17, 38, 53–54
   and employment 20–22
   extensive application of 18
   in fund industry 20
   legal and ethical issues 21–22
   origins and evolution 17
   provision in China 19–20, 53–54
   and regulatory practices 68–69
   weak and strong 17–19
   and the Web 3.0 127–128
Airwallex 57–58
Aldermore Bank 139–145
algorithms, use of
   algorithmic stablecoins 213
   algorithmic trading 38
   BTC mining 203
   in credit rating systems 98–99
   hashing 23
   P2P lending 174–175, 182–183
   regulatory frameworks 69–70
Alibaba 32–33, 51, 55–56, 94–95, 120
   cloud services 25
   MyBank 32–33, 89–90, 93–94, 97–98, 100–101, 151–152, 155
   partnerships 35, 97–98, 232–233
   use of AI algorithms 18
   use of big data 29–30, 98–99
   see also Alipay; Ant Group
Alipay 3–4, 32–33, 120, 199–200, 229–230
   BarCode Pay 88–89
   customer centricity 40
   dominant position of 43, 87–89, 93–94, 99–100, 232–234
   and mobile payment 94–95, 230–233
   origins and growth 85–88, 230
   vs. traditional banking 99

Yu'E Bao 89, 95–96, 99–100, 104–105, 233–234
Alphabet 120, 228
AlphaGo 18
Amazon 17–18, 26–27, 86, 120, 205
   Amazon Cash 120–121
Ant Fortune 32–33, 95–96, 104–105
Ant Group 32–33, 51, 55–56, 85–86
   business model 93–99
   history of 86–93
   regulation 90–93, 101–105
   vs. traditional banking 99–101
anti-money laundering (AML) 69–70
   and BTCs 206–207
   and CBDCs 216, 222–223
Apple 17–18, 119, 230–231
   Apple Pay 34–35, 43, 120–122, 198–199
application programming interface (API) 41
asset management 59–60, 62
   Nutmeg, in the UK 64
   regulatory practices 69–70
   and SME-focused digital banking 144
Assetz Capital 171–172
Atom Bank 35, 145, 149–150
Australia 51–52
   card payments 226
   regulatory framework 52, 101
Australian Prudential Regulation Authority (APRA) 52
Australian Securities and Investment Commissions (ASIC) 52, 73
Axa 82

Bank for International Settlements (BIS) 119–120, 198, 217–218
Bank of Canada 50, 209
Bank of England (BoE) 139–140, 153, 169–170, 185–186, 216–218
banking and digital banking 33–34, 161–162, 238–239

Index

in China 56–58, 82, 89–90, 97–98, 132–133, 149–152
and cloud computing 28
concept and rise of 137–141
deposit insurance 158–159
impact of e-commerce 33
regulatory framework 153–161, 238–239
security and data protection 160
supermarket-backed 138
too big to fail (TBTF) 133–137, 238–239
traditional *vs.* digital 99–101
in the UK 82, 132–133, 137–149
virtual, and the Metaverse 128
Barclays 13–14, 30, 119, 140–141
Basel III 122, 168–169
BBVA 35
big data *see* data
BigTech 34–35, 56–57, 75–76, 119, 129–131, 161–162, 237–238
and data-network-activities (DNA) 119–120
lending services 120–121
payment services 120
regulatory framework 79, 121–126
and SPACs 118–119
Bitmain 53–54
BlackRock 206–207
blockchain 3–4, 16, 120, 197
applications 24–25
decentralisation 22–23
regulation 24–25, 68–69
rise of 197
transparency and immutability 23
see also BTC; CBDC; cryptocurrencies; stablecoins
Boeing 25–26
British Bankers' Association (BBA) 159–160
British Business Bank (BBB) 166–167, 172–173, 179–181, 185–186
BTC 3–4, 50, 195, 213–214
invention of and concept 42, 197, 201
investment and trading 202, 205
mining 53–54, 200, 203–204
nature of 204–205
risks and regulation 203, 206–209
use of ICOs 202
ByteDance 53–54, 129–130

Canada 50, 209, 220–221
Cao, Yu 157

Cappitech 69–70
Caribbean 50
CashApp Investing 78–79
CBDC (central bank digital currency) 50, 58–59, 195, 198, 215–216, 223–224, 234–235, 240
anonymity, AML compliance 222–223
centralised, decentralised, hybrid 222
currency competition 218–219
definition and operating mechanism 216–218
M0 function 219–220
retail, wholesale, cross-border 220–221
token- and account-based 221–222
China
AI provision 19–20, 53–54
Beijing 52–54
BTC 203–204, 208–209
CBDCs 198
digital banking 132–133, 149–152, 155–157
'Fintech Development Plan' 52
Hangzhou 55–56
Hong Kong 57–58
mobile payment 94–95, 198–200, 227, 229–234
P2P lending 77, 100–103, 175–178, 184–185
regulatory system 85–86, 90–93, 101–105, 109–110, 125, 155–157, 184–185, 203, 207–209
Shanghai 54–55
Shenzhen 56–57
unicorn companies 83–84
see also Alipay; Ant Group; WeChat Pay
China Banking Regulatory Commission (CBRC) 97–98, 104–105, 155–156, 184–185
cloud computing 16, 41–42, 49–50, 62, 97–98, 122, 236
benefits 25–26
concept 25
in the finance industry 28
public, private and hybrid 27
and RegTech 69–70
service models 26–27
Clydesdale Bank 34
Coinbase 41, 116–117
Coinstar 120–121

corporate finance 15
   BigTech regulations 123–124
   capital market regulations 109–119
   DCSS 104–109
   equity and debt 109
   internal *vs.* external 167–168
   unicorn companies 82–84
Covid-19 pandemic 1–2, 39, 129–130, 132, 163–164, 167, 178, 196–197
   AI application 18
   and e-commerce 31–32
   and P2P lending in the UK 171–172, 186–187
   and the rise of digital banks 139, 141
   and SPACs 111–112
   use of digital payments 198–199, 201–202, 224
CreditEase 175–176
crowdfunding 43, 101–103, 146–147
   and UK P2P lending 163–165, 170–171, 181–182, 188–193
Cruikshank Report 136–137
cryptocurrencies 3–4, 22–23, 39, 201–202, 240
   definition and operating mechanism 200–201
   and disintermediation 37–38, 42
   and fund safety 77
   price volatility 195, 197, 202
   and scalability 41
   see also BTC; stablecoins
Current Account Switching Service (CASS) 154–155
customers/consumers
   centricity 40
   and digital banking 138, 141, 143, 145, 147–149, 151, 160
   inclusivity 43
   protection 60–61, 73–79, 91, 103–104, 122–123, 147–148, 161, 184, 188, 222–223, 239–240

data, big data 2–3, 16, 41–42, 236–237
   benefits 29–30, 41–42
   BigTech use of 119–123
   and blockchain 22–25
   Chinese companies 53–55
   and cloud computing 25–28
   concept 29
   and digital banking 90, 97–101, 141, 145, 150–151
   and digital payments 226–229
   and fraud detection 30–31
   Metaverse 128
   and P2P lending 182–183
   protection and regulation 30–31, 60–61, 68–72, 77–79, 103–104, 122–123, 125–126, 160, 222–223, 238–239
   Web 3.0 127–128
debt financing 109, 168, 178–179
decentralised finance (DeFi) 3–4
   vs. centralised 22–23
   and disintermediation 37–38
   and stablecoins 211–212
Deliveroo 106
Deloitte 46–47
   and AI 20
   and blockchain 24–25
Diem 34–35, 48–49, 120, 195, 197–198, 210–212
Dinero Electronico 220–221
Dogecoin 205
Du Xiaoman Financial 53–54
dual-class share structure (DCSS)
   advantages 107–108
   criticism 108
   and ESG investments 108–109
   regulations 106–107
   and trading shares 105–106
Dubai Financial Services Authority (DFSA) 65, 73–74

e-commerce 53–56, 86–88
   and big data 29–30, 122–123
   concept 31–32
   during Covid-19 31–32
   digital banking 33, 120–121
   payment systems 32–33, 85–89
   see also Alibaba; MyBank
Edison, Thomas 1
El Salvador 205
electric vehicles (EVs) 1–2
equity financing 90, 107–109, 168
Ernst & Young (EY) 45
Ethereum 42, 197, 200–201, 213–214, 240
eToro 128
Euronext 61–62
Europe
   Dublin 62–63

Frankfurt 62
  incentives for start-ups 83–84
  mobile payment 94–95
  Paris 61–62
  regulation 60–61
European Investment Bank 179–181
Ezubao 77, 101–103, 177–178

Facebook *see* Meta
Fannie Mae 135–136
FICO 98–99, 103–104, 174
Financial Conduct Authority (FCA) 64–65, 73, 101–103, 137, 147, 153–155, 161, 170–171, 182–183, 188
  regulation of P2P lending 188–194, 239–240
financial holding companies (FHCs) regulation 79, 85, 90–93, 101–105
  see also Ant Group
Financial Sector Development Programme (FSDP) 65–66
Financial Stability Board (FSB) 11, 136–137, 220–221
Financial Times Stock Exchange (FTSE) 142–144
FinHub (Strategic Hub for Innovation and Financial Technology) 47–48
Fink, Larry 206–207
Finland 135
Fintech 236, 240–241
  and accessibility 39–40
  and automation 38
  business models 33–36
  and customer centricity 40
  definition 2–3, 11, 236–237
  and disintermediation 37–38, 42
  diversity 35–36
  historical background 13–14
  hubs 45–67, 237–238
  impact of 2–3
  and innovation 37
  investments 15
  and scalability 41
  social and economic values 41–43
  vs. traditional finance 14–15
  and virtualisation 39
Fintech Saudi 65–66
Folk2Folk 171–172
Ford, Henry 1
Frankfurt Stock Exchange 62

fraud detection 33
  and big data 30–31
  cards and chip cards 225–226
  and cheque payments 224–225
  cheques 224–225
  and P2P lending 77, 175–178, 181–182, 184, 239–240
  regulatory mechanisms 69–70, 77, 101–103, 113–114, 147–148
Freddie Mac 135–136
FTX 77, 208–209
fund safety, regulation 69–70, 77, 104–105, 122–123
FundApps 69–70
Funding Circle 64, 171–173, 179–182, 187–188
Funding for Lending Scheme (FLS) 185–186

Golding, Andy 139–140
Goldman Sachs 85–86, 119, 121–122, 126–127
Gongsheng, Pan 92
Google Pay 34–35
Government of Singapore Investment Corporation (GIC) 59–60

hedge funds 20, 34, 38, 49–50, 108–109, 113–114, 116–117, 179–181, 202
Hikvision 55–56
HKEX 112–113
Hong Kong Monetary Authority (HKMA) 57–58, 73
HSBC 85–86, 135
Huatai 82

India 58–59, 134–135, 229–230, 236
Industrial and Commercial Bank of China (ICBC) 119, 134–135
Infrastructure as a Service (IaaS) 26–27
initial coin offering (ICO) 201–202
  regulatory concerns 207–208
initial public offering (IPO) 109–110, 168, 202
  Aldermore 142
  Ant Group 55–56, 90–92
  and DCSS 106–108
  in Hong Kong 57
  and online lending 174–176
  Shawbrook 143–144

initial public offering (IPO) (*Continued*)
    and SPAC listings 110–119
    and VC funds 84
Innovative Finance ISA 187
Instant Pay 88
insurance, insurtech 34, 36, 82
    and AI 38
    cloud services 28
    companies globally 49–50, 52–55, 57–59, 61–63, 65
    deposit 104, 158–159, 162, 181–182, 238–239
    payment protection, scandals about 132, 139–140
International Association of Deposit Insurers (IADI) 158

James, Letitia 214–215
Japan 134–135, 228–229
    'J-Coin' 209
JD Technology 53–54
JD.com 105–106
JFZ Capital management 56–57
Jiao Jiao 19–20
Jin, Xiaolong 152
JPMorgan 93–94, 135
    AI research 20
    digital banking 82
    use of big data 30–31

Kalifa Review of UK Fintech 12–13 n.6, 64–65, 106–107
Klarna International 33
Kookmink Bank 128

Latin America 50
Lee, Aileen 82–83
Lemonade 49–50
LendingClub 48–49, 173–175, 184
Li, Keqiang 157
Libra *see* Diem
London Stock Exchange (LSE) 41, 106–107, 112–113, 138, 143–144
Lufax 54–55

M-PESA 3–4, 39–40, 43, 66–67
MakerDAO 213
McCarthy, John 17
Meta (Facebook) 29–30, 126
    Diem/Libra 34–35, 48–49, 120, 197–198
    trading shares 105–106

Metaverse 8, 46
    concept 126–127
    criticism 130–131
    and NFTs 128
    regulation 129
    supporters 129–130
    use of VR 128
    and Web 3.0 127–128
Metro Bank 138
Microsoft 1, 25, 228
    Microsoft Azure 25–26
Middle East 46
    Dubai 65
    Riyadh 65–66
Moja 82
Monetary Authority of Singapore (MAS) 45n.2, 60
money and payment systems 3–4, 9–10, 240
    and BigTech 120
    cards 225–226, 233–234
    cash 224
    cheques 224–225
    direct debit 226–227
    evolution of 196–198
    fund safety, regulations 77
    and inclusivity 43
    mobile 94–95, 198–200, 227–235, 240
    NFC *vs.* QR codes 227–229
    and virtualisation 39
    see also Alipay; CBDC; cryptocurrencies; stablecoins
MoneyLion 50
Monzo 39, 146–147
MyBank 32–33, 89–90, 93–94, 97–98, 100–101, 151–152, 155

N26 62, 132–133
Nakamoto, Satoshi 42, 197
National Association of Securities Dealers Automated (NASDAQ) 13–14, 49–50, 106, 111–112
New York Stock Exchange (NYSE) 41, 49–50, 106–107, 112–113
NFC technology 94–95, 226–228, 230–231
non-fungible token (NFT) 128, 130, 141
Norway 135
Nutmeg 64

OneSavings Bank 139–140
Oracle 30

P2P lending 3–4, 22, 28, 33, 36, 95–96, 109, 193–194
　advantages 43, 179–183
　in China 77, 100–103, 175–178, 184–185
　and crowdfunding 163, 170–171
　and disintermediation 37–38, 42–43, 178–179
　and fraud 77, 175–178, 181–182, 184, 239–240
　regulation of 58–59, 183–193, 239–240
　and SMEs 36–37, 163–165, 172–173, 176, 178–183, 185–187, 239–240
　in the UK 63–64, 148–149, 163, 170–173, 179–182, 185–193
　in the US 48–49, 173–175, 184
Paipaidai 175–176
Paris Fintech Forum 61–62
Paxos 24–25
Pay.UK 154–155
PayPal 32–33, 41, 48–49, 89, 232–233
PE (private equity) funds 46, 73–74, 107–109, 113–114, 117–118, 146–147, 168
Peer-to-Peer Finance Association (P2PFA) 187–188
People's Bank of China (PBoC) 88, 230
　'Fintech Development Plan' 52
　digital currency 198, 209, 217–218
　regulatory measures 52–53, 85, 90–92, 207–208
Petro 220–221
Ping An Bank 19–20, 54–55
Platform as a Service (PaaS) 26–27
PPDai 54–55
Project Jasper 220–221
Prosper Marketplace 173–174, 184
Prudential Regulation Authority (PRA) 85, 145, 147, 153–154
　and capital requirements 159–160
　vs. the FCA 154–155

QR code technology 227
　Alipay use of 94–95, 230–232
　operating mechanism 228–229
　popularity 94–95, 228–229, 233

Rate Setter 187–188
Recovery Loan Scheme (RLS) 185–186
RegTech 46–48, 62–65, 80, 101–103, 161
　and big data 30–31
　concept 4–5, 67–68
　and cost saving on compliance 70
　features 68–69
　limitations 70–72
　and risk management 69–70
regulatory system 8, 46
　Ant Group 90–93, 101–105
　in Asia 51–53, 57–60, 109–110
　in Australia 52, 73
　BigTech 121–126
　blockchain 24–25
　BTC 206–209
　customer protection 76–79, 103–104
　DCSS 106–107
　digital banks 153–161, 238–239
　in Europe 60–62
　FHCs 79, 85, 90–93, 101–105
　and the Metaverse 129
　in the Middle East 65
　P2P lending 58–59, 183–193, 239–240
　sandbox regime 4–5, 33–34, 52, 57–58, 60, 64–65, 72–76, 101–103, 161
　SPACs 112–116
　start-ups 33–34, 47–48, 73–76, 78–79, 153
　systemic risks 79, 104–105
　in the UK 64–65, 73, 85, 101–103, 109–110, 153–155, 158–161, 185–193
　in the US 47–48, 116–117
　see also RegTech
Reserve Bank of Australia (RBA) 52
Reserve Bank of India (RBI) 58–59
Revolut 78–79, 148–149
Royal Bank of Scotland (RBS) 132, 135, 139, 153–154

Sainsbury's Bank 138
Santander 24–25
Securities and Exchange Commission (SEC) 24–25, 47–48, 184
Sesame Credit 89–90, 98–101, 103–104
Shangai-London Stock Connect (SLSC) 109–110
Shawbrook Bank 143–145
Silicon Valley 48–49, 84
Singapore 59–60, 83–84, 113–114
Singapore Exchange (SGX) 59–60, 112–113
Slam Corp. 111–112

small and medium-sized enterprises (SMEs) 43
 China financing 97–98, 100–101, 120–121, 149–150
 employee satisfaction 167
 P2P lending 36–37, 163–165, 172–173, 176, 178–183, 185–187, 239–240
 UK financing 139–140, 143–144, 164–170, 185–187
Small Business Administration (SBA) 47–48
smartphones 56–57, 120, 238–239
 Germany (N26) banking 132–133
 NFC technology 228
 and the popularity of digital banking 198–199, 224
 QR codes 228–232
 UK banking 145–149
Social Science Research Network (SSRN) 11–12
Software as Service (SaaS) 26–27
Sophia 18
South Korea 112–113, 128, 229–230
special purpose acquisition company (SPAC) 60, 110–111
 advantages of 116–119
 listing regulations 112–116
 media coverage 111–112
stablecoins 120, 195, 197–198, 215–216, 234–235, 240
 advantages and limitations 213–215
 algorithmic 213
 commodity-backed 212
 crypto-backed 213
 definition and operating mechanism 210–212
 fiat-backed 197–198, 212
Starling Bank 147–148
Start-Up Loans Scheme (SLS) 186–187
start-ups 28, 33–34, 39, 131
 African 66–67
 Chinese 57–58
 cooperation with large institutions 35
 cyber attacks on 78–79
 in Dubai 65
 EU assistance to 83–84
 German 62
 and ICOs 202
 Irish 62–63
 regulatory practices 33–34, 47–48, 73–76, 78–79, 153

Start-Up Loans Scheme (SLS) 186–187
unicorn 82–84
in the US 47–50
Suishou Technology 56–57
Sweden 199–200, 220–221
Switzerland 135–136

Taobao 29–30, 86–88, 98–99, 152, 230
Temasek Holdings 59–60
Tencent 56–57, 94–95, 120–121, 129–130, 231–233
 see also MyBank
TenPay 56–57
TerraUSD 211–215
Tesco Bank 138
Tesla 1–2, 205
Tether 195, 197–198, 210–212, 214–215
Tmall 29–30, 89, 152
Toyota 1–2

UK 63–64
 banking industry, traditional 132, 135–137
 banking, digital 82, 132–133, 137–149, 153–155
 cash payments 224
 cheque payments 224–225
 deposit insurance 158–159
 mobile payment 94–95, 199–200
 P2P lending 63–64, 148–149, 163, 170–173, 179–182, 185–193
 regulation 64–65, 73, 85, 101–103, 109–110, 153–155, 158–161, 185–193
 SME financing 139–140, 143–144, 164–170, 185–187
unicorn companies 3, 85–86, 110–113
 in Asia 53–54, 57–58
 criteria 83–84
 economic implications 84
 and Fintech investments 15
 global valuation 82–83
United Nations (UN) 11–12
US Federal Reserve 85, 198, 214–215, 217–218
USA 82–83
 banking sector 135
 BigTech 119, 125
 card payments and chip technology 226
 cash payments 224
 deposit insurance 158–159

mobile payment 94–95, 198–199
New York City 49–50
P2P lending 48–49, 173–175, 184
regulation 47–48, 125, 184
San Francisco/Silicon Valley 48–49
SPACs 110–111, 115–118
start-ups 47–50

venture capital (VC) funds 2–3, 15, 46, 73–74, 146–147
and DCSS 107–108
and equity financing 168
and SME financing 186–187
and unicorn companies 82–84
in the US 47–48
Vinnik, Alexander 206–207
Virgin Money 138

WeBank 56–57
customer recognition 155

loan services 120–121, 150–151
and P2P lending 174–175
WeChat Pay 3–4, 43, 94–95, 199–200, 229–234
and mobile payment 232–233
WeLab 57–58
World Economic Forum 79
World Fintech Show 65–66

Yirendai.com 175–176
Yorkshire Bank 34
YouBang Insurance 87–88
Yu'E Bao 89, 93–96, 99–100, 104–105, 233–234
Yu, Shengfa 151–152

ZA International 57–58
ZhongAn Insurance 54–55
Zopa 63–64, 163, 170–172, 181–182, 187–188